MECHANISMS OF MEMORY

Mechanisms of MEMORY

by

E. ROY JOHN

Brain Research Laboratories
Department of Psychiatry
New York Medical College
New York, New York

ACADEMIC PRESS/New York and London

1967

ACADEMIC PRESS, INC.
111 Fifth Avenue, New York, New York 10003

United Kingdom Edition published by
ACADEMIC PRESS, INC. (LONDON) LTD.
Berkeley Square House, London W1X 6BA

LIBRARY OF CONGRESS CATALOG CARD NUMBER: 66-29433

Third Printing, 1970

PRINTED IN THE UNITED STATES OF AMERICA

This volume is dedicated with love to
Suki, Sanyi, Penny, Andy, Miriam, and Mutti

PREFACE

Although the brain mediates much of reflex control and homeostatic regulation essential for life, the most important function of the brain is to process information. The brain mechanisms involved in storage and retrieval of memories are of peculiar interest, because memories are among the ingredients of thought. Understanding these processes will provide a uniquely intimate insight into the material bases of the human experience.

This field of science, the physiology of thought and memory, has yet to be structured as a discipline. The relevant facts from anatomy, chemistry, physiology, and psychology must be brought together and integrated with theoretical formulations which place them into functional perspective.

This book represents my attempts to perform that function. A set of facts from widespread domains has been assembled and placed into functional context relative to each other. A set of logical considerations has been proposed which provide constraints upon the theoretical reconciliation of these facts. Since this is an interdisciplinary area, many of the topics discussed are distant from my formal training or laboratory experience. It may well be that I have oversimplified or misunderstood some of this material. Hopefully, such errors will be quickly detected so others will not be misled. Although some of the arguments constructed herein may require correction or modification, I trust that the utility of the integrated perspective which has been provided will substantially outweigh these shortcomings.

In our initial efforts to construct a neural sciences curriculum for the Center for Brain Research at the University of Rochester, it became necessary to bring together materials which would permit a systematic presentation of some of these topics. As I gained familiarity with these areas, and as the research in my laboratories progressed, my friend, Dr. Samuel Sutton, suggested that I write a monograph to communicate the viewpoint of that work. Much as I appreciated his interest, the project seemed too difficult to undertake at that time. The opportunity to do so arose unexpectedly, shortly after I moved to New York Medical College. My good friend and colleague, Professor Kao-Liang Chow, decided to do a collaborative piece of research with me. While carrying out these experiments, he gave me the pleasure of staying in my home. Almost every night we discussed and argued about a variety of theoretical issues related to memory, citing evidence which came to mind. I reconstructed as much of the framework and content of these discussions as possible after each of these sessions, using a tape recorder. Those summaries were the first outline for this book. I wish to express my appreciation to K. L. Chow for the great stimulation which he provided me.

The original research described in this volume was carried out with a number of collaborators. It is a pleasure to acknowledge the many benefits I have derived from working with Daniel Ruchkin, Jorge Villegas, Samuel Sutton, Arnold Leiman, Eugene Sachs, Minoru Shimokochi, Jerzy Majkowski, Keith Killam, K. L. Chow, and Reginald Herrington. Much of that work was supported by grants from the United States Public Health Service and National Science Foundation.

I have benefited immensely from detailed criticisms of the manuscript which were provided by my friends and colleagues. I wish particularly to acknowledge my indebtedness to Endre Grastyán, Frank Morrell, Kao-Liang Chow, Neal Miller, Samuel Sutton, Daniel Ruchkin, Robert Galambos, J. Konorski, Asher Goichberg, Eugene Sachs, Bernard Schiff, and Arnold Leiman. Although I bear the responsibility for the inadequacies of the present formulations, their criticisms and suggestions eliminated many of the defects of early drafts of this work. The assistance of Asher Goichberg in all aspects of the preparation of this book has been invaluable. Daniel Ruchkin, Miss Hansook Ahn, Robert Nagel, and Noel Fleming have been responsible for much of the analysis of data from our own experiments. Without the careful work of Miss Reina Attias and Mrs. Marjorie Payne, the quality of this volume would have suffered severely.

Finally, I wish to express my gratitude to my wife and children, who patiently and lovingly endured the disruption of family activities caused by one of us writing a book.

E. Roy John

January, 1967

CONTENTS

Contents

Contents

CHAPTER I

INTRODUCTION

The brain is a marvelous mechanism. Our feelings of love and hate, of good and evil, our appreciation of ugliness and beauty in the world around us, the values toward which we aspire, the injustices which we strive to correct—all these mental riches which form the most treasured part of life for us are somehow generated by the interaction of present experiences with the residue of our past stored in the brain. Man could not grow from a child without learning, and learning is not conceivable without processes that achieve the storage of information and, perhaps even more remarkable, the deliberate retrieval and conscious remembering of past experience. It is astonishing to reflect on the fact that these intimate and compelling personal impressions, which we accept as a natural accompaniment of everyday life, are the products of delicate and complex electrical and chemical events in the myriad cells which constitute the brain. The way in which the context and continuity of personal experience arise from the interplay of these minute elements is still unfathomed.

For centuries philosophers have concerned themselves with how *mind* arises in us. For some time, the difficulties encountered in the experimental study of these processes sustained the so-called "mind-brain dualism." Whatever we have come to know of the brain, it has remained difficult to understand how *mind* arises from brain. It is perhaps the challenge of this age-old riddle which makes the study of memory so compelling. For, whatever the nature of the storage and retrieval of information in the brain, when we retrieve information, we may become

1

aware of it, we may *remember*. In that act resides an interface between our consciousness of the present and our consciousness of the past. Somewhere in the processes that generate *remembering* must lie a clue to the processes that generate the most remarkable feature of our brains —our subjective experience.

For these reasons, man has long been fascinated by memory. Until recently, because of technical difficulties, our investigation of the mechanisms by which such processes are mediated has been more or less limited to observation of the behavioral effects of the manipulation of environmental variables and the consequences of relatively gross brain damage, whether brought about experimentally or occurring naturally.

A vast behavioral literature has accumulated on phenomena related to learning and forgetting, the two major methods by which memory has been studied operationally. No attempt will be made to provide a systematic review of this literature, which is beyond the scope envisaged for this book. Neither is it our purpose to attempt the construction of a theory which will explain all these multi-faceted data; this would be pretentious and premature. The purpose of this volume is to present and discuss some of the facts and logical considerations which may guide our strategy in devising experimental approaches to the problem of the physical basis of memory. Data pertaining most directly to the chemical and physiological mechanisms which mediate memory are emphasized, and data of a purely behavioral sort are relatively neglected. The general topics to which this inquiry is directed are: (1) What is memory? How is information stored in neural tissue? (2) Where is memory? What role does anatomical distribution play in the process of information storage, regardless of the physical chemistry of the storage process? (3) In view of what and where memory seems to be, how is stored information retrieved? (4) How does remembering occur?

Because of the complexity of the techniques required to approach these problems on the various levels on which they can be attacked, the experimenter in this field is faced at the very beginning of his work with the necessity of selecting between the many possible approaches. Such a selection must be guided to a large extent by intuition, buttressed by whatever support logic can provide. There seem to be four fundamental functions that a memory mechanism must perform: (1) the configuration of external and internal stimuli impinging upon an organism, which constitute an experience, must somehow be coded into a neural representation; (2) the neural representation of that experience (coded information about the set of stimuli) must be stored; (3) it must be possible to gain access to the coded information in order to retrieve specific experiences from storage; and (4) the retrieved data must again be decoded into neural activity, which somehow recreates the sensations and qualities of the original experience and thus constitutes a "memory."

One must concede, at the outset, that these functions need not necessarily be discrete and separate. Perception may well be influenced by what has been previously stored, and retrieval may well reflect release due to input. In spite of such qualifications logical distinctions exist between these functions.

A. Localization of function

Implicit in many of the theoretical and experimental approaches to the study of brain mechanisms mediating memory has been the assumption that these functions are localized in particular anatomical structures. The widespread acceptance of such ideas is easily understood in historical terms. The naïve notions about localization of functions in various brain areas which culminated in the formulations of phrenology were replaced by more sophisticated analyses of the relation between structure and function as anatomical studies of the brain became more detailed. The observation of a characteristic gross morphology, together with increased knowledge about the anatomical interconnections between structures, lent further intuitive support to the proposition that specific functions were mediated by particular specialized structures.

The central nervous system must, in any species, cope with the tasks of receiving information about relevant events from a characteristic set of receptors, evaluating and integrating such information in the light of the previous experience and present state of the individual, and organizing the coordinated control and reaction of a limited set of effectors. The existence of a characteristic group of receptors and effectors, joined to the central nervous system by rather simple anatomical connections, imposes common input and output requirements on the nervous systems of different individuals belonging to the same species. These common requirements constitute sufficient constraint to make the gross similarity

3

of structures and connections within a species not particularly remarkable. Obviously, the mere existence of comparable morphology does not *necessarily* imply strict correlation of structures with function, even at the level of receptor input and effector control. If, in addition, one considers the great variation between individuals with respect to the uniqueness of relevant past experiences, as well as the temporal fluctuation of state and immediate relevance within a single individual, there seems no compelling logical reason to assume that integrative and evaluative processes are localized to particular brain structures. Even so primitive a device as a high-speed digital computer possesses considerable versatility in its ability to allocate different functions to different structures in turn, in accordance with its internally stored program, despite the fact that its circuit connections are specified and stable.

Further support for notions of the stable relationship between structure and function came from classical neurophysiology. A large part of our knowledge about neurophysiological processes has been obtained from studies of functionally truncated nervous systems: a vast literature exists on the characteristics of afferent input to or efferent output from various regions following various stimuli administered to anesthetized animals, to immobilized animals, to the cerveau isolé, the encéphale isolé, or the spinal cord or portions thereof. Such data have revealed impressive constancy of process under specified conditions and have further enhanced the credibility of notions of functional localization. It is not my intent to disparage such studies. They provided considerable information about the characteristics of basal process in the nervous system, without which further progress in understanding would be unthinkable.

The relatively invariant properties of response which are often displayed by the nervous system under reproducible basal conditions may sometimes mislead us into believing that comparable stability will necessarily characterize performance under more normal conditions. An instructive example of the hazardousness of such assumptions was provided quite long ago. In much of the early work upon the effects of electrical stimulation of cortical points from which movements could be elicited, such responses were viewed as the physiological expression of precisely localized structures possessing stable connections with lower motor neurons. Lashley (1923) mapped the precentral gyrus of a rhesus monkey, using electrical stimulation in a series of tests extending over a period of weeks. In each test, motor reactions to stimulation of a particular cortical point were essentially constant, and in different tests the general cortical fields from which movements of face, arm, or leg were elicited tended to remain constant although the borders of the fields varied somewhat. However, within the arm area, stimulation of the same point in different tests produced widely different movements and at different times the same movement was obtained from widely separated and shifting areas. Such results suggested that within the segmental areas the various parts of the cortex might be equipotential for the production of all the movements of that limb, and that the particular movements elicited in any test depended upon the momentary physiological organization of the area rather than upon any point-for-point correspondence between pyramidal and spinal cells.

Evidence increasingly accumulates from studies of the unanesthetized, unrestrained animal that many conclusions about functional localization must be seriously questioned. Data which contradict expectations based on "classical" cytoarchitectonic or neurophysiological evidence, as well as dramatic evidence of functional compensation, abound in the literature. To cite a few recent examples: (1) evoked potentials (Doty, 1958) or responses of single neurons (Burns, Heron, and Grafstein, 1960) to visual stimuli can be recorded from a widespread extent of cortex, far exceeding the *area striata* as defined cytoarchitectonically; (2) visual discriminations can be established after extensive ablations of cortical and collicular regions of the visual system (Winans and Meikle, 1966; Urbaitis and Hinsey, 1966) and ablations which produce severe sensory deficits in adult cats cause little or no permanent discrimination deficits when performed on kittens (Tucker and Kling, 1966);[*] (3) cats can perform visual pattern discriminations after destruction of as much as 98% of the optic tract (Norton *et al.*, 1966); (4) cats can relearn an auditory frequency discrimination after bilateral ablation of all cortical auditory areas, including A_I, A_{II}, E_p, S_{II}, insular temporal cortex, and the suprasylvian gyrus, which results in complete retrograde degeneration of the medial geniculate body (Goldberg and Neff, 1964); (5) extensive bilateral lesion of the thalamic and mesencephalic reticular formation does not produce unconsciousness, loss of arousal, inability to acquire new conditioned responses or loss of previously acquired conditioned responses, if such damage is inflicted in *multiple stages* (Adametz, 1959; Chow, 1961; Chow and Randall, 1964).

---

[*] Further, the severe visual impairment after unilateral removal of the visual cortex can be reversed by subsequent destruction of the superior colliculus on the other side (Sprague, 1966).

It is not my intention to suggest that *no* functions are localized to specific brain structures. Certainly, evidence exists to the contrary. My purpose is to point out that strict correlation of structure with function is difficult even with respect to such species-constant characteristics as sensory input and motor output. Extensive functional equivalence exists within the brain, so that *some* functions can be mediated by several structures or by different regions within a single structure.

B. The assumption of discrete memory circuits

Nonetheless, it is understandable that early formulations of the crucial events in learning, based upon a viewpoint derived from anatomical studies of the sensory and motor systems, observations of invariant physiological response, and also the associationistic philosophy of the British empiricists, were *connectionistic* theories. They were phrased in terms of the establishment of new pathways between brain structures mediating response to a sensory stimulus and regions controlling the performance of a particular movement. The changed relationship between stimulus and response observed during learning suggested a corresponding change in the organization of the conducting system. A new connection was presumably established between receptors and effectors. Since the postulated new connection or pathway must necessarily lie in particular anatomical regions, memory was perforce localized to whatever structures were the site of the connections or pathways.

Furthermore, these theories emphasized the implications of the gradual increase in response which often accompanies repeated performance. It was argued that early in learning there was a preliminary penetration of resistant neural pathways by propagation of sensory disturbances. Repeated stimulation caused further use of these new paths, leading to a gradual diminution of the synaptic resistance to passage of nerve impulses in particular circuits. As a series of elementary connections was successively facilitated or established, a new memory was acquired. Performance of the newly learned response was attributed to the conduction of nerve impulses arising from the sensory stimulus along this specific new pathway. These theories were therefore *deterministic,* in that the invariant discharge of specific cells in the new pathway was required in order to mediate the control of effector output by sensory input to the receptors.

An early attempt to discredit learning theories based on changes in synaptic resistance or efficiency was provided by Lashley (1924a), who constructed experiments in which the peripheral neurons in both centripetal and centrifugal paths were blocked during training in order to show that new conditioned responses may be established under conditions in which the passage of significant impulses over certain pathways is precluded. First of all, he showed that if a rat was trained to perform a visual discrimination while one eye was blindfolded, it displayed perfect discrimination when the blindfold was transferred to the other eye, thus compelling the use of the eye which was covered throughout training. Identical results were obtained after destruction of the visual area of both hemispheres. These latter observations, together with data showing that the cerebral hemispheres are differentially integrated with the two retinas, were used to exclude the explanation that corresponding points in the two eyes were connected to common cortical cells. In a second experiment, he destroyed the right precentral gyrus of a monkey. During the subsequent paralysis of the left arm and leg, the animal learned to open a series of latch boxes with his right hand. During training, the left arm and hand were used only as a stiff prop to support the body. At no time during training did the animal touch the latches with his left hand. When the training was complete, the left precentral gyrus was destroyed, with a resultant paralysis of the "trained" right hand. The animal was kept without further training until the paralysis of the right arm had substantially recovered. In the meantime, he had acquired facility in the general use of his left hand, which recovered from the earlier operation. When the problem boxes were presented, the monkey fumbled clumsily at the fastenings during a few trials with his lame right hand, and then released them dexterously and without random movement using the left hand which had been paralyzed during training. Lashley offered these two experiments as cases which could not be explained by the wearing down of synaptic resistance through the passage of nerve impulses during learning, as though the nervous system was a telephone switchboard.

Lashley (1934) summarized and criticized the theories of memory which were current at that time. The nature of the memory trace or engram envisaged in those various formulations could be divided into five major groups: the growth of new processes connecting active neurons, the increase in transmitter availability in active pathways, changes in the molecular structure of the synaptic membrane, reverberatory

7

excitation, and the timing of motor systems so as to become resonant to particular patterns of activity in sensory systems. It is extremely interesting to note the similarity between those hypotheses and much of the contemporary thinking on this problem. Most of these theories are concerned with the explanation of conditioning. However, the framework of conditioning fails to encompass many kinds of learning. For example, naive animals can acquire a new behavioral response merely by *watching* conditioned animals perform (Corson, 1966; John and Chesler, 1966). It is even more difficult to conceive of such cognitive learning as mediated by connections or pathways between inputs and outputs.

The fundamental assumption underlying most current approaches to analysis of the mechanisms mediating information storage and retrieval in the brain is that an experience causes certain alterations in particular brain cells. Subsequent recall of this experience requires the activation of these altered brain cells, and that discharge "stands for" the stored item of information. There are a number of present theories, differing with respect to the nature of the changes presumed to occur at the molecular level. A salient feature of many of these formulations is that the learning and storage of new experience involves the establishment of new connections between cells, as by growth of new synaptic contacts, so that cells which previously did not respond to some stimulus are subsequently caused to discharge upon occurrence of that stimulus. Other theories propose that the "thing in a place" which is to be considered as stored information is a macromolecule synthesized in a particular cell, an altered excitability or structure of a postsynaptic membrane in a particular cell, or the facilitation of the synthesis of transmitter substance in particular cells.

These proposals share the assumption that the storage of information is accomplished deterministically, by the establishment of specific mediating circuitry involving a restricted set of cells. The details of the information retrieval process postulated in these various theories differ, in order to reconcile the "readout" process with the particular cellular mechanism which has been chosen. In spite of this variation in detail, such theories have the common feature that readout requires the selective activation of the cells comprising the appropriate memory circuit(s), and must still cope with objections like those raised long ago by Lashley.

C. Objections to the concept of an anatomically localized engram

Existing data permit reasonable doubt that such functions as the integration of sensory input, the memory of specific past events, or the evaluation of present input in the context of previous experience are localized in particular anatomical structures, as implied by connectionistic theories. Even if some day it were to be unequivocally established that any of these abstract functions could be irreversibly disrupted by destruction of some brain region, this would not constitute definite localization of the function within that general region as connections between particular cells.

A number of kinds of arguments can be leveled against the strongly connectionistic point of view. Were the memory of an event stored in the brain as a thing or set of things in a fixed place or set of places, the many experiments which have attempted to interfere with the retrieval of stored information, usually measured by the amount of retention of conditioned responses following both localized and extensive brain lesions, should have provided substantial evidence that *specific* memories could be irreversibly eradicated by damaging localized regions of the brain. By and large, attempts to demonstrate such specific erasure have been unsuccessful. If any effect is observed from such damage, it has almost invariably been an effect on a *class* of memories, attributable to some relatively general consequence, such as impairment of some regulatory function, loss of motivation, disinhibition, change in set, increased distractibility, inability to orient, or a defect in short-term storage, rather than selective *erasure* of a specific memory.

This does not impugn the fact that some regions have been demonstrated to be implicated in the *elaboration* of certain kinds of memories. For example, although the evidence for hippocampal involvement still contains apparent inconsistencies and contradictions, there is appreciable support for the contention that hippocampal function may be involved in the "stamping in" of memories, although permanent storage does not itself seem to require mediation of this structure. Similarly, various regions have been consistently implicated in mediation of some of the general factors just enumerated.

From time to time, there have been assertions that particular structures were involved indispensably in the retention of certain experiences. Again, almost invariably, the effective lesion has extirpated a whole structure or system. Such evidence might well implicate the structure in mediation of the learned response, but hardly constitutes proof that retrieval of the relevant memory required activation of a particular cell or group of cells. After all, a structure in the brain contains an enormous population of cells. The storage function can as reasonably be attributed to some process performed within that population as to some unique property restricted to certain cells which belonged to that population. Aside from this fundamental objection, the assertion that a particular structure was crucial for an abstract function has generally been disproved with further careful investigation. This is not to say that the performance of a particular conditioned response cannot be demonstrated to deteriorate after a localized insult to the brain. However, if time is permitted for the brain to recover, or perhaps if retraining is utilized to study the savings in training time, it often becomes apparent that the interference has perturbed access or performance rather than accomplished "erasure" of a memory.

In his famous summary, "In Search of the Engram," Karl Lashley (1950) provided numerous examples to illustrate this point. So long as primary sensory receiving areas are left intact, it has been extremely difficult to obtain evidence that localized brain damage interfered differentially with specific memories. A case in point is relevant here. Some time ago, Heinrich Klüver (Klüver, 1942; Lashley, 1950) conditioned monkeys to perform serial discriminations between the brighter of two lights, between two patterns, between two tones, and between two different weights. After the animals had learned all these discriminations, the associative cortex around each of the relevant primary cortical areas was extirpated. Following recovery from surgery, the monkeys were tested in each of these tasks and it was found that none of the discriminations could be performed. Klüver then retrained his monkeys to perform the discrimination between two weights, selecting the heavier of two weights. During the retraining period, no further experience was given the monkeys in *any* of the other tasks. Once the discrimination of weights had been restored to its previous high level, the animals were again tested for retention of the performance of all the other discriminations. After retraining only in weight discrimination, Klüver found that the monkeys were again able to discriminate between all the various visual and auditory stimuli for which differential performance had been abolished following surgery. He concluded that what had been impaired by the operations was not the memory of the various responses but rather the "set" to compare. In summary, then, the extensive literature on the effects of brain lesions on the performance of previously acquired conditioned responses fails to provide conclusive evidence for the anatomical localization of memory about such learned behaviors. Were memory stored as a thing in a place, one might expect a less uniformly negative outcome to such research.

A major contradiction to the above conclusion may lie in the permanence of certain apparent memory defects in man, such as agnosias and apraxias, which are extremely discrete. These defects presumably arise from localized tissue destruction. Neural mechanisms which mediate the storage and access to elements of symbolic language in man may possess somewhat greater anatomical specificity than the mechanisms involved in storage of the very much less precise and probably multidimensional elements which represent a learned relationship in lower animals. Yet, marked improvement in many kinds of activity seems possible after most brain lesions in man, particularly if no projection area is involved. Learning in human adults is extremely dependent upon preexisting verbal associations, and man is particularly vulnerable to brain damage that abolishes verbal associations (Ojemann, 1966). Much of the difference between studies of the effects of brain damage in animals and man is probably due to the use of verbal mnemonic aids by man. We must acknowledge that the bulk of the data adduced in the foregoing argument comes from animal studies in which the stored information may well be so abundant as to provide much more diffuse representation.

The set of phenomena to which the name "state-dependent learning" has been assigned are also in disagreement with what one would expect if memory were mediated by a structural change localized in a place. Perhaps the earliest description of state-dependent learning was provided by Girden and Culler (1937), who conditioned animals under curare and showed that the conditioned response thus established could not be demonstrated in the same animal without the drug, but reappeared when the animal was again curarized. A group of such experiments now exists which shows that if a conditioned response is established under particular specified ancillary conditions, such as an altered concentration of electrolytes, a certain level of food deprivation, or a certain time of day, such responses can be elicited best or only if the ancillary conditions are present. Thus, restoration of the *state* of the nervous system when the stimulus was received, as it were providing the proper context of the stimulus, seems to facilitate greatly the retrieval of stored information about previous experience with that

11

stimulus. This implies a much more global process than could be mediated by changes or "traces" localized to some specific cells.

In particular, if the establishment of memory consisted of the growth of new functional contacts between cells, the phenomena of state-dependent learning would require the assumption that such synapses became selectively inoperative during the absence of the essential state and reestablished contact when the necessary state was restored. Such assumptions are sufficiently labored as to appear most implausible.

D. Objections to deterministic theories

The various considerations previously enumerated indicate the general bases on which the writer questions the validity of connectionistic theories, according to which memory must be localized in a region. Other workers may consider that such objections can be adequately answered by assuming that the postulated pathways are diffusely distributed and therefore are localized but extensive. Rather than debate this issue further, it would seem more profitable to address our attention to the assumption that specific memories are stored in specific cellular circuits which by firing indicate recognition of present input as previously recorded. Some of the objections raised in the previous section are relevant to this proposition.

Additional general shortcomings of the deterministic hypothesis can be pointed out. Numerous recent neurophysiological studies have indicated that neuronal processes at all levels involve a probabilistic element. Many workers have proposed quantitative neuronal models in attempts to account for the unit activity observed experimentally. As a rule, such models have postulated a random factor influencing spike discharge. Some theorists have endeavored to account for the unpredictable aspect observed in cellular firing by "noisy" processes intrinsic to the cell, such as random fluctuations in membrane potential or threshold level. Other workers have located the source of randomness outside the responsive cell, suggesting factors like unpredictability in the time of synaptic excitation. Developments in the statistical analysis of neuronal spike data have recently been reviewed by Moore et al. (1966).

It is well known that most cells in the brain are in incessant activity. Such cells may indicate the occurrence of some specific stimulus by a change in their characteristic "resting" pattern of discharge. Individual cells can only be described as responsive to peripheral stimuli in a statistical sense, with a variability in response rate and latency which is perhaps attributable to their irregular spontaneous activity (Burns *et al.*, 1960). Furthermore, the firing pattern of almost *any* arbitrarily selected cortical cell can be shown to change in response to local electrical stimulation of almost any accessible cortical area, as well as to a variety of peripheral stimuli (Burns and Smith, 1962; Burns and Pritchard, 1964), even though sequential responses may well be different. In view of this demonstration that many if not all neurons can be more or less directly influenced by most other neurons, no essential purpose would seem to be served by the assumption that new synaptic contacts are formed during learning. Burns and Smith have stated:

> . . . during one second, a single neuron does not provide the rest of the brain with sufficient information to identify the presence and nature of a stimulus. Our results suggest that sensory inputs to the brain set up a spatial and temporal pattern of activity which probably involves most of the cells in the cerebral cortex. It would appear that differentiation of the effects of a stimulus from the 'noise' of continual or 'spontaneous' activity is only made possible by the simultaneous, weak response of many neurons!

Thus, it seems that all brain cells fire occasionally in the absence of any specific input, and any arbitrary stimulus will affect the discharge of most (and perhaps all) brain cells within an anatomical system. Such observations provide the basis for formulation of a number of questions which seem crucial to an understanding of the mechanisms of information coding, storage, and retrieval in the brain: (1) From the viewpoint of a central nervous system neuron, how is activity arising from the influx of information to be stored differentiated from activity arising from spontaneous or background discharge? (2) How are memories selected for storage? Since all experiences do not seem to register in memory, how do discharges related to experiences which achieve registration differ from those elicited by experiences which will not be stored? (3) How are the cells selected which are to mediate a particular memory? Since any stimulus may affect the activity pattern of many cells, how are the cells which will store the occurrence of that experience distinguished from the cells which will not? (4) How is discharge of a cell due to spontaneous* causes distinguished from discharge due to

---

* By spontaneous we mean discharge due to ongoing background activity as well as discharge which may arise from local electrolyte fluctuations and other factors unrelated to synaptic input.

13

the arrival of afferent information similar to previous inputs stored in that cell? (5) How is the discharge of a cell due to the occurrence of a "new" event distinguished from discharge due to the recurrence of a previously experienced event, since most events will influence the discharge of many cells and since the response of a neuron to a given stimulus is often variable? (6) Whatever the basis for reconciliation of the problems raised by the foregoing considerations, once a memory has been laid down in a cell, how is it protected against the overlay of subsequent experience, which will also achieve discharge of the cell? Memories are well segregated, new memories do not often intersperse amidst the fabric of old memories. (7) Memories have multiple components arising from various aspects of the stimulus complex. These components seem to be stored separately and sequentially, not in an averaged form. Are all representational cells for an experience repositories of the full experience or only of constituent fragments thereof? If the former is true, how are the fragments reconstituted from the fact of subsequent cell discharge? If the latter is correct, how are the pieces of a memory, represented in separate cells, unified? (8) Since cells have a refractory period and are involved in discharges due to a variety of influences, how does the brain recognize an event which impinges upon the cell or set of cells responsible for its identification while such cells are in the refractory state?

Let us assume that memories are in fact stored in particular cells, and are evoked or "remembered" as a result of their discharge. If the *specific cells* in which a memory was stored were to discharge due to spontaneous causes, we would expect to be constantly bombarded by unrelated fragments of recollections. Yet, most of us do not live in a continuous kaleidoscope of our past. Were they to discharge due to ongoing new experience, we should similarly expect a confusing interlacing of present events with irrelevant past events, which does not occur. Since most central nervous system neurons discharge intermittently, if specific memories were localized in particular cells, we should expect such cells to be "busy" or refractory, a significant proportion of the time. If memories stored in such cells were interrogated during these busy intervals, readout of the stored information would fail to occur, and we should be plagued by failure to remember at irregular intervals; yet most of us are not troubled by *intermittently* inaccessible or evanescent memories. Although failure to recover stored material is certainly a

14

common experience, such inability usually persists for much longer than the expected refractory period.

The reader can undoubtedly pose further expected malfunctions in accordance with such considerations. Although these arguments do not conclusively demonstrate that remembering is not achieved by the discharge of specific cells in particular pathways, they indicate at least some of the objections that can be raised to such a proposition. At this stage of our knowledge, one's willingness to accept the deterministic formulation as plausible, or to reject it as implausible, must be partially influenced by arguments of the sort which have been raised above, and by what, for want of a better phrase, we will call scientific intuition. In this book, the author will attempt to account for the functions which a memory mechanism must perform in accordance with the constraints suggested by considerations such as those which have just been presented. An endeavor will be made to provide relevant data and tentative answers to the questions which have been raised.

E. The statistical hypothesis

A statistical formulation of the mechanism of information storage and retrieval can be constructed, almost diametrically opposed to the deterministic conception, and which appeals more to this author. Since cells can fire spontaneously, since the response of a given cell to a specified input may be variable, and since most if not all cells within a region are influenced by many different inputs into the region, unique informational significance cannot safely be attributed by the nervous system to such unitary events. *This uncertainty would be greatly decreased if the information provided to the brain from the activity of a group of cells were represented by the orderly behavior of the ensemble, compared with the random or characteristic basal discharge pattern.* The information content of the ensemble might consist of the emergence of organized patterns of response from random or rhythmic baselines. The average activity of the population through time might represent particular items of information, and the significance or reliability of the information might be related to the level of coherence in the underlying elements of the ensemble. The ensemble across which the average is effectively taken might be defined on an anatomical basis by the

15

boundaries of the architectonic region containing the group of cells or similar criteria.

Since it is assumed that the discharge of any particular cell cannot be adequate to represent an item of information, or event, it follows that the memory of an event cannot be stored in a fashion which makes the discharge of any cell necessary or sufficient for its recognition or recall. From this viewpoint, the ability of cells to achieve adaptive behavior which requires the recognition of previously experienced stimuli cannot be dependent on any single cell in the aggregate, but must arise from the patterned activity of the population.* If the coded information

---

* *Statistical Models:* Early theoretical models of brain function consisted largely of attempts to construct "nerve nets" of idealized neurons with connections capable of achieving some desired computation. Neurons were used in these models essentially as bi-stable switching devices providing simple logical functions. These endeavors received substantial encouragement from the development of stored-program digital computers, capable of performing extremely complex computations with simple elements. In a classical paper entitled "A Logical Calculus of the Ideas Immanent in Nervous Activity," McCulloch and Pitts (1943) established that any function which can be defined logically and unequivocally in a finite number of words can be realized by a formal neural network of two-state elements. Numerous subsequent papers provided detailed descriptions of deterministic networks designed to perform specific physiological or psychological functions. Rosenblatt (1962) has summarized some salient features of such models and listed some limitations of their utility. He concludes that, in general, such models have neither uniqueness nor generality, correspond poorly to known facts of neuroanatomy and neurophysiology, lack predictive value, and are not testable in detail because the postulated circuitry cannot be traced in neural tissue.

More recently, a set of models has been developed which are more consonant with the theoretical formulation presented in this book. These models provide numerous examples of networks which generate functionally equivalent processes differing in the details of the actual cells which are used. These models view the brain as a statistically organized system which displays certain classes of lawful behavior. One of the earliest endeavors of this sort was made by Shimbel and Rapoport (1948), vho characterized various parameters of a network by probability distributions and eveloped general equations for the probability of firing of a specified neuron unc r different conditions. In a pioneering study, Farley and Clark (1954) simulated a st. stically connected neural network and studied the response characteristics of the system, including its capability to modify responses or "recognize." Smith and Davidson (1962) have combined theoretical analysis and computer simulation of probabilistically interconnected networks of neurons. Such probabilistic networks can support self-maintaining activity which may have steady-state or oscillatory characteristics. Certain general patterns were observed which suggested that such networks tended to "organize" themselves from an initially disorganized state. Of particular interest were the cycling activity patterns which frequently emerged in these systems. A survey of statistical brain models is not within the

about events çausing afferent input to a region is contained in the non-random deviation of the ensemble from the random spatiotemporal pattern, the memory mechanism must achieve the stored specification of that orderly spatiotemporal process, so as to make that mode of ensemble activity *more probable*. When similar stimuli impinge upon the population subsequent to the storage of this memory, the most probable average behavior of the ensemble must correspond to the previous temporal pattern of deviation from the random distribution of ongoing activity. In this fashion, the coded representation of the previous input might be reproduced without requiring the participation of any specific cells.

In this view then, the memory of a past experience is not represented deterministically by the activity of any specific cell or group of cells in the population, but is specified by the average activity of the population through time, reflecting alterations in the spatiotemporal patterns of discharge as a result of past experience. This hypothesis will be developed more fully in subsequent chapters.

F. The material basis of memory

Whether truth about memory is represented by either of the views just stated, whether it lies someplace in between, partaking of both kinds of process, or consists of mechanisms not included in those alternatives, further specific questions can be posed. Whether memory is a thing in a place or a process in a population, the sustained change which we call memory must be mediated by some alteration of matter, some redistribution of chemical compounds.

What is the material of which memory is made? The same funda-

---

scope of this volume. Our purpose here is primarily to emphasize the existence of a large amount of intriguing and sophisticated theoretical work in this domain.

Good examples are provided by Ashby, whose "Design for a Brain" (1952) outlines a general approach to probabilistic models and illustrates how statistical mechanisms can achieve adaptive behavior; Beurle (1957), who has analyzed the characteristics of waves in a neuron mass with special attention to the ability of such a system to regenerate pulses; and Rosenblatt (1958), who has studied the capacity of statistically organized networks or perceptrons to accomplish a variety of psychological functions. Additional examples can be found in symposia on "Mechanization of Thought Processes" (National Physical Laboratory Symposium, 1959), "Self-Organizing Systems" (1960), and "Aspects of the Theory of Artificial Intelligence (Muses, 1962).

mental dichotomy encountered above can also be formulated with respect to the stuff of memory. If the substance providing the physical basis for two items of memories could be isolated chemically, two alternatives exist. Either the two memory substances would be chemically different, each reflecting in its structure the information which it represented, or the two isolated fractions would be identical, achieving the representation of information by distribution rather than by configuration. If memory is coded as a molecular configuration unique to each experience, how is the significance of discharge of a cell due to one molecular structure within it differentiated from that due to another? If spatial distribution of some common memory stuff is the vehicle of information storage, then we must face the questions raised earlier about the interpretation of discharge in a particular neuron or set of neurons.

Bypassing such problems temporarily, whatever the physical chemistry of the memory stuff, how is it made? There seem to be at least two stages in the elaboration of memory: an early labile phase in which representation of information about an experience is susceptible to erasure by perturbations of various kinds, and a later stable phase in which such perturbations have little or no disruptive effect. There must be an interface between these two phases, and it is important to inquire into its possible nature. Furthermore, once a memory has entered the stable phase there seems to be a gradual further stabilization. Such memories are not inviolate but can be made difficult of access. Amnesias are sometimes characterized by the fact that more recent memories become relatively less accessible, while quite early memories remain exceedingly durable. So memories seem to age, and somehow stabilize as they age. How might this occur?

The final problem relates to the spatial distribution of memory. Whether or not memory is localized as a thing in a place or a process in a population, there must be certain regions of the brain which are relatively more involved in this function at certain times than are others. It is possible that the locus of the neural tissue involved in various stages of the deposition of a memory shifts, and perhaps further shifts occur during the gradual stabilization with aging which has been referred to.

This book, then, will address itself to the foregoing questions, stressing what seems to the author to be relevant neurochemical and neurophysiological evidence.

CHAPTER II

THE LABILE PHASE IN MEMORY

A. The consolidation phase

Many experiments on the stabilization of memory suggest that there is a labile period, early in the registration of a memory, during which the fixation of experience is susceptible to external interference. Various kinds of perturbations have been demonstrated to accomplish erasure during this period, although they are ineffective some time later. Estimates of the duration of the vulnerable stage vary from a few seconds (Chorover and Schiller, 1965) to as much as days (Pearlman, Sharpless, and Jarvik, 1961) or even weeks (Flexner et al., 1963) depending on the nature of the test situation, the experimental species, and the strength and type of interfering agent. A survey of this phenomenon was published several years ago by Glickman (1961). A number of examples will be presented here which illustrate the evidence that there exists a period of time, whatever its length, during which a labile representation of experience gives way to a more stable long-term storage process.

Probably the earliest formulation of such a consolidation theory was provided by Müller and Pilzecker (1900) in an attempt to account for the observation that the ability to recall recently acquired verbal material deteriorated as a function of the interpolation of other tasks. They postulated the existence of a neural perseverative process, which was susceptible to external interference, in order to explain this retroactive inhibition. Alternative explanations, such as the concept of associative interference, were proposed to account for such behavioral phenomena,

19

which were not by themselves considered sufficient to compel acceptance of the perseveration theory.

More direct physiological evidence for the existence of a consolidation phase, however, was forthcoming from observations of retrograde amnesia resulting from cerebral trauma or anesthesia. The frequency of occurrence of retrograde amnesia is indicated by a survey of over 1000 cases of head injury, published by Russell and Nathan (1946). Over 700 of the individuals in this study reported amnesia for events occurring up to ½ hour before the injury, and 133 reported retrograde amnesia for the events during a period longer than 30 minutes. In most patients, the duration of the "erased" period was only a few moments. The authors concluded that the loss of memory of recent experiences was due to interference with a perseverative process.

With the introduction of electroshock therapy in 1937, many workers observed that electroconvulsive shock (ECS) resulted in amnesia for a brief period preceding it. Zubin and Barrera (1941) demonstrated that interpolated ECS abolished savings in the relearning of lists of paired associates originally learned before treatment, and showed that the severity of impairment of retention was an inverse function of the time lapse between initial learning and ECS. These conclusions from human studies were extended and confirmed in animal experiments by Duncan (1949), Ransmeier (1953), and other workers. The results of these various studies indicate that there is a marked deterioration of performance after ECS, and the magnitude of the effect increases as the interval between the learning experience and ECS decreases.*

The most serious objection to interpretation of these results as evidence for consolidation arises from the data of Miller and Coons (1955), indicating that ECS has punishing effects, and attributing the post-ECS decrement in performance of rewarded behaviors to production of a conflict situation. Although such an interpretation is logically possible, the use of control groups receiving painful but nonconvulsive shocks in studies like those cited above has showed that painful shocks produce a smaller decrement of performance over a much shorter posttrial period than the decrements observed after ECS (Coons and Miller, 1960). In more recent publications, Miller and his colleagues have conceded that the retention deficits caused by ECS are sometimes the result of a true amnesia (Quartermain et al., 1965). Attempts to test the generality of

---

* Although the data of Chevalier (1965) suggest that ECS effects are permanent, under certain conditions recovery can occur (Zinkin and Miller, 1967).

conclusions about the time course of consolidation which have been proposed by some of these workers show that a temporal gradient of retrograde amnesia as long as 1 hour can be observed in some but not other one-trial learning situations (Kopp, 1966; Kopp *et al.*, 1966).

Strong rebuttal of the conflict explanation of the post-ECS decrement has been provided by experiments such as those of Essman and Jarvik (1961) in which the conflict and consolidation interpretations have in essence been opposed in one-trial learning situations. In these studies, the experimental animal is placed on a small platform above a shock grid. The time which elapses before he steps off the platform onto the grid is ascertained by a number of control trials. The animal is then shocked when next he steps off the platform. Normally, this single experience results in a large increase in the amount of time he will remain on the platform. Posttrial administration of ECS or a number of chemical agents, including both anesthetics and convulsants, abolished this increase, so that the animal stepped onto the shock grid with the same short latency as before the shock trial. This selection of a behavior which has resulted in punishment would seem decisive evidence that a consolidation process has been interrupted by the ECS.

Other experimental studies have explored whether a variety of perturbations of the nervous system could achieve interference with the registration of recent experience, of a comparable sort to the deficit produced by ECS. Cerf and Otis (1957) showed that heat narcosis immediately after massed avoidance training impaired the subsequent performance of goldfish more severely than identical treatment administered several hours after training. Ransmeier and Gerard (1954) failed to find evidence that lowered body temperatures interfered with the retention of a maze habit in the hamster, although anoxia was effective in producing decrements in learning. Baldwin and Soltysik (1965) have shown that cerebral ischemia, causing cessation of brain electrical activity, can be continued for a period of 90 seconds, beginning 50 seconds after a training trial, without impairing acquisition of a classical defensive reflex. This suggests that if reverberatory activity is involved in short-term memory, consolidation must be substantially completed within 50 seconds. Gerard (1955) has reported, however, that hypothermia extends the period during which ECS can produce deficits in performance. This suggests that the rate of the processes responsible for permanent storage of experience can be slowed by lowering brain temperatures. As mentioned previously, anesthetic and convulsant agents

21

have also been shown to impede consolidation. Some of the failures to achieve effects with ether anesthesia reported in the literature may be accounted for by the interesting observation of Jarvik that the temperature at which the ether is volatized is an important variable (1964).

B. Localization of consolidation process

Experiments of the sort which have been summarized thus far provide evidence that gross interference with ongoing brain activity, shortly after an experience, prevents the permanent registration of that experience in memory. However, such experiments fail to provide any insight into the possible anatomical locus of the consolidation process.

A number of experiments, particularly the dramatic observations of Milner and Penfield (1955), have directed attention to the possible role of the hippocampus in the "stamping in" of experience. This proposition seems to receive support from such studies as those of Bureš (Bureš, Burešová, and Weiss, 1960a) which show that hippocampal spreading depression can block retention of avoidance learning, and Hunt and Diamond (1957), who reported that bilateral hippocampectomy interferes differentially with performance of avoidance responses to visual and auditory cues, and that the effects disappear with overtraining.

Yet Grastyán and Karmos (1962) have shown that bilateral removal of the hippocampus in the cat does not interfere with the ability to acquire either alimentary or defensive conditioned reflexes. Flynn and Wasman (1960) demonstrated that a defensive reflex could be established during bilateral afterdischarge of the hippocampus following electrical stimulation. A number of investigators have concluded that various behavioral deficits observed after hippocampal disturbance are not due to recent memory loss, but can be attributed to discrimination failure (Cordeau and Mahut, 1964), motivational changes (Grossman and Mountford, 1964), complexity of task (Drachman and Ommaya, 1964), or inability to alter previously established behaviors (Webster and Voneida, 1964). These inconsistencies indicate the necessity of using a variety of response measures and methods of intervention in attempts to assess the anatomical localization of memory processes.

Studies too numerous to review here have explored the effects of localized brain lesions on such tasks as delayed response or alternation,

22

interpreting observed deficits as due to interference with short-term memory or consolidation. For our purposes, it suffices to emphasize that a variety of regions has been thus implicated as necessary for consolidation of particular experiences to occur. The desirable control features provided by more reversible types of interference lead us to turn to other experiments which utilize temporary local stimulation or depression in an effort to localize regions involved in the consolidation process.

C. Interference by local stimulation

A number of workers have attempted to interfere with consolidation of learning by localized electrical stimulation of various brain regions (Zeigler, 1957). Mahut (1962, 1964) tested the effects of electrical stimulation of the nonspecific thalamic nuclei on perceptual learning in rats and cats, obtaining a deficit in animals receiving such stimulation as compared with unstimulated animals or animals stimulated in the midbrain tegmentum. Glickman (1958) has studied the effects of stimulation of the mesencephalic reticular formation on acquisition of an avoidance habit, observing that stimulated animals revealed poorer retention than unstimulated controls. Olds (1959) has described an ingenious learning set paradigm in the rat, enabling him to explore the effects of electrical stimulation upon acquisition or upon subsequent performance of the correct response for a given day. He found severe interference with acquisition resulting from stimulation of hippocampus, anterior thalamus, and periamygdaloid cortex, although stimulation of most cortical points was ineffective. Performance of previously established responses was disrupted by stimulation of periamygdaloid cortex, although stimulation of hippocampus or anterior thalamus had little effect. However, Burns and Mogenson (1958) and Stamm (1961) have reported that electrical stimulation of various cortical areas interferes with acquisition of certain conditioned responses.

The observations of Zuckermann are also relevant to the role of the cortex (Zuckermann, 1959). Following establishment of classical defensive reflexes to a visual stimulus, Zuckermann caused local seizure discharge in various areas by direct electrical stimulation, and tested the ability of the visual conditioned stimulus (CS) to elicit the conditioned response (CR) during local afterdischarge. Presentation of the visual

23

CS during afterdischarge of motor cortex elicited performance of the CR, although no evoked potentials seemed to be elicited in the *visual* cortex by the stimulus. Similarly, presentation of the CS elicited the CR during afterdischarge of the mesencephalic reticular formation (MRF) although intrinsic brainstem reflexes were abolished. Conversely, presentation of the CS did *not* result in performance of the CR during afterdischarge of the visual cortex. This suggested that performance required an intact functional relationship between the sensory projection area and subcortical regions, presumably thalamic and/or limbic.

Many criticisms have been leveled against experiments of the sort that have been cited, on grounds ranging from the possible interference with registration of reinforcement due to ongoing stimulation, through interference with registration of sensory experience or maintenance of set or orientation, to the possibly reinforcing and therefore competing effects of central stimulation. In spite of such ambiguities, which hopefully will be resolved by future experimental results, if one considers the existing data as a whole, it is striking that *interference with registration has been obtained by stimulation of a widespread set of brain regions,* including representatives of the various major functional systems. Whether the observed effects are in fact directly due to interference with consolidation, or less directly to the various kinds of competing activity suggested in the alternative explanations, it seems that severe disturbance of the activity of a goodly portion of the brain is often not compatible with concurrent consolidation, although the precise nature of the interference undoubtedly varies, depending on the disturbed region. Effects obtained by a particular type of interference probably depend as well upon the nature of the task.

Although the contradictions in the data argue against the suggestion that any single brain region or system could be responsible for mediation of consolidation of all learned experiences, the results suggest that particular regions may well play a salient or critical role in the consolidation of memories about certain specific classes of events.

D. Interference by local depression

Another approach to localization of the consolidation process is the transitory depression of function. Just as local stimulation establishes a disturbance which propagates elsewhere, while lesions may release otherwise inhibited areas which leads to difficulty of interpretation of results, similarly depression of local function does not produce locally confined effects. Yet the strategy is an interesting one, in view of the fact that general depression of nervous system activity has been demonstrated to interfere with registration of experience. Perhaps the most promising approach to this problem has been provided by the use of spreading depression, ingeniously utilized by Bureš and other workers (Bureš, 1959; Bureš and Burešová, 1965; Russell and Ochs, 1963).

Spreading depression (SD) is a reaction displayed by neural tissue to a variety of agents, ranging from electrical stimulation to topical application of KCl. The reaction seems to consist of a gradually spreading potential change, accompanied by a flattening of the EEG, a disappearance of evoked responses, and impedance changes, apparently resulting from a marked intracellular chloride shift (Van Harreveld and Schade, 1959) and a massive extracellular potassium shift (Křivánek and Bureš, 1960) accomplishing a massive depolarization of involved neurons. Bureš has observed that cortical SD is accompanied by an increase in firing of units in the MRF, and a decrease in certain thalamic areas (Bureš, Burešová, Weiss, and Fifková, 1963; Burešová, Bureš, and Fifková, 1962a). Cortical SD has little effect on spontaneous or evoked hippocampal electrical activity, and, conversely, hippocampal SD does not exert marked effects upon the cortex. There has been some controversy as to whether or not SD itself required prior tissue damage due to dehydration, but the work using chronically implanted electrodes indicates this is untrue (Van Harrevald et al., 1956; Ochs et al., 1960).

Bureš (1959) has demonstrated that a conditioned animal will stop displaying conditioned responses (CR's) to the conditioned stimulus (CS) during cortical SD, although unconditioned responses (UR's) continue to be elicited by the unconditioned stimulus (US). The dependence of performance upon cortical-subcortical relationships is suggested by an ingenious study by Burešová et al. (1962b). A unilateral lesion was placed in the hypothalamic "feeding center." An alimentary conditioned response was then established, with both hemispheres intact. After acquisition of this response, these workers showed that cortical SD contralateral to the hypothalamic lesion blocked performance of the CR, while cortical SD ipsilateral to the lesion had no effect.

Pearlman and Jarvik (1961) have demonstrated that bilateral cortical

SD after a one-trial learning task blocks the consolidation of the experience, indicating that the cortex is crucially involved, quite like the results with ECS or anesthetics. This conclusion is compatible with the results of Bureš (1959) and Russell and Ochs (1963) showing that SD in a cerebral hemisphere prevents the participation of that hemisphere in the formation of a trace, while not affecting an already established memory. A chemical "split-brain" can be achieved so that if a conditioned response is established while SD is applied to one cortical hemisphere, no performance is displayed during subsequent testing in which the previously intact hemisphere is depressed while the previously depressed hemisphere is intact. Transfer of information between the two hemispheres can be accomplished by one trial with both hemispheres intact.

One is reminded of Morrell's demonstration that a discharging epileptic focus in the region of the CS prevented establishment of cortical conditioning (1958) while a lesion in the cortical region responding to the US did not interfere. This buttresses Lashley's emphasis on the importance of the sensory projection areas for modality specific learning. Conversely, Bureš found complete abolition of CR following hippocampal SD, after *massed* training, while *minimal* defects were observed after cortical SD (Bureš, 1959). The duration of the massed training was sufficient to permit the possibility that considerable consolidation occurred before cortical SD was administered. The differential results obtained suggest a differential *time rate* of susceptibility in various regions that is reminiscent of similar differences found with various chemical agents.

It is difficult to provide evidence that a localized disturbance or damage can interfere with performance of a given task without at the same time affecting the subject's ability to acquire the same performance.

The mechanisms of temporary information storage and retrieval, consolidation, and long-term information storage and retrieval are difficult to separate experimentally although they are readily distinguished logically. These mechanisms presumably mediate the ability to learn, to recall past experiences, and to perform learned acts. We try to infer facts about the underlying mechanisms from observations of these functions. The recall of past experience may be mediated differently before and after consolidation. The mechanisms mediating retrieval and readout may well involve a multiplicity of anatomical structures and may well differ from task to task as well as between stages of learning. These considerations highlight the caution necessary in interpretation of experimental findings in this domain and indicate some possible explanations for the apparent inconsistency and contradiction that exist between many reports. However, the apparent contradictions and inconsistencies in the data cited above also serve as evidence suggesting that there is no unique anatomical locus crucially responsible for consolidation. Multiple loci seem to be involved that vary according to the particular sensory and motivational characteristics of the test procedure utilized, that is, the content of the information to be stored. Since most tasks are multidimensional with respect to the attributes of relevant sensory information, motivational parameters, and necessary effector involvement, it is reasonable to expect that widespread neural regions must participate in the over-all consolidation process. However, if some of this evidence were interpreted as compelling the interpretation that a specific brain region were uniquely necessary to achieve consolidation of a particular experience, this would not constitute proof that permanent storage of the memory resides in the region or in a unique set of cells therein.

E. The reverberation hypothesis

These various data, no matter how unsatisfactory they may be from the viewpoint of establishing regional responsibility for consolidation, do provide an adequate demonstration that there is a period following the occurrence of an event during which disturbance of the nervous system will interfere with registration of the experience. The assumption most frequently encountered as an explanation for this phenomenon of consolidation is that it depends upon the ability of specific neuronal circuits to sustain a reverberatory activity. This hypothesis originates from the anatomical studies of Lorente de Nó (1938). It was explicitly proposed by Hilgard and Marquis (1940), Hebb (1949), and numerous other workers who suggested that *reverberatory activity sustains the representation of an experience until permanent structural or chemical storage has been accomplished.* This "trace" theory has been reviewed by Gomulicki (1953).

Some evidence that stimulation results in a transient reverberation of neural activity has been directly provided by Verzeano and Negishi (1960), who recorded from multiple microelectrodes in the thalamus of the cat. They reported the appearance of recurrent *patterns* of unit discharge following sensory stimulation which they interpreted as evidence for continued circulation of a representation of the stimulus through a responsive neural network. The pattern of discharge that was observed varied as the stimulus was changed. Additional evidence for the existence of reverberatory activity has been provided by Burns (1954, 1958) who studied the electrical activity of cortical slabs that were isolated neurally from the rest of the brain while retaining an intact blood supply. Such slabs display a marked diminution of spontaneous electrical activity. However, Burns has observed that a single electrical stimulus train can initiate bursts of electrical activity in these slabs which last for 30 minutes or longer. These bursts can be blocked by a subsequent massive electrical interference, but become easier to elicit if the stimulus is repeated. This burst activity seems to involve reverberatory circuits.

F. Self-selection of representational neurons

The existence of the consolidation phase, together with the reverberation hypothesis, may provide the basis for an answer to two of the questions raised in Chapter I: (1) How are memories selected for storage, since all experiences do not seem to register in memory? (2) How are the cells selected that are to mediate the storage of a particular experience, since most stimuli affect the activity of many cells?

The answer to the first question might be that only those experiences are stored in memory which can achieve excitation in a significant number of neurons, under conditions which permit reverberatory activity to persist during the period necessary for consolidation to take place. This implies the existence of a "storage threshold." Although random variables may contribute to the storage threshold, it seems subject to systematic influence since it is possible to "direct one's attention" effectively to stimuli that are to be remembered. Perhaps the effect of such attentional focus or set is to change the excitability of a population of neurons so that a more coherent response will ensue, thus achieving the storage threshold more readily. Certain situations may sharpen attention in a particularly reliable fashion, and therein may lie the explanation of why some kinds of learning consistently occur with rapidity.

28

With respect to the second question, consider the consequences of excitation of a number of neurons in an extensively interconnected network, due to some input "stimulus." Each of the initially responsive cells has access to a number of neural pathways, a proportion of which are reentrant and form loops around which an impulse might circulate. The path length of the loops might be as short as two neurons, each stimulating the other, or might be extremely long. The circulation time in a given loop depends on the number of synapses in the circuit, the path length, and transmission times in the fibers which are involved. In any anatomical region, the *distribution* of possible path lengths and the corresponding circulation times would depend upon fine anatomical structure, regional microchemistry, and blood supply, and might be expected to be characteristic for that region.

At the instant of arrival of a specific afferent barrage, certain cells in the population are refractory while others are responsive. The selection of the initially responsive neuron set, therefore, must reflect some fortuitous factors. This initially responsive set now propagates the disturbance into the available set of pathways. Certain of these possible routes are blocked due to refractoriness, while others are momentarily facilitated or inhibited by ongoing activity. The cumulative effects of these constraints plus the inhibitory consequences of the input itself act to terminate the propagation of the disturbance along certain of the possible paths, while other paths sustain propagation long enough to succeed in becoming reentrant. Only cells in pathways which become reentrant can participate in reverberatory activity. Since we assume that sustained activity or inhibition is a prerequisite for permanent storage of information to be accomplished, and furthermore that the effect of reverberation must be upon the cells which mediate circulation of activity, *these cells and those which they inhibit are selected as the only set of neurons which could serve to store a representation of the original afferent stimulus configuration.* Multiple reentrant pathways undoubtedly exist in parallel, and may be thrown into activity at different times. However, all cells that do not belong to some such pathway or receive its influences would seem to be necessarily excluded from participation in the storage process.

However, the achievement of reentry is not *sufficient* for a loop to participate in storage. If we assume that the mean time required for a neuron in the central nervous system to respond to stimulation of its

29

dendrites by depolarization of the soma, the generation of an action potential propagated along its axon to the terminal arborization, and passage of that impulse across the synapse is (on the average) 5 milliseconds, and if we assume that 20 minutes is often the duration of the consolidation phase (since that is the most frequently encountered estimate of the time involved), a crude estimate of the number of neural discharges which must go on during the consolidation period in such a reverberating loop would be on the order of 240,000. (Values of transmission time and duration of consolidation existing in the literature suggest that this estimate might well be erroneous in either direction by as much as one order of magnitude.) Since this is not a number which represents a significantly large percentage of the brain (according to Chow, Blum, and Blum, 1950), the cell population of the visual cortex of monkeys is approximately 140,000,000 cells), it is possible that a group as small as several hundreds of cells undergoes a thousand recirculations during the consolidation period, or that a group as large as 240,000 cells undergoes one sequential ordered discharge. Reverberation in pathways of interconnected loops might reduce the number of participating cells even further.

An objection can be raised on logical grounds to the proposition that storage of information is achieved by *one* iteration around a network involving any number of neurons. It is difficult to understand how a cell in such a sequence would alter itself *differently*, as a result of participation in such a circuit, from the alteration resulting from spontaneous discharge not due to membership in a representational set. Actually, a continuum of possibilities must exist in any anatomical region between two extremes: Small loops involving only a few neurons might reverberate at high frequencies many thousands of times, and long loops involving a large number of cells might reverberate at lower frequencies only several times. The distribution of loop lengths between these extremes would depend upon regional factors as discussed above.

The minimum loop length might be estimated from data on spike frequencies in single cells, and the maximum frequencies observed in brain electrical rhythms. Although occasional events at higher frequency can be observed, few cells fire more than 100 times per second, and relatively little brain electrical activity can be observed above that rate. Most activity is at appreciably slower frequencies, below 50 per second. The maximum loop length cannot be well estimated, yet one would expect it to be much smaller than 240,000 neurons. Whatever might be the details of the activity during consolidation, appreciable time is required to achieve long-term information storage in neurons. Most chemical reactions proceed rather quickly. Why then does consolidation require such a comparatively long time?

G. Critical substance and critical shift

Perhaps the reaction which produces the stuff which stores memories requires achievement of a minimum change in the concentration of a critical substance or catalyst inside the nerve cell, and this change is more than is accomplished by a single neural discharge. Furthermore, the change in concentration due to a single discharge may be dissipated by diffusion or by destruction of this necessary substance. Unless this hypothetical product of discharge is to swamp the cell, the normal rate of cell activity and metabolism must maintain the concentration at a steady state level. Nonrandom or *sustained* alteration in the pattern or rate of activity in a neuron would tend to shift this balance. Define the change in the rate of production of this critical substance in a neuron per unit time after a discharge as ΔF, and the required net change to initiate the storage reaction in any cell i as K_i, the *critical shift*. Then those cells which could participate in the representation of that experience are those cells for which $\Delta F \times T \geqslant K_i$. T is equal to the consolidation time for the corresponding cell. Cells in extremely long loops would be unable to shift concentration sufficiently to outstrip homeostatic regulation since the unitary increment occurs infrequently. Furthermore, the longer the loop, the greater would be the chance that a participating cell might be captured by competing circuits. The briefer the interval between firings due to reverberation, the more likely is a cell to be preempted by representational activity and thereby protected during the consolidation period.

Although the preceding discussion directs attention to the effects of a sustained increase in the rate of activity of a given neuron, the same consequences can be envisaged for a sustained decrease in activity. Critical shifts in concentration in some cells might result from accumulation during inactivity. Furthermore, critical shifts might consist of lowering the concentration of certain substances. The occurrence of

31

inhibition contains possible informational significance. Inhibition of neural activity is probably an essential aspect of learning, and a parallel formulation should be assumed for the simultaneous inhibitory influences, although it will not be explicitly constructed here. It is also necessary to realize that the critical substance need not be a specific molecule common to all cells. Various substances may serve such a regulatory role and they may differ from time to time and from cell to cell. Furthermore, the threshold for critical shift may not be the same for all neurons involved, nor need it be the same under all metabolic conditions. Thus, the achievement of consolidation in a group of cells participating in shared activity may proceed at varying rates in different cells.

These assumptions create a picture of a network in which certain cells participate in reverberations after an afferent barrage. Each cellular discharge is considered to contribute a unitary increment toward a concentration change in a critical substance. Since discharge occurs at varying rates in various loops, increments accumulate at varying rates in different neurons. The *rate* of change of concentration must exceed some minimum in order to outstrip the homeostatic mechanisms of the cell. This adequate rate must be sustained for a sufficient time to achieve a critical shift in concentration necessary to trigger the storage reaction. Since only the net shift is considered crucial, this model depicts consolidation as a process occurring at different rates in circuits reverberating at different frequencies, *all of which participate in the representation of the original event.* Since these cells are the only neurons in the nervous system which have been altered by the event, the memory of that event must *necessarily* be somehow stored in this neural subset.

Learning often takes numerous trials although it can occur with a single experience. Certain events seem to register with reliable rapidity. The process that has been described is such that if the necessary shift in concentration occurs in some or all the neurons of a particular mediating loop after a specific trial, for those cells consolidation can be considered to be accomplished as a consequence of that experience. In many cells, the effects of that trial fail to achieve the critical shift before neural activity returns to the usual level. The residual concentration changes would thereafter be expected to dissipate gradually because of factors related to metabolism and diffusion. Unless the cell is again set into sustained activity before normal concentration levels are restored, there will be no lasting effect of the experience in that neuron.

After a particular trial, some neurons are postulated to achieve an altered state (consolidation) in the nonincremental manner which has been outlined. On subsequent trials, stimulus conditions and neural excitability will be somewhat different. Presumably, additional sets of neurons will achieve consolidation in a similar way each time the event is repeated. The ability of these neural sets to alter behavioral performance, *which is the usual operational criterion that learning has occurred,* will depend on a variety of factors. These probably include the percentage of neurons in the population which have achieved consolidation by the relevant time, the variability of state of the system, and the complexity of the stimulus input and of the operationally defined response. The ability of these altered sets of neurons to mediate altered behavioral response in a reliable way might be expected to increase more or less gradually, i.e., incrementally, depending upon the response criterion. In this view, information storage can occur without affecting overt behavior. Whether one chooses to call such storage learning becomes a matter of definition.

Any neuron may have access to numerous potentially reentrant paths of varying length. An impulse may well circulate around first one loop and then another, crossing over at some cell which constitutes a *nodal* point between these alternative paths. Changes in local excitability, convergence of impulses, and inhibitory effects might be expected to play a major role in shifting activity from circuit to circuit in this way. The previously cited work of Verzeano and Negishi (1960) shows, however, that such factors are not so overwhelming as to preclude sustained circulation in a network. From the foregoing discussion, we might expect consolidation to proceed at different rates in nodal cells, and in nonnodal cells in loops of varying length. Conceivably, the results of a particular input might be such that only certain nodal cells could achieve consolidation.

The regional fine structure or the point at which a perturbation entered a network might determine the ratio of nodal to nonnodal cells in a given population. A cell need not belong only to one loop of a specified length, but might have membership probabilistically in loops of all the possible lengths represented in the population distribution, in addition to a number of nonreentrant pathways. Therefore, the activity observed in a cell which is participating in a process of the sort de-

33

scribed here need not be rhythmic, but need only contain an iterated pattern embedded in other activity. Statistically, the average ensemble activity during a fixed interval and the pattern of unit discharge integrated over a sufficiently large sample of activity might well converge, at a rate depending upon the diversity of processes in which a single cell might be involved.

Does critical shift imply deterministic function?

The reader may possibly conclude at this point that the foregoing argument outlining the processes by which changes in specific cells would occur after an experience actually provides support for the deterministic formulation which it is my intention to challenge. If changes occur in specific cells due to reverberation, so that a consolidation process can take place only in those cells, they therefore participate discretely in the storage of information. Clearly, no theory could hope to explain memory without invoking permanent alterations in a finite set of brain cells. Information cannot be stored in a vacuum. Certainly, changes must take place in certain cells, and such changes might even consist of synaptic alterations. The crucial question under examination is *how* such changes represent the storage of information, and whether activation of a memory or readout of the stored information requires the discharge of unique cells whose activity represents the past experience in a deterministic way.

The essential feature of the model being developed in these pages is that information about an experience is stored as changes in specific brain cells, but does not influence behavior deterministically.

In the preceding discussion, a process has been described by which a large number of cells, located in multiple brain regions, is affected by the occurrence of an experience in such a way as to bring about some long-lasting consequence, the functional details of which remain to be clarified. These cells are presumed to have been selected fortuitously, and to be distributed in parallel diffusely throughout the brain. The modification of future behavior of the organism as a result of this stored information, involving readout of the stored memory, need not require the participation of any specific cells so that activation of a particular pathway mediates the learned response. The essential feature of the proposed mechanism is that readout may be accomplished probabilistically, that different cells may control the same behavior on different occasions, and any given cell may contribute to the storage of multiple experience and to the performance of a variety of learned responses. The effect of an experience is postulated to consist of alteration in the properties of many cells in various anatomical regions. The consequence of this alteration is suggested to be a change in the probability of *coherent* activity in neural populations when a particular stimulus is subsequently presented. The replacement of baseline or random activity by coherent activity in an ensemble of cells is proposed as the informationally relevant event. In this view, the activity of any single cell is important from an informational viewpoint only insofar as it contributes to such coherence. The argument to be developed in subsequent chapters is that the coherence or signal-to-noise ratio represents the *significance* or reliability of the information, while the specific information *content* is reflected by the average activity of a cellular ensemble through time. These hypotheses remove the representation of experience from any particular cell, and free the identification of familiarity from dependence on any pathway. At the same time, the proposed mechanism demands that definite changes occur in a discrete group of cells.

H. Possible intermediate holding mechanisms

A substantial contradiction of the picture described above has recently been provided by the work of Albert (1966a,b,c). Although those experiments have not yet received confirmation in other laboratories, they possess an internal logic and elegance which require that they be described and considered at this point. Albert has made ingenious use of the technique of spreading depression, in conjunction with application of electrical polarization of cortex and subcortical injection of local anesthetics. The basic paradigm which he used involves depression of one hemisphere by cortical SD while an avoidance task is learned. Normally, one trial with both hemispheres intact suffices to transfer the conditioned response to the previously depressed hemisphere, so that appropriate performance is displayed on subsequent tests with the initially intact hemisphere subjected to SD.

First of all, Albert used localized lesions of the intact hemisphere to show that transfer of this task between the hemispheres required the mediation of the medial region of cortex (1966a). Next, by applying SD to the medial region of the trained side at varying intervals after the transfer trial, he showed that transfer of the stored information from the *transmitting* trained side to the *receiving* untrained side required approximately 3 minutes. During this 3-minute interval, a labile process of reverberatory nature was presumed to mediate representation of the transmitted information in the receiving side.

Spreading depression applied to other regions of the transmitting cortex was ineffective. Similarly, SD of the hippocampus, and depression of the amygdala and the midline thalamic nuclei by local procaine injection were not adequate to disrupt transmission. Therefore, he concluded that the intact medial cortex of the trained hemisphere was necessary and sufficient for transmission of the stored information to the untrained receiving side.

Albert then investigated the temporal course of consolidation of this transmitted information in the receiving side. First, he showed that consolidation could be blocked by applying cortical SD to the receiving side, resulting in failure to display conditioned responses when tests were conducted with the initially trained side depressed. Such interference could be demonstrated for a period up to 2 hours after transfer depending upon the *length* of the applied SD. Brief periods of SD showed slowing of consolidation but not complete disruption, while longer periods completely blocked retention.

Albert argued that short SD periods, known to cause extreme changes in neural firing patterns, must suffice to disrupt completely any sustained patterns of neural discharge mediating temporary representation of the transmitted information. *His subsequent conclusions depend heavily on this assumption, which may or may not prove correct.* This question cannot be resolved without demonstration of what constitutes *adequate* disruption of a representational pattern. Arguing that SD also alters potential gradients in cortex, he applied pulsating cathodal dc polarization to the receiving medial cortex and found that this maneuver also blocked consolidation. Surface anodal polarization caused no loss of retention.

Next, he provided evidence that a brief period of SD slowed consolidation, since it greatly increased the period during which a second period of SD could be effective. A single SD application could block retention up to 2 hours, as did surface cathodal dc polarization. These effects could only be obtained when the intervention was applied to the receiving medial cortex.

In later work (1966b), Albert showed that surface anodal polarization of medial cortex seemed to speed up consolidation. SD, usually effective up to 2 hours after transfer, was ineffective 30 minutes after transfer if preceded by a 10-minute period of anodal polarization. Thus, the *rate* of consolidation seemed to be accelerated by this maneuver. It was interesting that application of slowly pulsating current was much more effective than constant current. The speeding up of consolidation was proportional to the *duration* of anodal polarization.

The fact that consolidation could be slowed but not abolished by cathodal polarization or brief periods of SD suggested that the mechanism *holding* information during the consolidation phase can resist influences which disrupt the consolidation process itself. For this reason, Albert proposed the notion of *separate processes mediating the holding and consolidation of information.* The most intriguing portion of his investigations on consolidation consists of his attempt to demonstrate the existence of these two separate processes.

Pursuing the apparent antagonism between the effects of surface cathodal and anodal polarization, he showed that it was possible to block the consolidation process with SD or cathodal polarization of the receiving medial cortex, and *to restart consolidation by a subsequent application of surface anodal polarization to the same region.* Thus, although the conditions for consolidation had been abolished, the information *holding* mechanism was not destroyed. Therefore, he concluded, the two processes of holding and consolidation must be mediated by separate mechanisms. Neither SD nor cathodal polarization destroyed the holding mechanism. Yet, he adduced the evidence cited earlier that SD caused massive changes in neural firing patterns as justification for the conclusion that the holding mechanism could not depend upon a sustained reverberatory process.

The next question was whether the holding mechanism was capable of mediating recall while the consolidation mechanism was blocked. Using SD, Albert succeeded in showing that the recall of the transmitted information was blocked, and no retention could be displayed. However, if consolidation was blocked with cathodal polarization, recall was unimpaired. This evidence suggested the existence of two holding mechanisms subserving somewhat different functions. One, sensitive both to SD and

37

cathodal polarization, seemed to be involved in the actual consolidation of experience, perhaps serving a template function for the synthesis of a permanent storage mechanism. The other, sensitive to SD but *not* to cathodal dc, seemed to mediate recall during the consolidation period. Recall was not possible during the effects of SD, which blocked consolidation. Yet, this interference did not destroy the holding process since subsequent anodal polarization could reverse the effect, allowing consolidation to proceed. Recall was possible during the effects of cathodal polarization, which also blocked consolidation. Again, the holding process was not disrupted since anodal polarization reversed this effect, allowing consolidation to proceed.

If consolidation were blocked by cathodal polarization, recall of the transmitted information could be demonstrated for a period up to 3 hours. Thus, the lifetime of the mechanism mediating recall in the absence of consolidation was 3 hours. The lifetime of the second holding mechanism, serving as a template for consolidation, was estimated by blocking consolidation by SD, and testing the effectiveness of application of surface anodal polarization to restore consolidation as a function of time. The estimate of the lifetime of the template holding process was thus ascertained to be 11 hours.

The differential susceptibility of recall and of consolidation to interference with cortical SD and surface cathodal polarization, plus the different lifetimes suggested by the results described, suggests that two different holding mechanisms may exist. One of these mechanisms may mediate recall but does not suffice for consolidation. The second process may serve as a template for consolidation.

Finally, Albert argued that when SD alone no longer blocks recall, the permanent retention mechanism built during consolidation must have become operative. Pursuing this line of inquiry, he found that after 5 hours SD was no longer effective in blocking performance, and suggested that interval as the necessary time for the consolidation process to be completed.

I. Implications of recent work

Full acceptance of the salient results of the very recent work described above must await replication and confirmation. Yet, the internal consistency and apparent adequacy of the reported experiments warrant examination of the implications for the present discussion. The evidence just presented suggests that the process described earlier in this chapter, in which permanent storage was assumed to result as a direct consequence of reverberatory activity, may require modification. The additional features of this process suggested by the present evidence, still restricted to one particular task, are the following:

1. Transmission of information to a neural population may require an initial phase of 3 minutes, a relatively short time compared to most other estimates, during which representation is accomplished by sustained reverberatory activity.

2. The reverberatory activity may give rise to two temporary information holding mechanisms of unknown nature, which may not involve reverberation. The first of these mechanisms seems capable of mediating recall although it is inadequate for consolidation. It appears to have a lifetime of approximately 3 hours. It is disrupted by spreading depression but not by cathodal polarization. This feature suggests that it neither involves synaptic change nor chemical shifts at the synapse, but may well involve ionic shifts.

3. The second holding mechanism is inadequate for recall but is sufficient for consolidation, and has an apparent lifetime of 11 hours. It is disrupted both by spreading depression and cathodal polarization, and may involve the maintenance of established potential gradients.

4. The consolidation process itself seems to depend upon the second holding mechanism and requires about 5 hours.

Although we regard the conclusions summarized in the last section as tentative until confirmed and extended to other situations, the implication for our theoretical formulation is that intermediate holding mechanisms of two sorts may exist and must ultimately be explained. Further work is needed to clarify the nature of these mechanisms. However, the fundamental propositions outlined earlier with respect to critical shifts would still apply, and the nondeterministic role envisaged for particular cells remains unaffected. The primary implication of these results relates to the nature of the coupling of initial reverberation to the terminal stage of storage. The results under discussion suggest that the initial reverberation couples to two holding mechanisms.

One of these holding mechanisms may involve sustained ionic shifts, and mediates recall. The other mechanism may serve as a template for information specification during the elaboration of the permanent storage process. Suggestions as to how anodal polarization serves to restart the consolidation process after interruption by SD or cathodal polarization are extremely difficult to propose if it is true that reverberatory activity has been disrupted. These data pose an interesting new problem. The massive shifts in extracellular potassium which occur in spreading depression may well be of central importance in the set of phenomena just described, as will be seen from Chapter III.

Further implications of this chapter will be examined in later portions of this volume. We have outlined tentative answers to some of the questions raised earlier in this book, and generated further questions. What chemical shifts might the unitary discharge accomplish? What might be the substance whose synthesis occurs when a critical shift of concentration occurs? How might the synthesis of storage substance serve to represent the stimulus whose action constituted the experience for that cell?

CHAPTER III

CHANGES IN SPEED OF CONSOLIDATION

A small group of experiments bear further upon the nature of the activity of the labile phase, providing evidence of a different sort which is as informative and as interesting as the data showing interference with storage as a consequence of various kinds of disruption. There are a number of studies that indicate that the speed with which animals acquire conditioned responses can be increased, as well as decreased.

A. Genetic studies

Perhaps the earliest and best known of these studies is the work of Tryon (1940) on so-called "maze-bright" and "maze-dull" rats. Tryon tested rats for speed of acquisition of a maze, and selected those who learned most rapidly and most slowly, and separated them from the original population. Those which learned rapidly were bred to each other, those which learned slowly were bred to each other, and the F1 generations were again tested in maze acquisition. From the F1 generations, again the maze-bright animals and the maze-dull animals were segregated out. Thus, by selective breeding, maze-bright and maze-dull strains of rats were developed, the so-called S_1 and S_3 strains. Once these strains were established, their performance remained distinctly different. As a group, the maze-bright animals acquired maze performance rapidly. They were characterized from the maze-dull animals by a number of

41

differences. Those differences included body weight, tail length, thickness of fur, and over-all general activity.

B. Hypothesis behavior

Additionally, the maze performance of the two groups was demonstrated by Krechevsky (1935) to involve the utilization of different sorts of cues. The maze-bright animals seemed to depend primarily on spatial cues, the maze-dull animals primarily on visual cues. Using an insoluble maze, Krechevsky showed that the hypothesis used by the "bright" group of rats to solve the maze was a spatial hypothesis; the hypothesis used by the other strain of rats was a visual hypothesis. Krechevsky then showed that lesions of visual and somasthetic cortex in these two groups had different effects on maze hypothesis behavior. Following this work up, many years later, Krech, Rosenzweig, and Bennett (1956) subjected animals from these various strains to analysis with respect to cholinesterase (ChE) levels in various regions, and asserted that these levels were characteristically different. Chow and John (1958) challenged the interpretation that the difference in behavior was *caused by* a difference in distribution and concentration of this enzyme, based on their failure to change "hypothesis" behavior after localized cortical injection of anticholinesterase. Whatever may be the basis for the differential behavior of maze-bright and maze-dull animals, the primary relevance of this study for our purpose is that it constitutes one of the early clear demonstrations that the rate of learning a task by a given animal can be manipulated, in this case by the selection of groups bred for certain characteristics. It seems reasonable that the genetic differences between these inbred strains have, as their neuronal counterpart, some differences in brain chemistry and/or structure.

C. Enriched environment

In a series of studies, Krech and his colleagues have extended these initial observations. Most recently (Krech, Rosenzweig, and Bennett, 1962a,b), their endeavors have focused on an analysis of the effects of "enriched" or "impoverished" environments upon the chemistry and anatomy of the brain, following the earlier observation of Hebb (1949, p. 298) that such differences in environment were attended by establishment of differences in learning ability. These studies have been reviewed by Epstein (1964). It is not clear whether the demonstrated differences in learning ability are related to factors such as temperament and emotionality, which secondarily result in increased resistance to distraction by novel stimuli and greater speed of habituation, as seems to be the case in some studies of the effects of early experience, or whether the differential performance is to be attributed primarily to a more effective neurochemical mediation of consolidation.

These workers have found that, concurrent with the maintenance of increased environmental complexity for 75 days, there was an increase in the weight of the cortex and a decrease in the specific activity of the ChE, together with a greater total cortical ChE activity. Similar changes occurred during a 30-day period introduced after weaning. It is of interest, in this regard, that Altman has investigated the effects of manipulation of these environmental variables on neuronal and glial proliferation in the rat (Altman and Das, 1966). Using tritiated thymidine as an index of nuclear division, and tritiated leucine as an indication of general permeability, Altman has concluded that these procedures are accompanied by a large increase in the number of recently divided glial cells in the cortex, with no evidence for generally increased permeability, and no apparent effects on neuronal growth. Thus, the anatomical and chemical changes reported by Krech *et al.* may largely result from the stimulation of glial division. It is unclear from these various data whether or not the alterations in brain anatomy and chemistry reported have any relationship to the changes in learning displayed by these animals. It has recently been reported that food deprivation and over-stimulation led to ChE increases in the medulla and cerebellum, while operant conditioning was accompanied by as much as 23% increases in the ChE content of the cerebral hemispheres (Saunders, 1966). These results suggest that behavioral and environmental manipulations may cause regional shifts in ChE activity.

Other studies have explored the behavioral effects of experimentally induced increases in the density of cortical neurons. Zamenhof *et al.* (1966) have demonstrated that injection of pituitary growth hormone into pregnant rats causes a significant increase in the final number of cortical neurons in their offspring. Although the offspring of injected animals had unchanged body weight, they displayed significant increases in brain weight, brain DNA content, cortical cell density, and in the ratio of neurons to glia. Using essentially identical procedures, Clendinnen and Eayrs (1961) observed a significant increase in the mean number and mean length of dendrites associated with each cortical neuron in the experimental animals. These workers observed an increase in the area occupied by neuronal perikarya, although they found no significant increase in cell density. Dendritic fields were computed and these data were used to estimate the probability of interaction between an extended axonal system and the characteristic dendritic field. Experimental animals showed a significant (55%) increase in the statistical probability of interaction between neurons. The authors suggested that the probability of neuronal interaction was an important factor regulating the cortical mediation of adaptive behavior, consistent with their observation that the experimental animals showed an earlier appearance of the placing reaction and significantly enhanced performance in the closed-field Hebb-Williams test. The maturation of other innate and reflex behavioral responses was relatively little affected.

Using smaller doses and a simpler task, Block and Essman (1965) showed that the offspring of rats treated with growth hormone during pregnancy showed more rapid extinction of a conditioned avoidance response than controls. These results were interpreted as a more rapid return to adaptive behavior, since avoidance was no longer appropriate to the situation. The results of these experiments cannot be definitely attributed to increased numbers of neurons or probability of interaction, since growth hormone injections may well have other effects. However, these findings provide some suggestion that learning may be enhanced by increasing the *number* of the nerve cells that are involved.

D. Effects of drugs on learning and memory

The effects of chemical substances on learning and memory storage have received substantial attention in the laboratory. Early studies focused upon thiamine, glutamine acid, barbiturates, and amphetamine. Since then, a large number of compounds has been tested for possible effects in this regard. Reports of drug-induced impairment and facilitation of learning and memory storage are numerous and have recently been thoroughly reviewed by McGaugh and Petrinovich (1965).

Such studies provide clear evidence that drugs can influence learning. The observed effects in some cases seem likely to be due to drug influences on mechanisms involved in attention, perception, and motivation. However, many of the results indicate clear modification of processes involved in the storage or retrieval of information. Interpretation of the results in terms of the neural mechanisms of memory is particularly difficult in view of the existing limitations of our knowledge about the pharmacological basis of action of most of the substances found to be effective.

A tentative generalization about the results of these studies, with a number of exceptions, might be that anticholinergic substances, barbiturates, or compounds with depressant action tend to impair learning or retention. Conversely, anticholinesterase drugs, stimulants, or convulsant drugs in subconvulsive doses tend to facilitate learning or memory storage. Many substances which have been found facilitatory, such as strychnine, picrotoxin, nicotine, pentylenetetrazol, physostigmine, caffeine, amphetamines, and diphenyldiazadamantanol, to cite a few, share an excitatory effect on the activity of the central nervous system (CNS), but are believed to possess different mechanisms of action. Other substances for which positive findings have been reported do not seem appropriately classified as either stimulants or depressants.

For those findings which suggest effects on information storage or retrieval processes, the interpretations tend to be of two sorts: (1) the results are primarily explained on the basis of alterations in transient neural processes initiated by a stimulus; or (2) the results are viewed as indication of direct modification of the specific biochemical processes involved in permanent memory storage. For purposes of our analytic endeavors in this volume, particular interest is attached to the line of experiments represented so well by McGaugh and his co-workers, who have shown that injection of a systemic excitant such as strychnine (McGaugh, 1961; McGaugh and Petrinovich, 1959; Petrinovich, 1963) facilitated maze learning and successive discriminations. Both maze-bright and maze-dull rats showed facilitation (see Fig. III-1). Similar results had been provided by Lashley (1917). These data suggested that strychnine enhanced consolidation by facilitating reverberatory activity.

45

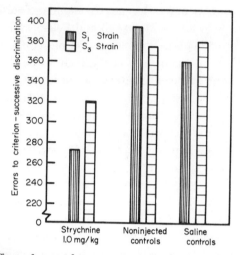

Fig. III-1. The effect of pretrial injections of strychnine sulfate on successive discrimination learning. Injections were given each day before the rats received ten massed training trials. Rats were from Berkeley S_1 and S_3 strains. Facilitating effects of strychnine injection are apparent. [Based on data from Petrinovich (1963).]

In these experiments, the injections preceded the training runs. Alternative explanations existed, related to the effects of the injection on attention or sensory responsiveness *during* the subsequent trials.

E. Posttrial injection effects

In subsequent work, Breen and McGaugh (1961) showed that *post-trial* injections of picrotoxin enhanced the rate of learning of mazes by rats. Westbrook and McGaugh (1964) ruled out the possibility that the rewarding effects of drug injection per se were responsible for the observed facilitation. These workers also studied the effects of posttrial injection of 1757 I.S., a systemic excitant, upon the latent learning of a maze by a group of rats permitted free exploration of the maze without reward. When reinforcement was introduced, following the exploration and posttrial injection, the experimental group displayed fewer errors than the controls. Thus, it appeared that subjects injected with the analeptic drug learned more about the floor plan of the maze during free exploration than did controls, yet no difference in behavior developed until the introduction of reinforcement. These data suggest that the drug improves learning by facilitating memory storage.

Petrinovich *et al.* (1965) have explored the effect of posttrial injections of analeptic drugs on the duration of nonrandom delayed alternation performance in the rat. These injections enable extension of the interval between alternation responses from the normal maximum of about 3½ hours to as long as 8 hours. This indicates that information about a previous single choice can be retained for a markedly prolonged period.

The fact that both strychnine and picrotoxin facilitate storage is informative. Strychnine blocks *post*synaptic inhibition, while picrotoxin blocks *pre*synaptic inhibition (Eccles, 1962). The common effects of these two substances in spite of their different locus and mode of action indicate that the release of inhibition per se may be the crucial factor, rather than the particular cellular structure at which this occurs. However, pentylenetetrazol injection has been reported to cause more marked and reliable facilitation of learning than either strychnine or picrotoxin (Irwin and Benuazizi, 1966). This substance neither blocks presynaptic nor postsynaptic inhibition, but seems to achieve excitatory effects by decreasing the time required for neuronal recovery after discharge. The action might accelerate neuronal transmission or increase maximum firing rates.

In related work, Stratton and Petrinovich (1963) investigated the effects of *post*trial injection of an antiChE drug, physostigmine, on the rate of maze learning. These investigations were partially spurred by the earlier demonstrations by Platt (1951) and Russell (1954) that anticholinesterase drugs facilitated learning. In the present study, Stratton and Petrinovich explored the effects of posttrial injections of physostigmine on the learning of maze-bright and maze-dull rats. Both maze-bright and maze-dull rats showed facilitation of learning after physostigmine injection, with the effect markedly greater on the maze-dull rats. The differences in performance between strains tended to be erased by the drug injection. It is perhaps relevant here that McGaugh, Jennings, and Thomson (1962) found that the differences between maze-bright and maze-dull animals could also be eliminated by distributed rather than massed practice, suggesting that the animals differ in the time rate of consolidation. Stratton and Petrinovich proposed not only that this study provided further evidence for the role of perseverative activity in the "fixing" of the memory trace, but also that the ratio of acetylcholine to cholinesterase was an index of the probable time course of perseverative activity. A similar hypothesis has been offered by Ross (1964) in the interpretation of his experimental results. This worker observed that strychnine facilitated maze learning in maze-bright animals whether injected 1 minute or 1 hour posttraining, while maze-dull animals showed facilitation only when injection occurred 1 minute after training.

In related work, Pearlman *et al.* (1961)* investigated the effects of strychnine injection immediately following a shock trial in a one-trial learning procedure. Ether anesthesia administered 10 minutes after the strychnine had little effect upon retention, indicating that consolidation was already complete. In contrast, normal animals anesthetized 10 minutes after the learning trial showed severe impairment of retention. Thus it appeared that the effect of strychnine was to enable the more rapid elaboration of the structural or chemical basis for long-term storage. These results cannot be attributed to mere lengthening of the reverberatory process which might be offered as a possible explanation for the previous results. The speeding up of consolidation by strychnine resembles the effect of anodal polarization of cortex that was described in Chapter II. Bishop and O'Leary (1950) have presented evidence that the physiological effects of these two agents are markedly similar (see Chapter IX).

It seems reasonable, in view of these results, to conclude that these procedures either *intensified* the reverberatory activity, resulting in a greater amount of consolidation per unit time because more neurons were involved, or *accelerated* the rate of the chemical processes mediating consolidation.

F. Role of electrolyte shifts in neural excitability

It is well known that the membrane potential of nerve cells is related to differences in the concentration of various electrolytes, notably sodium and potassium, across the cell membrane. The potassium concentration inside the resting nerve cell is higher than outside. Within limits, increases in extracellular potassium decrease the membrane potential and increase neural excitability. It is also well known that potassium release from nerve cells takes place during neural activity.

---

* See Pearlman, C. A., Some aspects of localization of the consolidation process. A.P.A. Symposium on Consolidation, Annual Meeting, 1961.

The phenomenon of post-tetanic potentiation, namely, the observation that rapid firing of impulses across synaptic junctions can result in increased excitability of such synapses for periods lasting from seconds to hours, has been described by Lloyd (1949) and numerous other workers. In his review of the phenomenon of post-tetanic potentiation Hughes (1958) summarized evidence that facilitation of neural circuits ensued for a period of time following intense synaptic activity. This phenomenon has been demonstrated at all levels of the nervous system. Hughes speculated on the possibility that this potentiation was due to the local release of acetylcholine (ACh) or of potassium. It is perhaps relevant that MacIntosh and Oborin (1953) have provided evidence that neural activity in the central nervous system (cortex) is accompanied by the release of ACh, in an amount proportional to the integrated neural activity. The released material seems to diffuse through the neural tissue, and can be detected in exudate entering a cylinder filled with solution containing anticholinesterase, and resting on the cortex. It is also interesting that Colfer and Essex (1947) demonstrated alteration in the extraneuronal potassium after intense neural activity, using microincineration techniques. Similarly, Cicardo and Torino (1942) have shown an increased potassium level in the venous outflow of the brain after intense neural activity. Direct release of radioactive potassium has been measured from cortex previously loaded with the isotopic tracer (Brinley et al., 1960; Křivánek and Bureš, 1960). This release has been observed to increase greatly over its resting value during spreading depression. Grafstein (1963) has calculated the expected relationship between changes in brain extracellular potassium concentration and periods of stimulation at various rates. The calculations indicate that the effects of potassium shift due to local cortical activity can cause membrane depolarizations ranging from a few millivolts, leading to increased excitability, to about 10 mV, causing spontaneous firing, to even greater depolarization as in spreading depression. Significant shifts in the level of extracellular potassium can be caused by massed firing of groups of neurons at a rate of 7 to 8 impulses per second, a rate often exceeded by single cortical cells.

Tschirgi (1952) has proposed a scheme whereby such processes might alter neuronal microenvironment by regulating the permeability of the blood brain barrier. Cholinesterase is known to occur in high concentrations in glial cells, as evidenced by measurements of astro-

49

cytoma tissue. Electron microscopy shows astrocyte end feet closely plastered around central nervous system neurons and surrounding all capillaries. It has been proposed that the blood brain barrier is actually a secretory process, anatomically localized in the perivascular glial membrane of Held.

Tschirgi suggested a mechanism acting as follows: ACh, released by neurons as a result of discharge, begins to diffuse away from the region of high concentration. Little ACh hydrolysis occurs until the ACh reaches the glial membrane around capillaries in the region. Grieg and Holland (1951) have shown, in the red blood cell, that the *hydrolysis* of ACh by ChE, but not either ACh nor its breakdown products, alters the permeability of these cells to radioactive potassium in the surround. In analogous fashion, Tschirgi (1952) has proposed that the action of ACh upon the astrocytic perivascular membrane effects an alteration in the local permeability for potassium.

The increased influx of potassium into the region in which the cell fired might enhance the probability of that cell's subsequent firing due to a number of factors. These include a direct increase in excitability, activation of acetylcholine synthesis, change in the free-bound ratio of ACh, and changes in protoplasmic viscosity enabling easier migration of fine axonal processes. Although such systems have not directly been demonstrated in the brain, their existence is possible. Finally, the suggestion that these various considerations are relevant to the evidence previously cited receives support from work which shows that *a number of substances alter CNS excitability by accomplishing a redistribution of electrolytes* (Woodbury, 1954, 1958). Among such substances are several that have been found to facilitate the acquisition of learned responses (Stille and Kröger, 1957).

These various considerations suggest that an alteration in regional microchemistry, particularly with respect to extracellular potassium, may be involved in consolidation.

G. The role of central electrolyte shifts in learning and retention

The evidence that one of the salient features of neural activity is redistribution of electrolytes suggested that electrolyte shifts might somehow be involved in the coupling of the early labile phase of learning to the ensuing stable storage of information. In early work (John, Tschirgi, and Wenzel, 1959), we found severe, prolonged, and sometimes differential deterioration of previously well-established conditioned responses after small intraventricular injections of potassium or calcium chloride. However, central injections of various pharmacological substances did not appreciably impair learned performance, although massive increases or decreases of general excitability were achieved. These results suggested that brain electrolyte concentration played an important role in conditioned response performance, in a fashion somewhat more complex than mere alteration of excitability.

These findings also suggest that the variability in rates of learning, observed in a normal population, might arise partially from chemical influences upon the coupling between labile and permanent representational mechanisms or upon the ability of neural systems to achieve certain kinds of nonrandom organization. Changes in excitability might alter the ratio of relevant signal to nonrelevant background activity, or facilitate the maintenance of reverberating activity. It is possible that the various manipulations which facilitate consolidation, described above, share the common feature that they somehow alter the potassium-to-calcium ratio in the extracellular fluid, which would achieve a modification of neural excitability.

Sachs (1962a) has studied the effect of intraventricular injections of small amounts of potassium and calcium on the acquisition of avoidance responses by the cat. He found that animals systematically receiving a central injection of potassium (25 to 37.5 microequivalents), shortly before the beginning of a training session, acquired the conditioned avoidance response as rapidly as the *most* rapidly learning animals in a large control population. All potassium injected cats seemed to be "bright." In contrast, animals receiving a comparable calcium injection (22.5 to 33.75 microequivalents), immediately before each training session, all learned significantly more *slowly* than the average cat in a control population. Calcium injected cats seemed to be "dull" (Fig. III-2).

The sensitivity of acquisition rates to small variations in central electrolyte concentration provides some support for the earlier suggestion that electrolytes may somehow be involved in the coupling of the early labile phase of learning to the late stable storage of information, although other possible explanations certainly come to mind. The facili-

III. Changes in speed of consolidation

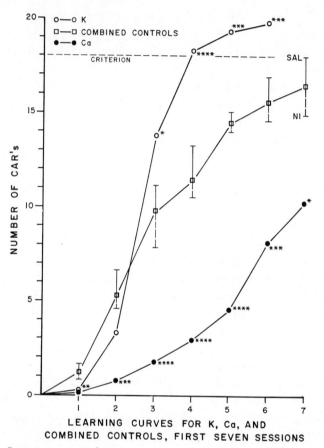

Fig. III-2. Learning curves from a group of cats ($n = 8$) which received intraventricular injections of potassium (K), a group ($n = 8$) which received intraventricular injections of Calcium (Ca), a group ($n = 10$) which received intraventricular saline (SAL), a group ($n = 7$) which was intraventricularly cannulated but not injected, and a group ($n = 9$) of unoperated animals (NI). The SAL and NI data were combined into a pooled control group for this figure. The data show that the K group acquired the conditioned avoidance response significantly more rapidly than did the controls, while the Ca group learned significantly more slowly. The interval shown about the control curve represents one standard deviation. (*p*-values: * = .05, ** = .02, *** = .01, **** = .001.) [Based on data from Sachs (1962a).]

tation of learning observed in animals with increased central potassium concentration may be due to a number of factors, among which are: (1) Increase in the mean excitability of neural populations may enable a stimulus to elicit a more phased discharge, thus achieving an improvement of the ratio of activity relevant to the signal to unrelated ongoing neural processes. (2) The alteration in ionic surround with its consequent increase in excitability may enable *more cells* to be recruited into a reverberating loop or set of loops, and may permit a longer perseveration of that reverberating trace. (3) The ionic shift may exert its effect by *facilitation of the synthesis* of the stable storage compound itself. (4) Sachs (1965) has proposed a mechanism whereby the growth *of new synaptic processes* might be facilitated by the release of potassium by intensely discharging cells, or by the injection of high potassium solutions. The effect of increased potassium concentration is a tendency toward *solation* of protoplasm, while an increased calcium or decreased potassium concentration facilitates *gelation.* Thus, ionic gradients caused by the release of potassium from stimulated neurons or central injection may solate the terminals of neural fibrils, facilitating movement along the potassium gradient, while raised calcium concentrations may diminish or abolish processes which might change the spatial relationships of synaptic membranes.

Admittedly, the available data do not permit a conclusive choice between these various alternatives. Furthermore, these alternatives do not include all conceivable formulations, but represent the most probable from the viewpoint of the writer. It should be noted that there is nothing differential about any of the four possibilities listed. The consequences are not unique to activity relating to the signal about which information is to be stored, but are equally pertinent to unrelated neural events occurring during the same period. It might seem preferable to search for mechanisms that have the capacity to distinguish between relevant and nonrelevant neural activity. There is no compelling *a priori* reason to assume that relevant and nonrelevant neural discharges possess an intrinsic difference, other than the earlier probabilistic suggestion that relevant activity in a neuron will tend to be temporally coherent with other relevant neural activity in the network. Such coherence should tend to increase the likelihood of maintenance of reverberatory activity. One might expect that repeated experience might result in the emergence of an invariant aspect in the time course of coherent activity. The development of this invariance might provide a basis for the "learning" of relevant activity and the "nonlearning" of irrelevant activity. It should be noted that activity not directly related to the stimulus but related to consistent features of the context in which the stimulus occurs, such as neural reflections of motivational processes, behavioral responses, or constant features of "figure-ground" relationships, would gradually be incorporated into this characteristic pattern.

[Findings of the sort described here raise the question of whether learning difficulties in various clinical populations might not be due to abnormal brain electrolyte concentrations. It may be worthwhile to mention that occasional ionic shifts of the magnitude involved in these experiments can arise physiologically as a consequence of minor environmental events such as a drop in room temperature (Benjamin *et al.*, 1961). If central electrolyte concentrations can fluctuate readily, sustained malfunction of regulatory mechanisms might have severe functional consequences.]

H. Localization and duration of electrolyte effects

Undoubtedly, diffusion of the injected ionic solutions from the ventricles to other brain regions is great during the period of training. One cannot conclude that the effects described above are localized to the immediate vicinity of the ventricular system of the brain. The proximity of the hippocampus to the ventricular system indicates the desirability of exploring this question with isotope and impedance techniques. On the other hand, evidence for a long-term inhomogeneity of distribution has been observed after potassium injection (John *et al.*, 1959). A series of potassium injections was given to a number of cats, the interval between intraventricular injections being 15 minutes. After two to three injections, some of those animals displayed a similar syndrome: a tic developed in the contralateral hind leg, gradually increased in intensity, and involved adjacent portions of the musculature. This involvement extended anteriorly up that side of the body until it reached the neck where it crossed over to the ipsilateral facial musculature. This clonic contraction sometimes developed into a full-blown epileptiform seizure. Such a seizure could be stopped almost instantly, by intraventricular injection of an amount of calcium identical in its equivalency with the total potassium injection which was administered. On a number of occasions, potassium injection was terminated before seizure, and the animal was returned to his home cage after all signs of clonus vanished. Under these circumstances, an interesting phenomenon could be observed on the next day. When the animals returned to the experimental situation, they appeared perfectly normal. Avoidance training was then initiated, and shock delivered to the animal. After 5 or 10 minutes of such stress, a twitch often developed in the contralateral hind leg, *the same limb which showed convulsive movement on the previous day, after potassium injection.*

It is known that avoidance training constitutes a stress. The level of 17-hydroxycorticosterone in the circulating plasma of an animal has been reported to increase sharply during avoidance training (Mason *et al.*, 1961). This may well have been the case in the experiments under discussion, although no steroid measurements were made. It has been shown by Woodbury that this type of steroid shift causes an increase in the extracellular potassium concentration of the brain (1954).

Thus, the extracellular fluid of the brain may gradually have been flooded with a potassium increase due to the steroid release. The potassium concentration at the region where the clonic discharge was initiated on the previous day perhaps again reached a critical level and discharge resumed, although the level elsewhere was not sufficient to cause such an effect. This suggestion admittedly involves a number of unsubstantiated assumptions, yet these observations indicate that a long-term aftereffect of potassium injection persists. Even 24 hours later, some inhomogeneity of potassium distribution, or of heightened excitability, may have endured. The injected potassium, therefore, cannot be assumed to diffuse freely. Some portion of it may perhaps still be bound. About 80% of the potassium in brain seems to be labile, based on measurements with radioactive potassium (Katzman and Liederman, 1953). This implies that the remaining 20% is not freely exchangeable and exists in a bound form (Folch-pi, 1952). It is not known to what substances the binding occurs, nor whether any function is served thereby.

I. Electrophysiological effects of CNS electrolyte shifts

A number of experimental findings are relevant to the effects of CNS electrolyte shifts on acquisition of conditioned responses. In a pilot experiment, the effect of these central ionic injections on the electrophysiological responses to flickering light were explored (Sachs, 1962b).

III. Changes in speed of consolidation

A cat with chronically implanted electrodes in the lateral geniculate was subjected to repeated flashes of light, and the evoked potentials were displayed in superposition on oscilloscopic film. The normal response in the lateral geniculate and the visual cortex displayed a primary component with little variability and a later component with moderate variability. When this naïve animal received an intraventricular potassium injection, the variability of the primary component was unaffected, but the late component displayed *decreased* variability. This animal, under conditions which should facilitate learning, showed a diminution in the variance of the secondary component of the evoked potential caused by the stimulus. In contrast, the effect of an intraventricular calcium injection was essentially opposite to that of potassium. While the primary response still showed no alteration, the variability of the late component was tremendously *increased*. Under conditions which could be expected to decrease the speed of learning, this animal showed a huge increase in the variance of the late component of the evoked potential elicited by the stimulus.

These data suggest that the intraventricular ionic injections may have accomplished an alteration in the reproducibility of the neural response to the conditioned stimulus.

Previous findings on the electrographic effects of ionic shifts have been reviewed by Heppinstall and Greville (1950). Other reviews of the effects of altered central electrolyte balance include Tschirgi (1960) and Sachs (1962a). Small increases in central potassium ion raise the frequency and decrease the amplitude of the EEG, which is usually interpreted as an increase of cortical excitability. Investigations of both evoked and spontaneous potentials have revealed a differential susceptibility of these to changes in potassium and calcium concentration. Small intracarotid injections of potassium chloride have no effect on the primary response of the auditory cortex to clicks, but they intensify the afterdischarge. The size of cortical responses to a continuous sound is also increased with low potassium chloride doses. Increased central calcium· ion decreases the frequency and increases the amplitude of the EEG, which is usually interpreted as indicative of a decrease in cortical excitability. Work on both evoked and spontaneous potentials indicates that raised central calcium ion concentration has no effect on the primary evoked cortical response, but blocks the afterdischarge.

Heppinstall and Greville conclude that neither potassium nor calcium ions can influence direct sensory transmission to the cortex. However, neurons which respond indirectly to the arrival of afferent impulses at the cortex, probably internuncial neurons in upper cortical layers, can be excited or depressed by these ions. In contrast, Horsten and Klopper (1952) suggest that the cortical effects of ionic shifts are not achieved via direct cortical action, but rather via the effects of these ions on the reticular formation. They argue that all effects of altered cerebrospinal fluid ionic composition on brain electrical responses in the literature can be viewed as consequences of ionic action on brain-stem centers, and that the observed cortical waves arise from *synchronous* fluctuations in membrane potentials governed by subcortical centers.

J. Comparable effects of reticular stimulation

It may be interesting, in the context of the interpretation provided by Horsten and Klopper for the electrographic consequences of ionic shift, to recall two further experimental findings. Studying the acquisition of differential conditioned responses in the cat, Zuckermann has shown that the ability of the cat to distinguish between two different stimuli can be markedly enhanced in the period following electrical stimulation of the mesencephalic reticular formation (Zuckermann, 1959). Similarly, Fuster (Fuster, 1958; Fuster and Uyeda, 1962) has reported that the time required for monkeys to achieve recognition of differential conditioned stimuli in a pattern discrimination task when the stimuli are presented tachistoscopically drops sharply in the period following electrical stimulation of the reticular formation. Mahut has described facilitation of visual discrimination in cats by stimulation of the brain stem tegmentum or intralaminar and midline thalamic nuclei (1964). There is some indication from such studies of differential effects of stimulation upon avoidance and approach behaviors. Carbachol injections into regions of the mesencephalic reticular formation before approach or avoidance training show facilitation of CAR (conditioned avoidance response) acquisition and performance together with retardation of approach behaviors (Grossman, 1966). Lesions in these regions produce the opposite effects. No effects on escape, eating, or drinking behavior were observed, nor were sensory or motor deficits apparent. Such electrical or chemical stimulation may well influence arousal or motivation, but might act by facilitating coherence in the response of widespread neural regions to the subsequent stimulus presentations.

CHAPTER IV

THE GROWTH, SHUNT, AND MODE HYPOTHESES

Evidence has been presented to support the contention that there is an early phase, immediately after an experience, during which the representation of that experience is mediated by a labile process, possibly reverberatory in nature. During this period, disruption of ongoing activity by various types of intervention interferes with the registration of that experience in more permanent storage. As time elapses after the actual experience, these various interventions gradually lose their ability to prevent registration. Conversely, substances which increase neural excitability seem to facilitate registration, even when injected after the experience. The substances that have been found effective in this regard may influence central levels of acetylcholine and potassium. Systemic injection of anticholinesterases and intraventricular potassium also facilitate registration. Alteration of one of these substances in the brain probably influences the concentration of the other markedly, because of influences on permeability, synthesis rates, and other factors. The common capacity of these various substances to affect consolidation may either be due to the consequences of changes in excitability or to direct chemical influence on the mechanisms involved in the synthesis of the substances which mediate long-term information storage. Such mechanisms will be evaluated further in Chapter VI.

A. Possible facilitatory mechanisms

In what fashion might the increase in excitability after an experience facilitate the storage process? A number of possibilities can be suggested.

Assume that some subset of cells in a neural population retains residual coherent activity resulting from a prior experience. A general increase in the mean excitability of the whole population is then established by the action of the drug. (1) One possible consequence of this shift might be to augment the group of cells in coherent activity by facilitating the recruitment of additional neural elements responding to the circulating representation. An action of this sort would increase the *local coherence,* i.e., the number of neural elements in a volume of tissue that were in coherent activity. (2) A second possibility is that the density of coherent activity is unaltered but the *total time* that such activity might persist is prolonged. (3) A third possibility is that the number or density of cells in coherent activity remains constant, but the *rate of circulation* of reverberatory activity is increased. (4) A fourth possibility is that neither the number of neurons in reverberation, the total time of reverberation, nor the rate of reverberation is altered, but the contribution to the stable storage process which is made by each relevant neural event is enhanced. In other words, *the chemical reaction responsible for permanent storage is accelerated.* (5) Finally, it is possible that *the rate of growth of synaptic connections is facilitated.*

Pearlman *et al.* (1961)* have provided evidence, cited earlier, that indicates that analeptic drugs decrease the time required to accomplish permanent storage. Mice exposed to a one-trial learning situation show no retention of the experience if they receive electroconvulsive shock 10 minutes later. However, animals which receive injection of strychnine immediately after the single-learning trial are unaffected by ECS 10 minutes later and display perfect retention afterward. Thus, consolidation has been completed in *less time* than that required by control animals. This evidence permits us to rule out the second possibility listed above. Although prolongation of time of reverberation might facilitate learning, it is not a *necessary* condition for more effective storage of information.

Similarly, the author has difficulty in accepting the last alternative as an explanation for the facilitation of consolidation by increased excitability. A number of criticisms have already been leveled at the growth hypothesis, which suffers from the vulnerability of all models requiring the mediation of memory by establishment of fixed neuronal pathways.

---

* See Pearlman, C. A., Some aspects of localization of the consolidation process. A.P.A. Symposium on Consolidation, Annual Meeting, 1961.

In addition to the difficulties of accounting for many of the phenomena described earlier with such an explanatory concept, if all neurons are affected by all stimuli, the growth of new synaptic processes or the swelling of end feet would seem at best to achieve an elaboration upon preexisting connectivity. Such processes seem redundant, and are considered unlikely to accomplish susceptibility of a neuron to previously ineffective influences. However, quantitative increase in response to marginally effective input might thus be accomplished. In any event, the consequence of growth of new processes would seem likely to be an increase in the *rate* of response of a given neuron to a specified event. Although the growth hypothesis cannot be invalidated conclusively, it seems to be functionally equivalent to the third alternative in that it achieves more intense neural response per unit time. Yet it remains a distinct possibility. The remaining alternatives, other than acceleration of the rate of chemical synthesis of a hypothetical storage substance, are that the action of analeptics to facilitate learning is either due to (1) an increase in the *number* of neurons involved in representational activity, or (2) an increase in the *rate of circulation* of reverberatory activity involving a *fixed number of neurons.*

We have assumed that the permanent storage of information is somehow accomplished as the *result* of the sustained neural processes taking place during consolidation, since disruption of ongoing activity blocks permanent registration of experience. We assume further that a *unitary* contribution to permanent storage during reverberatory activity results from each discharge of a participating nerve cell.

Conceive of a network in which reverberations are circulating in neuronal loops after some event. The network can be expected to contain a number of such loops of varying size. A number of circulation times should exist, ranging from high-frequency circulations in short loops to low-frequency reverberation in long loops. The distribution of loop sizes ought to reflect the characteristic morphology of the anatomical region containing the population of neurons. The time course of coherent activity, averaged across the ensemble of cells, should be a function of the distribution of loop sizes in which the effects of a given stimulus circulate. *It is proposed that the evoked electrophysiological response to a stimulus represents the averaged time course of activity in a responsive ensemble.* This suggestion will be developed in further detail in Chapter XI. The electrophysiological events which contribute to the average represented by an evoked response, however, are primarily the postsynaptic potentials in the neurons, rather than the action potentials. Action potentials transmit excitation from synapse to synapse, and thereby both reflect the influence of postsynaptic potentials and are responsible for their occurrence. The relationship between the two is increasingly apparent from recent research, which suggests that the integrated postsynaptic potentials reflect the probability that action potentials will occur in the members of the neuronal ensemble. Fox and O'brien (1965) have shown that the frequency distribution of single nerve cell discharges averaged over many poststimulus intervals correlates well with the averaged evoked potentials recorded from that region. Since the neurons for which this relation was shown cannot be considered unique, the same relationship should hold for the frequency distribution during a single poststimulus interval averaged across many cells in an ensemble. Therefore, it seems justifiable to consider the evoked response as a reflection of the average temporal distribution of activity in a neural network. The amplitude of the evoked response should be related to the coherence of neural activity.

If the effect of an analeptic agent were to increase the number of neurons in an ensemble which participated in *coherent* response to a stimulus, *the amplitude of the average evoked response waveshape should increase.* Increased excitability of other neurons in the population, not responsive to the stimulus, might result in generally increased activity but would not be coherent with the representational set. Conversely, if a population of a (more or less) fixed number of neurons achieved more rapid circulation of activity within loops with the same length distribution, the number of circulations per unit time around a loop of given size should increase, *and the frequency distribution of the set of loops should be shifted toward a mean of higher frequency.* The evoked potential waveshape should thus show a corresponding *decrease in latency* for each component. Although analeptic drugs cause some decrease in evoked response latency, the most striking effect of these substances is to cause a marked increase in evoked response *amplitude.*

B. More neurons or faster circulation

The two alternatives under consideration are: (1) analeptic drugs accelerate storage by causing *more neurons* to participate in reverberation, thus increasing coherence. *The number of unitary "storage" events occurring in each participating neuron per unit time remains the same.* (2) Analeptic drugs accelerate storage by causing *more rapid circulation* of impulses within loops of fixed length. The number of participating neurons remains the same, but *the number of unitary "storage" events occurring in each participating neuron per unit time is increased.* The electrophysiological data adduced suggest that *more rapid storage is accomplished by increasing the number or density of neurons involved in coherent representation of the event.* The conclusion that learning may be accelerated by involving *more* cells in the process seems contradictory to the suggestion that memory is mediated by establishment of a circuit involving a specific set of cells. Of course, the conclusion that analeptic drugs probably achieve their effects by increasing the local coherence of participating cells does not contradict the suggestion that increased rate of reverberation might facilitate storage. However, increased rate of reverberation is not *necessary* for more rapid storage to occur.

How might the *rate* of storage be accelerated by increasing the *number* of cells involved? Clearly, an increase in the number or coherence of participating cells will enhance the "signal-to-noise ratio" (S/N) in the population. While this might be expected to have some effect on detectability of the process, it seems unlikely that change in signal-to-noise ratio in the ensemble itself is responsible for the apparent facilitation of storage in its constituent cells. Some increase in S/N can be accomplished by manipulating intensity of the conditioned stimulus in a training situation, which does not produce facilitation to the same striking extent as analeptic drugs.

Although it remains possible that the increase in internal S/N is somehow directly responsible, it is extremely difficult to understand how this fact by itself could result in acceleration of the storage process. It seems necessary to assume some intervening process. Might that process be our fourth alternative? In other words, is it possible that the action of the analeptics is to accelerate some chemical reaction critical for permanent storage?

In the foregoing development, it was implicit that *the involvement of a greater number of neurons increased the number of circulating loops in parallel rather than altering the average number of neurons per loop.* In order to account for acceleration of the storage rate under

63

these circumstances, it seems necessary to postulate some *interaction* between these various loops, in terms other than direct synaptic influence. Although direct synaptic interactions might ensue, if these effects were primary they should alter the effective average number of neurons per loop, with resulting shifts in latency. Perhaps the effect of massive local neuronal coherence is to accomplish some alteration in the extraneuronal microenvironment of the whole population, facilitating the critical chemical reactions involved in storage.

C. The growth, shunt, and mode hypotheses

Whatever the reasons why the rate of acquisition of new responses, or storage of information required therein, can be facilitated, three tenable alternatives have been distinguished for the changes which might be accomplished during the labile phase and result in the establishment of long-term memory. (1) An experience may result in the formation of new neural connections. The pathways established by the growth of these connections constitute the stored memory. *Performance of behaviors requiring access to the stored information is subsequently mediated by conduction through these pathways.* We will refer to this as the *Growth Hypothesis*. (2) A pathway selectional mechanism might operate in an extensively interconnected network in which the connections remain essentially fixed. The temporal and spatial configuration of stimuli during an experience activates particular cells in the network. Interaction of these cellular discharges with ongoing activity in the network selects particular pathways through the network along which the information propagates. *Differential facilitation of conduction of particular temporal patterns along the selected pathways constitutes the stored memory.* Stimuli producing comparable spatial and temporal patterns of input will subsequently propagate along these same pathways. We will refer to this as the *Shunt Hypothesis*. (3) A *mode*-selectional mechanism might operate in an extensively interconnected network, in which the connections remain essentially fixed. The configuration of activity in the cells of the network at any time defines the *state* of the network. The temporal sequence of states in the network defines a *mode of activity*. Modes of activity involving greater coherence than is characteristic of ongoing background activity in the individual cells

64

of the network constitute information. This will be termed *nonbasal coherence* to avoid the implication that background activity need be random. The temporal and spatial configuration of stimuli impinging upon the network during an experience activates a particular mode of response. *Increase in the probability of coherent activity in that mode constitutes the stored memory.* Behaviors requiring utilization of the stored information involve activation of the corresponding mode of response within the network. Transfer of the information through the nervous system is accomplished by the coupling of *compatible* modes of response between interacting networks. We will refer to this as the *Mode Hypothesis.*

The Growth and Shunt Hypotheses differ in that the first requires growth of new connections while the second assumes the preexistence of connections, with pathway selection achieved by spatiotemporal patterning. The two hypotheses are functionally similar in that both postulate that information storage facilitates neural activity in particular pathways. Information storage and retrieval are mediated deterministically in a fashion necessitating activity in particular neurons.

Both the Shunt Hypothesis and the Mode Hypothesis require a mechanism at the cellular level which facilitates the response of the cell or set of cells to the occurrence of a specified temporal or spatial pattern of afferent input. This might occur by virtue of an increase or decrease in the synaptic effectiveness of a given input. Increased availability of transmitter or synaptic swelling (Eccles, 1965) might accomplish facilitation at the presynaptic level. Facilitation at the postsynaptic level would seem to require a method to "tune" the cell effectively to a specified time course of input.

Such tuning might be accomplished by changes in membrane characteristics which facilitated particular spike-interval patterns of response by the unit. Alternatively, tuning might be accomplished by specification of the configuration of some sensitive substance in such a way that a stipulated pattern of input activated the sensitive substance and thereby initiated a reaction leading to the discharge of the cell.

Both Shunt and Mode Hypotheses share the requirement of tuning the representational cells. They differ in that the Shunt Hypothesis postulates that information storage achieves transmission through some one or more members of a set of parallel pathways in a deterministic fashion, while the Mode Hypothesis proposes that information storage

65

increases the likelihood of a particular mode of coherent oscillation in a network in a *probabilistic* fashion.

Were tuning accomplished by a modification of membrane response characteristics, there would seem to be no need to postulate *specific* coding on the molecular level to represent stored information. It is sufficient to assume that cell discharge with a given temporal pattern facilitates the synthesis of some substance, *selected* from the class of ongoing reactions in the cell, which permits the cell membrane to participate in that response pattern more readily. This assumption implies that the storage of all memories is based upon the *same* chemical substance or upon a group of substances which have a common property. However, specification of the molecular configuration of a substance that will subsequently "recognize" a given pattern of input in a deterministic fashion would seem to require the *instruction* of a unique synthetic process. This assumption implies that different memories are stored by different compounds. We shall return to these problems in Chapters VI and VII. Unfortunately, considerations such as those presented up to now do not permit conclusive resolution between these hypotheses. Fortunately, further insights are afforded by electrophysiological data of the sort which are presented in Chapters IX–XVI of this book.

CHAPTER V

STATE-DEPENDENT LEARNING

The reader may be aided in his attempts to evaluate the relative plausibility of these various hypotheses by a consideration of the phenomenon of "state-dependent" or "dissociated" learning. These terms have been applied to a body of data which indicates that retrieval of information stored in the brain while a special "state" of the organism was maintained is made more difficult or even impossible if this critical state is altered. When the specified state is restored, retrieval occurs as usual. Obviously, the fact that performance may deteriorate after change in the conditions under which a response was acquired need not imply interference with central information processing mechanisms. Studies of stimulus and response generalization are numerous, and they indicate the variation of performance with changes in input and output conditions.

However, appreciable insight into the central mechanisms mediating performance based on previously acquired information may be provided by studies which explore effects of alterations of central state, while leaving stimulus and response characteristics unaltered. Obviously, deficits produced by some agents on the performance of responses acquired in the *normal* state may merely indicate a general impairment of function. Deterioration of performance after an experimental intervention cannot be attributed to specific interference with information retrieval unless adequate controls exist to rule out explanations based on more generalized actions, such as changes in sensory input systems, attention and arousal mechanisms, motivational levels, or muscular coordination. However, the deterioration of performance established in an *abnormal* state, when tested under normal conditions, seems more paradoxical. Perhaps the most convincing demonstration of state-dependent performance would be provided by evidence that an animal behaved adaptively in a specified situation under both *normal* and *abnormal* conditions, but that the type of behavior displayed was determined by which state was imposed. Even under such circumstances, some assurance is desirable that the differential performance is not based upon changes in sensory cues, whether exteroceptive or interoceptive. A number of examples of phenomena which seem to illustrate state dependency will be provided, including instances in which variations in internal or drive stimuli cause marked changes in performance, as well as data revealing striking dissociation between learning and performance in the presence or absence of particular drugs. Recent reviews of such phenomena are available (Sachs, 1962a; Overton, 1964).

A. The stimulus change interpretation

We will not attempt to review experiments in which the deficit in performance arises as a consequence of change in the configuration of stimuli presented to the organism. The literature relevant to the effects of stimulus change on response has been well reviewed by Bindra (1959). However, in passing, it is worthwhile to point out that numerous data exist which demonstrate decrements in various aspects of the performance of acquired behaviors, when alterations take place in the stimulus conditions. Bindra attributes a major role in response decrements accompanying changes in the stimulus complex to the distracting and competing features of response to novelty. Although it is necessary to concede the relevance of competitive responses, particularly in the rat, they do not seem to account adequately for all examples of performance decrement with stimulus change, particularly in other animals less prone to "freeze" in response to novelty.

For example, in our own experimental work it has often become necessary to move behavioral apparatus from one room to another, or to change what appeared to be secondary features of the apparatus for experimental convenience. It has been commonplace in our experience that previously well-trained cats display a decrement in performance after these changes, minor though they may seem to us. Such deterioration has been observed in a variety of behavioral situations involving both approach and avoidance tasks. Although the causes of these disturbances have not been analyzed systematically, the impression is given that the animal is somehow confused by the change in the total stimulus context although the conditioned stimuli and instrumental responses have not been altered. In differential response situations in which discriminative behavior is required, such animals perform erroneous responses, rather than being immobilized or "freezing." These observations indicate that the total stimulus complex, including data from various sensory modalities providing information about "ground" as well as "figure," possesses cue value for the organism. Although such casual evidence is admittedly far from conclusive, it suggests that a fairly complex multiple set of input requirements must be satisfied in order for a conditioned response to be elicited upon stimulus presentation. Since the primary stimulus is unchanged, such phenomena seem to be somewhat more difficult to explain in terms of the Growth Hypothesis in comparison to the other two alternative formulations.

B. Dissociation phenomena

Perhaps the first example of apparent state-dependent learning was provided by Lashley (1917), who trained rats in a maze after administration of strychine or caffeine. He found that strychnine enhanced the rate of acquisition of the maze habit, while caffeine resulted in slower acquisition. Both groups took longer to relearn the maze, when tested subsequently without drug injection, than the undrugged control group. In a well-known series of studies, Girden and Culler (1937) and Girden (1942a,b,c; 1947) conditioned a number of autonomic and muscular responses in dogs, cats, and monkeys injected with crude curare or dihydro-β-erythroidine HBR. The conditioned response thus established could not be subsequently demonstrated in the undrugged state, but reappeared following administration of the drug. Case and Funderbunk (1947) reported similar dissociation with physostigmine. Conditioned responses acquired under the influence of one of these drugs could also be elicited after medication with the other, but were absent in the undrugged state. These findings suggest that severe response decrements can be produced by a chemically induced change in the state of the central nervous system, but do not decisively rule out the stimulus-change explanation.

Carson (1957) showed that rats could acquire a conditioned avoidance response (CAR) quite rapidly in the period following ECS, but demonstrated no retention when tested several days later. Presumably, this effect is due to gradual return of the perturbed nervous system to a more normal state. The stimulus change argument might be offered in explanation for this result. However, Hunt and Brady (1951) have shown differential decrements in behavior after ECS that demonstrate temporary disappearance of a conditioned emotional response while an appetitive learned response was unaffected, showing that stimulus changes, if caused by ECS, are not so massive as to disrupt both behaviors.

Otis (1956, 1957) conditioned three groups of rats to perform an avoidance response while satiated with food, after 6 hours of food deprivation, or after 24 hours of food deprivation. All three groups were subsequently tested under each condition. Performance of the avoidance response was best in each group under the test conditions that corresponded to those under which acquisition took place. Similar effects were obtained using a conditioned emotional response. It would appear that the level of a biogenic drive which had been associated with a noxious stimulus became a determinant of state in these animals. For these animals, one might think of the drive level plus the noxious stimulus in order to define a compound conditioned stimulus that provides a basis for differential response.

Perhaps the "switching" experiments reviewed by Asratyan (1961) are also compatible with such an explanation. In such experiments, the same stimulus serves as the CS for *either* an appetitive *or* an aversive CR, depending upon variables such as the time of day when the test trials occur, or the room in which the tests are administered. The use of two sets of stimuli in an analogous fashion reveals reciprocal inhibition of antagonistic conditioned responses. Asratyan adduces such data as evidence that the locus of the stored information is neither in the sensory nor the motor "analyzers" (cortex), but must lie in intermediate regions. He also provides data that, if both contextual cues are brought together, the behavior resulting from the presentation of the CS can be determined by alterations in stimulus intensity or reinforcement intensity. Furthermore, extinction of the conditioned response elicited by the CS in one contextual situation results in enhancement of the opposite CR to the same CS in the second situation. Such data would seem to indicate extensive interactions of two mediational systems responding to the same CS, involving reciprocal inhibition, and reflect incomplete isolation of the different states. Stimulus-change or state-dependency interpretations of these results might be considered equally plausible in the absence of further data.

(Similar conclusions about interaction arise from the studies of Grastyán, Lissák, and Kékesi (1956) on the effects of central electrical stimulation on the performance of appetitive and aversive responses to two conditioned stimuli. Those studies revealed a set of placements in the brain stem where stimulation at a lateral position inhibited one response and facilitated the other while stimulation at a medial position had the opposite effect. However, such effects were not elicited if the two CR's were concurrently established in the same environment.)

Some indication that the phenomenon involved in switching experiments may be illustrative of state dependence is provided by the data of Sakhiulina (1955, 1960), who established a flexion response of the right paw when the CS was presented in one situation, while the same CS elicited left paw flexion in another situation. Electrographic data obtained in both situations revealed a sustained desynchronization of one motor cortex in one situation, while the opposite motor cortex was desynchronized in the second situation. The proposition that a change in the excitability of the motor cortex effectively constitutes a change in the characteristics of the sensory stimulus would seem logically equivalent to the argument that if the stimulus has a different effect, it is by definition a different stimulus. Such reasoning here seems far-fetched, since the stimulus encounters rather than elicits the sustained desynchronization.

Anokhin (1960, 1961) has presented data that in the so-called "dynamic stereotype," a well-practiced and overlearned routine, the CS plays the role of a nonspecific activator or releaser of the CR. Presentation of any strong stimulus at the proper point in a behavioral sequence will elicit performance of the CR, independent of the CS. The electrographic response to presentation of an indifferent stimulus (bell), at the point where the CS (light) usually occurs, causes

71

cortical desynchronization similar to the response to the CS, while presentation of the tone at other times does not elicit this effect, nor does it elicit the CR. Similarly, the expected EEG sequence can occur in the absence of any marked stimulus (see chapter XII). Anokhin concludes that situational differences in switching experiments create subcortical dominant foci (see Chapter IX), which he attributes to activation of the reticular formation.

One can, in this fashion, construct an explanation for the effects of stimulus change in state-dependent terms. Different aspects of the stimulus complex cause changes in the dynamic features of CNS response to the over-all situation. The processing of information about environmental events involves interaction of phasic input with the tonic features characterizing the central excitatory state reflecting the situation. In this view, a change in stimulus complex will cause a change in state, thereby altering the processing of information about the stimulus.

Anokhin provides evidence that chlorpromazine, which displays preferential interference with performance of defensive but not appetitive responses to conditioned stimuli, also blocks EEG activation to the defensive CS, leaving the desynchronization response to the alimentary CS unimpaired. John et al. (1958a,b) have provided similar evidence for differential effects of reserpine on approach and avoidance responses, both mediated by visual cues. Wenzel (1961) has provided similar evidence showing that reserpine will block performance of a lever-pressing response to avoid shock after presentation of one auditory CS, leaving unimpaired the performance of lever-pressing response to obtain food after interspersed presentations of another auditory CS. Such data indicate the participation of drive-relevant systems in CR mediation, perhaps by a contribution to maintenance of the necessary central state, and are of particular interest because of the differential nature of the effects.

In general, interference with performance of so-called "existential discriminations" (John, 1961) is less convincing evidence of interference with information retrieval than selective blockade of differential discriminations. *Differential* effects of the sort enumerated above are difficult to explain on the basis of a stimulus change argument or general depression of function, and seem to provide evidence for functional dissociation reflecting an alteration in state of the central nervous system. In the absence of differential effects, some of the findings thus far cited might be interpreted to result from alteration in the effective stimulus. It is admittedly difficult to prove that hypothetical differences in the effective stimulus arising from change in drive level, change in features of the surround, or the gross effects of drug action do not constitute the basis for apparent state dependence. Our conclusions must include an evaluation of whether the effects can *reasonably* be attributed to stimulus change. Such evaluation might legitimately include human report as to whether or not the relevant conditions accomplish a noteworthy change in the apparent characteristics of the stimulus. Some manipulations which have been found to be effective in producing dissociation do not seem to cause such subjective effects.

C. Transfer as a criterion for dissociation

Somewhat more compelling evidence for evaluation of the stimulus-change argument is available from the relative ease of transfer of response, with reinforcement, from the inital acquisition state to the subsequent test state. The effects of rather marked change in stimulus characteristics can be overcome fairly readily when reinforcement is provided after presentation of moderately altered stimuli. In a number of the studies of dissociation which have been reported, such ease of transfer could not be demonstrated.

An example may be provided from the work of Bloch and Silva (1959), who used a latent learning design. Rats were permitted unrewarded maze experience under the influence of pentobarbital, meprobamate, or under control conditions. Based on measures of frequency of arrival at the goal box, mean number of cul entries, or time spent to traverse the maze, the pentobarbital group manifested superior acquisition of the maze habit while drugged in comparison with the other groups. When tested in the undrugged state, with reinforcement introduced, the pentobarbital group showed no evidence of prior experience in the maze in contrast with the other two groups.

Particularly convincing evidence against the stimulus-change explanation for dissociation of learning has been provided in a careful series of experiments by Overton (1964). First, this worker

73

trained one group of rats to turn in one direction to escape shock in a T-maze, after the injection of sodium pentobarbital. A second group was trained to escape shock when saline was injected. Subsequently, the direction of the escape response displayed by these animals depended on whether or not pentobarbital had been injected. When drugged, the animals trained under pentobarbital performed almost perfectly, while performance without the drug was at the random level. Conversely, animals who were trained without the drug showed random performance when treated with pentobarbital, but performed well when undrugged.

Additional groups were trained to turn in one direction when drugged, and in the other direction when nondrugged. If dissociation between drugged and nondrugged states had not occurred, training would have been expected to generalize from one state to the other. The results showed clearly that these animals displayed behaviors completely controlled by their state, indicating essentially complete dissociation of learning. These results are illustrated in Fig. V-1.

Next, Overton used the method of savings to evaluate the degree of state dependence. Rats were trained to perform a response in the drug state and, after acquisition, training was continued in the nondrug state. Relearning without the drug was essentially identical in speed with the rate of acquisition displayed by a naïve undrugged control group. The results showed no savings during relearning by the group originally trained under drug. Thus, no transfer of training occurred between the drug and nondrug state, indicating that dissociation of learning between the two states was essentially complete.

As a further demonstration of the completeness of dissociation under these conditions, Overton showed that it was possible to develop two opposite response tendencies concurrently under drugged and nondrugged states, by alternating training trials under the two conditions. Evaluation of the extent of transfer was based upon comparison of errors committed by animals undergoing such concurrent training with errors committed by a control group. Incomplete dissociation between states should have resulted in increased errors in each drug state due to interference. Differential responses in the drugged and nondrugged states were acquired by the experimental group with no more errors than evidenced by comparable control groups learning only a single response, indicating a complete absence of transfer between the two

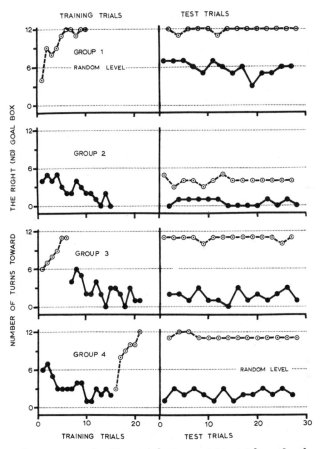

Fig. V-1. Performance in the T-maze during training trials and subsequent test trials. *Group 1* was allowed to escape shock while undrugged by running to the *right* goal box. After ten such training trials, twenty-eight test trials followed. These were performed alternately in the drugged and nondrug states. Each rat received only one trial per day. The drug state was produced by injections of sodium pentobarbital (25 mg/kg) 15–45 minutes before the trial for the day. *Group 2* was trained for fifteen trials while drugged to go to the *left* goal box. Training was then stopped and twenty-eight test trials followed as for Group 1.

Rats in *Groups 3* and *4* were trained first to turn toward one goal box while in one state, then trained to turn toward the other goal box while in the other state, and finally tested the same way as Groups 1 and 2.

There were twelve rats in each group. Closed circles indicate drug trials; open circles indicate undrugged trials. These results demonstrate essentially complete dissociation of learning in the two states. [Based on data from Overton (1964).]

states. Experiments in which stimulus parameters are manipulated to establish differential responses seldom show such absence of transfer. Further work showed a graded amount of transfer as a function of drug dosage, indicating that the extent of state dependence of the acquired response could be systematically manipulated. These findings are summarized in Fig. V-2.

Perhaps the most useful experiment in the careful evaluation of dissociation provided by Overton was the examination of the extent to which changes in exteroceptive or interoceptive stimuli produced by the drugs might account for the apparent response control. The effectiveness of drug states to control differential responses was compared with that of various exteroceptive stimuli, interoceptive stimuli, and drive states. Marked peripheral discriminative stimuli in three modalities, sound, light, and electric foot shock, a single strong visual cue, muscle flaccidity due to gallamine triethiodide administration, extensive autonomic nervous system blockade with tetraethylammonium chloride, and 23-hour food and water deprivation were compared with pentobarbital as agents for establishing differential response control (see Fig. V-3). Pentobarbital was significantly more effective than any of these manipulations ($p < .001$). These results establish rather unequivocally the fact that response control by massive exteroceptive or interoceptive stimuli was much more difficult to establish in this experimental situation than by administration of pentobarbital. In view of these thorough investigations, it seems exceedingly unlikely that the dissociation of learning achieved by pentobarbital can reasonably be attributed to changes in sensory cues. A more parsimonious explanation would seem to be that information which is stored in the central nervous system while it is in a specified state is most easily retrieved when the same state is again imposed, even if some normal functions of the system are severely disrupted by that state.

In a second study (1966), Overton provided evidence that not all dissociation phenomena are the result of some single process, such as changes in arousal level. A set of depressant drugs including pentobarbital, phenobarbital, alcohol, urethane, and meprobamate produced a state in which learning was partly dissociated from learning in the nondrug state. These substances were approximately equivalent in their actions and were interchangeable. A second set of anticholinergic drugs including atropine and scopolamine was found to produce a state in which learning

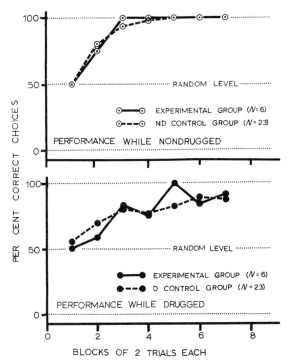

Fig. V-2. The animals in the experimental group were trained to turn right while undrugged and to turn to the left goal box while drugged. They received two training trials per day, one undrugged trial in the morning and a drug trial in the evening. A nondrug control group was given one training trial per day in which a right turn was required. A drug control group received one training trial per day in which a left turn was required. The drug state was produced by injection of pentobarbital (25 mg/kg) 15–45 minutes before drug trials.

If learning in the drug and nondrug states is completely dissociated, it should be possible to develop different response tendencies in the two states concurrently by alternate training trials under the two conditions.

These data show clearly that rats in the experimental group learned to turn toward one goal box when drugged and toward the opposite goal box when not drugged. Differential response was effectively controlled by the drug state. Furthermore, the learning curves for the experimental group in each state are very similar to those of the comparable control groups; no significant differences were found. Therefore, no transfer of training occurred between the two experimental conditions, which indicates virtually complete dissociation. [Based on data from Overton (1964).]

was partially dissociated both from the nondrug and the depressant drug states. The effects of atropine which produced this state neither mimicked nor antagonized the dissociative effects of the depressants. This study also showed that the amount of dissociation of learning caused by a particular

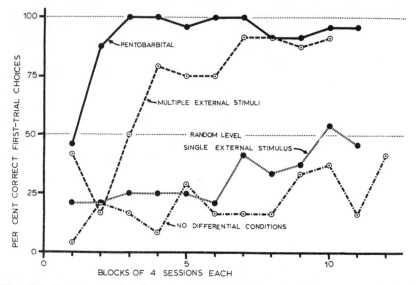

Fig. V-3. Learning curves for the acquisition of differential responses controlled by drug states or by external discriminative stimuli ($N = 6$ per group). The multiple external discriminative stimuli consisted of "bright light plus loud tone plus high shock intensity" versus "dim light plus no tone plus low shock intensity." The single discriminative stimulus consisted of bright versus dim light. Additional control groups received gallamine, tetraethylammonium, water deprivation, or food deprivation versus saline.

Note that the difference between pentobarbital and saline rapidly established control over differential responses. Multiple external stimulus changes also acquired differential control, but more slowly than pentobarbital ($P < .001$). None of the other groups of animals displayed good differential response within 40 training sessions; performance curves for food, water, tetraethylammonium, and gallamine groups are not shown.

These results show that the response control achieved by pentobarbital versus saline was not due to sensory cues resulting from muscle flaccidity, changes in apparent stimulus intensity, autonomic effects, etc. It seems unlikely that pentobarbital dissociation is due to direct change of either exteroceptive or interoceptive stimuli. [Based on data from Overton (1964).]

substance may vary sharply from task to task. Since there is no reason to believe that the action of a given drug on the state of various brain regions will vary with the task, this finding illustrates that the involvement of brain regions in the mediation of learned responses varies from task to task.

In another clear demonstration of dissociation of learning, Sachs *et al.* (1966) have observed rapid learning of the CAR by rats following medication with chlordiazepoxide (librium). When tested subsequently without drug injections, the experimental animals performed uniformly at essentially the zero level. It is noteworthy that in each test session a number of shocked "reminder" trials were, inserted. In spite of these trials, response in the undrugged state remained at near zero levels, indicating poor transfer of training to the undrugged state. Injection of the drug quickly restored performance to high levels, with severe deterioration again after the drug effects wore off. Control animals displayed a small performance deficit when tested under drugged conditions.

D. Dissociation and brain electrolytes

In previous work, John, Tschirgi, and Wenzel (1959) had explored the effect of intraventricular injection of small amounts of potassium or calcium on the performance of a battery of conditioned responses by cats. Cats were trained to perform an avoidance response to tone, an avoidance response to light, pattern discrimination for food, and to run an elevated runway for visible food. These responses were acquired in counterbalanced order. These animals were then studied in an effort to determine whether it would be possible to delete performance of particular responses from the repertoire of an animal, after intraventricular injection of electrolyte solutions, without affecting the remainder of the battery. Results showed it was possible to achieve quite specific interference with performance of conditioned response in reproducible fashion. Almost every configuration of differential deficit which was possible was, in fact, obtained.

The effects of calcium injections provide perhaps the most striking and consistent example of the differential deficit which could be achieved. Following calcium injection these animals, fully trained in the four responses described above, almost invariably behaved as follows: Presentation of the auditory conditioned stimulus for avoidance resulted in well-coordinated performance of the conditioned avoidance response, hurdle jumping, with the customary latency which had been established by training. Presentation of the visual stimulus, interspersed with the auditory stimulus according to a random schedule, resulted in what looked like a "conditioned emotional response." The animal crouched and hissed at the onset of the visual stimulus. However, no attempt was made to jump the hurdle, although well-directed escape occurred when shock was delivered. On occasion such an animal, upon the presentation of the visual CS, would not only crouch and hiss, but might attempt to climb up the walls of the box. This behavior was observed most frequently in animals who had displayed similar escape attempts during the course of conditioning. Test sessions with pattern discrimination, interspersed during avoidance testing, revealed the performance of visual pattern discrimination for food was excellent, and motor coordination was not impaired, as evidenced by the continued ability to run the elevated runway, and leap a hurdle to get visible food.

The following considerations indicate some of the possible interpretations of these results. One cannot attribute the failure of the visual CS to decreased motivation for avoidance as a consequence of the injection, since the latency to the interspersed auditory aversive stimuli was unchanged. The response mechanism was manifestly intact, since avoidance behaviors continued to be elicited by auditory stimuli.

Furthermore, the lack of impairment of visual processes was evidenced by the continued perfect discrimination between squares and circles for food. Thus the relevant sensory input pathways remained functional. Further evidence that this was the case was provided by the strong conditioned emotional response, frequently displayed by these animals upon the onset of the visual stimulus.

The conditioned avoidance response can be considered to consist of three components: (1) An instrumental hurdle jump, learned initially as a response to shock; (2) a classically conditioned emotional response, with strong autonomic components, pupillary dilation, and change in respiratory and heart rates, is established to the conditioned stimulus, light or tone in this case; (3) a process analogous to "second-order" Pavlovian conditioning links these two components, so that the classically conditioned response to the CS comes to serve as the stimulus for performance of the instrumental response, which was originally established to shock. The configuration of behavior following intraventricular calcium injection, which has just been described, suggests that both the classically conditioned autonomic response component to the CS, as well as the instrumentally conditioned escape component established initially to shock, remain intact. However, the bond between these two, so that the classical conditioned response releases the instrumental conditioned behavior, has been dissociated by the calcium injection.

From this viewpoint, the effects of calcium injection described above seem to constitute an example of dissociation due to a relatively specific interference with information processing. The differential nature of the deterioration of conditioned avoidance response to gross visual stimuli, with simultaneous retention of another avoidance response and an appetitive response based on the discrimination of fine details of the visual cues, seems to rule out explanations based upon stimulus changes or generalized motivational or muscular factors in favor of a dissociation explanation.

Related indications of state-dependent performance were obtained by Sachs (1961, 1962a). Groups of animals, who had received intraventricular injections of potassium or calcium just *before each training experience* in a shock avoidance task, were tested in the absence of ionic injections. All groups performed *worse* when tested with normal brain ionic concentrations, that is, without injection of the substance received during training. Injection of potassium into calcium-trained cats or of calcium into potassium-trained cats also resulted in severe performance deficits. The concentrations and volumes of intraventricular injections were comparable to those used by John *et al.* in the preceding study, although multiple injections were often used in the earlier work.

When an animal trained with elevated brain calcium is tested without calcium injection, one might expect that the excitability of neural regions should be somewhat greater than when calcium was present. Those neurons which could respond to the stimulus in the presence of calcium should now be even more excitable, and should continue to remain responsive. In addition, other neurons, biased to cut-off by the calcium injection, can now come into play. It is possible that the disruption of performance in calcium-dependent animals in the absence of calcium injection is due to the "noise" introduced into the system by newly responsive neurons. It seems, nonetheless, surprising that these effects are so great. Although similar effects are observed in animals who are potassium dependent, the calcium effect seems more potent, is more generally observed, and is longer lasting.

In Sachs' experimental design, there were several control groups to estimate the extent to which ionic effects arose from simple accommodation. Such animals were first trained normally to criterion, and were then subjected to a series of ionic injections, some animals receiving potassium and others calcium, equal to the course of injections received

81

by one of the animals in each experimental group. These matched controls were subsequently tested, immediately after ionic injection, to see whether performance would occur. Both potassium-control and calcium-control animals, thus prepared, showed significant deterioration of conditioned response performance in test sessions which were preceded by injection of the substance they had received during the accommodation period. The deterioration of performance was most striking in the animals which received calcium. Recently, Wang *et al.* (1966) have reported striking changes in hippocampal impedance after such injections.

Control animals showed little performance deterioration after intraventricular injections of hypertonic sodium chloride. This fact, together with the resistance of conditioned responses observed after central or systemic injections of other substances which alter excitability (John *et al.*, 1958b), suggests that the properties described here for potassium and calcium may derive from factors unrelated to their direct influence on neural excitability.

These findings suggested that the calcium state dependency was specific to its presence during the period of acquisition, rather than arising from the accommodation of this system to calcium. Furthermore, this susceptibility to ionic injections on the part of accommodated controls indicated that the ability of the experimental groups to acquire and perform conditioned responses after ionic shifts could not be explained merely on the basis of acquired tolerance to the altered central ionic environment. However, it was not possible to decide whether the calcium effect was due to its general action during the period of training, which took place in the presence of raised calcium, or arose from the specific consequences of raised calcium during the actual experiences.

As discussed earlier, deterioration of conditioned response when some aspect of the environment is altered is a familiar observation in more orthodox behavioral situations, sometimes referred to as "stimulus generalization decrement." When the stimulus complex present during conditioning is altered and behavior is observed to deteriorate, it is usually possible to reestablish performance at a high level rapidly, by reinforcing the new stimulus complex. The conditioned response is *transferred* to the new stimulus complex. Usually, transfer of this sort, even to stimuli of other modalities, can be readily achieved. It seems unlikely that this factor constitutes an explanation of the state-dependent performance of animals who received ionic injections during learning. Test conditions consisted of a mixture of so-called "reminder" trials, "R," of which two occurred at the beginning, two in the middle, and two at the end of each session, and so-called "extinction" trials, "E," bracketed by the former as follows: RR-EEEEE-RR-EEEEE-RR. In reminder trials, after stimulus presentation for the period permitted before reinforcement during training, the animal was shocked, until behavior occurred or until a series of four shocks was received, one every 5 seconds. In the extinction trials, no shock was delivered until 30 seconds elapsed without the appropriate performance, and the trial was then concluded *without* shock. Response latency was measured only using the data from the extinction trials. The reinforced "reminder" trials actually constitute trials in which transfer of the conditioned response to the new condition is taking place. The failure of the state-dependent animals to show marked transfer, in spite of the reinforcement received under the new condition during the reminder trials in test sessions, strongly militates for the interpretation of the ionic effects as due to dissociation.

E. Relative specificity of ionic effects

Additional experiments (John, Bartlett, and Sachs, 1963a) have attempted to clarify these phenomena further. It should be noted that in this work, as in the previous studies by Sachs, injections were received *every 4 days,* and training sessions were similarly spaced. Two additional groups of animals were trained, under conditions essentially identical with those used by Sachs, except that injection no longer *preceded* each training session. Instead, one group received its calcium injection intraventricularly *1 minute after each training session was concluded.* The other group received an intraventricular calcium injection *48 hours after each training session was concluded.* Because 4 days intervened between training sessions, injection of the second group occurred *midway* between successive sessions. The 1-minute group learned even more slowly than the animals who received calcium preceding each training session. The animals who received calcium 48 hours later learned somewhat more rapidly, but were still slower to acquire the response than the group receiving calcium injections before each training session.

Following acquisition of the conditioned response, all groups were tested immediately *after* calcium injection. The only group showing consistently adequate performance was the group which received calcium injection before each training experience. Although one or two of the animals in each of the other groups could perform adequately in the face of calcium injections, both posttrial injection groups showed significantly poorer performance ($p < .001$) immediately after central calcium injection. Thus, the data suggested that calcium dependency required the presence of raised brain calcium levels during the actual experience, and could not be achieved by intercurrent injection and experience which were not congruent. Possibly, the ability of a few animals to perform under these circumstances could be explained by extension of consolidation processes sufficiently into the posttraining period to be affected by subsequent injection, or by persistence or accumulation of calcium injected during the interval between training periods so that a raised level was present in the following session. These shortcomings could be overcome by carrying out analogous experiments using "one-trial" learning situations to see whether raised calcium must be present during some specified portion of the consolidation phase, in order for retrieval in the presence of calcium to be possible.

Some aspects of the data suggested that accumulation of calcium may have occurred during the injection period. Some animals revealed marked improvement in the ability to tolerate calcium injections before performance tests, when simply permitted a longer period of time with no central injection. A more adequate test might have consisted of estimation of the amount of calcium necessary to achieve complete blockade of performance in each group. For some animals, however, the dissociation appeared to be relatively complete. Clear alternation between performance and nonperformance in a sustained series of test trials without and with preceding calcium was displayed by several animals who were trained with calcium injection 1 minute after each session. This alternation showed that little transfer occurred.

A small number of pilot experiments provide an interesting suggestion that the reported effects of intraventricular calcium injections may involve significant chemical specificity (Bartlett and John, 1963). Animals which had been trained with calcium injections preceding each training session could *not* perform after intraventricular injection of comparable amounts of strontium. Systematic exploration of functional equivalence or the lack thereof between various substances might provide worthwhile insights into the mechanism underlying such phenomena.

With these various qualifications in mind, the data nevertheless suggest that the ability of an animal to recover information stored in the presence of a particular internal ionic milieu is dependent upon restoration of a corresponding neural environment. This dependence appears to involve relatively specific factors rather than general consequences of ionic shifts.

F. Implications of dissociation for growth, shunt, and mode hypotheses

Although almost any one of the experiments cited in this chapter might conceivably be challenged on some grounds as insufficient evidence for the existence of "state-dependent" learning, in sum they provide strong support for the proposition that certain responses, if acquired under specific conditions, are thereafter best elicited when those conditions are reestablished. This body of data further supports the contention that the observed changes in performance levels are often due to alterations in crucial states of the central nervous system related to the processing of information, rather than to alterations in stimulus characteristics, or other factors of a more general sort. The stimulus-change argument seems effectively controverted by a number of examples provided, in which the measurement of savings and the substantial failure of transfer between states when reinforcement was introduced shows virtually complete dissociation. Consideration of the known effects of the agents involved in some instances, from the viewpoint of human subjective report, and evaluation of relevant electrographic evidence, provides further support for this interpretation.

In agreement with the arguments of Bindra, Sachs (1965) has suggested that many of the situations involved in these studies are such that one can account for the observed decrement as a result of competing responses due to novelty and fear. He has accumulated strong evidence for a relationship between the ability of certain agents to achieve dissociation, change in arousal, orienting, and fear responses, and alteration of hippocampal theta rhythms. In many cases, it may be possible to contend that the crucial difference in state relates to the suppression or release of systems in the brain responsive to novelty. Such an explanation seems contradicted by the placidity displayed by animals in some situations in which no performance of the learned response can be elicited. The strongest objection to these suggestions, however, arises from consideration of experimental procedures in which the same generic behavioral response is performed in one fashion in the drugged state and another fashion in the nondrugged state. Response mode varies with state, in such studies, but performance occurs in both states.

As with much of the data presented thus far, interpretation cannot conclusively be accomplished on the basis of the available evidence, and personal intuition influences analysis. Whether or not factors such as change in stimulus characteristics or competition from novelty responses contribute to some of the phenomena which have been described, the author finds great difficulty in reconciling this set of findings with the assumptions of the Growth Hypothesis. If the performance of the relevant learned responses were normally mediated by growth of new synaptic connections, established between nerve cells to constitute a memory pathway built during the learning experience, it seems highly unlikely that the various maneuvers shown to achieve dissociation would cause reversal of that growth. Furthermore, why should just those particular connections be detached from each other, while the connections held by such a formulation to mediate other behaviors remain in contact? These considerations raise severe doubts about the validity of the Growth Hypothesis.

It seems more plausible to conclude that these interventions alter the excitability of neuronal populations that are required to interact in relatively reproducible manner whether one assumes the validity of either the Shunt or Mode Hypotheses. Some readers may feel that excitability changes might also account for inactivation of new connections postulated by the Growth Hypothesis. If one assumes that excitability changes can cause functional inactivation of these connections, one can argue equally well that functional activation of connections be accounted for in similar terms. The Growth and Shunt Hypotheses would thereby become logically indistinguishable.

The excitability formulation proposes that a set of neurons capable of adequately sustained response to the stimulus is selected as a consequence of state-induced changes in the microenvironment of the brain. Alterations in excitability accompanying subsequent changes in state respecify the set of neurons which can respond to the stimulus, thereby altering the probability of readout mediated by the initial representational set.

The ionic studies discussed in this chapter offer the advantage of reasonable confidence in the fact that the chemical substances responsible for the observed phenomena are those which were injected. Such studies revealed extreme sensitivity of the mechanisms of information storage and retrieval to small shifts of brain potassium and calcium, whether imposed systematically during the learning experience or as obstacles to retrieval of information stored under normal conditions. A vast literature, well summarized by Tschirgi in the "Handbook of Neurophysiology" (1960), shows that potassium and calcium have antagonistic effects on many biological systems. Specifically, the effects of one of these substances on many processes in the nervous system are well antagonized by the effects of the other. Examining the full configuration of conditioned response deficits obtained by injections of potassium, of calcium, and of equivalent potassium and calcium mixtures, it becomes clear that the behavioral effects of potassium and calcium are *not* antagonistic. In some of the behaviors which have been studied, the deficits following the potassium injection were *similar* to, rather than opposite from, the defects caused by calcium injection. Were deficits due to simple shunting of signals in a network, altered by changes in excitability due to the potassium or calcium injections, it seems surprising that injection of a balanced mixture of these substances did not antagonize the behavioral effects.

What may be involved in the recovery of stored information for the appropriate performance of a conditioned response is the precise *timing* of neural impulses, which must arrive at particular places appropriately synchronized for interaction with other neural events. Since potassium injection causes decreased chronaxie and earlier time of discharge to an adequate stimulus, impulses from a system that is "potassium-biased" might be expected to arrive at a junction slightly in advance of their normal time. Conversely, a system biased with calcium should have a higher chronaxie, and impulses might be expected to propagate to some junction point somewhat later than the usual time. The equivalence of behavioral effects obtained in some performances by equivalent injections of potassium or of calcium suggests that

87

when precise timing is necessary, too early may be as inadequate as too late. The depression of neural responsiveness with raised calcium level may seem an obvious basis for poorer performance, but it is not obvious how the increased neural responsiveness with raised potassium level could be equally disruptive.

Perhaps it should be mentioned that the absence of obvious state dependence when responses are normally acquired is not remarkable. During the usual duration of learning, central chemical systems may fluctuate through an appreciable range. Responses elaborated under such conditions can be expected to display the characteristics which Ashby (1960) has termed *multi-stability*. That is, these responses must, of necessity, be compatible with *each* of the states extant during the learning process.

G. Inadequacy of the excitability explanation

The adequacy of explanations of state dependency or dissociation based on changes of excitability is placed in question by a number of facts. The observed ineffectiveness of central or systemic injections of various pharmacological substances known to alter excitability, or of shifts in central sodium levels, shows that change in excitability is compatible with perfect retention of conditioned responses. Animals can perform conditioned responses correctly while at seizure threshold after injection of anticholinesterases (Chow and John, 1958).

In such contradictions lies support for the suggestion that perhaps excitability changes are not the only dimension which accounts for the phenomena under discussion. The stable representation of information which is synthesized during consolidation may somehow include a representation of the neural milieu as part of the stored configuration of variables. The microenvironment of a neural system receiving stimuli may constitute part of the functional context, and retrieval may occur best when the total context is well approximated. The surprising inability to substitute strontium for calcium in calcium-dependent animals may reflect such readout specificity. Considerations such as those just presented may be relevant to an analysis of the mechanism responsible for permanent information storage, but do not contribute to attempts to evaluate the relative merits of the Shunt and Mode Hypotheses. Although the accumulation of data on the facilitation of learning during the consolidation phase, as well as the phenomenon of dissociation, pose severe challenges to the assumption that information storage is accomplished by the growth of new connections, they also constitute an inadequate basis for a choice between a pathway-selection versus a mode-selection mechanism. Hopefully, additional facts influencing the relative plausibility of these two alternatives will emerge in later sections of this book when relevant electrophysiological data will be presented for the reader's examination.

Some of the facts cited above are relevant to evaluation of the relative plausibility of selectional versus instructional mechanisms required to mediate long-term storage by both the Shunt and Mode Hypotheses. Further data bearing on this point will be presented in the next chapter, dealing with experiments and formulations concerning chemical mechanisms of long-term storage of information in the brain.*

* Further experiments of possible interest, although not relevant to the problem of information storage mechanisms, were conducted on the ion-dependent animals discussed earlier in this chapter.

The study of rates of equilibration of various substances between the plasma, brain tissue, and cerebrospinal fluid, long ago generated the concept of the "blood brain barrier." Data relevant to this phenomenon are summarized in the "Handbook of Neurophysiology" (Tschirgi, 1960). In essence, the chemical milieu of the brain seems to be derived from the plasma by a process which differs from passive diffusion and involves the active secretion of particular concentrations of material in the brain. Concentrations of some substances, notably potassium and calcium, deviate from that which would be expected according to the Donnan equilibrium and show active regulation. A number of studies, including my own (John, 1956), show that the mechanisms regulating this active secretion are not invariant in their function and do not produce a precisely regulated, constant neural microenvironment. Under certain circumstances, these homeostatic mechanisms can deviate from their usual regulatory levels. Realization that such fluctuations in chemical milieu might occur in the nervous system stimulated inquiries as to whether or not such fluctuations in electrolyte concentration might be of *functional* significance in behavior.

Other workers have explored the question of whether or not these fluctuations in extracellular fluid composition occurred after the administration of various pharmacological agents, and might explain some aspects of the action of such agents. Some pharmacological substances bring about a change in the extracellular-intracellular distribution of potassium in the brain.

Since we have demonstrated the functional consequences of artificially imposed ionic shifts, it seems plausible that endogenously generated electrolyte shifts resulting from the fluctuation of regulatory mechanisms might also have marked functional consequences. Such shifts, then, might play a role in various clinical manifestations, and conversely, drugs of clinical utility might exert their actions by either achieving or reversing specific, more or less local, ionic shifts. From this viewpoint, it was noteworthy that animals in our experiments, after receiving ionic injections, displayed behaviors reminiscent of those observed after injections of some common drugs.

Many similarities can be observed between an animal which has experienced several central potassium injections over a brief period of time, and an animal who has received a high dose of methamphetamine. Conversely, some similarities exist between animals who have received calcium injections and moderate doses of reserpine. A calcium-injected animal tends to be passive and relatively quiescent. With high doses of calcium, it is sometimes possible to achieve an immobilization of voluntary movement, although righting reflexes remain undisturbed. Animals can be observed to maintain uncomfortable postures for long periods of time without movement, following calcium injection. Perhaps more striking is the observation that calcium-injected animals, receiving shock for failure to perform a previously established conditioned avoidance response, display a tendency to purr loudly in the interval between stimulus presentations instead of manifesting the excitable agitated behavior commonly observed in cats under such shock conditions.

These considerations and observations suggested that it might be possible to estimate the extent to which ionic shifts might be an aspect of the mode of action of some drugs by studying the interaction of ionic and drug injections in variously state-dependent populations. Extensive studies of this sort have been carried out, using the various groups of animals described above, trained with potassium or calcium preceding each session, as well as the corresponding "ionic accommodation" controls (John, Sachs, and Bartlett, 1963b).

Months after state-dependent training was completed, groups of animals, who were made state dependent on different ionic substances, displayed differential sensitivity to certain drugs. For example, the effect of chlorpromazine on animals trained with saline injections preceding each training session was not significantly different from the effect on potassium controls or calcium controls. All three control groups showed a deterioration of conditioned response through time following the injection of chlorpromazine, an increase of latency to a maximum value, and a gradual return of the conditioned response. Potassium-trained animals were significantly more susceptible to the effects of chlorpromazine, showing an earlier disappearance of conditioned avoidance response and a longer duration of the behavioral blockade following a chlorpromazine dose. In contrast, calcium-trained animals, who performed poorly in the absence of calcium, performed as well with chlorpromazine as if they had received calcium. Such data suggest that chlorpromazine administration may be attended by an increased central calcium concentration. Calcium-dependent animals, who require calcium for good performance, act as though chlorpromazine met that need. Vertua and Poggi (1960) have demonstrated an altered permeability to calcium, using radioactive calcium, following chlorpromazine administration. Conversely, Christenson has demonstrated a decreased permeability to potassium using radioisotopes, after chlorpromazine administration (Christenson et al., 1958).

Such findings, then, are consistent with the suggestion that some drugs of clinical interest may achieve their effect by bringing about a central ionic shift. Conversely,

---

the possibility must be considered that the conditions which are ameliorated by the administration of such drugs have as a significant aspect the perturbation of blood brain barrier regulation, so that the homeostatic regulatory mechanisms are displaced to an abnormal control point, with a resulting sustained ionic shift in some anatomical regions.

CHAPTER VI

POSSIBLE MECHANISMS OF STABLE INFORMA-
TION STORAGE: EXPERIMENTAL EVIDENCE

A. Logical considerations

What mechanism might mediate the storage of information in the stable phase? Since memories are extremely resistant to erasure, persisting through sleep, unconsciousness, and excitement for a good part of a lifetime, once consolidation has been completed, it seems reasonable to argue that during the consolidation phase something must be "made." Although reverberatory neural activity may be the basis for short-term representation during the labile phase, long-term memory cannot be attributed to enduring reverberation. The concept of "neurobiotaxis," enunciated many years ago by Kappers (1917), concretized this common-sense argument with the proposition that new neural processes grew between active cells as they responded to stimuli: new synaptic connections were formed, new boutons laid down, better contact was achieved, and the storage of experience was mediated by such structural changes. No direct evidence is available as to whether or not such growth does in fact take place in the central nervous system, although reservations about this concept have been presented in previous chapters.

Whether information is stored by the actual growth of new connections between nerve cells or the synthesis of substances inside neurons or glial cells, or whether the responsible mechanism operates in a deterministic or a statistical manner, these processes must require changes to occur in the matter of which the brain is constructed, changes in struc-

93

ture or composition. So the question can be raised: What might be the chemical nature of the change which makes for stable storage?, without having to resolve the detail of the structure which is involved or the means by which the change is wrought. Since information stored in the nervous system can often be retrieved throughout an individual's lifetime, it is appropriate to ask: Can one detect or demonstrate a stability in the matter of which brain is made, which provides a counterpart of the stability of information storage in the brain?

Although the gross morphology of brain seems to be fairly characteristic and stable, radioisotopic turnover measurements and other methods provide insight about whether or not any of the molecular species composing this structure are in fact static, and persist throughout a lifetime once they are laid down. Such isotope turnover data are available for most of the compounds of brain. There seems to be no significant compound of brain which does not display a remarkably high rate of turnover (Lajtha, 1961; Palladin, 1964).

The permanence of memory, therefore, cannot reasonably be attributed to the establishment of new intra- or extracellular structures laid down by *permanent* chemical molecules. It seems necessary, then, to explain the stable representation of experience as due to some change in configuration or substance mediated by a chemical system which, although itself not stable, is characterized by the fact that the molecules which break down are resynthesized in a specified way, so as to maintain the essential features of the change. Such template functions are known to be served by the nucleic acids. Furthermore, instinctive behaviors arise because of the influence of DNA and RNA on the cells of the nervous system. Since learning can produce long lasting patterns of behavior as stable as instincts, it seemed plausible that analogous mechanisms might be involved. Deoxyribonucleic acid, or DNA, is almost completely localized to the nucleus. Ribonucleic acid, or RNA, is found not only in the nucleus, but is distributed on the microsomes and throughout the cytoplasm of the cell, in various forms. Since stimuli impinge on the cell at its outer surface, the chemical systems which permanently alter the cellular response to presentation of such stimuli probably modify substances which are found in proximity to cellular surfaces or in the subjacent cytoplasm. Considerations of this sort have led various workers, both in theoretical formulations and experimental explorations, to turn to the possible role of RNA or proteins in the mediation of long-term information storage. Substances located in the cell nucleus may well mediate such changes. In spite of the nuclear localization and greater resistance of DNA to alteration, there is no reason to assume that modification of DNA *action* may not also play a role. A central question which must be considered in this general context is whether the hypothetical mechanism is more likely to be *instructional,* so that the structure of the representational molecule is somehow specified by the information to be stored, or *selectional,* so that one of a preexisting set of possible structures is allocated for a given representational function.

Perhaps the first suggestion in the literature that information storage might involve macromolecules was made by Von Foerster (1948), who pointed out the large information capacity which might be afforded by base sequences in a macromolecule. Several years later Katz and Halstead (1950) proposed a set of hypotheses suggesting that changes in brain nucleoproteins might be the basis for memory.

In this chapter we will review the experimental data presently available which are most relevant to such speculations and consider a number of the theoretical formulations which have recently been proposed.

B. Effects of neural stimulation on RNA and protein turnover

In 1952 Brattgård utilized a variety of exceedingly precise methods to investigate the alteration in ribonucleic acid and protein content of ganglion cells in the rabbit retina as a function of light stimulation (Brattgård, 1952). He reported that, with light deprivation, the concentration of RNA in the ganglion cell dropped rapidly to an exceedingly low level, although there was relatively little short-term change in the protein concentration. Upon stimulation the rate of synthesis of ribonucleic acid in the ganglion cell was proportional to the total light stimulation received by the cell. In related research, Rasch et al. (1961) showed that normal light stimulation was a major factor controlling the development of normal ribonucleoprotein levels in retinal cells of rat, cat and chimpanzee. In numerous works thereafter, Hydén and his colleagues established the fact that a chemical concomitant of neural activity was a stimulation of ribonucleic acid and protein synthesis. It is of interest that

Shtark (1965) has observed enhancement of the surface positive component of dendritic potentials after topical application of RNAase to the cortex, which suggests that a membrane transport system may be dependent on RNA.

Since that time other workers, for example Weiss (1961), have suggested or demonstrated that protein moves from the cell body down the axone in the course of neural activity. Geiger, in time lapse studies of neural tissue cultures, has demonstrated the movement of microsomes down the axone (Geiger *et al.*, 1960). The fate of the synthesized protein migrating down the processes of a nerve cell when the boundary of the cell is reached is not known.

C. Effects of learning on RNA synthesis

In addition to demonstrations that RNA synthesis is increased in nerve stimulation, a number of studies have attempted to demonstrate more directly that there is an increase in RNA synthesis in a learning situation. Some years ago Palladin described the work of Smirnov, utilizing radioisotope methods to study RNA turnover during conditioning (1964). Smirnov (1955) found that after establishment of a conditioned response presentation of an auditory conditioned stimulus caused an increased turnover of RNA in the auditory cortex but not in adjacent cortical regions, while such increased turnover was not elicited by neutral stimuli.

Morrell has studied RNA changes associated with the so-called "mirror focus" as a prototype of learning (1961a). If an epileptogenic focus is caused by irritation of regions of cortex, the symmetrically located area on the contralateral hemisphere displays response to discharge volleys arising in the irritated regions. This so-called "mirror focus" remains "dependent" for the first several weeks after its appearance, in that removal of the primary irritative lesion results in diminution and disappearance of the activity in the mirror focus. However, if several weeks are permitted to elapse, the mirror focus becomes independent and epileptiform discharge of the mirror focus persists, following removal of the primary irritative region. The independent mirror focus seems to provide, then, an example of sustained alteration in the activity of a neural region as a consequence of a particular type of neural input, experienced over a period of time.

Following the establishment of an independent mirror focus, Morrell circumscribed and undercut the region containing it, so that the mirror focus resided on a chronically isolated cortical slab. Under these conditions the electrical activity of the slab became quiescent. However, it was possible subsequently to demonstrate that hypersynchronous discharges induced on adjacent normal cortex by Metrazol application would spread across the neural gap to the isolated slab where the mirror focus had been. This transfer of disturbance across the neural gap did not take place in normal cortex which was chronically isolated, and was taken as evidence that the isolated slab bearing the mirror focus retained a characteristic hyperexcitability. Using methyl green pyronin, a stain selective for RNA, Morrell demonstrated that the chronically isolated mirror focus was characterized by dense staining of the cytoplasm, including the apical dendrites, which indicated higher concentration of RNA in that region than was found on normal isolated cortex.

Eiduson, Geller, and Beckwith (1961) have studied the concentration of a number of substances in the brain of chicks, following the establishment of imprinting. Imprinting is a phenomenon in which a chick, upon hatching out of its egg, is exposed to a moving stimulus, and, if that exposure occurs for a period of time sufficiently soon after birth, the chick subsequently will follow that moving stimulus when it becomes an adult. Eiduson and Beckwith found a negative correlation between the effectiveness of imprinting and the amount of ribonucleic acid in chick brain. This result suggests that, as the amount of available RNA increases, the more possible it becomes for the chick to establish alternative behaviors to the relatively rigid response which is represented by the following which results from imprinting.

Corning, working together with Freed, has studied the incorporation of P^{32} into RNA during the establishment of a conditioned response by planaria, as light and shock were systematically paired (Corning and Freed, 1963). Corning found that conditioned worms revealed a higher P^{32} incorporation during certain stages in the conditioning process than was obtained in control worms experiencing randomly presented light and shock, who failed to acquire any new behavioral response to light.

Using labeled uridine, increased RNA synthesis has been demonstrated in the brains of goldfish learning a CAR, but not in the brains of control fishes receiving the same total stimulation at random (Glassman et al., 1966). Analysis of RNA from nuclear and ribosomal fractions of

97

centrifuged brains from mice trained to perform the CAR showed greater incorporation of labeled uridine than the same material from control animals (Wilson *et al.*, 1966). No change in cellular or regional permeability to the labeled precursors was found. Further analysis suggested that the rate of synthesis of a messenger-like RNA in brain increased during learning.

D. Effects of learning on RNA base ratios

Hydén and Egyházi exposed young rats to a learning situation, requiring them to balance on a wire in order to reach a platform where food was located (1963). The number of times that a young rat performed this tightrope walking in a session increased rapidly with repeated sessions. When a terminal running rate was achieved, after about 8 days, the rats were sacrificed and the cytoplasmic and nuclear RNA of Deiter's nerve cells from the lateral vestibular nucleus was analyzed. Cytoplasmic RNA did not differ in rats who had learned the balancing response from the RNA of controls who were not stimulated or from functional controls who received passive vestibular stimulation. However, significant difference in base ratios were found in the nuclear ribonucleic acid, with the experimental group showing a greater amount of adenine and less uracil than the other two groups. These results were taken as an indication that the base ratios of RNA changed during learning. Since identical stimulation was not presented to the control animals, it is possible that the observed effects reflect neural response to increased stimulation rather than the consequences of learning as such.

In subsequent experiments (Hydén and Egyházi, 1964), these workers studied the changes in RNA content and base composition in the cortical neurons of rats using an ingenious paradigm involving the transfer of handedness. The basis of these studies was the observation that rats forced to reach for food using the nonpreferred paw for a few days experience a shift in handedness and will proceed with the "new hand" when tested months later. Evidence has been presented indicating that a critical region of rat cortex is involved in the control of handedness, and tissue from this region was utilized for biochemical assay. A significant increase in the amount of RNA was observed when the learning cortex was compared to the control cortex. Furthermore, the purine to pyrimidine ratio was significantly increased in the RNA of the presumed learning neurons compared to that of the controls. Rats not subjected to transfer experiments showed no difference between the right and left side of the cortex. Rats which used the preferred hand in their habitual fashion with the same number of movements over the same time period as was alloted in the transfer experiments showed a slight RNA increase in neurons of the active side, but no base ratio changes were found. These studies provide more thorough controls and seem to constitute substantial evidence that the RNA changes in neurons that are involved in a forced motor task take place because of factors other than neural activity per se.

In other work, Hydén has demonstrated a reciprocity between glial and neural chemical processes (1962). Conditions which cause an increase of certain compounds in neurons seemed to cause a decrease of such compounds in glia and vice versa. On such evidence, Hydén has suggested that the glial cell serves as a satellite of the neuron, providing it with the substances which it needs. The base composition of glial nucleotides is opposite to that of the neuron, with respect to guanine and cytosine. Hydén has pointed out that glial molecules transferred to the neuron might act as inhibitors of neuronal repressor RNA. By blocking a repressor RNA in the neuron, enzyme induction and specific protein synthesis might occur, which would meet the functional demands. Hydén has further suggested that the RNA produced in the neuron might partly be used to synthesize the enzymes involved in sodium and potassium transport at the membrane.

In a later experiment, Hydén and Egyházi reported that base ratio changes occurred in the RNA of Deiter's cell glia during learning (1963). These changes were similar but not identical to the nuclear changes previously reported in nerve cells under similar conditions. Ribonucleic acid synthesis was also reported to increase in nerve cells of the brain-stem reticular formation. However, these cells displayed no changes in base ratio. These workers suggested that the glial cell and glial RNA might be the substrate for short-term memory, while the neuron and its RNA might be the substrate of long-term memory. An acid protein, so-called S100, has been found which is unique to brain. This protein is located in glial cell membranes and cytoplasm and in the nucleus of the neuron. Hydén has suggested that this substance moves from glia to neurons, since the loss of glial RNA in activity exactly balances the increase in neuronal

RNA with the same base ratio. The glia cells might thus specify part of the neuronal protein synthesis (Hydén, 1966).

In recent unpublished works, workers in our laboratories have collaborated with those of Hydén's in an attempt to provide tissue for base ratio analysis from behavioral situations in which pseudoconditioning controls were included (Hydén et al., 1966). We selected the conditioned response of the planarian as well suited for this purpose. Barnes and Katzung have described a method for the establishment of flexion reflexes in planaria which may provide better reproducibility than previous methods (1963). The earlier methods used the pairing of light and shock to establish the conditioned response, with the shock delivered from an inductorium. The wave shape of an inductorium output is a biphasic potential of varying frequency content, reminiscent of the ringing of a misused transformer. Barnes and Katzung substituted a monophasic shock from a laboratory stimulator for the inductorium output. They reported that, if planaria were trained under conditions so that whenever shock was delivered the head of the planarian was oriented toward the cathode, a conditioned flexion response would rapidly be established to the light paired with such a stimulus. In contrast, if shock was delivered to other animals while the head was oriented toward the anode, no such increase of response to light took place. We succeeded in substantially corroborating this observation, except that some increase in the response of anodally oriented worms was observed, which stabilized at an intermediate level. In this work, parameters such as shock current proved to be critical for conditioning to occur.

Once this technique had been validated in our laboratory, the following groups of worms were prepared, fixed after training, and sent to Hydén's laboratory for analysis of base ratios in nerve cells of the anterior ganglion: Group A received systematic pairing of light with monophasic shock delivered while the planarian was oriented with its head toward the cathode. Group B was treated similarly, except that shock was delivered while the head was toward the anode. For these animals, the light stimulus lasted for 2 seconds, shock was applied for 1 second, and shock and light were then terminated together. Group C received light and shock in random sequence, with random variation of anodal or cathodal orientation as well. Group D received random presentations of light and cathodal head shock. Group E rested in the home environment during the conditioning sessions of the other groups. Total light and shock received by all groups was identical, with variation only in shock orientation and temporal relationship between stimuli. Figure VI-1 shows the learning curves of these five groups. It is obvious that Group A acquired a conditioned response. The other four groups did not differ significantly from each other, but displayed consistently lower performance than Group A.

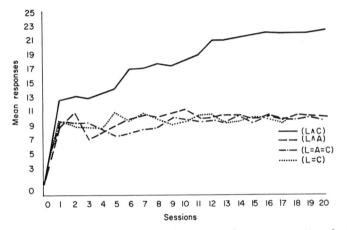

Fig. VI-1. The four curves shown above represent the mean responses displayed by each of the four experimental groups in the training sessions. Group A (L ∧ C) consists of animals which received light paired with shock delivered so that the head of the animal was toward the cathode (N = 13). Group B (L ∧ A) consists of animals which received light paired with anodal head shock (N = 13). Group C (L = A = C) consists of animals which received light which was randomly associated to shock which was sometimes anodal and sometimes cathodal (N = 13). Group D (L = C) consists of animals which received light randomly associated with cathodal head shock (N = 10). Group E, composed of resting controls, showed no systematic changes throughout and is not illustrated.

As each animal in Group A achieved the criterion level of performance, it was killed and fixed in Carnoy's solution. At the same time, a previously matched control in each of the other groups was killed and fixed identically. After imbedding them in paraffin, random numbers were assigned to each animal, and they were then sent to Hydén's laboratory without further identification. Nerve cells from the anterior ganglion of each of these animals were removed by dissection by Hydén and his collaborators, and base ratio analysis was carried out. After the results were obtained they were returned to our laboratory, where the numbers which had been assigned to the experimental animals were

101

decoded and the data assigned to the various experimental groups. The group of worms which was systematically conditioned with light and cathodal shock, Group A, showed a significant change in the adenine to guanine ratio, as compared with the resting controls, Group E, and the anodal shock Group B, neither of which acquired a conditioned response. *However, animals from Group C in which randomized cathodal and anodal shock were randomly paired with light, and also those from Group D in which light and cathodal shock were randomly paired, showed the same changes in base ratio, although neither of these groups acquired a new behavioral response.* This experiment shows that the observed base ratio changes are not specific to learning but may also occur in animals subjected to a pseudoconditioning procedure in which the total amount and type of stimulation are carefully equated. These findings raise the question of the extent to which other reports of chemical changes in conditioning situations may reflect the general activity caused by stimulation rather than specific changes related to learning. Careful examination of many of the studies of this genre reveals that provision of pseudoconditioning controls has often been neglected.

Admittedly, there is no reason to assume that the cells selected arbitrarily from the anterior ganglion need be crucially involved in mediation of the conditioned response. Perhaps base ratio studies conducted on other regions of the planarian would show changes specific to situations in which conditioning took place. With that reservation, however, the present data do not provide evidence for a change in base ratio unique to the acquisition of new response.

E. Effects of decreased RNA on learning or performance

1. Destruction of RNA

A number of studies have explored the effects of interference with RNA synthesis or destruction of RNA on the storage and retrieval of information. In early experiments, John and his co-workers (unpublished work, 1958c) investigated the effects of small intraventricular injections of ribonuclease into trained cats and found that pattern discrimination performance deteriorated for a period of time following the injections, and well-trained animals reverted to a position habit. The difficulty of devising adequate controls to demonstrate that these effects might be due specifically to the destruction of RNA in brain was sufficient to cause temporary termination of the experiments, while a better experimental preparation was sought.[*] The report of McConnell, Jacobson, and Kimble (1959) that conditioned planaria displayed retention of the conditioned response following transection and regeneration whether the tested animals regenerated from head or tail segments suggested a somewhat better preparation for a continuation of these experiments. Corning and John (1961) first replicated and confirmed the observation of McConnell *et al.* that the retention of conditioned responses was equally good in planaria regenerating from either head or tail segments of previously conditioned worms. Conditioned animals were then transected and head segments and tail segments permitted to regenerate in a solution containing a low concentration of ribonuclease. The concentration of ribonuclease employed was determined by finding the maximum concentration in which regeneration could occur without grossly apparent morphological deformation of the animals. Various control groups were provided to test the effects of regeneration per se upon retention, to check the effect of the addition of ribonuclease to the pond water in which trained animals rested during the period required for regeneration by the experimentals, and so forth. The results showed that worms which regenerated from head segments retained the conditioned response equally well, whether they regenerated in the presence of ribonuclease or in ordinary pond water. In contrast, tail segments which regenerated in solutions containing ribonuclease performed the conditioned response at the random level while tail sections which regenerated in ordinary pond water performed indistinguishably from head segments. Trained animals which rested in ribonuclease during this period showed no deterioration of conditioned performance beyond that observed in trained animals who rested in pond water. Interfering effects, then, were obtained when regeneration by tail segments occurred in the presence of ribonuclease in the surround. Since these animals are dominated in their behavior by the cephalic ganglion, it would seem that as the regenerating tail

[*] In recent work, Krylov *et al.* (1965) have shown that intracerebral injection of RNAase, but not DNAase, trypsin, or serum albumin, blocked retention of a conditioned defensive reflex in white mice.

produced head tissue which contains a cephalic ganglion, the information which has somehow been stored in the tail segment during training is transferred to the new cephalic ganglion tissue being formed.

Three possibilities exist for the mode of transfer from a trained tail segment to the regenerating head tissue: (1) "trained" cells migrate from a position in the tail to the cephalic ganglion being formed in the regenerating head; (2) the chemical configuration of molecules being synthesized to constitute the regenerating head is specified by "trained" RNA in the tail tissue; (3) patterns of nervous discharge, established by training in nerve cells in the tail segment, are transmitted to nerve cells formed in the regenerating head segment, thus "teaching" the new head tissue.

The experimental results in the work of Corning and John indicate that when a trained tail segment regenerates in the presence of ribonuclease the process of information transfer to the head is disturbed. A number of qualifications must be made. First of all, the almost global nature of the contracting and twisting conditioned response produced by this training procedure makes it necessary to question whether discretely coded information relating a specific conditioned response to a specific conditioned stimulus is actually transferred from the trained tail segment to the head during regeneration. More generalized effects might be involved, such as increased sensitivity of regenerated tissue to light. The fact that untrained animals did not display these responses to light after transection and regeneration is somewhat reassuring. Unequivocal information on this question would require evidence, not yet obtained, that a planarian trained to perform a *differential* conditioned response can be transected and will display differential performance by the animals regenerated from the head and tail segments.* The level of specificity of the information transmitted by the tail segments in these experiments cannot yet be adequately evaluated.

However, it seems clear that a behavioral response, based on information of unknown specificity, has been transferred from the trained tail to the regenerating head. Since we have no basis of selecting between the three possible transfer mechanisms listed above, we cannot stipulate the level at which the ribonuclease interference was accomplished. Thus,

---

* Since this was written, Corning (1966) has published a report of retention of a right-left discrimination by both the anterior and posterior segments of transected trained worms after regeneration.

we cannot assert that the failure of the regenerating tail segments to transfer the conditioned response when regeneration occurred in the presence of ribonuclease was due to the destruction by ribonuclease of ribonucleic acid serving a function in the storage of learned information. The observed effects might be due to some less specific interference.

Equally possible, however, is a change in the mobility or the ability of certain kinds of cells to migrate from tail tissue to head tissue in the presence of ribonuclease, or interference with patterned neural discharges at the regenerating interface because of some reaction related to alterations in protein composition, which were secondary effects of the enzyme. In other words, interpretation of the experimental results requires considerably more data relating to the effects of other substances on the mechanism which mediates information transfer from regenerating tissue to new tissue. Until such information is available, no firm conclusion about the specificity of the ribonuclease effect can be made legitimately.

2. Interference with RNA synthesis

Other workers have approached the question of RNA mediation of information storage by interfering with the synthesis of RNA. Dingman and Sporn utilized 8-azaguanine for that purpose (1961). It is known that 8-azaguanine is an inhibitor of RNA synthesis. The work of Dingman and Sporn utilized chromatographic procedures to confirm that the base analog had been incorporated into the RNA of brain. The effect of administration of this substance was tested in rats on maze learning. There was no significant difference in the running time of groups of experimental animals injected with 8-azaguanine and controls, showing that the motor performance of the animals was not affected by the drug. However, the number of errors of the experimental group was increased as the maze was learned. Experimental animals did not show significantly poorer retention, however, when tested on a previously learned maze. Thus, Dingman and Sporn concluded that RNA may be involved in learning, but a response, once learned, does not depend on RNA for retention. 8-Azaguanine may have interfered with metabolic processes which affected other substances as well as RNA metabolism, and it is not possible to attribute the results exclusively to the action upon RNA.

Chamberlain, Halick, and Gerard (1963) have described an experiment involving the fixation of experience in the spinal cord of the rat, which is an extension of the previous work of Di Giorgio (1929). This experiment involves the production of a unilateral cerebellar lesion in the rat. Following such a unilateral lesion, the hind legs of the rat demonstrate a postural asymmetry. If the spinal cord of the rat is sectioned at the upper cervical level, following the cerebellar lesion, the hind-leg asymmetry disappears, and the position of the legs once again becomes symmetrical. However, if the symmetry is permitted to persist for a period of 45 minutes after the cerebellar lesion before the cervical transection is performed, the asymmetry is found to have stabilized. Chamberlain and Gerard demonstrated that the administration of 8-azaguanine increased the time at which cervical transection would result in restoration of hind-leg symmetry. That is, interference with RNA synthesis extended the period of time required for this asymmetrical cerebellar influence on the spinal cord to have a long-lasting effect. In that sense, then, the influence of the asymmetrical cerebellar input to the spinal cord is a learning experience which brings about consolidation of a new pattern of activity in the spinal cord, and the consolidation time for this experience, normally about 45 minutes, is lengthened by interference with RNA synthesis.

F. Effects of increased RNA on learning and performance

1. Facilitation of synthesis of RNA

Conversely, Chamberlain et al. found that the administration of a dimer of malononitrile decreased the consolidation time of the hind-leg asymmetry to about 30 minutes. This malononitrile dimer, TCAP,* is known to facilitate RNA synthesis. Other experiments by Gerard and Chamberlain investigated the effects of TCAP injection on more orthodox behavioral indices. Lower avoidance latency and a higher number of avoidance responses per day were obtained with TCAP injection than in control groups ($p = .05$), although no effects were observed in the Hebb-Williams maze.

Essman (1965, 1966) has provided additional evidence that TCAP facilitates the rate of consolidation. Two experimental groups of mice

* Tricyanoaminopropene.

were injected with this compound for 3 days, while two groups of control mice received saline. On the third treatment day, all animals received a single training trial in a passive avoidance task. One experimental and one control group received ECS immediately after the learning experience. The other two groups received ECS 1 hour following training. All groups were tested for retention 24 hours later. Eighty per cent of the experimental group, receiving shock immediately after training, showed retention of the conditioned response, while the corresponding controls showed the characteristic retrograde amnesia ($p < .02$). Both groups receiving ECS 1 hour after training showed good retention of the response. Analysis of brain tissue from various sites showed a significant elevation of RNA levels in the drug treated animals. ECS caused reduction of RNA levels in some structures, confirming prior observations by Mihailovich et al. (1958). These data suggest that chemical stimulation of RNA synthesis accelerated the rate at which consolidation was achieved.

Increase in the speed of consolidation with facilitation of RNA synthesis is analogous to the strychnine effects discussed in Chapter III. A number of papers are relevant to this parallelism. Strychnine prolongs the action potential and produces repetitive spike discharge in isolated nerve cells (Washizu et al., 1961). The known increase in RNA synthesis with nerve activity suggests that hyperactivity of nerve cells due to strychnine may lead to changes in RNA (Ahmed and McKenzie, 1963). Datta and Ghosh (1964) have reported an effect of strychnine sulfate on the secondary structure of RNA in ribosomes of slices of brain cortex, with marked diminution of hydrogen bonding. The work most directly bearing on the parallelism, however, has been done by Carlini and Carlini (1965). These experimenters carried out a study based on the reports by McGaugh of facilitation after posttrial injection of strychnine. They investigated the effects of strychnine and of marijuana, injected before or after learning trials, on consolidation and also on brain RNA content. They found that strychnine facilitated consolidation whether administered before or after the learning experience. Marijuana facilitated learning only when administered before the training session. On this basis they concluded that the facilitation by marijuana was due to general factors and was not related to direct effects on the consolidation process. Chemical analysis showed that strychnine increased the concentration of brain RNA but not DNA, while marijuana raised the concentration of brain DNA with no effects on RNA. These results suggest that the speeding of consolidation by strychnine may be mediated by an increase in the RNA content of nerve cells due to their increased rate of activity. It would be extremely interesting to know whether all agents known to facilitate consolidation also cause increases in brain RNA, and whether all excitants which cause increased brain RNA can facilitate consolidation.

Magnesium pemoline, which stimulates true RNA polymerase activity *in vivo* (Glasky and Simon, 1966), enhances acquisition and retention of an avoidance response in rats (Plotnikoff, 1966a). Methylphenidate and metamphetamine administration did not affect the gross operant behavior studied in this experiment, although they facilitate the acquisition of some instrumental responses (Gollub and Brady, 1965). The fact that facilitation of learning by some drugs may be restricted to certain tasks but not to others suggests an unspecific action on anxiety levels or arousal rather than on mechanisms specifically related to learning or memory. Claims of facilitation of learning should be supported by evidence of widespread generality of effects in a variety of learning tasks. Using the same task as in the initial demonstrations of enhancement by magnesium premoline, it has been reported that animals pretreated with magnesium pemoline relearned the CAR faster than control animals receiving no injection, following disruption of conditioned performance by ECS administered immediately after completion of training (Plotnikoff, 1966b). This effect may reflect enhancement of consolidation. Further studies on retention, savings on retraining, and generality of effects are necessary before these findings can be interpreted.

2. Injection of "naïve" RNA

Other experiments exist suggesting that increase in RNA facilitates the storage of information and its retrieval. Cameron and Solyom (1961) at McGill University have administered massive doses of RNA and of DNA to aged individuals. They found that patients receiving RNA showed marked improvement in memory, whereas this was not true of patients receiving DNA. The changes which were reported involved almost total retention in some cases. However, defects in memory recurred on termination of the RNA injections. It is possible that these effects reflect alterations in metabolism due to improving the nutritional state of these individuals, and are not due specifically to the effects on the RNA content of brain; or it may be that the constituents of RNA, the nucleotides themselves, are the responsible agents.

108

Kral and Sved have also reported improvement of memory with the injection of yeast RNA (1963). These workers suggested that the improvement resulting from these injection studies occurred because the injected RNA served to preempt much of the ribonuclease available in these patients, and allowed more of the *endogenous* RNA to survive and accumulate. Clearly, these effects need not imply any direct utilization of such substances as yeast RNA for the storage of information in human neural tissue. It is highly doubtful that the injection of yeast RNA causes a change in the yeast RNA content of the brain. It may be that the yeast RNA is hydrolyzed and is utilized as the constituent nucleotides rather than as RNA. If the reported effects are due to accumulation of RNA in brain, some such mechanism as the one suggested by Kral and Sved would seem to be inescapable. It remains to be demonstrated, however, that more general effects other than on the brain are not responsible.

The work of Cameron and Solyom, and of Kral and Sved has been confirmed in rats by Cook *et al.* (1963). These workers tested the rate of acquisition of conditioned avoidance responses in rats who were injected intraperitoneally with yeast RNA before learning sessions, throughout the learning period. Injected animals acquired the conditioned avoidance response significantly more rapidly than controls receiving saline injections. Furthermore, animals who were trained after RNA injections were then tested for the resistance of such responses to extinction after termination of the RNA medication. RNA-injected animals showed a significantly greater resistance to extinction than did controls. Similar facilitation after subcutaneous injection of yeast RNA has been reported on maze learning in rats (Goren, 1965). However, other workers have studied the effects of these injections on a variety of tasks requiring spatial discrimination, pattern discrimination, escape by running, and other kinds of responses (Corson and Enesco, 1966). No enhancement of the acquisition of any of these behaviors was observed, *except* the facilitation of the pole-climbing response used by Cook *et al.* Again, it appears that the response required of the animal is a critical variable in the determination of RNA effects. It is particularly interesting that the RNA used in a related study was $C_2C_8{}^{14}$-labeled prior to injection. No radioactivity was detected in the brains of the injected animals, suggesting that unspecific factors may be responsible for the observed effects. (Enesco, H. E., Fate of ^{14}C-RNA injected into mice. *Experimental Cell Research* **42**, 640–645, 1966.)

In recent work, Solyom has explored the effects of systemic injection of 10% RNA solutions on the acquisition of avoidance responses by rats in the so-called "master" situation. In this situation, naïve animals are placed in a Skinner box with a trained animal and acquire the conditioned response by observation and imitation. RNA-injected rats acquired the conditioned response significantly faster than control animals (Solyom, 1965).

Such data indicate, then, that the ease of acquisition of new responses and the retrieval of stored information may be increased as the availability of RNA is increased. The information available thus far does not permit evaluation of whether the observed effects of RNA injection are due to influences exerted directly on mechanisms involved in the storage of information, or arise from more general factors such as increased excitability or even improved nutrition. It seems particularly important to emphasize that no data have yet been adduced from injection experiments to show resulting changes in brain RNA.

G. Evidence for specific molecular coding of information

The potential theoretical relevance of studies similar to those described in this and the following section compels a fairly complete review of the evidence.

1. The cannibalism experiment

McConnell (1962, 1964) and his collaborators have reported that worms which were fed fragments of conditioned worms acquired that conditioned response more rapidly than other worms which ingested fragments of naïve worms. These experiments have been repeated in our laboratories using a "blind" procedure, and significant differences between the experimental and control groups were found on 8 out of the first 15 days of testing following the cannibalistic ingestion ($p = .01$) (John, 1964). In our experiments, 24 hours were permitted to elapse between performance of the conditioned responses by a "diet" worm and its subsequent fragmentation and feeding to the experimental group. This period was considered adequate to permit the dissipation of after effects of general excitation and movement in the training situation. In spite of these precautions, however, the experiment suffers somewhat from the fact that the diet of the control group consisted of fragments of *resting* worms, rather than fragments of "pseudoconditioned" worms which had received randomized light and shock without acquiring a conditioned response. The possibility has not been unequivocally ruled out that some long-lasting effect of shock or light per se was responsible for the changed reactivity of the cannibalistic group. Nonetheless, this seems relatively improbable, in view of the long delay period between behavioral testing and feeding.

Analogous results have been reported by other workers (Fried and Horowitz, 1964). The contraction response can be established quite readily in planarians belonging to species normally refractory to such training after ingestion of planaria from more easily conditionable species. A replication of the original cannibalism experiment was performed, with delays as long as 1 week interposed between the last learning session of the trained worm and subsequent ingestion by a cannibal worm. In spite of the long delay, the learning rate of the cannibals was significantly faster than the learning rate of the cannibalized (Feldman and Capretta, 1965). In a study involving differential response, planarians learned a T-maze faster when allowed to cannibalize trained worms in a yeast RNA solution rather than in plain water (Pickett *et al.*, 1965).

Some indication as to a possible explanation for these findings has been provided by the work of Hartry *et al.* (1964). Cannibal planarians were fed other planarians which had previously been exposed to light only, shock only, handling, a light-shock conditioning procedure, or no experimental manipulation. All cannibalistic groups performed significantly better than naïve animals. Ingestion of planarians which had been handled, exposed to light, or conditioned proved equally effective in enhancing the performance of cannibal worms. These results suggest that the cannibalism effect may be due to nutritional factors or changes in activation or sensitization which are unrelated to the transfer of specfic memories.

As with the previous discussion of the regeneration experiment, the evidence from cannibalism experiments does not permit any decision as to whether information about a specific learned stimulus-response relationship has been transferred, or whether sensitization to shock or light or generally increased reactivity is responsible. Even if the latter explanations were found true, the phenomenon would be of more than super-

111

ficial interest. Whether the transferred information is specific or general, it represents a long-lasting effect of experience. For theoretical purposes, however, it would be crucial to know which explanation is more correct.

2. Injection of "trained" RNA

The cannibalism experiments suggest that the tissue of a trained planarian may contain a substance which, when ingested, transfers information to the ingesting organism. This conclusion may at first seem farfetched, since it is natural to assume that digestive processes would disrupt the chemical structure of ingested substances. Such apparently reasonable objections may well not be relevant since the digestive system of the planarian is not highly specialized. Particulate ingested matter is distributed through the body of the organism, and engulfed by the cells. Further breakdown occurs within the cells. If planaria are placed in a suspension of carmine particles, microscopic examination some time later shows that the particles are inside cells throughout the organism. Therefore, planarian cells may be capable of absorbing food without gross alteration of its macromolecular structure.

The possibility that substances carrying information were to be found in nervous tissue led to attempts to extract RNA from trained animals and evaluation of the effects of injecting the "trained" RNA into naïve animals. The first report of success in such endeavors was provided by Zelman et al. (1963). Planaria were trained in a classical conditioning situation, and RNA was extracted from the trained worms and from untrained worms. An experimental planarian group received injections of "trained" RNA; a control group received injections of "naïve" RNA. Some tendency was observed for the experimental group to respond more frequently to the conditioned stimulus than the control group, following these injections.

These preliminary experiments, although inconclusive, attracted much interest, since they were the first to provide *any* experimental support for the suggestion that specific experiential information might be represented as a code on the molecular structure of RNA. The results stimulated a number of attempts to obtain supporting evidence. Interestingly, the equivocal nature of the conditioned response of planarians used in the early work, as well as interest in whether comparable phenomena might exist in mammals, seem to have led a number of workers to attempt analogous investigations with the rat. A series of intriguing results has been obtained.

Babich et al. (1965a) trained rats to approach a food cup at the sound of the pellet magazine. After completion of training, RNA was extracted from the brains of the conditioned animals and injected i.p. into naïve rats. Rats receiving "trained" RNA injections showed a greater approach tendency when tested in the same situation than control rats who received injections of RNA from naïve animals.

Gross and Carey (1965) were unable to replicate the results reported by Babich et al. although the procedures followed were identical in most respects. However, other workers have reported positive findings in analogous experiments. In work done at the same time as the experiments of Babich et al., Fjerdingstad et al. found that rats receiving intracisternal injection of RNA from trained rats showed significant transfer of training when compared with controls (1965). Subsequently, Rosenblatt, Farrow, and Herblin (1966a) have confirmed the transfer effects reported by Babich et al. Incubation of the extract with ribonuclease did not block the transfer effect, which led these workers to suggest that a small protein or polypeptide might be responsible. Cerebellar extract was just as effective as cerebral extract. In later work (Rosenblatt, Farrow, and Rhine, 1966b,c), some indication of transfer of a bar-pressing response in a Skinner box by injection of brain extract from trained animals was reported. They estimate the molecular weight of the mediating substance in the range of 1000 to 5000, excluding any known form of RNA.

Reiniš (1965) has reported effective transfer of alimentary conditioned reflexes to tone and to light in rats. Rats trained to perform these responses were decapitated, the rostral portions of brain homogenized, and injected i.p. into two experimental groups, "Hungry" and "Not Hungry." Two control groups received injection of brain homogenate or liver homogenate from naïve animals. The effects of injection of brain homogenate from trained animals into the "Not Hungry" experimental group were not significantly different from the controls. However, the animals in the "Hungry" group showed enormous enhancement of both latency and accuracy of conditioned responses in subsequent training sessions, when compared with the other groups.

In subsequent work, Reiniš (1966) has posed a most important question. The brains of trained animals were made radioactive by administration of radioactive phosphorus. After injection of radioactive brain homogenate into naïve animals, no radioactivity could be detected in the brain tissue of the injected group. This experiment represents the first attempt to ascertain whether the substances injected in such transfer experiments actually succeed in reaching the brain. Unfortunately, the experiment under discussion cannot be considered decisive. Although radioactive phosphorus binds itself to RNA, it is possible that the radioactive tracer in the phosphate group was separated from the organic portion of the RNA molecule by metabolic processes before entry into the brain. A more conclusive demonstration would entail radioactive labeling of the constituent nucleotides of RNA. Nonetheless, these preliminary experiments provide no evidence that the injected material successfully penetrates the brain, and thus it is essential to pursue this question further. In a comparable study, in which a variety of extraction procedures and learning tasks were used, Luttges *et al.* (1966) completely failed to observe any transfer effects, nor could they detect entry of P^{32}-labeled RNA into the brain after intraperitoneal injection. Since publication of negative findings is less likely than positive reports, one suspects that a large number of unpublished failures to replicate the transfer phenomenon already exist (Byrne *et al.*, 1966). The published contradictions of this controversial experiment are sufficient to indicate that, at the very least, transfer by injection is a rather labile phenomenon.[*]

Additional support for the transfer of information by injection has come from other laboratories. Ungar and Cohen (1965) investigated the question of whether morphine tolerance could be induced in animals with no previous contact with morphine, proposing that morphine tolerance represents a kind of memory since it is based on previous experience by the individual. Morphine tolerance could be transferred to drug-naïve animals by injection of brain extracts from animals made tolerant by repeated morphine injections. The responsible substance was identified as a peptide. In related work (1965), Ungar and Oceguera–Navarro showed the transfer of habituation by injection of brain extracts from habituated animals to naïve animals. In subsequent investigations by this worker, it has been found that the transfer of habituation is stimulus specific (Ungar, 1966a). Some animals were habituated to air puffs and others to sound. Injection of brain extracts from trained animals to naïve animals conferred only habituation to the response acquired by the donor.

[*] One author has published negative and positive findings within 2 months (Byrne and Samuel, 1966).

Again, the responsible factor was found to be a peptide. Other work (Ungar, 1966b) explored the transfer of experience on a Y-maze, with effective transfer accomplished by injection of brain extract, in this case a protein. Transfer of a conditioned avoidance response by injection of brain extracts has also been observed, with the responsible factor in this case identified as RNA. Ungar reconciles the varying chemical nature of the substances in the brain extracts identified as mediating transfer in these different situations by proposing that the primary action may be mediated by protein and RNA plays an intermediate role.

Aside from the absence of direct chemical demonstration that the injected materials actually reach the brain, which would seem to be a prerequisite for any possible influence to be exerted on the behavior of the injected organism, most of the experiments thus far cited do not involve the transfer of differentiated responses. For this reason, the observed results might reasonably be attributed to general consequences of injection, such as metabolic influences, changes in over-all reactivity to stimuli or excitability, or similar factors which might be subsumed under the rubric of sensitization.

However, it should be noted that differential response was involved in the studies of transfer of habituation carried out by Ungar. Further demonstration of differential effects has been provided by Jacobson et al. (1965). In this work, two groups of rats were trained to approach a food cup in the presence of a discriminative stimulus. The click of the pellet magazine was the stimulus for one group, and a blinking light served as the stimulus for the second group. After establishment of the conditioned response, RNA extracts were made from the brains of the trained animals. Eight hours later, these extracts were injected intraperitoneally into naïve rats, which had previously been habituated to show no behavioral response either to click or light. Subsequently, these naïve animals were tested for response to mixed sequences of click and light. Animals which received the injection of RNA from click-trained rats approached the food cup more frequently in response to clicks than to light, while animals which received RNA from light-trained rats responded more frequently to light than to clicks. The difference in the response of the two groups after injection was considered significant at the .001 level. These results suggest that the transfer of information by injection may be specific to a particular learning experience, and may not be due to general factors of the sort discussed above. Nissen et al. (1965) have also reported transfer effects of a differential nature, using lighted or dark alleys

115

as the cue for a water reinforcement. Intracisternal injection of RNA extracted from the brains of rats trained to choose one cue caused recipients to show a significant preference for the *other* cue. The difference in the outcome of these two experiments further highlights the lability of these phenomena. Other reports of positive findings in transfer experiments have recently appeared, including effects in forward but not backward conditioning (Jacobson *et al.*, 1966), cross-species transfer (Babich *et al.*, 1965b), and an unspecific motor transfer phenomenon (Essman and Lehrer, 1966).

One of the most interesting and detailed studies of the transfer of experience by injection of brain tissue has been conducted by Albert (1966c), who exploited the results obtained in work on spreading depression discussed previously. As demonstrated in those earlier experiments (Albert, 1966a), removal of the medial cortex of one hemisphere blocks retention of an avoidance response by a rat which learned that response while the other cortical hemisphere was disturbed by spreading depression. After the ablation, these animals failed to perform the conditioned response when tested with the remaining hemisphere functioning normally. If the removed tissue were homogenized and injected intraperitoneally, significant savings in learning were obtained on retraining. Injection of other cortical regions did not produce this effect, indicating that the results were not due to general consequences of tissue injection, and savings were specific to the previously learned task, indicating that the results did not reflect general increases in excitability or other nonspecific factors.

Furthermore, savings were not obtained after injection of homogenized medial cortex unless consolidation processes were permitted to continue for several hours in the initially trained hemisphere. Injection of tissue removed immediately after the acquisition session was without effect. Centrifugation of the excised tissue and injection of various fractions showed that the substance responsible for these effects was found in the water insoluble portion of cell nuclei. Degradation by heating destroyed the ability of this substance to influence the rate of retraining. Treatment with proteolytic enzymes did not abolish the effect, but treatment with ribonuclease prevented transfer from occurring. However, in apparent contradiction to the other injection experiments described in this section, negative results were obtained when these substances were injected into animals other than the individual from which the tissue had been removed. This may be due to the fact that RNA was not extracted from the tissue for injection unaccompanied by other substances.

As indicated by the experimenter, these results suggest that it is unlikely that information is stored as synaptic modifications in specific multisynaptic pathways connecting separate areas of brain. If this were so, it would be necessary to conclude that injected material reached specific cells in the second hemisphere and altered their connections in such a way as to reconstruct the multisynaptic network which stored the experience in the first hemisphere when training initially occurred. Such a proposition appears to be extremely implausible. Were the evidence provided by such experiments sufficiently well established, it would constitute almost incontrovertible proof that deterministic and connectionistic hypotheses about the mechanism of information storage in the brain are not correct.

Albert suggests that it is more likely that certain areas of brain are equipotential, and that the injected molecules need only migrate to certain brain regions. He cites evidence that large molecules can enter the brain (Sherwin et al., 1963), and argues that the lesion will disturb the blood brain barrier so as to increase the ease of entry of the injected substances into brain (Lajtha, 1962). He suggests that the relevant molecules may be labeled in a fashion which accomplishes migration to specific parts of the brain, pointing out that intraventricular injection of antibodies formed in response to specific brain nuclei has been shown to cause specific disruption of the electrical activity of the corresponding brain regions (Mihailovic and Jankovic, 1961). Other evidence suggesting chemospecificity of neurons has been summarized by Roberts (1965). On this basis, it is suggested that RNA molecules on which information about the learning experience has been coded may enter the brain and be guided to the appropriate region of the untrained hemisphere, by the influence of specific chemical affinities, where they somehow function as stored memory.

Since it is highly unlikely that such restoration of function is accomplished by establishment of specific new neuronal interconnections, it seems reasonable that they involve changes in the reception or emission of temporally patterned neural activity. The basis for such functional changes is not clear. Since the RNA molecules which these experiments suggest may mediate the storage of information seem to be in the nucleus, far from the cell membranes, it is probable that they do not influence neural behavior directly. As Albert has pointed out, it is reasonable to expect such influence to be achieved via resulting alterations in protein structure. The ability of RNA to enter a variety of cells has been demonstrated (Niu *et al.*, 1961; Amos and Moore, 1963). Once inside the cell, these molecules have the capability of directing the synthesis of corresponding proteins by the host cell, and may achieve long-lasting consequences by influencing the cell nucleus to initiate independent biochemical processes capable of producing the new proteins (Niu *et al.*, 1962; Niu, 1963; Cohen and Parks, 1964).

These various considerations provide a relatively plausible set of initial assumptions with which to explain the information transfer apparently achieved by injection of substances from the brains of trained animals. Direct isotopic confirmation of entry of the injected substances into the brain of the recipient animal, with evidence of selective migration to homologous brain regions, and incorporation into cells within that region are required in order for these suggestions to be accepted as adequate. It is emphasized that all the evidence from isotope studies thus far available has been negative and indicates no penetration of the brain by the injected substances. The phenomena which have been described pose many unresolved problems in addition to those focused upon in this discussion. Not the least of these problems relates to the dilution of the relevant RNA, representing the particular learned response selected by the experimenter, by the enormous volume of irrelevant RNA which must be presumed to represent all the other learned experiences and innate processes which are also stored in the same neural tissue. Even if we were to concede that the injected substances reach and enter the brain, migrate to corresponding brain regions, enter the cells, and influence their responses appropriately, perhaps the most remarkable feature of the numerous unusual processes which must be postulated is the ability of the "relevant signal RNA" to prevail in the presence of overwhelming "irrelevant noise RNA."

Taken as a whole, these experiments seem to provide support for the belief that nervous tissue from trained animals may contain chemical substances which encode information relevant to the learning experience, and that this information may be effectively transferred to other neural tissue by appropriate introduction of these substances. Such a proposition may strike many as extremely improbable, and certainly all evidence offered to support it must be subjected to extremely critical scrutiny.

118

Even if absolute adequacy of technique and data evaluation are presumed, the results are extremely difficult to reconcile with a great variety of considerations. Whether or not future investigations reveal errors in the experimental studies which have thus far been carried out, the increasing effort and interest directed to these studies makes it necessary to evaluate the possible merits of this proposition seriously and objectively.

H. Effects of blockade of protein synthesis on memory

The work of Flexner, Flexner, and Stellar (1963) suggests that perhaps RNA is not the primary responsible agent for information storage, but represents an agent for the *transfer* of information to protein. These workers conditioned mice to run a maze, using a particular solution. Once that solution had been established as the running pattern, reversal training was carried out, so that different choices were established at the various choice points. Puromycin, which is known to block protein synthesis, was then injected intracerebrally into various brain regions. Bilateral injection into temporal cortex and hippocampus caused the mice to revert to the maze solution which had been established first, but injection into other regions was ineffective. The recently acquired alternative solution was no longer employed by these animals; although they continued to run the maze, they used the *initial* learned pattern. Since the original maze habit was retained, the effects cannot be attributed to incapacitation of the animals.

These experiments have interesting implications. Puromycin is not known to affect the synthesis either of ribosomal RNA or of transfer RNA. Recently, Sells (1965) has shown that puromycin also does not interfere with synthesis of messenger RNA. The interference with protein synthesis accomplished by puromycin therefore would seem to involve minimal interruption of RNA synthesis. The puromycin blockade of protein synthesis lasts about 6 hours; thereafter, protein synthesis returns to previous levels. Were the information about the recently acquired maze pattern stored as a stable RNA configuration, the resumption of protein synthesis following the termination of puromycin blockade should permit the representational RNA to resume synthesis of the corresponding protein. The abolished mode of maze response should thereafter return. In

119

fact, recovery of the blocked response did not appear as protein synthesis was resumed. Therefore, retention of the maze performance appears to have been somehow dependent upon protein and continued protein synthesis, rather than primarily upon a coded RNA. In this regard, it seems anomalous that Heinrich Waelsch, whose recent death was a severe loss to neurochemistry as well as to his many friends, failed together with several colleagues to demonstrate any difference in the incorporation of tritium into the proteins of brain areas on the "conditioned" side of the split-brain monkey (Cuenod *et al.*, 1966). Classical conditioning based upon simple light-shock pairing was established with only one eye uncovered. Since some transfer to the other side may occur under these circumstances, this ingenious experiment should be repeated using a task such as pattern discrimination for which absence of transfer between sides has been established. A combination of these methods with puromycin and actinomycin injection might be particularly interesting.

Another interesting feature of these experiments suggests that additional phases of information storage may exist, beyond the two which we have emphasized in our analysis thus far. Flexner *et al.* showed that retention of the original maze solution which had been learned 3 weeks earlier could be severely impaired by bilateral injections into frontal plus temporal regions, buttressed by intraventricular injections. These results indicate vulnerability of memory to interference by puromycin long after the time when most investigations have indicated that stable storage of information has been achieved. Furthermore, the results reveal an apparent shift in essential mediating processes from the temporal areas to other brain regions, which seems to occur over a period of 6 days. Further stabilization of stored information may take place after the initial consolidation period, and this stabilization implicates tissue in multiple brain regions. Similar inferences can be drawn from lesion experiments in which damage to a given region interferes with retention of a response just learned to criterion but is ineffectual after overtraining. Observations of this sort, which suggest that the processes responsible for mediation of information storage may extend and shift their anatomical locus during time, pose major theoretical difficulties. Such anatomical mobility involves cells in a representational role over long periods of time, apparently in the absence of exteroceptive stimulation or the need for further training. These cells seem almost to acquire information passively, by

120

infection rather than by experience. How such "diffusion" of information might occur is extremely intriguing.

Agranoff *et al.* (Agranoff and Klinger, 1964; Agranoff *et al.*, 1965) have confirmed the disruptive effects of puromycin on performance of conditioned responses, showing interference with retention of avoidance behavior in the goldfish as a result of intracerebral injections of the drug. Subsequently, Brink and Agranoff (1966) provided evidence indicating that the behavioral effects of puromycin might be more crucially related to the time of onset rather than to the extent or duration of inhibition of protein synthesis. It is extremely interesting that the recent work of this group (Davis and Agranoff, 1966) indicates that puromycin blocks retention of the avoidance response by goldfish if injected immediately after the training session, but not if injection occurs 1 hour later. The blocking phenomenon seems very reliable, judged by the ability of these workers to obtain dose-response curves. The puromycin does not seem to interfere with short-term memory, but blocks transfer to long-term storage as if preventing consolidation. Although numerous obvious differences exist between the procedures of the Flexner and Agranoff groups, it is very difficult to reconcile the two sets of studies. The results of Flexner *et al.* show disruption of memory *after* relatively long periods of time, while the results of Agranoff *et al.* suggest that puromycin is *only* effective when injected immediately. Perhaps the most interesting feature of these recent findings (Davis and Agranoff, 1966) is the observation that if the goldfish are left in the training tank for as long as 3 hours after completion of training, the period of puromycin susceptibility is correspondingly lengthened. This suggests that the onset of the actual consolidation phase is triggered by removal of the fish from the training tank. The implication of the delay is that "completion" of the learning experience effectively disinhibits the process of consolidation.

Further confirmation of the puromycin effects has been provided by Barondes and Cohen (1966) in an interesting extension of the Flexner study. These investigations were designed to provide information on the time when the puromycin-sensitive processes become necessary for memory storage. Puromycin was injected bilaterally into the temporal area of mice. Five hours later, at a time when protein synthesis had been massively inhibited for several hours, the mice received maze training for shock avoidance. Puromycin-injected animals learned the maze just as rapidly as saline-injected controls. Thus, blockade of protein synthesis does not impair acquisition of a learned response. Retention of memory was then tested by retraining animals at various time intervals after initial learning, and measuring savings. When tested 15 minutes after they finished learning the task, puromycin-treated animals behaved the same as saline-injected controls. However, in the next few hours the performance of the animals who received the drug gradually deteriorated and savings were less than 7% after 3 hours. The difference between the puromycin and saline groups was significant at the .001 level after that time. Since a total of 8 hours had elapsed since drug injection, tests were carried out demonstrating that other animals learned normally and showed normal savings when trained 8 hours after bitemporal puromycin injections.

These experiments indicate an initial phase of information storage which does not involve protein synthesis and which is capable of mediating recall of this task for a period of less than 3 hours. A second phase of memory storage, which mediates long-term performance, seems to be dependent on protein synthesis.

In earlier experiments, Barondes and Jarvik (1964) achieved 86% inhibition of cerebral RNA synthesis after brain injection of actinomycin-D, based upon measurement of uridine incorporation. This antibiotic is believed to inhibit DNA-dependent RNA synthesis directly. Under these conditions, no evidence was obtained that any unique RNA species was uninhibited. Yet, in spite of the severe perturbation of RNA synthesis, no significant interference with retention of learned responses occurred. Cohen and Barondes (1966) have found that 94 to 96% inhibition of cerebral RNA synthesis by actinomycin-D does not interfere with retention of the solution to a maze within 4 hours after training. These results suggest that, *if protein synthesis is really required for the second phase of memory storage, such protein synthesis would seem to be mediated by a stable messenger RNA which was itself synthesized before acquisition of the learned response.*

Taken together, these experiments suggest that the stable storage of information requires the synthesis of protein but, at the same time, the messenger RNA required for that synthesis must be a stable form which existed before the learning experience and was, therefore, independent of it. *If these conclusions were accepted, they would indicate that the experience is not coded as an instructed macromolecular configuration, since the template utilized in the synthesis of the representational substances existed before the experience took place.* Coding involving pro-

122

tein synthesis would then seem selectional in nature, with mediation based upon stimulation of an existing synthetic mechanism. These experiments seem particularly important because they possess strong theoretical implications, and they also seem to contradict much of the evidence presented earlier in this chapter which indicates that RNA synthesis is important for learning and which implies an instructional process. These contradictions require careful study to achieve resolution and clarification of the underlying questions.

Because of the relevance of these studies, an explanation of failure to obtain positive results in related experiments is particularly desirable. In earlier work, severe inhibition of protein synthesis in brain was achieved by Flexner et al. (1962) without significant impairment of learning or retention in the same behavioral situation. Measurement of valine incorporation indicated that approximately 83% inhibition of protein synthesis had been achieved. It seems anomalous that negative results were obtained in these experiments. The diminution of protein synthesis was comparable to that achieved in the experiments with positive outcome (Flexner et al., 1965a,b). It seems unlikely that inhibition must be essentially complete in order to be effective. This would imply a tremendous margin of safety in the mediating processes, so that only a small fraction of the capacity of the system is essential. Were this true, it would become extremely difficult to understand the marked behavioral effects reported when less major shifts in RNA concentrations were achieved in other studies discussed in this chapter.

Such inconsistencies suggest the desirability of further exploration along these lines involving other drugs, species, and behavioral situations. Results already available from the work of Deutsch et al. (1966) provide further indication that additional complexities remain to be unravelled. These workers pursued the phenomenon reported by Flexner et al. in the context of evidence that puromycin alters ChE activity (Burkhalter, 1963). Rats were trained in shock avoidance in a Y-maze, using a visual cue. Bilateral injection of the anticholinesterase drug, DFP, into the hippocampus 30 minutes after training impaired retention on tests 1 day later. Recovery of performance was observed in animals tested over a period of several days after injection. These results indicated that the injection interfered with performance, not with retention. Tests of the effect of increasing the interval between completion of training and DFP injection revealed an initial period of susceptibility, followed by resistance to disruption by hippocampal injections 3 days later. These results appear to correspond with those reported by Flexner et al. with

123

respect to shift in the locus of vulnerability. However, injection of DFP into the hippocampus 14 days later revealed that performance was again severely impaired. These results raise the question of whether the puromycin effect responsible for the behavioral impairment is solely by virtue of blockade of protein synthesis or whether alteration of ChE activity may not also be involved. They also emphasize the need for careful study to determine whether the effects are on retention or on performance. Measurement of savings on retraining will be necessary to resolve this issue.

Barondes and Cohen (1967) used cycloheximide to inhibit protein synthesis as much as Flexner *et al.* achieved with puromycin, and found no amnesic effect several hours later. Similarly, Flexner and Flexner (1966) found that puromycin, but not acetoxycycloheximide, interfered with memory in mice one day after training. Because of the different effects of these two drugs on memory, Cohen, Ervin, and Barondes studied their effects on hippocampal activity (1966). Cycloheximide caused no discernible changes, while puromycin produced marked abnormalities, including suppression of rhythmic activity. Thus, the effects of puromycin on consolidation cannot simply be attributed to interference with protein synthesis. The differences in effects of the two drugs on consolidation may be related to their different effects on hippocampal activity. These results do not necessarily indicate that the hippocampus plays a unique role in memory, since the drug may have produced electrical abnormalities elsewhere.

These findings not only cast doubt on whether protein synthesis was crucial for consolidation in these situations, but highlight the hazardousness of interpretation of findings in this research area. Although numerous facts suggest that macromolecular synthesis may well play a role in consolidation, new experimental findings may easily recast our understanding of those facts into a completely different mold. Although it is essential to attempt continuously to devise a theoretical framework which can encompass the facts, it is necessary to recognize that such formulations are extremely tentative and derive utility largely as temporary springboards for fresh experiments.

In the writer's opinion, none of the experimental results which have been described is sufficient by itself to warrant the conclusion that stable information storage in the brain is mediated by the structure of macromolecules. Yet, it must be conceded that a wide variety of experimental procedures have yielded an impressive quantity of data strongly pointing toward RNA and protein synthesis as deeply implicated in the functions of memory.

CHAPTER VII

POSSIBLE MECHANISMS OF STABLE
INFORMATION STORAGE: THEORETICAL
FORMULATIONS

A. Mechanisms of protein synthesis

In order to provide a better frame of reference from which to evaluate the body of data presented thus far, as well as the various theoretical formulations which are to be discussed, it may be worthwhile to summarize current notions about the mechanisms of protein synthesis. Proteins are large polymers, or macromolecules, which are assembled from a large number of building blocks called amino acids. The enzymes that are essential for the production of those substances required by cells are proteins. The properties of a protein depend upon the particular sequential arrangement of amino acids in the macromolecule. The specification of amino acid sequence on a synthesized protein is controlled by a system involving deoxyribonucleic acids (DNA) and ribonucleic acids (RNA).

DNA molecules are primarily confined to the nucleus of the cell where they are the major constituents of the genes. Each DNA molecule is a long, unbranched chain of nucleotides, usually chemically bonded to another DNA molecule to form a double helix. In cell division, the two strands of the helix separate and serve as templates for the synthesis of new polynucleotides to form two new helices. DNA molecules in the nucleus of a nerve cell are believed to be permanent structures since replication of DNA occurs only during cell division. DNA can be formed only on a template and spontaneous coupling of nucleotides does not occur. Kornberg (1960) has demonstrated that the base sequence of a DNA molecule is determined by the base sequence of the template on which it was formed, and no polynucleotide synthesis occurs in the absence of a template.

As pointed out by Briggs and Kitto (1962), these considerations seem to rule out the possibility that experiential information is stored by changes in the base sequence of nuclear DNA molecules, since there is no known way in which neural activity could interfere with the process of DNA synthesis to produce a new base sequence. Even if nuclear DNA molecules were somehow disrupted by the consequences of a nerve impulse, the fragments would not recombine into polynucleotides of altered base sequence.

The synthesis of messenger RNA (mRNA) in the nucleus is dependent upon DNA. The base sequence of the DNA serves as a template, specifying the structure of the RNA which is constructed upon it (Weiss and Nakamoto, 1961). The spatial or steric constraints imposed by the DNA template absolutely specify the particular bases which can be sequentially assembled in the RNA molecule (Abrams, 1961). The rigidity of this specification precludes any possibility that neural activity can interfere with the synthetic process to give rise to an mRNA of base sequence not determined by its DNA template.

Messenger RNA leaves the nucleus and forms a temporary complex with ribosomes. This complex has the capability of synthesizing protein. The sequence of amino acids in any particular protein molecule is determined explicitly by the base sequence of the RNA on which it forms (Speyer *et al.*, 1962). It appears extremely unlikely that neural activity could disrupt these template mechanisms so as to alter the base sequence in the protein molecule. Even if the base sequence were altered by some mechanism, no matter how improbable that may seem, the alteration must either be great or small. If great, the cell must experience severe disruption due to the reaction to a foreign protein. If small, the enzyme would either be unaffected or would lose its catalytic properties. For these reasons, it seems necessary to conclude that it is extremely unlikely that experiential memory is stored by alteration of base sequences in brain proteins. The constraints of biosynthesis seem to preclude such changes. Even if they occurred, large alterations would lead to cata-

126

strophic disruption of cell activity and small ones would have no significant effect.

Most of the investigations of such mechanisms have been conducted with non-neural tissue. It is possible that the specification of polymers by template mechanisms in neural cells is somehow different than in other cells and that neural polymers are more amenable to structural alteration. Some evidence supporting this possibility has been summarized by Gaito (1963).

B. Operators, repressors, and effectors

However, other avenues can be discerned for modulation of this synthetic system which do not require the postulation of processes which defy the steric constraints required by these template mechanisms. The following outline is based upon the overview provided by Stent (1964). In 1961, Jacob and Monod (1961) suggested that segments of the DNA molecule, which were called *cistrons,* served as templates for the synthesis of messenger RNA molecules. The cistronic polynucleotide sequence was transcribed to the mRNA. The mRNA-ribosome complex synthesizes the polypeptide specified in the parent cistron as a succession of *codons.* Each codon represents a particular amino acid. Each mRNA molecule has a limited lifetime and thus serves for the synthesis of only a limited number of protein molecules.

Furthermore, Jacob and Monod proposed that a set of cistrons located in adjacent regions of the DNA molecule constituted an *operon* because of their functional control by their common *operator.* This operator, located nearby, is a gene that can occupy two states: open and closed. While the operator is open, every cistron of the operon synthesizes the mRNA, resulting ultimately in synthesis of the corresponding polypeptide. When the operator is closed, no cistron of the operon can be active. The operator closes when it is engaged by a specific cytoplasmic *repressor,* which is itself the product of a *regulator* gene. The work of Huang and Bonner (1962) and others suggests that the genetic potentials present in every cell are for the most part repressed: *derepression must occur for this potential to be realized.*

The cytoplasmic concentration of specific metabolites, or *effectors,* controls the activity of various repressors. Effectors can either induce or

127

repress the synthesis of particular proteins, due to two modes of inter-action with repressors. One kind of repressor is inactivated by the pres-ence of its effector and is thereby prevented from closing the responsive operator. In this case, the effector *induces* previously repressed synthesis of the polypeptides coded in all cistrons of the corresponding operon. *Thus, adequate concentration of some substances in the cytoplasm can, by feedback to the nuclear DNA, achieve the synthesis of substances in the cytoplasm.* Conversely, another kind of repressor is activated by the presence of its effector, and consequently closes the operator which it inhibits. In this case, all cistrons of the related operon cease to participate in production of polypeptides. *Thus, concentration of certain substances in the cytoplasm, by feedback to the nuclear DNA, can terminate the synthesis of particular compounds.*

C. Feedback in protein synthesis

These notions provide a much more flexible picture of cellular syn-thesis. While the capacity for synthesis is genetically determined by the DNA structure, the instantaneous expression of these chemical poten-tialities is continuously regulated by feedback from the cytoplasm. Clearly, this feedback loop provides an attractive mechanism whereby alteration of metabolites in a neuron due to neural activity might raise or lower the concentration of an effector substance. The synthesis of polypeptides found in the cytoplasm might thereby be regulated in four possible ways: (1) raising the concentration of an effector which inac-tivates a repressor would result in induction of previously repressed synthesis; (2) lowering the concentration of that effector would activate the repressor, terminating ongoing synthesis; (3) raising the concentra-tion of an effector which activates a repressor would terminate ongoing synthesis; (4) lowering the concentration of a substance which activates a repressor would initiate previously repressed synthesis.

Obviously, feedback reactions of this sort could serve as homeostatic mechanisms that act to maintain the cytoplasmic concentration of par-ticular reactants in a chemical reaction within well-regulated limits. Such homeostatic feedback systems would possess the general feature such that the shift in effector concentration which altered the state of an operator would result in the synthesis of compounds which would alter the rate

of the effector-producing reaction to *oppose* the direction of the concentration change. However, a class of possible *regenerative* feedback reactions can be recognized in which the shift in effector concentrations alters
the state of an operator which acts to drive the rate of the effector producing reaction further in the *same* direction. In such a case, the effector
concentration would shift to a new level which would thereafter be
self-sustaining. In this fashion, one can conceive of extremely long-
lasting and stable changes in the chemical and physiological properties
of a neuron that are brought about by a relatively brief period of neural
activity.

Of particular interest is the possibility that the state of a repressor
might be altered by two different substances: (1) a low molecular weight
metabolite such as an ion, whose concentration might rapidly alter with
neural activity and (2) a high-molecular-weight polymer whose synthesis
rate was shifted as a consequence of the action of the repressor on the
responsible operator. Thus, an ionic shift sustained during reverberatory
activity in the consolidation phase might produce a sustained change in
the cytoplasmic concentration of a polypeptide.

D. Action of repressors

This possibility is sufficiently attractive to arouse our interest in the
status of the concept of the postulated regulator gene. Thus far, experimental attempts to identify or isolate the repressor synthesized by that
gene or to obtain evidence as to how it manages to "close" the associated
operator have failed. Stent (1964) has published a detailed analysis of
this question. He suggests that the salient feature of the repressor substance is that in its active form it inhibits enzyme synthesis, rather than
failing to promote the reaction. In other words, it acts negatively. Present
belief is that the chemical nature of the repressor is protein. Jacob and
Monod (1963) have proposed that chemical affinity of the repressor
for the specific metabolic effector causes combination of the two substances, thereby altering the affinity of a second site on the repressor for
the nucleotide sequence of the operator gene.

Recent evidence, summarized by Stent, confirms that the presence of
a particular effector influences the intracellular concentration of the
specific mRNA produced by the relevant operon. These experiments

129

indicated that the mode of action of the repressor is via inhibition of mRNA *formation*, rather than the inhibition of mRNA *function* in protein synthesis. Experimental data based upon the size of mRNA molecules showed that the messenger molecule was *polycistronic*, and resulted from the action of the operon rather than individual cistrons. Furthermore, calculation of the relative numbers of messenger molecules and ribosomes led to the realization that single messenger molecules contact several ribosomes simultaneously. Apparently, the mRNA and the ribosomes are in constant relative motion during protein synthesis. The ribosome advances step by step along the messenger adding one amino acid to the growing polypeptide chain at each segment and releasing the synthesized protein when it reaches the end of each cistron.*

* However, evidence relating to *differential* synthetic activity of cistrons in an operon as a function of distance from the operator shows that the operon is polarized and does not truly function as a unitary synthetic mechanism. This differential synthesis cannot be reconciled with the assumption of uniform control of all cistrons in the operon. This apparent contradiction led to the suggestion that polypeptide synthesis once begun by a polycistronic mRNA molecule might come to a halt before transcription of the last cistron was completed. The effect of the contradiction, thus, was to suggest that some regulation of enzyme synthesis must occur at the level of messenger function, and, therefore, the postulated action of the repressor to inhibit mRNA formation is inadequate. Amino acids in the cytoplasm are known to be activated by certain enzymes, and to be carried to the ribosomes by *transfer RNA,* sometimes called soluble RNA (sRNA). It is believed that the mRNA-ribosomal complex specifies a series of codons, each corresponding to a particular species of sRNA. Some amino acids are represented by more than one kind of codon because of the degeneracy of the genetic code and thus can be transferred by more than one species of sRNA. If the cytoplasmic availability of different sRNA species capable of transferring a particular amino acid differs widely, then the rate of protein synthesis by a polycistronic mRNA must *also* depend on the relative occurrence of coded representations of the different sRNA species in the cistrons. These cistronic variations would then correspond to codon changes calling for switches in sRNA species as well as in amino acid sequence. This dependence of protein synthesis rate on the relative abundance of different sRNA has been called *modulation*. Thus, the availability or absence of a particular species of transfer RNA might regulate protein synthesis by a polycistronic mRNA in much the same functional fashion as the postulated regulation by the repressor produced by a regulator gene. The difference between the two mechanisms lies in the level of the supposed interference. Pursuing this line of reasoning, Stent suggests the possibility that there is a feedback connection between mRNA synthesis and function, and provides evidence that synthesized mRNA is not freely liberated from its DNA template but requires an active liberation process. This active process supposedly involves the ability of the mRNA to move over the appropriate ribosomes. Since this movement can be blocked by absence of the required sRNA species, he proposes that the primary agent in the release is the availability of sRNA. The suggestion of Jacob and Monod that regulator gene action involves the produc-

E. The derepressor hypothesis

The structure of DNA, the steric constraints on RNA synthesis by DNA, and the steric constraints on protein synthesis by RNA in the nerve cell impose severe restrictions on the cellular processes which they control. These processes must be assumed to possess extreme resistance to modification except by mutagenic influences. Therefore, arbitrary alteration of base sequences in the products of these processes would appear an improbable if not impossible candidate for mediation of the storage of information about previous patterns of cell discharge. However, the initiation, termination, or gradation of processes which conform to the specified constraints may be influenced by cellular activity. The modification by cellular discharge of the rate of processes qualitatively constrained by the preexisting operon repertoire may provide an alternative mechanism for information storage that is more consonant with present beliefs about macromolecular synthesis. The capacity for synthesis is determined and constrained by the DNA structure, but the momentary expression of these potentialities is regulated by cellular activity.

The aspect of the protein synthesis system most vulnerable to events related to neural discharge seems to be the feedback loop from the cytoplasm to the nuclear DNA whereby changes in concentration of an effector can activate or inactivate a repressor. If we assume that the repressor is inactivated by the cytoplasmic metabolite, the repressed DNA operator is released and the corresponding operon begins to produce the appropriate mRNA. This mRNA migrates to the ribosome where it makes the cognate protein. *Let us assume that this protein has*

---

tion of a repressor substance which inhibits messenger synthesis by operator closure is reexamined, and the alternative suggestion is made that the primary action of the repressor is at the level of messenger *function,* by regulating the supply of various sRNA species. This also leads to the notion that the nucleotide sequence of the polycistronic mRNA produced by an operon must contain one or more modulating codons calling for specific sRNA molecules. This requirement then makes that mRNA susceptible to the action of specific repressor substances produced by regulator genes.

Although these ambiguities have not been resolved, they do not alter the fundamental picture of feedback between cytoplasm and nucleus. Whether or not the operator is a gene which in fact synthesizes modulating sRNA, and the regulator gene governs sRNA activity, two kinds of regulatory units are still involved. Further work in this field will clarify whether the critical control site is at the level of messenger synthesis or messenger action.

two properties: first, it has the capacity to substitute for the action of the initial effector so that the new synthesis becomes independent of the original metabolic state which inactivated the repressor; *second,* it alters the probability of particular discharge patterns in the nerve cell. (Alternatively, if we follow the Stent proposal, the effector substance initiates the synthesis of a deficient sRNA species.)

Thus, we propose the following scheme, which we call the *Derepressor Hypothesis:*

(A) In any cell, much of the potential for synthesis of specific substances inherent in the DNA structure is repressed.

(B) Sustained participation of a neuron in representational activity causes a shift in the concentration of cytoplasmic materials, resulting in the derepression of an inhibited synthesis.

(C) The resulting alteration in cytoplasmic constituents has two consequences:

(1) Derepression of that synthesis is thereafter sustained.
(2) The reactivity of the neuron to patterns of stimulation is altered.

This scheme is illustrated in detail in Fig. VII-1. Thus, the feedback loop

becomes self-sustaining and changed neural reactivity (step 11) is postulated to be a by-product of this loop.

There are several essential features to this hypothesis. It is assumed that the postulated changes do not occur as a consequence of mere neural activity, but that the activity must be sustained for a sufficient time and at a sufficient rate to achieve a critical shift in the concentration of a critical substance. The basis for this assumption was outlined in Chapter II. Since the sustained activity underlying the critical shift arose from participation in a reverberating loop, the neuronal input presumably involved only a portion of the many synaptic contacts of the cell and was characterized by a particular temporal pattern. Thus, the input possessed particular spatiotemporal characteristics. The resulting neuronal discharge reconciled the various spatial influences at different synapses, integrating these into a temporal pattern of neural response.

There seems to be no compelling reason to require that the change in neural reactivity resulting from the released synthesis necessarily accomplish altered probability of neural response to the arrival of im-

THE DEREPRESSOR HYPOTHESIS

(1) Spatio-temporal pattern of neural impulses impinging on cell

(2) Sustained neural activity with particular pattern

(3) Critical change in cytoplasmic concentration of reactant in system producing effector substance

(11) Change in neural reactivity to input with the specified temporal pattern

(4) Inactivation of repressor ◄——— (10) Effector-mimic action
in nucleus

(5) Release of operator in DNA

(9) Production of new protein at ribosome

(6) Coordinate activity of operon in DNA

(8) Release of new m RNA to cytoplasm

(7) Synthesis of new m RNA

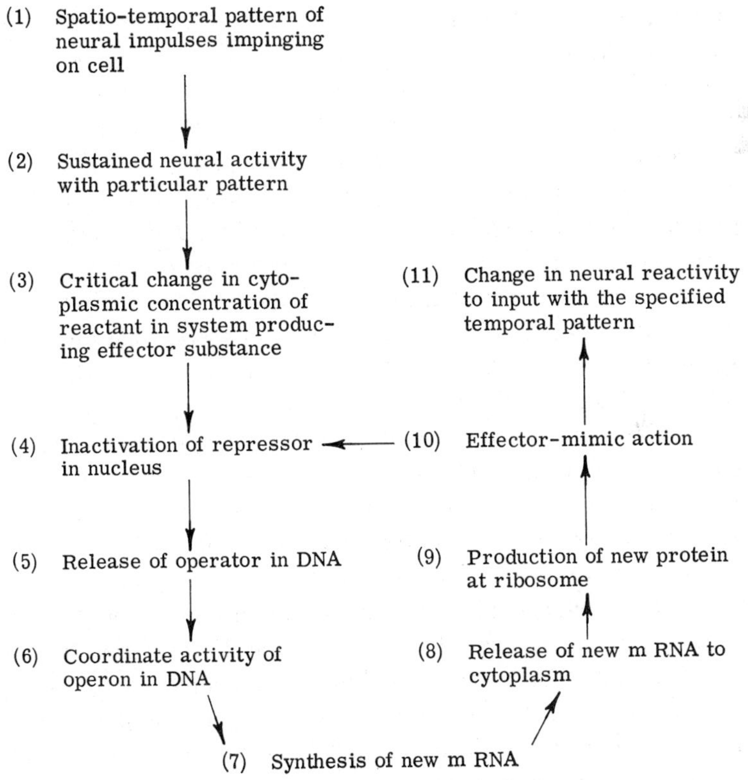

Fig. VII-1. The Derepressor Hypothesis.

pulses with *specified temporal distributions at specific synapses*. The integrative nature of neuronal response to multiple synaptic inputs might well result in a "smearing" of the contribution of individual synapses. A great deal of specification would seem to be accomplished if the cell becomes effectively "tuned" to some temporal pattern integrated over all the synaptic inputs which influence cytoplasmic chemical concentrations during the relevant time period. This tuning would not require faithful reproduction of the events at each synapse, and would also alter response tendencies to partial reproduction of the initial set of input events. Furthermore, it would permit alternative inputs to be accepted if temporal constraints were satisfied over the full set of stimuli which occurred. This formulation seems to provide advantages of flexibility and over-all accuracy while conforming to the probabilistic nature of many of the propositions set forth earlier in this book.

At the same time, the mechanism outlined previously might equally well provide the basis for changing the conductivity or efficiency of a specific synaptic connection. This requirement poses much more severe demands on the detailed specification of tuning which must be achieved by the consequences of the derepressor action. Instead of tuning the whole neuron to an altered reactivity to a particular temporal pattern integrated over the ensemble of inputs, providing unitary reconciliation of a multiplicity of factors, it becomes necessary to achieve separate tuning of many members of a group of synapses, each one to its idiosyncratic input pattern. This requirement imposes what looks like a staggering burden on the suggested mechanism, and thereby must be considered relatively unlikely.

Even if one were to assume that individual synaptic conductivity were altered by some such mechanism, it seems necessary to maintain the requirement that such synaptic tuning be specific for some temporal pattern. If this requirement is abandoned, the cell has been made more responsive to *any* input at that synapse. Change in synaptic effectiveness as required by connectionistic formulations might be accomplished by a mechanism similar to that described by the Derepressor Hypothesis. Nonetheless, unless increased excitability is accompanied by some basis for discrimination between various events at the same synapse, the system either loses the capacity for differentiation or must be limited to one synaptic input per memory.

F. Evaluation of experimental data

The salient features of the body of experimental evidence presented in Chapter VI can now be reevaluated in the joint context of this picture of protein synthesis and the proposed Derepressor Hypothesis. The observed enhancement of protein and RNA synthesis by neural activity, and the decrease in the amount of these substances resulting from sustained inactivity, suggest the existence of rate-limiting factors to these reactions. One such factor might be the accumulation of certain reaction products that tend to inhibit the reactions if neural activity does not lessen their concentration. A related factor might be the shift in electrolyte or metabolite concentrations accompanying neural discharge, which tends to facilitate the reactions. These factors might directly modify cytoplasmic reaction rates as a function of neural activity, independent of the mechanism suggested in the Derepressor Hypothesis. The postulated nuclear feedback loop may become effective only when neural activity alters sufficiently to achieve a critical shift in an effector substance. The increase in RNA content and synthesis rate reported to accompany learning may additionally reflect the activation of new feedback loops involving derepression. Changes in the base ratio of neuronal RNA, reported during learning, would be interpreted from this viewpoint as reflecting production of a new RNA with its own characteristic composition rather than alteration in the base ratios of existing RNA species.

The interference with learning observed by blockade of RNA synthesis might be due to prevention of new synthesis after temporary derepression, so that the feedback loop failed to become established. Effects on retention or transfer after ribonuclease injection might be attributed to effective disruption of a feedback loop previously established. Similar disruption might explain the puromycin results. Puromycin blockade of protein synthesis would interrupt the loop at step 9. Some time afterward, the mRNA in step 8 would decay, having remained intact for a brief period. The inactivated repressor in step 4 becomes activated due to effector deficiency. The operator in step 5 closes, and production of the specific RNA by the operon in step 6 terminates. The loop has been opened and when protein synthesis resumes after puromycin effects wear off, no effector is available. Thus, the loop remains open, and the "memory" is destroyed.

The facilitation of learning and consolidation reported after enhancement of RNA synthesis may reflect greater ease in establishment of sufficient new RNA after derepression to accomplish stabilization of the feedback loop. The hypothesized effector-mimic substance must achieve sufficient concentration to be comparable to the initiating critical shift; the time required to build up this concentration would presumably

135

contribute to the length of the consolidation period. Consolidation might be considered to end when the critical concentration necessary to close the feedback loop is attained. The positive effects of injection of "naïve" yeast RNA that have been reported may be viewed as an alternate method to accomplish the same end, by lowering the effective available ribonuclease concentration so that new RNA is destroyed more slowly.

The fact that such ad hoc explanations can reconcile the reported spectrum of experimental findings with the proposed hypothesis obviously does not establish the correctness of the hypothesis. It merely indicates that the hypothesis is not incompatible with the data. One of the most severe challenges to the speculations above is provided by the cannibalism and injection experiments which seem to suggest a specific informational coding on the new RNA produced as a result of experience. Possibly future research will show that those observations reflect methodological errors or fortuitous factors which are not presently apparent.

In order to consider the implications, let us assume that the evidence for information transfer in these studies will eventually be adequately substantiated. Functional access to the past experience of certain neurons seems to be transferred to new neurons by the incorporation of substances from "trained" neural tissue, perhaps RNA. This may incline some to conclude that the information is represented by a specific molecular configuration and the memory resides in the cell containing that representational molecule, so that its subsequent discharge will constitute "recognition" of the event about which information has been stored. We cannot reasonably assume that the new host cells possess connections replicating those of the cells in which these hypothetical molecules were initially formed. However, we do assume that numerous molecules of this type must have entered a large number of host cells, and that chemical affinities make it likely that many of these cells are in anatomical regions grossly corresponding to the original production sites of the molecules.

It may be possible to interpret the "trained" RNA injection results by assuming that the "trained" RNA essentially "infects" the host cell, inducing the DNA to initiate synthesis of new mRNA. The new cytoplasmic substances resulting from this change may alter reactivity of the whole neuron to the specified temporal pattern of input, independent of the particular synaptic terminals by which such afferent influences arrived. Many cells might conceivably be tuned to a particular temporal

136

pattern in this way, so that the over-all probability of sustained response in the network containing them became altered. An explanation along these lines might help to account for the reported results if one assumed that the inputs, interconnections, and outputs of a network were effected in statistically comparable fashion from animal to animal within a species in such a way that the temporal patterns of activity within different networks bore a statistical resemblance when similar stimulation occurred. The basic similarity which exists in the characteristics of many electrophysiological phenomena among different members of the same species may offer some justification for such speculation.

The reader may be disturbed by the introduction of such extreme hypotheses to account for phenomena not yet unequivocally established, and he may well be justified. The author is faced with the choice between ignoring a substantial body of remarkable data which seems to contradict the theoretical position laboriously constructed here, or of attempting to provide some explanation of those phenomena in terms of present knowledge and speculation. It seems preferable to try to deal with the facts as adequately as possible under existing limitations of knowledge in the hope that reasonable lines for further investigation can be suggested.

G. Interface between labile and stable process

Regenerative feedback of cytoplasmic effectors to regulator genes in the nucleus of the nerve cell may provide a mechanism potentially capable of achieving long-term alterations in the chemistry and reactivity of the neuron. The salient features of experimental findings about the effects on learning and performance which result from manipulation of the processes of RNA and protein synthesis seem to be compatible with the Derepressor Hypothesis which has been offered as a formal description of this mechanism. Two major tasks remain: first, to indicate in more detail some reasonable process by which the participation of a neuron in representation of an event during the labile phase might activate such a feedback reaction, thereby coupling the two stages of storage; second, to outline in some detail how retrieval of stored information might occur from such a representational mechanism.

Whether we assume that the mechanism which mediates the early labile phase of information storage is a frequently repeated reverberation

137

of a loop involving relatively small numbers of neurons or the circulation of impulses through a network first in this loop and now in that loop, it seems necessary to assume that at least certain cells, if not all, maintaining this ongoing activity are in repeated discharge throughout the consolidation period. These cells, whether they constitute the full reverberating circuit or only the nodes between loops, must somehow be protected against "capture" by circuits engaged in the other ongoing activities of the brain. How can such protection be achieved? The longer the interval between the recovery of a neuron from its refractory period and the arrival of another impulse from the circulating activity representing an experience, the higher the probability that the neuron will be diverted from its role in representation. Conversely, the shorter that interval, the higher the probability that the neuron will be available. Protection of a participating cell, therefore, would seem best provided if that cell fires at a rate which is maximum or near maximum. (Equivalent protection might be afforded if the afferent barrage were to cause a shift in membrane potential which increased its threshold for other incoming volleys for a period of time, effectively extending the refractory period so that firing rate diminished sharply between circulations of activity. This inhibition would have to be phasic, with an interval coinciding with reverberation time.) If we assume that numerous cells are initially involved in response to an input, that many possible loops can be set up, and that on successive passages around the loop, first some cells and then others will drop out because they will become "captured" by other circuits, gradually, one of two things must happen. Either the circulation of impulses arising from some previous input must gradually dwindle and disappear long before the consolidation period terminates (in which case it seems necessary to assume that these cells make a negligible contribution to the storage of information about the previous stimulus); or else some subset must select itself by continuing to participate. Even if reverberation were maintained first by one loop, and then by another, certain nodal points must exist at which crossovers may occur between these interlaced groups, and these considerations must apply to the cells at such nodal points. Therefore, it seems reasonable to conclude that at least for some and perhaps for all the cells in the subset mediating the continued circulation of neural activity after an experience throughout the consolidation phase, there must be an altered pattern of discharge which is sustained over an extended period. This altered pattern would seem likely to consist either of a relatively constant high rate of discharge or intervals of intense discharge followed by inhibition in an orderly fashion. Diverse consequences can be expected from this sustained pattern of discharge. As one effect, certain metabolic processes providing the energy for neural discharge must go on at an altered rate.

H. Metabolites or electrolytes as the critical substance

Another consequence of a sustained rate or pattern of discharge should be a shift in the mean intracellular electrolyte concentration for cells participating in such activity. As the mean interspike interval changes with altered activity, the flux of electrolyte across the membrane must also change. If the change in activity of the neuron during this period were a sustained increase in discharge rate, the mean intracellular concentration of potassium during this period might be expected to shift to a lower level, while intracellular sodium concentration increased. If the altered activity consisted of bursts of activity alternating with inhibition in a characteristic pattern sustained over time, the effect on electrolyte concentrations might be either to stabilize them at a different level or to cause patterned fluctuations in concentration. Probably both effects occur, depending on the size of the volume inside the neuron which is considered. Local volumes may experience phasic fluctuations, while effects on the cell as a whole were smoothed.

It is difficult to make a precise estimate of the shift in intracellular potassium level which might occur within a CNS neuron participating in such representational activity. Measurements of the fraction of intracellular potassium which moves extracellularly per impulse vary from 1/40,000 to 1/100,000 in various peripheral nerves. However, the usually accepted values for intracellular potassium in the central nervous system are about 155 μmol/ml, and calculations indicating the potassium shift per impulse to be 0.20 μmol/ml have been published (Grafstein, 1963). Considering the fact that 20% of the potassium seems to be bound (Katzman and Leiderman, 1953), sustained neural activity may well cause an appreciable movement of potassium out of the cells. It is most difficult to estimate the extent to which this movement is easily reversible in the central nervous system, where glial packing and other anatomical features may provide "traps" for extra-neural potassium. Clearly, the reversal requires appreciable time as noted when the measurements of potassium efflux were cited earlier in Chapter III.

Hertz (1965) has presented evidence for the presence of a potassium-activated ATP-ase on the outer surface membrane of glial cells. Addition of potassium to the incubation medium caused a sharp increase in the respiratory rate of brain slices, with an exponential decline. The increase of O_2 uptake was attributed to stimulation of K^+-activated ATP-ase known to exist in brain. The effect was found to be specific to brain gray matter. Microdissection techniques were used to show that the respiration of neurons was unchanged under these conditions, while glial cells showed changes comparable to intact brain slices. These results were interpreted to mean that glial cells comprise a system capable of active potassium uptake and transport. The presence of this process in glial cells intimately surrounding CNS nerve cells might lead to appreciable changes in intracellular potassium during increased and sustained excitation. *Not only might neuronal potassium concentration be decreased, but marked increases in glial potassium might occur.* The discussions in this and subsequent sections apply to *both* kinds of cells, although neural activity is emphasized. The demonstrations of changes in both glial and neural cells during stimulation and learning (Hydén, 1962; Hydén and Egyházi, 1963) are relevant to this point. It might be worthwhile to consider the possible changes within the *glia-neuron unit.* Galambos (1961) has suggested that the glia may play an important role in modulating neuronal responses.*

* Considerations of the sort raised above bring to mind some early work by Marui (1919). This worker studied the changes in the Mauthner's cell synapse of teleosts during sustained vestibular stimulation. The fish was confined in a long narrow tank and received a rotatory torque about its midline from two jets of water: one jet was directed high on one side, the other jet was low on the other side. These pressures constituted a force tending to rotate the fish around its center line, belly over back. Resistance to this vestibular stimulus was compelled for long periods of time. After about 12 hours of this stress, the fish began to display deviations from the normal orientation. These displacements gradually became greater and more prolonged. After between 20 and 24 hours of continued stress, the fish irreversibly lost the ability to orient itself with respect to the vertical plane. It rotated helplessly in the water jets and did not regain the ability to orient properly when permitted to rest.

The Mauthner cell synapse in teleosts is enclosed in a glial reticulum. Marui carried out histological studies on this structure in groups of fish at varying time intervals after the onset of stimulation. As vestibular stress was prolonged, the glial reticulum gradually swelled and seemed to become turgid. At the time when the capacity to orient properly was irreversibly lost, *the glial reticulum ruptured.* Small

I. Effects of a critical shift in potassium

It is even more difficult to estimate how large a shift might be "big enough." Some considerations relevant to this were outlined in an earlier chapter. Either metabolites resulting from neural discharge or electrolytes might be the critical substance. Let us assume that potassium is the critical substance, and that a critical shift in potassium concentration, K, takes place in the subset of neurons which reverberate during the consolidation period, or in the glial cells which surround each of these neurons. How might the electrolyte shift affect the stable storage of information in that group of cells?

The messenger RNA molecule, and the ribosome to which it is attached, carry side chains which by virtue of their spacing and charge distribution serve as acceptor sites for particular amino acids carried by transfer RNA molecules in the environment. In this fashion, the synthesis of a particular polypeptide is specified. The side chains of the messenger-ribosome complex, however, are also capable of accepting potassium or calcium ions. Rudenberg and Tobias have shown that calcium is bonded to RNA in axoplasm (1960). Calcium ions may also change protein configuration (Gurd and Wilcox, 1956). The distribution of electrolytes between the cytoplasm and the template can be expected to be a function of the potassium concentration of the system. As the intracellular potassium concentration of the neuron changes during sustained activity, the binding of ions should also change. The charge distribution of the complex may therefore change as a function of neural activity, with a consequent change in bond-to-bond angles between the side chains. The ability of a particular transfer RNA to fit into the template may be affected thereby.

Change in electrolyte concentration thus may serve as a rate-determining factor in the synthesis of proteins. This is equivalent to the suggestion that electrolyte concentration is able to *modulate a codon*. Alteration of firing pattern over a sustained interval due to incorporation

---

ameboid glial fragments remained. No structural changes could be observed in the nerve cell or synapse itself during this period. These observations suggest that some substance may be released by nerve cells during activity and taken up by glial cells, and that some aspect of the glial-neural relationship is essential for neural function.

Additionally relevant to the ideas discussed above is the fact that neuroglia contain about the same potassium concentration as neurons; much of it is probably in bound form (Koch *et al.*, 1962).

141

of a neuron into circulating reverberatory activity may affect the amount of certain types of protein synthesized by the cell. This protein might be the critical substance which serves as the cytoplasmic effector when a sufficient concentration change takes place. Conceivably, the effector function might be served directly by the altered electrolyte shift, perhaps by changing the affinity. between a repressor and DNA. However, it seems more probable that the effector is protein in nature.

J. Influence of electrolytes on protein synthesis

A crucial question for an evaluation of the proposed mechanism would seem to be whether or not the synthesis of macromolecules or molecular complexes by a cell can be significantly affected by the concentration of the electrolyte in the surround.

Recently, Lubin (1963, 1964) provided evidence that the rate of protein synthesis in various bacterial cell types was selectively affected by decrease in intracellular K^+ concentration, although RNA synthesis was maintained at close to the normal rate. The relationship between rate of protein synthesis and potassium ion concentration, over the range studied, seems to be approximately linear. These findings were presented as a plausible mechanism by which *extracellular* influences might govern protein synthesis or cell growth through the regulation of potassium transport. Investigating this finding, Lubin and Ennis reported (1963) that the effect of the ammonium ion was frequently even more marked than that of potassium. It may be relevant that ammonium ion is a by-product of neural activity. During excitation, there is an increase in the ammonia content of brain (Vrba *et al.*, 1964). Vladimirova showed considerable increase in brain ammonia (44 to 60%) during conditioning and differentiation. After completion of differentiation, presentation of the negative conditioned stimulus caused no change in brain ammonia (Vladimirova, 1964).

Consistent with Lubin's reports, Conway (1964) confirmed these observations and demonstrated that the function of these ions was to fix amino acyl sRNA to the ribosome. Spyrides (1964) confirmed this report and provided evidence that the specific binding appears to be the initial and sometimes rate-limiting step in amino acid polymerization, a conclusion compatible with the interpretation of Haselkorn and Fried (1964).

K. Retrieval mechanism

The evidence that protein synthesis is responsive to electrolyte concentration lends some plausibility to the assumption that the ionic shift resulting from a sustained pattern of neural activity may act as an effector, or that the effects of ionic shift on enzyme activity or protein synthesis may play this role. The change in protein synthesis resulting from release of a repressed operator must effectively mimic the initial effector action to maintain the feedback loop. Furthermore, the altered protein synthesis must alter the response characteristics of the neuron in such a way as to provide for retrieval of the stored information which it represents.

Actually, what is that information? A subset of cells (one of many constellations which might share a common activity over a period of time in this population) received afferent input under such conditions that the members of the subset shared a sustained pattern of increased or decreased activity. The configuration of activity in this fortuitously selected group of neurons constituted a particular mode of response. Sustained activity in that specific mode, a nonrandom occurrence in the network, was a representation of the effect of the afferent input on the population of neurons and constituted the information to be stored. The postulated derepressor mechanism must alter neural response characteristics so as to enhance the probability that this mode of shared activity will again be displayed by this group of cells at some time in the future when stimulated by a comparable input. This reasoning requires that the change in protein synthesis caused by sustained activity in a mode of response must alter the membrane characteristics of the neurons in the representational subset so as to make the cells more capable and likely to display sustained response with those particular temporal patterns. If tuning to a particular pattern could be established in the members of the subset, the probability of coherent activity in the relevant mode when the total population subsequently received that input would be increased.

It is difficult to see just how such tuning might be accomplished. A possible way might involve the binding of potassium by the newly synthesized protein, analogous to the well-known potassium binding by muscle protein. As potassium is thus bonded, its mobility decreases and the activity coefficient would effectively change. In this way, the potassium flux during neural discharge might be diminished, and the recovery

143

time of the depolarized membrane decreased. The optimal mean inter-spike interval of the neuron might thereby be shifted, tuning it to respond most effectively at a preferred frequency. Since the binding of potassium would probably be proportional to its concentration, the changes in various cells of the representational subset would differ, each neuron being tuned to a preferred frequency reflecting its characteristic response when participating in the representational mode. Although this tuning would not endow the individual neuron with the capacity to reproduce complex syncopated discharge patterns, the resulting changes in effectiveness of excitatory and inhibitory drives on the individual neurons in the system, and the interaction of those effects, might increase the reliability with which coherent response in a particular mode was displayed by the total network upon later repetition of the input. That is, increase in coherent response, in a particular mode, above random levels would constitute the essential feature of information retrieval in the neural network.

Increased probability of association, in a particular mode, of the subset of cells previously involved in the representation of an event during the labile phase may seem like an extremely fragile mechanism on which to base a proposed information storage scheme. Nevertheless, it is this association that defines the information that must be stored.

Probabilistic processes, furthermore, can be exceedingly lawful. If we assume that the number of functional systems in which the process just described occurs is quite large, and that the number of cells involved in any system is also large, then perhaps the mechanism which has been described might be quite stable. Once such changes in protein synthesis have been achieved in a set of cells, the cells will continue to respond to other influences that are impinging upon them since neurons participate in many systems. Although in the short term, the rate of activity of some cells of the subset will be higher than random, and the activity of other members lower than the mean for the group, over any substantial period of time these short-term fluctuations should average out. For a period of time, the consequences of involvement in other processes might shift the preferred frequencies of some cells, which might drift away from the distribution of characteristics that reflect the shared experience of the group, but gradually they should drift back in as homeostatic regulation occurred. If the number of cells and the number of loops in the representational group were sufficiently large, then these fluctuations should not impair the capacity of the network to display a

144

characteristic mode of shared activity when the same stimulus configuration again impinged on the system. Thus, random activity in the network would not destroy the altered preference for particular interspike intervals that has been established in the set of cells. Similarly, uniform influences on the full population—massive activity such as that during convulsion, or relative silence as during anesthesia—will not destroy the organization which has been achieved because the system will experience a common increase or decrease in the baseline, a shift shared by all cells. The system would not be destroyed unless orderly activity involved a significant portion of the set for a sufficiently large period of time to impose a shift in protein synthesis and bound charge differentially on a portion of the system. Neither random activity, nor massive activity, nor systematic and differential activity could affect this set unless it were of sufficient duration to modify the synthesis of protein. The representation achieved by the proposed scheme could be altered effectively only by the same process that established it, that is, by new learning. Finally, each time stimulation reoccurs, additional neural elements can be recruited into loops parallel with those previously established. Thus, the memory can be expected to stabilize further and gradually spread into additional anatomical regions as it ages.

One possible advantage of this model over some of the alternative formulations, to be discussed later, is that the proposed mechanism for memory involves the alteration in rate of one of the potential processes of chemical synthesis in the cell by *selection*, rather than requiring the different input to the cell somehow to *instruct* the arbitrary synthesis of a unique representational configuration (Morrell, 1962).

The proposed mechanism achieves an increased coherence in the discharge of a group of neurons associated in a particular mode of responses. We assume that these associated groups of cells are being constructed not only *within* the boundaries of the various anatomical regions of the brain, but also that afferent and efferent circuits *between* these various regions join them into an anatomically extensive larger system. The circulation of impulses throughout these systems must have a characteristic time course, reflecting the distribution of cells within each region and the length of the pathways between such regions. The summated consequences of nonrandom association of activity in these groups of cells should be reflected as phase-locked oscillations in the electrical activities generated in such a network. One might expect to see

145

characteristic electrical patterns emerge in various places during learning as these volleys of neural activity presumably circulate.

Indeed, one might speculate whether the patterns elicited in certain plastic regions by afferent stimuli might not, after modification of those regions in the fashion described, come to be emitted by such regions when "familiar" stimuli impinged upon them. Evidence relating to these topics will be presented in later chapters.

L. The need for a comparator mechanism

1. Inadequacy of a simple tuning mechanism

Suppose we concede that electrolyte shifts might serve as effectors to initiate changes in protein synthesis which tuned neurons to respond to some preferred frequency, thereby increasing the ability of a network to display a particular mode of oscillation or to respond more markedly to a specific input. A mechanism of this sort would achieve a quantitative increase in a qualitative mode of neural response which existed before. How might this influence the activity of the nervous system so as to alter behavior, due to the effect of previously acquired information? How might the nervous system distinguish between heightened response to a previously experienced event due to specific memory readout and enhanced response to a new event due to general increase in excitability? Mere quantitative increase of the probability of neural response in a given mode seems inadequate to account for the qualitative changes which accompany learning. Intuitively, it seems desirable for a mechanism to exist which distinguishes the response to novel events from the response to familiar events in terms of more definite and distinct qualitative features. Furthermore, the proposed storage mechanism represents an item of information as a specified mode of oscillation in a network. This type of coding would seem to impose an extremely severe if not impossible burden on the ability of the nervous system to recognize and distinguish between temporal patterns of activity.

2. Differential plasticity and comparator hypothesis

Thus, even if our speculations about the nature of the interface between neural activity and the mechanism of information storage and

146

retrieval were correct, they do not provide an adequate basis for understanding how functionally significant readout might occur. Additional features of the readout process seem necessary in order to account for the two major deficiencies mentioned previously. It seems possible to remedy both of these apparent shortcomings by postulation of another characteristic of the system—anatomical differentiation and organization. Matters become simpler if we assume the existence of two kinds of cells or cell organizations in the brain: (1) *stable cells or networks which display a relatively constant and invariant response to specific afferent inputs*—perhaps these might be conceptualized as stimulus-bound and their responses primarily determined by extrinsic influences; (2) *plastic cells or networks which display variable response to specific afferent inputs*—these may be conceptualized as responsive to extrinsic influences, but with the previous history and state of the system playing a major role in the determination of their activity.

The observations of Yoshii and Ogura (1960) are relevant to this suggestion. These workers observed that 38% of the neurons studied in the reticular formation were not influenced by presentation of three different types of stimuli, 29% were influenced by only one type of stimulus (monovalent), and 33% were influenced by two or more types of stimulus (polyvalent). Relatively regular discharge patterns were observed in 49% of the cells studied, while 51% displayed irregular and intermittent spontaneous activity. Differentiated conditioned responses were then established by pairing one (but not another) type of stimulus with the third: mild electric shock to the foot. Little change in response of regularly firing monovalent neurons was observed. Irregular monovalent neurons showed fairly consistent changes. The majority of polyvalent neurons showed changed responsiveness to the stimuli after conditioning, particularly those with irregular patterns. Altogether, 46% of the neurons studied showed altered response patterns in relation to conditioning. These results provide support for the suggestion that there may be two types of nerve cells with regard to plasticity. These findings also show that the patterns of discharge in large numbers of cells change during conditioning. Similar conclusions follow from the work of Morrell *et al.* (1966).

Consider the nervous system to be composed of these two kinds of components in functional parallel. Stable and plastic networks receive the same input. The output of the stable network consists of a particular mode of oscillation in specific regions of the brain. The output of the plastic network will depend on previous history and state of the system.

147

Assume that these two outputs converge. If they are of compatible mode and of nonrandom magnitude, this would indicate that the stimulus which produced the activity in the stable network was a known, familiar event. Convergence of stable and plastic networks would occur in regions throughout the brain on many levels. However, significant coincidence between the two modes of activity would occur only in some regions. The specific afferent input to those regions would define the *content* of the information.

The various assumptions of the system can now be summarized:

(1) The information in a neural network is the deviation of the average response of the network from baseline activity over a period of time.

(2) The time course of the average activity reflects a mode of oscillation. A particular mode of oscillation in certain structures represents a particular event.

(3) Information storage consists of enhancement of the probability that a plastic network will display a particular mode of oscillation. Initiation of that mode of oscillation constitutes retrieval of the stored information.

(4) Stable and plastic networks exist in functional parallel in many anatomical regions throughout the brain. The output of the two kinds of networks travels to a comparator which estimates the congruence between the mode of oscillation in the two networks.

(5) Coincidence between the two modes constitutes identification of a present event as one which occurred before.

(6) Coincidence beween the two modes will occur only in some anatomical regions. The specific nature of the input to the stable networks in regions in which coincidence occurred defines the *unique content* of the retrieved information, and thereby provides the reference for decoding or readout.

A system possessing these features (particularly 5 and 6) would seem to be free of the two major shortcomings of a storage process based only on the suggested tuning mechanism which were pointed out previously. The coincidence detection mechanism required by the comparator hypothesis might be located in regions which specially served that function, upon which the two kinds of network which have been postulated converge. Alternatively, one might conceive of stable and plastic networks

148

within relatively local volumes of neural tissue, which also contained comparators. The output of the local region might consist of transmission of information about the afferent input into the region, plus an attached sign of some sort indicating whether the information represented in that mode of oscillation was novel or familiar. Evidence bearing on possible comparator functions in brain as obtained from electrophysiological studies will be presented in the second part of this volume.

M. Current theoretical formulations: a critique

A number of theoreticians have proposed models for a memory mechanism which relate to data of the sort which have been presented. Schmitt (1962) has proposed that the synthesis of a macromolecule by RNA is a sequential process that can be abruptly terminated at whatever stage it has reached when a pattern of nervous impulses *impinges* upon a cell. The resulting partially completed moiety is assumed to be a specific representation of the stimulus sequence during which it was produced, although a previously ongoing synthesis was terminated by the stimulation. This moiety is assumed to bond to transmitter molecules. On subsequent excitation of the cell with that same stimulus pattern, the complex composed of the moiety and the transmitter substance decomposes, with a consequent availability of transmitter substance. Thus, this "tape recorder molecule" concept involves the representation of particular experiences by particular fragments. However, the cells containing these fragments bonded to transmitters must fire under numerous conditions. Any input which releases any transmitter substance from the complex with any moiety can result in discharge of the cell. This would seem to result in considerable ambiguity, so that information which has been placed on the "tape recorder molecule" cannot be played back with any specificity. Indeed, to play it back at all requires the invocation of processes for which there is little evidence. Furthermore, our knowledge of protein synthesis offers little basis for the assumption that partially completed protein fragments can be released by ribosomes.

Hydén (1960) has proposed a model which is very similar to that of Schmitt. The sequence of stimuli impinging upon a cell is presumed to alter the base sequence of RNA in some fashion. This new RNA then synthesizes protein with a particular configuration. The synthesized specific protein is hypothesized to dissociate when the cell subsequently is stimulated with the same temporal pattern of influences. The protein fragments resulting from this dissociation facilitate the release or the synthesis of transmitter substances. Again, this theory envisages a cell that will fire when a given impulse pattern impinges upon it. Yet it would appear that other impulse patterns can also make it fire. It is not easy to see how such firing constitutes a *unique* readout event. In addition to vagueness about how the information is to be retrieved, there is little evidence supporting the various steps of coding and decoding which are postulated. This model assumes synthesis of a specific protein in contrast to Schmitt's model which involves the synthesis of a specific fragment. Both of these models seem to have similar shortcomings.

Elul (1966a) interprets the evidence provided by Hydén and others as indicating that learning is accompanied by changes in DNA and/or RNA which will result in alteration of membrane proteins in certain nerve cells. Elul has addressed himself to the problem of how retrieval of information stored in this fashion might be accomplished. He bases his proposals upon his observation that the application of extraneous current will displace cells in tissue culture and calculations which indicate that comparable current densities occur during normal synaptic activity. During synaptic activity, the interaction of the electrical field with the polarized ionic layer adsorbed to the membranes of the synaptic region should increase the width of the synaptic cleft in excitatory synapses and narrow it in inhibitory synapses, according to this theory. The deformation of the cleft by the first pulse in a train of impulses would influence the flow of current and the diffusion of transmitter substance, thus modulating the amplitude of the postsynaptic potential. The postulated effects depend upon the affinity of the membrane surface for specific ionic groups, and the adsorption of particular polar groups. Changes in the protein covering of the surface of the subsynaptic membrane are considered likely to alter these effects. Thus, the postsynaptic potential will be of different amplitude than before learning, and the response of the postsynaptic neuron to input at that synapse will change. A number of experimental observations of altered neuronal reactivity which are difficult to explain in terms of changed transmitter mobilization or presynaptic hyperpolarization are adduced in support of these formulations. If the various assumptions of the argument were conceded, the net result of the proposed mechanism seems to be long-lasting facilitation or inhibition of a particular synaptic connection, which serves to store information about previous activity of that neural interface. Retrieval of the stored information represented by the changed excitability would seem to be rather indiscriminate since all subsequent presynaptic inputs to that junction will have altered effects independent of their origins. Also, no provision exists in the theory for decoding or readout of the neural discharge which takes place.

Briggs and Kitto (1962) have presented a number of objections to formulations involving the synthesis of specific proteins by specifically coded RNA. As mentioned earlier, they point out that, if these proteins are synthesized in a fashion determined by the new RNA sequence, cells will be continually bombarded by an input of foreign proteins. The reactions against such foreign proteins could be expected to disturb the regulatory functions of the cell severely, and they might well imperil the viability of the cell. Furthermore, many of the substances being produced by RNA are enzymes which are essential for the regulation of the cell. If the availability of these substances were endangered by modifications of the RNA responsible for their synthesis, this would become another threat to cell homeostasis. In view of these objections, Briggs and Kitto suggest an alternative formulation. They suggest that, as a cell becomes involved in the response to systematic stimulation during learning, the increased demands made on that cell for release of transmitter deplete the endogenous store of transmitter substance. This depletion, with the consequent change in gradients, is assumed to alter the precursor concentrations in such a fashion as to create a situation that is analogous to enzyme induction, in some ways similar to the Derepressor Hypothesis formulated previously. The consequences of altered concentrations of transmitter and precursor feeding back on the DNA in the nucleus inhibit repressor sites on the DNA and permit the synthesis of new RNA which will, in turn, make greater amounts of transmitter substance available.

This model offers an alternative to the representation of information by the unique specification of bases on a macromolecule. Among the deficiencies of this model are the fact that the hypothetical increase in the intensity of neural response lacks specificity. Synaptic inputs are not differentially facilitated. Furthermore, no mechanism is indicated which would be capable of sustaining the postulated inhibition of the repressor sites. In the terms defined earlier, the described feedback loop is homeo-

151

static rather than regenerative and will act only temporarily until the appropriate transmitter concentrations have been restored.

A rather similar enzyme induction hypothesis has been proposed by Smith (1962), who also suggests that the crucial event may be alteration of transmitter concentration. It should be noted that Elkes (1964) and Hechter and Halkerston (1964), have suggested that "recall" in neuronal memory might involve an immunological reaction of antibody with amine-coded protein. These workers suggest that patterns of biogenic amines, combining with a neuronal protein, might act as haptenes to form specific antigens that induce the formation of antibodies in certain kinds of neurons. When the "familiar" pattern of amines is later received at the synapse, a characteristic amine-protein is formed and recognized in an ultrafast reaction by antibody. The resulting reaction leads to firing of the cell. The theory of Szilard (1964) somewhat similarly suggests the induction of a specific memory "antibody" in certain neurons, with an increase in synaptic efficacy. Although these various theories will not be discussed further at this time, thoughtful consideration of their details may suggest experimental manipulations to the reader, by which they might be subjected to evaluation.

Although they differ in the details by which alteration of neuronal responsiveness to subsequent input is accomplished, these models share the assumption that the discharge of particular cells mediates the retrieval of stored information. Whether the postulated changes increase the intensity of neural discharge or merely heighten the excitability, it must be borne in mind that afferent impulses can reach presynaptic terminals of such cells under a variety of circumstances. Most of the models presented do not endow the cell with altered reactivity to some, but not all, inputs. Therefore, these cells can transmit efferent impulses to their axonal terminals under various conditions. How are those discharges which arise from spontaneous activity and from the action of inputs related to novel events to be distinguished from neural output due to retrieval of stored information? How is activity related to retrieval to be decoded into informationally significant readout? The proposed models do not offer any criterion by which such discrimination between various neural discharges is to be accomplished. Those models which provide specificity by unique RNA or protein configurations synthesized in specific nerve cells not only invoke mechanisms which are difficult to reconcile with current ideas about the synthesis of these substances, but also require recognition of particular temporal patterns of synaptic input by the coded molecules, a reaction for which no more evidence exists than for the model proposed herein.

Almost all of these models postulate that the retrieval of the stored information is basically mediated by the enhanced release of a transmitter substance. It therefore becomes necessary to ask what that transmitter might be. Intraventricular injection of massive amounts of acetylcholine, norepinephrine, epinephrine, dopamine, γ-aminobutyric acid or serotonin in conditioned cats failed to cause any marked effects on the performance of previously established approach or avoidance responses (John et al., 1958b). These substances include the most popular candidates for a role in central transmission. Injection of substances such as atropine, DFP, eserine, and iproniazid, which might be expected to alter the concentrations of some of these transmitter substances in brain also failed to disrupt performance of these learned responses.

It must be conceded that intraventricular injection of these substances may not be an effective route for altering their concentration inside the relevant nerve cells. It may be that they reach some regions of the brain, but that those regions are not the regions responsible for the deposition of memory. Altman and Chorover (1963) observed that after intraventricular injection, radionucleotides were restricted to a narrow periventricular band two to six mm. in width from the ventricular walls, suggesting that this route is a poor one for supplying the brain uniformly with various nucleotides. However, Snyder et al. (1965) report that tritiated norepinephrine introduced into the lateral ventricle appears to mix with endogenous norepinephrine, since its regional and subcellular distributions parallel those of the natural amine. These results suggest that the efficacy of the intraventricular route varies for different substances, and is quite adequate for norepinephrine, and possibly others. Bearing these qualifications in mind, it is nonetheless possible to see marked systemic changes, for example in autonomic responses, following the intraventricular injection of these substances. This indicates that these substances have clearly had extensive effects on neural tissue, and that for such effects, at least, intraventricular injection is an effective mode of introducing these materials.

A conclusive evaluation of the role of transmitter substances in this function must await evaluation of the effects of demonstrated alteration of transmitter concentrations inside central nervous system neurons which are widely distributed throughout the brain. However, the fact that an animal can perform conditioned responses while in seizure following intraventricular eserine injection makes it difficult to give much credence to the notion that a particular acetylcholine concentration is crucial for the performance of such responses. Until clear effects of altered transmitter availability on retrieval of stored information have been reported, the failure of the attempts made to date would seem to argue against formulations based on that premise.

The deterministic models discussed above do not afford insight into the organization of stimuli impinging on the organism, so that some stimuli are represented in memory, while others apparently have only a transient effect. They ignore the expansion and contraction of the number of structures mediating retrieval and performance which seems to occur during the life history of a memory. They also do not account for the protection of stored memories against subsequent overlay by other events which cause discharge of relevant neurons. This protection certainly must be provided somehow, since serial memories are not pooled to produce an average memory but are kept relatively distinct. These and other considerations make it difficult for the author to accept formulations which suggest that the storage of coded information is accomplished by mere modification of the efficacy of given synaptic transactions, and that retrieval depends upon the changed threshold or increased intensity of synaptic response. However, this skepticism is not shared by Eccles and others (e.g. Eccles, 1964, 1965; Konorski, 1948; Hebb, 1949), who have considered that plastic changes in the potency of synaptic transmission provide the most plausible neurological basis for learning.

Earlier in this chapter, the Derepressor Hypothesis was suggested in an attempt to provide a model which could be reconciled both with the data and with considerations such as those raised previously. Speculation along the lines sketched out in that section suffers from its own shortcomings. Although it accounts somewhat laboriously for many of the salient factors with which it must cope, it relies heavily upon the postulated, but not demonstrated, ability of the nervous system to discriminate between modes of activity in neural ensembles. Furthermore, it invokes the synthesis of new RNA as a result of derepression of DNA, in spite of the evidence that learning can occur while new RNA synthesis is prevented by actinomycin D.

A somewhat similar proposal has been put forward by Landauer (1964). This author suggests that the glial cells in the surround of active neurons release RNA, in accord with the evidence of Hydén and Egyházi (1962, 1963). Concurrently active neurons are assumed to establish a potential gradient resulting in electrophoretic migration of glial RNA into the simultaneously active neurons. This invasion is analogous to a viral RNA infection, which results in modification of the invaded neurons so as to produce proteins specified by the invading RNA. The newly synthesized protein is assumed to "tune" cellular membranes to a frequency-specific sensitivity corresponding to the temporal pattern of stimulation caused by the represented event. Although this model does not require the synthesis of new RNA configurations, it is not at all clear why the invading RNA should possess the capacity to accomplish the required specific neural tuning. Actually, the theory displaces the coding problem to the glial cell, but fails to propose a solution to it. This theory also relies heavily upon the ability of the nervous system to discriminate between temporal patterns of activity.

Robinson (1965) has constructed a model which has many attractive features, and which lacks most of the shortcomings of the formulations discussed thus far. The uniqueness and logical adequacy of this theory make it desirable to examine in some detail. A number of steps are postulated to be involved in the information storage process. (1) Afferent input to a neural region is assumed to activate a group of neurons so that they fire "together," that is, within a short time interval of each other. This neural group includes some so-called pattern neurons, whose joint activity is to be recorded in memory. (2) Pattern neurons contain reservoirs of pattern molecules. All the pattern molecules in a given pattern neuron are the same and differ from those in any other pattern neuron. Thus, the pattern molecule is the "signature" of the pattern neuron. (3) Whenever a pattern neuron fires, it releases a burst of pattern molecules, which diffuse in the extracellular space to the nearby locus of a hypothetical "open" storage unit, perhaps a glial cell. (4) The open storage unit incorporates all the pattern molecules which appear within a short interval of time. If the concentration of these pattern molecules is insufficient, no consequences ensue and they are dissipated. However, if the concentration of pattern molecules exceeds a critical threshold, the storage unit "closes" and no further pattern molecules can enter. Thus,

155

the storage unit contains a sample of pattern molecules from all the nearby pattern neurons set into sustained activity by the original stimulus input. (5) During the closed period, the storage unit produces sets of pattern co-molecules, each of which is complementary to an incorporated pattern molecule. All pattern co-molecules within a set are identical and can react only with the unique pattern molecules to which they are complementary. At this stage, the recording of memory is assumed to have been completed and the recorded storage unit now reopens. Although pattern molecules can again enter the storage unit no new types of co-molecules will be synthesized in it.

Retrieval of the stored information proceeds as follows: (1) Subsequent neural activity releases pattern molecules from the pattern neurons in the regions which are activated. These pattern molecules diffuse through the extraneuronal space to the storage units in the vicinity. (2) Entry of pattern molecules into a recorded storage unit has no effect unless a sufficient number which are complementary to the pattern co-molecules confined within the storage unit impinge on that cell within a short interval. If the concentration of such complementary pattern molecules is sufficient, the storage unit is triggered. Thus, triggering occurs if a nonrandom level of coincidence is achieved in the sustained activity of the set of pattern neurons, adequately approximating the configuration of neural events which accomplished the closing of the storage unit during the recorded experience. (3) When triggered, the storage unit releases a burst of pattern co-molecules, which diffuse throughout the region and penetrate the pattern neurons which they encounter. If the penetrated pattern neuron contains pattern molecules which are complementary to the entering pattern co-molecule, a "recognition" reaction occurs, and the neuron discharges. Thus, triggering a storage unit leads to recurrence of the neural activity which was initially recorded, and constitutes retrieval.

At the same time, decoding of the retrieved information can be considered to have occurred. Nonrandom activity or information arising in the neural network because of some input event involves a set of pattern neurons in shared activity. The resulting diffusion of pattern molecules into the environment constitutes an interrogation of the regional storage units: Has this constellation of pattern neurons been associated in sustained activity before. Triggering of recorded storage units and the back-diffusion of pattern co-molecules causes the corresponding pattern neurons to fire again: The information represented by the set of pattern neurons which now discharge was previously stored.

The model just described possesses numerous advantages and interesting features. It does not require direct discrimination between different temporal patterns of activity in a tuned network; it does not localize memory to discrete pathways between particular cells; it does not depend on increased availability of transmitter substance; it does not code information as base sequences on instructed molecules which are tuned to particular temporal patterns of stimulation; and it does not imply a deterministic mode of action. It is a probabilistic mechanism. While it is not vulnerable to many of the criticisms leveled against the other formulations presented in this chapter, it is based upon the postulated existence of pattern neurons, pattern molecules, storage units, pattern co-molecules, and a number of interactions between these components, none of which has been demonstrated. Yet none of the requirements seems utterly contrary to known processes. The model possesses a reasonable amount of plausibility. The comparator mechanism asserted as necessary earlier in this chapter becomes, in this formulation, a comparison between the input to pattern neurons and the output from storage units in the same region, registered on the pattern neurons themselves. Note also that triggering of a storage unit by activation of some partial subset of pattern neurons, under certain conditions, may result in reproduction of a configuration of neural activity corresponding to a particular stimulus, in the absence of that stimulus. A particularly interesting feature of this formulation is that the pattern neurons in a region should display different responses to novel and familiar stimuli. Novel stimuli should cause a single burst of response in activated pattern neurons, constituting the "interrogation pulse." Familiar stimuli should cause a double burst of response in activated pattern neurons, corresponding to the interrogation pulse and the "retrieval pulse." Electrophysiological phenomena have been observed which can be reconciled with these requirements, and will be presented in later chapters of this book. Although such observations do not confirm the theory, they lend it somewhat more plausibility.

None of the theories that have been outlined can be accepted as satisfactory. Many reservations can be expressed against all of them, some of which have been discussed. Undoubtedly, the reader can think of many more. The reader may even object to effort he considers ill-spent on the serious consideration of theories which seem to him premature, based on *ad hoc* arguments and invoking unknown processes, and which can at best be reconciled with only a portion of the factual and logical constraints. Yet, the formulations which have been presented provide a reasonable survey of the present state of theory in this field. Certain salient features of these theories can be discerned. They can be categorized into classes with respect to their basic assumptions about storage, retrieval, and readout processes. As we turn to the evaluation of other evidence on information storage mechanisms from electrophysiological studies, it may become possible to judge whether certain classes of theory seem more compatible with such data than do others. Hopefully, such analysis at this time may help us to focus on the avenues which lead to clearer formulations, subject to definable experimental tests.

The material which has thus far been presented summarizes the bulk of the presently available neurochemical data and theory bearing upon mechanisms of information storage and retrieval in the nervous system. On the basis of these considerations it seems appropriate to propose that the mechanism of memory may involve the specification of statistical processes in neural populations, which achieve a unique temporal patterning of the deviation from random or baseline activity. Further understanding of these processes requires study of the results of ablation and electrophysiological investigations, which will be presented in the second part of this book.

CHAPTER VIII

THE STATISTICAL APPROACH: (1) HEBB AND CONTIGUITY

A. The ablation method

The method of ablation has been the traditional technique used by those who wish to correlate brain structure with function. The reports of ablation studies have been voluminous, and a detailed review of this literature is beyond the scope of this book. The interested reader is referred to the review article by Diamond and Chow (1962) in Volume 4 of "Psychology, A Study of a Science," edited by Koch, which provides an excellent general survey. The fundamental assumption underlying most ablation studies is that regional differences in the anatomical and histological characteristics of the central nervous system imply the mediation of distinct functions by these regions. This concept of the localization of function is derived from a "trait" psychology which pays little attention to the detailed processes by which behaviors are accomplished. The assumption that particular neural structures are uniquely responsible for specific elements of behavior is not logically dictated. This interpretation is well exemplified in a comment by Tizzard (1959), who says, "A lesion x presents symptom y. This represents damage to the psychological trait z which must be located at x." The position described is analogous to the assertion that two people engaged in a telephone conversation are localized in a piece of wire which disrupts that conversation when it is cut. The appearance of a deficit in learned response after a brain lesion sim-

159

ply warrants the conclusion that the damaged region also participates in the mediation of some function necessary for successful performance. This hardly constitutes evidence for exclusive localization of a necessary function in the structure, or for the conclusive localization of the *memory* of the learning experiences which established the behavior. Even if one were to concede that evidence compelled the localization of crucial stores of information about certain specific experiences within a particular structure, this would still not suffice to conclude that the memory was deterministically represented in certain cells, whose firing constituted retrieval of the stored information.

More sophisticated examples of this position exist in the current literature. It may be worthwhile to refer to a recent theoretical work, "A Model of the Brain," by J. Z. Young (1964). After acknowledging that the storage of information *may* be based upon the maintenance of particular discharge patterns. Professor Young chooses to assume that coding depends upon the initiation of action in distinct neural pathways, selected by restrictions on connectivity resulting from anatomical and physiological properties. Coding depends upon isomorphism between stimulus and responsive structure. Professor Young goes on to suggest that memory is a characteristic of the network itself, primarily based upon the geometrical locus of dendrites. The connections which constitute a memory are assumed to be widely distributed and thus resistant to lesions. Synaptic changes are proposed as the mechanism which opens or closes pathways, possibly dependent upon changes in synaptic volume. Finally, the reduction of redundancy in alternate pathways by inhibition is proposed as the fundamental process in learning (pp. 267–285).

Observation of the actual behavior of an animal engaged in performance of a well-practiced conditioned response provides intuitive contradiction of the notion that the memory of the response is localized in a discrete mediating region. If such an animal is repeatedly challenged to perform a response, such as lever-pressing on presentation of a test stimulus, many *varieties* of response can be observed. The lever will at first always be pressed with a particular forepaw, say the right forepaw. After a while, the animal will switch to the left forepaw. Later, he may press with his chin or his shoulder. If the session is sufficiently tedious, he may even lie on his back under the lever and reach up to press it. This variety of response forms must involve neural populations which differ greatly. The mediating pathways cannot be identical. There can be no single specific output region to which the afferent input from the CS gains access. These responses are functionally equivalent, but one cannot reasonably insist that they involve the same identical set of neurons. At the same time, it must be pointed out that Miller (1959)' has suggested the possibility that this flexibility of behavior is achieved by a cybernetic control mechanism involving specific connections. This possibility must be acknowledged.

B. Mass action and equipotentiality

In spite of these logical limitations, which have been discussed more completely by Chow and Hutt in their paper on the association cortex (1953), the ablation technique has provided a number of important conclusions about the mechanisms involved in memory. Lashley summarizes these in his paper "In Search of the Engram" (Lashley, 1950). First of all, the hypothesis that learning involved the establishment of connections between sensory and motor areas of the cortex was refuted by experiments which showed little or no deficit in the acquisition or retention of learned responses in animals which had received lesions separating sensory regions from motor regions, or even after extensive removal of motor cortex.

Second, much of the vast literature on the effects of lesions and ablations reports little or no deficit in learned behaviors after localized brain damage, provided that primary sensory receiving areas were spared. Much of the literature that reports deficit after damage also describes the gradual restitution of function as time elapses after the damage occurs. Often, this restitution of function occurs without the necessity of retraining. Brain regions undoubtedly exist that are crucial for certain functions, particularly those dynamic regulatory processes that involve homeostatic mechanisms. For example, there can be little doubt that lateral and medial hypothalamic areas are essentially involved in the regulation of food intake. Again, the fact that some functions appear to be structurally localized does not warrant the conclusion that similar regional localization holds for all functions, nor that information storage requires deterministic mediation by discharge of specific neurons in certain regions.

Third, interpretation of that portion of the literature which reports clear-cut deficits in performance of learned behaviors following brain

161

lesions raises the necessity of distinguishing between many possible contributing factors. Failure to perform a previously established response or to acquire a new response after a brain lesion may be due to interference with sensory input, interference with motor coordination, deficits in motivation, interruption of transmission lines conveying stored information between brain regions, disruption of the process of information storage, blockade of information retrieval, or interference with the set to perform a response.

Lashley's research led him to conclude that performance of conditioned reflexes was dependent upon the sensory areas and upon no other part of the cerebral cortex. In a series of well-known experiments, Lashley showed that rats could retain a pattern discrimination if as little as one-sixtieth of the visual cortex were spared (1950). This small preserved percentage of tissue might be anywhere within the boundaries of visual cortex. The response seemed independent of the particular sensory nerve fibers or any specific part of the cortical receiving area. The various parts of this region seemed to be functionally equivalent with respect to their capacity to mediate a habit based upon a visual discrimination. The generalization that neither required afferent nor efferent pathways are fixed by habit is often referred to as the Law of Equipotentiality.

These conclusions referred particularly to habits requiring an association between a specific sensory stimulus and a motor response. With other types of learning, the deficits observed after cerebral destruction were approximately proportional to the amount of tissue destroyed. The loss was independent of the locus of the destruction, provided that the damage to both hemispheres was comparable. This rough quantitative relationship led to the formulation of the so-called Theory of Mass Action. This formulation states that the activities of any part of the cortex in the acquisition, retention, and performance of more complex integrative functions are conditioned by the activities of all other parts (Lashley, 1931, 1933).

These conclusions have been questioned by some workers on the basis that Lashley used rather complex situations in which animals probably utilized a variety of cues so that multiple sources of information were available. Furthermore, the argument neglects possible replication of circuits in various brain regions, each involving specific connections. In recent work, Gross et al. (1965a) have suggested that some of the evidence adduced by Lashley in support of the Hypothesis of Mass Action may be partially due to encroachment upon an anterior region critical for alternation behavior and a posterior region critical for visually guided behavior. In these studies, it was found that alternation behavior was impaired by lesions of the caudate nucleus, hippocampus, anterior cortex, or dorsomedial regions of the thalamus, while Hebb-Williams maze performance was impaired by lesions of posterior cortex, lateral geniculate bodies, or the medial thalamus. Interestingly, these authors pointed out the fact that lesions of similar location and size made by dissimilar methods may exert different effects. It is noteworthy that they concluded that their results could not be accounted for in terms of memory deficit, but were relatively nonspecific. Whether or not one accepts the proposed explanation for the data compiled by Lashley, this study does not provide evidence for localization of memory in any of the lesioned structures. Rather, particular structures are suggested to mediate generic types of behavior. Perhaps it should be reiterated that although the argument constructed herein does not decisively rule out mechanisms based upon replication of parallel deterministic circuits in various brain regions, neither does the available evidence prove that such connectionistic mechanisms actually operate.

C. The expansion of representational systems

Perhaps more important than the Law of Equipotentiality is the inference therefrom that the organization of the system mediating pattern discrimination must be diffuse and ultimately involve the bulk of the cells in the visual system. Although a small group of cells might conceivably mediate the initial reactions to the patterned stimulation, the effects of experience upon these cells must somehow be reduplicated in numerous other regions and ultimately spread so extensively throughout the structure that any group of cells of adequate size can mediate the discrimination. The experimental literature contains numerous examples of the spread of mediating processes through the nervous system with time. For instance, Chow and Survise (1958) showed that bilateral temporal lobe lesions produced severe deficiencies in pattern discrimination if inflicted as soon as criterion performance was achieved, but did not produce deficiencies if inflicted after overtraining. Hunt and Diamond (1957) showed deficits in conditioned avoidance responses to

163

auditory stimuli if bilateral hippocampal resections were performed as soon as criterion performance was achieved, but not if overtraining was carried out prior to surgery. Flexner *et al.* (1963) observed that bilateral puromycin injection into hippocampal regions blocked retention of a recently acquired maze habit, but had no effect after 6 days, although injection into other regions was still effective.

These data indicate that the memory function is not localized to a particular area of the brain, but that mediation by anatomical regions shifts during time. These phenomena may well reflect the gradual recruitment of neurons in regions relatively remote from those initially responsive to afferent stimulation during a particular experience, and the slow spread of participation in the representational process into additional regions as consolidation proceeds and as the learning experience is repeated. Gradually, such recruitment might engage neurons in widespread areas.

D. The structural trace

However, in addition to providing evidence of extensive and diffuse participation of brain regions in learning, lesion studies have focused attention upon the necessity to devise techniques for the study of the detailed processes by which learned behaviors are established and subsequently mediated. A number of workers have speculated upon the nature of the physiological mechanisms logically required for the performance of learned responses on the basis of the psychological data obtained from studies of this sort. Some of these formulations, notably those of Hebb and Lashley, are so relevant to the line of argument which will be advanced in later portions of this book that it seems preferable to quote extensively from the most relevant portions of their writings, rather than to attempt to paraphrase their arguments. The first passages to which I wish to refer are to be found in the superb book by D. O. Hebb, "The Organization of Behavior" (1949, pp. 12–16).

> The assumption we must accept is that the memory trace, the basis of learning, is in some way structural and static; and the difficulties in the way of making the assumption are mainly in the facts of perceptual generalization that have been emphasized by Gestalt psychologists (Koffka, 1935; Köhler, 1929, 1940; and Lashley, 1938, 1942). The problem raised by these writers is crucial and must be disposed of before we touch anything else.

Lashley has concluded that a learned discrimination is not based on the excitation of any particular neural cells. It is supposed to be determined solely by the pattern, or shape, of the sensory excitation. Köhler, also stressing the apparent fact that the pattern and not the locus of stimulation is the important thing, has developed a theory of electrical fields in the brain which control cerebral action. Like Lashley, he explicitly denies that the same cells need be excited to arouse the same perception.

This suggests that the mnemonic trace, the neural change that is induced by experience and constitutes 'memory,' is not a change of structure. Other facts, at the same time, are an even stronger argument that it *must* be structural. A structural trace, as we shall see in a moment, must be assumed; but when we do so we have to find some way of fitting in the facts of perception.

If it is really unimportant in what tissue a sensory excitation takes place, one finds it hard to understand how repeated sensations can reinforce one another, with the lasting effect we call learning or memory. It might be supposed that the mnemonic trace is a lasting pattern of reverberatory activity without fixed locus, like some cloud formations or an eddy in a millpond. But if so it seems that the multitudinous traces in the small confines of the cerebral cortex would interfere with one another, producing a much greater distortion of earlier memories by later ones than actually occurs.

Moreover, violent cortical storms can occur (as in *grand mal* epilepsy or cerebral concussion) without a detectable effect on earlier memories. That the trace should be purely 'dynamic'—a pattern of activity not dependent on structural changes for its permanence—thus seems in the highest degree unlikely. No one has explicitly made such an assumption; yet how otherwise are the known properties of a learned discrimination to be accounted for, with its inevitable tendency to be generalized beyond what has already been experienced by the animal—its apparent independence of excitation in specific cells?

In addition to the facts of perceptual generalization, two other forms of evidence might make it difficult to postulate a structural trace as the basis of memory. One is from Lashley's (1929b) extirpation experiments, showing that the removal of blocks of the rat's cerebral cortex does not affect habits selectively. If one habit is affected, others are also. From this, Lashley has concluded that memory traces are not localized in the cerebral cortex, but himself has pointed out (Lashley, 1929a) another possible interpretation. His evidence is consistent with the idea that the trace is structural but diffuse, involving, that is, a large number of cells widely spaced in the cortex, physiologically but not anatomically unified. This is not, consequently, crucial evidence for or against the notion of structural traces in the cortex.

The other evidence that seemed once to prevent postulating a structural trace is found in the work of Wulf (cited by Koffka, 1935) and later investigators who have interpreted their studies of human memory for patterns to mean that the trace is spontaneously active, and does not lie dormant or merely deteriorate with the passage of time. Hanawalt (1937), however, effectively criticized the earlier evidence for this idea; and Hebb and Foord (1945), having obtained data inconsistent with Wulf's hypothesis, re-examined the later work that managed to avoid Hanawalt's criticism.

165

They have shown that there is no evidence to even faintly support the idea of slow, spontaneous changes in the trace. This conception must be abandoned.

Thus the only barrier to assuming that a structural change in specific neural cells is the basis of memory lies in the generalization of the perception of patterns. Man sees a square as a square, whatever its size, and in almost any setting. A rat trained to look for food behind a horizontal rectangle will thereafter choose almost *any* horizontal figure, such as an interrupted line or a pair of circles side by side. Trained to choose a solid upright triangle and to avoid an inverted triangle, he will discriminate consistently between outlines of triangles; triangles with confusing figures added (such as circumscribing circles); and triangles of different size, which cannot thus excite the same retinal cells simultaneously (Lashley, 1938). Rats reared in darkness, then trained in the same way, show the same perceptual generalizations (Hebb, 1937).

These are concrete, undisputed facts of behavior. They have been interpreted as meaning that perception is independent of the locus of excitation; and this interpretation has been tacitly accepted as inescapable. The result is an awkward dilemma for theory, since, as we have seen, it is hard to reconcile an unlocalized afferent process with a structural (and hence localized) mnemonic trace.

Lashley's (1942) hypothesis of interference patterns is the one explicit attempt to solve this difficulty and to deal adequately with both perception and learning. As such it deserves special mention here, although we shall see that in other respects it faces great difficulties.

Other writers have had to choose one horn of the dilemma. Köhler (1940), for example, starts out with the facts of perceptual generalization, in his theory of cerebral fields of force, and then cannot deal with learning. He has no apparent way of avoiding a fatal difficulty about the nature of the trace, its locus and structure. This is another aspect of the difficulty for Gestalt theory raised by Boring (1933), who pointed out that at *some* point the perceptual process must act on specific cells in order to determine a specific response.

The theory elaborated by Hull (1943), on the other hand, is to be regarded as providing first of all for the stability of learning. It then has persistent difficulty with perception. The principle of 'afferent neural interaction' appears to be a concession extorted by the facts of perceptual generalization. With this, there is some danger that the entire system may lose its meaning. The great value of Hull's theory is in showing how one may conceive of variable behavior as determined by constant causal relationships between stimulus, intervening variables, and response. This is brilliantly achieved, for an important segment of behavior. But then the postulate of afferent neural interaction adds that anything may happen when two sensory events occur at the same time—which of course they are always doing. Evidently no prediction is possible until the limits, and the determinants, of afferent neural interaction can be given in detail. This it seems demands that the neurological reference, already present in the theory, be made explicit, and detailed. For our present purposes, at any rate,

Hull must be regarded as not yet having solved the problem of dealing with the perceptual process in a theory of learning, although it remains possible that his program (Hull, 1945) will do so in the future.

E. The mode of attack

How are we to provide for perceptual generalization *and* the stability of memory, in terms of what the neuron does and what happens at the synapse? We must suppose that the mnemonic trace is a structural change; the difficulty, in supposing it, is a conflict with the idea that only the pattern, and not the locus of sensory stimulation is important in perception; so let us begin by asking whether that idea is, after all, securely established.

The fundamental problems with which Hebb was concerned in the passages just quoted are closely related to questions and theoretical formulations presented in earlier chapters of this book. The central question under analysis is whether the trace of a memory is a structural change in a particular neural cell or set of cells, which must discharge when remembering takes place. Hebb argues against the contention by Lashley and others that the same cells need not be excited in order to arouse the same perception. How, he asks, can repeated sensations reinforce one another to cause learning, if it is not important what neural tissue responds to each sensation?

This objection is based on an incremental model of learning. Yet we know that learning can occur in one trial. This suggests that the underlying neural processes may involve threshold mechanisms which must be exceeded for storage to occur. The model of the consolidation process presented in Chapters II and III suggested that those cells which could achieve a critical shift K in the concentration of a critical substance as a result of sustained response to a particular afferent stimulus would thereby undergo a change in state. The postulated change in state was subsequently mediated by a chemical feedback system, and altered the reactivity of the cell to certain temporal patterns of afferent input. For the set of cells undergoing a change of state after a particular event took place, learning was incremental during the accumulation of the concentration shift leading to the nonincremental change in state. Performance might or might not be altered by the change in state after the first sensation of that specific event. On repetitions of that event, additional responsive neural sets will presumably achieve the change in state resulting during consolidation. Variations in the over-all stimulus complex and local excitabilities will cause variation in the reliability with which stabilized sets of loops respond to the event with a characteristic mode of oscillation. Gradually, this increased system reliability will cause increase in the probability of a given performance. In this view, repeated sensations do not lead to learning by incremental effects upon certain cells which gradually acquire a new structural relationship. Rather, learning is a nonincremental change in a subset of cells responsive to an event with sufficiently sustained reverberation, and performance appears when the size of this subset becomes sufficiently large to constitute a significant portion of the population.

Hebb argues, in this and later passages, against the representation of a trace as a lasting reverberation. He dismisses the failure of extirpation experiments to provide evidence for a structurally localized trace by invoking the suggestion that traces are structural but diffuse and constitute a physiological but not an anatomical unit. He poses the facts of perceptual generalization as the major obstacle to acceptance of a structural basis for memory, because those facts suggest that the interaction of present and past experience must be independent of the excitation of specific cells.

Yet the basis of the trace can be structural without requiring the deterministic excitation of specific cells to retrieve particular memories. The facts of consolidation support the conclusion that a durable change must take place. Presumably this change is in the matter of which nerve cells are composed, and therefore is a structural change. Whether or not that structural change is an actual growth of new synaptic junctions, as Hebb suggests, or a membranal change tuning the cell to respond more reliably to a particular frequency or pattern of afferent input, as suggested above, is not the central question. The fundamental question, recognized by Hebb, is: Does the discharge of a particular set of cells stand for one memory, while the discharge of a different set of cells stands for another memory; or does the emergence of a particular organized temporal pattern of activity in a population of cells stand for a specific memory, no matter which cells are momentarily active? Is memory the tendency for specific cells belonging to a given representational set to discharge deterministically under specific conditions, or is it the tendency for a population of neurons to display certain statistical

168

processes? In one view, information is represented by the locus of the active neurons. In the other view, the same set of neurons might represent two or more events, by different temporal patterns of activity.

In retrospect, the facts of generalization do not seem to provide an adequate basis for decision about this problem. The configuration of stimuli comprising a particular perceptual experience can be conceptualized as a set of discrete values assigned to a number of descriptive parameters that define the dimensions of which the perception might be composed. Presumably these various parameters define substimuli which constitute the effective afferent input to different neural regions. In each of these regions, consolidation processes construct the corresponding portions of a representational system. Other stimuli more or less overlap with a given stimulus in terms of the values for each relevant parameter. To the extent that the values of specific parameters correspond for two different stimulus configurations, they possess comparable ability to provide similar afferent input to some neural regions. This similar input might activate the portion of a representational system within that region, either by activating specific cells or by generating specific modes of activity. Generalization behavior may occur when the overlap between the parameter values for two stimuli is sufficient to achieve such activation for a critical proportion of the total system representing one of the stimuli. To this author, no irreconcilable contradiction is posed by the phenomena of generalization, and either of the alternatives under discussion may be acceptable.

F. Growth of the cell assembly

A second relevant passage entitled *"Growth of the Assembly"* from Hebb's book follows (1949, pp. 60–74):

> . . . It is proposed first that a repeated stimulation of specific receptors will lead slowly to the formation of an 'assembly' of association-area cells which can act briefly as a closed system after stimulation has ceased; this prolongs the time during which the structural changes of learning can occur and constitutes the simplest instance of a representative process (image or idea). The way in which this cell-assembly might be established, and its characteristics, are the subject matter of the present chapter. In the following chapter the interrelationships between cell assemblies are dealt with; these are the basis of temporal organization in central processes (attention, attitude, thought, etc.). . . .

The first step in this neural schematizing is a bald assumption about the structural changes that make lasting memory possible. The assumption has repeatedly been made before, in one way or another, and repeatedly found unsatisfactory by the critics of learning theory. I believe it is still necessary. As a result, I must show that in another context, of added anatomical and physiological knowledge, it becomes more defensible and more fertile than in the past.

The assumption, in brief, is that a growth process accompanying synaptic activity makes the synapse more readily traversed. This hypothesis of synaptic resistances, however, is different from earlier ones in the following respects:

1. structural connections are postulated between single cells, but single cells are not effective units of transmission and such connections would be only one factor determining the direction of transmission;

2. no direct sensori-motor connections are supposed to be established in this way, in the adult animal; and

3. an intimate relationship is postulated between reverberatory action and structural changes at the synapse, implying a dual trace mechanism.

G. The possibility of a dual trace mechanism

Hilgard and Marquis (1940) have shown how a reverberatory, transient trace mechanism might be proposed on the basis of Lorente de Nó's conclusions, that a cell is fired only by the simultaneous activity of two or more afferent fibers, and that internuncial fibers are arranged in closed (potentially self-exciting) circuits. Their diagram is arranged to show how a reverberatory circuit might establish a sensori-motor connection between receptor cells and the effectors which carry out a conditioned response. There is of course a good deal of psychological evidence which is opposed to such an oversimplified hypothesis, and Hilgard and Marquis do not put weight on it. At the same time, it is important to see that something of the kind is not merely a possible but a necessary inference from certain neurological ideas. To the extent that anatomical and physiological observations establish the possibility of reverberatory after-effects of a sensory event, it is established that such a process would be the physiological basis of a transient 'memory' of the stimulus. There may, then, be a memory trace that is wholly a function of a pattern of neural activity, independent of any structural change.

Hilgard and Marquis go on to point out that such a trace would be unstable. A reverberatory activity would be subject to the development of refractory states in the cells of the circuit in which it occurs, and external events could readily interrupt it. We have already seen . . . that an 'activity' trace can hardly account for the permanence of early learning, but at the same time one may regard reverberatory activity as the explanation of other phenomena.

There are memories which are instantaneously established, and as evanescent as they are immediate. In the repetition of digits, for example, an interval of a few seconds is enough to prevent any interference from one series on the next. Also, some memories are both instantaneously established and permanent. To account for the permanence, some structural change seems necessary, but a structural growth presumably would require an appreciable time. If some way can be found of supposing that a reverberatory trace might cooperate with the structural change, and *carry the memory until the growth change is made,* we should be able to recognize the theoretical value of the trace which is an activity only, without having to ascribe all memory to it. The conception of the transient, unstable reverberatory trace is therefore useful, if it is possible to suppose also that some more permanent structural change reinforces it. There is no reason to think that a choice must be made between the two conceptions; there may be traces of both kinds, and memories which are dependent on both.

H. A neurophysiological postulate

Let us assume then that the persistence or repetition of a reverberatory activity (or 'trace') tends to induce lasting cellular changes that add to stability. The assumption can be precisely stated as follows: *When an axon of cell A is near enough to excite cell B and repeatedly or persistently takes part in firing it, some growth process or metabolic change takes place in one or both cells such that A's efficiency, as one of the cells firing B, is increased.*

The most obvious and I believe much the most probable suggestion concerning the way in which one cell could become more capable of firing another is that synaptic knobs develop and increase the area of contact between the afferent axon and efferent soma. . . . There is certainly *no direct evidence that this is so, and the postulated change if it exists may be metabolic, affecting cellular rhythmicity and limen* (italics, E. R. John); or there might be both metabolic and structural changes, including a limited neurobiotaxis. There are several considerations, however, that make the growth of synaptic knobs a plausible conception. The assumption stated above can be put more definitely, as follows:

When one cell repeatedly assists in firing another, the axon of the first cell develops synaptic knobs (or enlarges them if they already exist) in contact with the soma of the second cell. This seems to me the most likely mechanism of a lasting effect of reverberatory action, but I wish to make it clear that the subsequent discussion depends only on the more generally stated proposition italicized above.

. . . The changed facilitation that constitutes learning might occur in other ways without affecting the rest of the theory. To make it more specific, I have chosen to assume that the growth of synaptic knobs, with or without neurobiotaxis, is the basis of the change of facilitation from one cell on another, and this is not altogether implausible. It has been demonstrated by Arvanitaki (1942) that a contiguity alone will permit the excitation aroused in one cell to be transmitted to another. There are also earlier experiments, reviewed by Arvanitaki, with the same implication. Even more important, perhaps, is Erlanger's (1939) demonstration of impulse transmission across an artificial 'synapse,' a blocked segment of nerve more than a millimeter in extent. Consequently, in the intact nervous system, an axon that passes close to the dendrites or body of a second cell would be capable of *helping* to fire it, when the second cell is also exposed to other stimulation at the same point. The probability that such closely timed coincidental excitations would occur is not considered for the moment but will be returned to. When the coincidence does occur, and the active fiber, which is merely close to the soma of another cell, adds to a local excitation in it, I assume that the joint action tends to produce a thickening of the fiber—forming a synaptic knob—or adds to a thickening already present. [The next relevant passage begins on p. 69.]

I. Mode of perceptual integration: the cell assembly

In the last chapter it was shown that there are important properties of perception which cannot be ascribed to events in area 17, and that these are properties which seem particularly dependent on learning. That 'identity' is not due to what happens in 17 is strongly implied by the distortions that occur in the projection of a retinal excitation to the cortex. . . . Perception must depend on other structures besides area 17.

But we now find, at the level of area 18 and beyond, that all topographical organization in the visual process seems to have disappeared. All that is left is activity in an irregular arrangement of cells, which are intertangled with others that have nothing to do with the perception of the moment. We know of course that perception of simple objects is unified and determinate, a well-organized process. What basis can be found for an integration of action, in cells that are anatomically so disorganized?

An answer to this question is provided by the structural change at the synapse which has been assumed to take place in learning. The answer is not simple; perceptual integration would not be accomplished directly, but only as a slow development, and, for the purposes of exposition, at least, would involve several distinct stages, with the first of which we shall now be concerned.

The general idea is an old one, that any two cells or systems of cells that are repeatedly active at the same time will tend to become 'associated,' so that activity in one facilitates activity in the other. The details of speculation that follow are intended to show how this old idea migh be put to work again, with the equally old idea of a lowered synaptic 'resistance,' under the eye of a different neurophysiology from that which engendered them. . . .

The fundamental meaning of the assumption of growth at the synapse is in the effect this would have on the timing of action by the efferent cell. The increased area of contact means that firing by the efferent cell is more likely to follow the lead of the afferent cell. A fiber of order n thus gains increased control of a fiber $n + 1$, making the firing of $n + 1$ more predictable or determinate. The control cannot be absolute, but 'optional' (Lorente de Nó, 1939), and depends also on other events in the system. In the present case, however, the massive excitation in 17 would tend to establish constant conditions throughout the system during the brief period of a single visual fixation; and the postulated synaptic changes would also increase the degree of this constancy. . . .

It is, however, misleading to put emphasis on the coincidences necessary for the occurrence of such a simple closed circuit. Instead of a ring or hoop, the best analogy to the sort of structure which would be set up or 'assembled' is a closed solid cage-work, or three-dimensional lattice, with no regular structure, and with connections possible from any one intersection to any other. Let me say explicitly, again, that the specificity of such an assembly of cells in 18 or 20, to a particular excitation in 17, depends on convergences. Whenever two cells, directly or indirectly controlled by that excitation, converge on another cell, the essential condition of the present schematizing is fulfilled; the two converging cells need not have any simple anatomical or physiological relation to one another, and physiological integration would not be supposed to consist of independent closed chains.

. . . The sort of irregular three-dimensional net which might be the anatomical basis of perceptual integration in the association areas would be infinitely more complex than anything one could show with a diagram and would provide a large number of the multiple parallel (or alternate) units which are suggested . . . If so, an indefinite reverberation in the structure might be possible, so long as the background activity in other cells in the same gross region remained the same. It would not of course remain the same for long, especially with changes in visual fixation; but such considerations make it possible to conceive of 'alternating' reverberation which might frequently last for periods of time as great as half a second or a second. . . .

This then is the cell-assembly. Some of its characteristics have been defined only by implication, and these are to be developed elsewhere, particularly in the remainder of this chapter . . . The assembly is thought of as a system inherently involving some equipotentiality, in the presence of alternate pathways each having the same function, so that brain damage might remove some pathways without preventing the system from functioning, particularly if the system has been long established, with well-developed synaptic knobs which decrease the number of fibers that must be active at once to traverse a synapse.

J. Statistical considerations

It must have appeared to the reader who examined figures 8 and 9 carefully that there was something unlikely about it being arranged at the Creation to have such neat connections exactly where they were most needed for my hypothesis of perceptual integration. The answer of course is statistical: the neurons diagrammed were those which happen to have such connections, and, given a large enough population of connecting fibers distributed at random, the improbable connection must become quite frequent, in absolute numbers. . . .

The diagrams and discussion of the preceding section require the frequent existence of two kinds of coincidence: (1) synchronization of firing in two or more converging axons, and (2) the anatomical fact of convergence in fibers which are, so far as we know, arranged at random. . . .

It is not necessary, and not possible, to define the cell-assembly underlying a perception as being made up of neurons all of which are active when the proper visual stimulation occurs. One can suppose that there would always be activity in some of the group of elements which are in functional parallel: . . . When for example excitation can be conducted to a particular point in the system from five different directions, the activity characteristic of the system as a whole might be maintained by excitation in any three of the five pathways, and no one fiber would have to be synchronized with any other one fiber.

There would still be some necessity of synchronization, and this has another aspect. In the integration which has been hypothesized, depending on the development of synaptic knobs and an increasing probability of control by afferent over efferent fibers, there would necessarily be a gradual change of the frequency characteristics of the system. The consequence would be a sort of fractionation in recruitment, and some change in the neurons making up the system. That is, some units, capable at first of synchronizing with others in the system, would no longer be able to do so and would drop out: 'fractionation.' Others, at first incompatible, would be recruited. *With perceptual development there would thus be a slow growth in the assembly,* understanding by 'growth' not necessarily an increase in the number of constituent cells, but a change. How great the change would be there is no way of telling, but it is a change that may have importance for psychological problems when some of the phenomena of association are considered.

This then is the statistical approach to the problem. It is directly implied that an 'association' of two cells in the same region, or of two systems of cells, would vary, in the probability of its occurrence, over a wide range. If one chose such pairs at random one would find some between which no association was possible, some in which association was promptly and easily established when the two were simultaneously active, and a large proportion making up a gradation from one of these extremes to the other. The larger the system with a determinate general pattern of action, the more readily an association could be formed with another system. On a statistical basis, the more points at which a chance anatomical convergence could occur, the greater the frequency of effective interfacilitation between the two assemblies. [The next passage begins on p. 95.]

K. The development of superordinate perceptions

We can now turn to the question of an integration of the several parts of the figure into a distinctive whole, as contrasted with the amorphous whole that is perceived in first vision.

The most direct way of accounting for the superordinate integration is as follows, as long as this is still recognized as frankly schematic. Activity in the assembly a, aroused by fixation on an angle A of a triangle, can occur independently of b or c. When A, B, and C are looked at successively, in any order, but in a short period of time, activity may continue by reverberation in two of the structures while the third is sensorily aroused. . . . In these circumstances, conceivably, there is a frequent occurrence of activity in the three assemblies, a, b, and c at the same time. These lie interlaced with each other in what is grossly the same tissue of the cerebrum, and according to the assumptions of the last chapter the simultaneous activity would result in an integration of the three systems. . . .

According to the assumptions made earlier, simultaneous activity in a, b, and c would establish facilitation between them, through their chance anatomical interconnections and the enlargement of synaptic knobs. An effective facilitation from one system on another means a change of frequency characteristics in the system receiving the facilitation. It therefore means some fractionation and recruitment in the constituent units. With three extensive systems involved, each facilitating action on the other two, these growth changes must be considerable. The resulting superordinate system must be essentially a new one, by no means a sum or hooking together of a, b, and c. Instead of abc, which might suggest such an idea, a better notation for the new structure is t: the assembly of cells whose activity, in the schema, is perception of the triangle as a distinctive whole. As Gestalt writers would say, this is something other than the sum of its parts; but, unlike Gestalt theory, the schema derives the distinctiveness of the whole from perception of the parts. . . .

The argument up to this point can be summarized in general terms. Reasons have been given for believing

(1) the fixation on each of the several parts of a figure would have an increasingly determinate effect, as arousing one specific structure;

(2) that these structures, each corresponding to a frequently made fixation, are anatomically diffuse and interlaced with one another in the same gross cerebral tissue; and

(3) that the several activities may coexist, and be aroused in any order. It is a reasonable inference

(4) that two of these determinate actions simultaneously would have a determinate effect, tending to excite specific transmission units, and that the action of these units would tend to organize in the same way that the earlier established systems were organized. *Activity in a superordinate structure . . . is then best defined as being whatever determinate, organized activity results from repeated activity in the earlier-developed or subordinate structures giving rise to it. . . .*

L. The phase sequence in perception

Next, let us consider the temporal relationship of activity in these various structures. During the development of the assemblies a, b and c, arousal of a as we have seen is accompanied by two motor activities. Of these, one always becomes liminal (producing a change of fixation) before b or c is sensorily aroused. The sequence of events can be schematized as a-b-c-b-a-c-a-b-a-etc. Each of these events is associated with two specific motor excitations. One of them at least is subliminal, and one becomes liminal as an event intervening between a and b, for example, or between c and a.

This 'ideational' series with its motor elements I propose to call a 'phase sequence.'

When the assembly t has become organized, the psychological evidence indicates that its activity intervenes between the activities of the subordinate assemblies a, b, and c and does not supersede them. The sequence now becomes something like this: a-b-t-a-c-t-c-t-b-. . . .

It follows that the integration of t, the basis of perceiving a distinctive total figure, essentially involves a sequence of cortical events with motor components. Activity in a facilitates the arousal of both b and c, with the appropriate intervening eye movement, and activity in b or c facilitates the arousal of a in the same way. Whether b or c is aroused following a would depend on the momentary conditions of excitability. Activity in a would also facilitate that in t. In the early stages of perceptual development, t might be excited only after repeated activations of a, b, and c, but later . . . might be aroused following sensory activation of a alone, so that the triangle would be recognized with a single glance at A. But the activity so aroused must be transient, as we have seen; perception of the whole as such is momentary, and alternates with perception of the various parts. Instead of an indefinitely prolonged reverberation, interrupted only by some event outside of the system, excitation in one of the assemblies a, b, c, and t is an unstable equilibrium which moves readily into another phase.

. . . The stability of a perception is not in a single persistent pattern of cerebral activity but in the tendency of the phases of an irregular cycle to recur at short intervals.

Thus, Hebb argues that a set of cells, perhaps in the appropriate association area, acts as a closed system in which activity continues to circulate for a brief period after stimulation. The association of activity in two adjacent cells, whether by synaptic action of one upon the other, or by ephaptic facilitation due to proximity of cellular surfaces, causes alteration in membranes in such a way that the influence of one cell upon the other is facilitated. In this fashion, the ability of the afferent cell in the circuit to control the efferent cell is enhanced. In effect, the result of the postulated change is to increase the probability that an impulse will be conducted along certain pathways.

This dual-trace mechanism achieves the structural change as the result of an unspecified process activated by the reverberating activity.

Whether or not one accepts the details of the scheme proposed to establish the cell assembly, it bears strong resemblance to certain aspects of the representational system discussed in earlier chapters. The selection of cells that participate in the cell assembly is fortuitous and depends upon statistical considerations to achieve the necessary convergences of fibers upon cells, the necessary facilitatory and inhibitory relationships, and the proper timing of impulses. Although the cell is presumed to become responsive to a discharge with a particular temporal pattern of input, the basic effect of the postulated synaptic growth is to alter the timing of cell discharge. Reliability of response is achieved by assuming a large number of parallel paths, rather than by requiring the invariant involvement of certain cells. Thus, precise synchronization of activity in specific cells is not crucial. The mediating subset of cells undergoes a gradual evolution, certain cells drop out while others are recruited.

Although the details whereby these changes are accomplished differ in many aspects from those which we proposed in the opening chapters, some functional features of the Hebbian formulation correspond to the mechanisms which are proposed in this volume. Some of the major distinctions relate to the invocation of deterministic versus statistical mechanisms to accomplish various functions. Although Hebb proposes that the selection of neurons for membership in a cell assembly is fortuitous and is based upon the statistical incidence of the required interconnections between neurons in a large population, the representation of information is proposed to involve the determinate excitation of certain specific cell groups which comprise discrete transmission units, in contrast to our proposal that information is represented by the deviation of the average activity of a neuronal ensemble from baseline over a period of time. In the quoted passages, Hebb is largely preoccupied with explaining how the perception of a stimulus is mediated by mechanisms established during prior presentations of that input. Perceptual development is assumed to involve growth of these mechanisms, and in that sense perception requires the readout of stored information. The deterministic activation of experientially established cell assemblies sequentially organized into a phase sequence is proposed to mediate perception. Readout thus consists of the occurrence of activity in a discrete, although distributed, set of transmission units. In contrast, we assume that readout involves the achievement of adequate coincidence between two com-

177

pared modes of activity, one of which represents the stimulus input while the other reflects the retrieval of previous experience stored in a neural network.

One of the most distinctive features of Hebb's formulation is its reliance upon associative mechanisms related to the temporal contiguity of activity in adjacent neural systems. Not only the establishment of the cell assembly, but the integration of several cell assemblies into a phase sequence, which constitutes a superordinate structure or organization, is mediated by mechanisms which he suggests are based upon contiguity. Whether one prefers to assume that the informationally significant events in local neural regions are deterministic or statistical in nature, it is necessary to envisage some mechanism whereby the anatomically dispersed activities which represent different aspects of a unitary stimulus complex become integrated into a comprehensive total representation. We believe that the temporal contiguity of organized activity in various brain regions may provide the basis for such integration. Therefore, it seems worthwhile to examine some of the evidence about the neural consequences of contiguous activity, most of which has become available in the period following Hebb's theoretical formulations.

CHAPTER IX

EFFECTS OF CONTIGUITY

Ablation studies and observation of the widespread changes in the electrophysiological activity of various brain regions during the course of conditioning suggest that many areas of the brain are involved in the mediation of conditioned response performance. Although deficits in behavior following localized damage to the brain may be interpreted as evidence that the damaged structure plays a role in the performance of the previously established response, such evidence does not constitute a demonstration that memory for that experience is localized in such a region. The ability to reestablish conditioned response performance upon retraining, usually with substantial savings, suggests that the memory mechanism is distributed between at least a number of brain regions. This implies some process by which the representation of information about an experience in each of a number of anatomical regions becomes coordinated, so that an extensive system mediates the function of information storage and retrieval. How might such a system be established?

Fundamental to the theoretical formulations about the conditioning process made by Pavlov and other workers in this field is the idea of "temporary connection formation," namely: During the process of conditioning, functional relationships are somehow established between two anatomical regions, in such a way that functions originally mediated by activation of one region are subsequently elicited as a result of stimulation impinging on the other region. Sustained memory for simple learned behaviors such as conditioned responses, then, would require the stabilization of this temporary connection. A number of phenomena seem to illustrate a fundamental property of the central nervous system related to this function: namely, under certain specific circumstances, more or less permanent functional relationships can be established between two central regions, so that stimulation of one of these regions acquires the capacity to evoke activity in the second region.

A. Early observations

Probably the earliest description of this phenomenon was provided by Brown-Sequard (1884) who wrote, " . . . in dogs and rabbits I have excited energetically the cerebral cortex, using two Du Bois Reymond apparatuses. The stimulators of one of them were applied at the maximum intensity on the occipital portion of the cerebral cortex, those of the other, at a lesser power, were applied to the motor zone. Two important effects have been observed numerous times. The first is that, during the passage of current, which continued about 20 seconds, there occurred in the trunk, in the forelimbs, more energetic movements than those which I produced if the currents of the two coils were applied only to the motor area; the second is that, after the passage of current in the two areas, the zone called non-motoric has become motoric. On stimulating it weakly with a low setting of the DuBois Reymond apparatus, I have seen repeatedly at each stimulation, movements completely similar to those which follow the application of a current of the same intensity to the motor areas. This part, (the occipital and sphenoidal areas primarily) became then just as motoric as a portion of the cortex which one considers as the seat of the motor control of the limbs. I have seen the face, the neck and the tail move also under these circumstances by a weak stimulation of the occipital cerebral cortex. These experiments were carried out more frequently in the dog than in the rabbit" (translated by E. R. John).

In 1897, Wedensky reported a similar finding. If, in a dog under light narcosis, shortly after electrical stimulation of the motor point for the extensors of the forepaw (Center A), stimulation is applied to the motor cortex region of the flexors of the forepaw (Center B), it is possible to observe a paradoxical effect. The result of stimulation of Center B is the same as if Center A had been stimulated, and extension rather than flexion of the forepaw occurs (Wedensky, 1897).

In 1905, in a startlingly elegant series of experiments in which chronically implanted electrodes were used to study the effects of cortical stimulation in unrestrained dogs, Baer confirmed and extended the earlier findings of Brown-Sequard. The conclusions to which Baer came, as well as his methods, merit more careful consideration than they have received. "Now that I have completed the presentation of my experimental work, it remains, in conclusion, to summarize the findings which have been obtained. The outstanding finding was that it suffices, to make an inexcitable region of the cortex excitable, that one stimulate an excitable region of the cortex simultaneously with a brief electrical current. . . . On the basis of the observations reported above, that, from all regions of the cortex, all voluntary muscles can be excited, we must conclude that each region of the cortex is connected to every other region through an extensive network" (translated by E. R. John).

Were we to accept the suggestion that the ramification of connections in the central nervous system is such that some pathway exists from any arbitrarily selected point to any other point, the necessity to invoke a concept such as neurobiotaxis in explanation for the storage of new functional relationships becomes superfluous. Rather, if it is possible for one region of this extensively interconnected network to achieve significant functional control over the activity of another region, simply as a consequence of simultaneous nonrandom activity in the two areas, it would suffice for the storage of this new relationship merely to facilitate the coupling of excitation between the two interacting systems via preexisting pathways between the two areas.

The reports of Brown-Sequard, Wedensky, Baer, and others indicate that for some time after stimulation of some region I of the central nervous system, a physical state may exist such that other input to region I, via diffuse irradiation from some more directly stimulated location II in the extensively interconnected network that comprises the brain, now results in the discharge of region I although it would normally be ineffective. These changed functional relationships might be due either to previously subthreshold influences of the second region upon the first becoming suprathreshold, because of enhancement resulting from the prior stimulation of the first region, or might indicate the formation of new "temporary connections" when these influences were previously absent or occluded.

[An alternative possibility, which is functionally equivalent although anatomically different, might be pointed out. Stimulation of the first region may exert a sustained but subthreshold effect on some third region, so as to raise its excitability. Input from the second region,

181

previously ineffective, may now converge upon and cause the discharge of that third region.]

In 1929, Zal'manson (1929) showed such an altered functional state could be produced by strychninization. After establishing a conditioned defensive reflex of the left rear paw to the beat of a metronome, he placed strychnine on the motor cortical representation of the right forepaw. Subsequently, presentation of the metronome beat which was the conditioned stimulus was found to elicit vigorous flexion of the right forepaw, rather than the left rear paw. These results showed that creation of an excitable region may in a sense dominate the hierarchy of responses of the animal, so that afferent input which has normally been processed in a particular fashion, learned or non-learned, now has a different consequence.

B. The dominant focus

Ukhtomski assigned to the central state assumed to underlie these phenomena the term *"dominant focus"* (1926). Ukhtomski characterized the condition of excitation in "dominance" by four aspects: (1) relatively heightened excitability of a neural center; (2) temporal stability of the local nervous excitation; (3) capacity of the excited center to summate input from the stream of indifferent afferent impulses; (4) excitation inertia, that is, the capacity of this mechanism to retain excitation, once established, and to be able to persist in that state when the original stimulation has disappeared.

The dominant focus can be considered as an aggregate of neurons, sharing a sustained state of altered excitability. The excitability of a population of neurons in a region would normally tend to be randomly distributed, ranging from refractoriness to hyperexcitability. An afferent input to the region would be expected to cause a diffusely distributed response throughout the network. The percentage of responding cells in any unit volume would be that fraction of the total population which was in a nonrefractory state of excitability, which received that afferent input, and for which the input was supraliminal. The establishment of a dominant focus in an area of this region would make the excitability of neurons in that area more uniform. An adequate afferent input to the region would cause a diffusely distributed response throughout the region as before, except in the area of the dominant focus where a massive synchronized response would occur, which involved a high percentage of the neurons. The coherent nature of this response would amplify the informational "significance" of the input, by causing a greater departure from baseline activity patterns than would otherwise occur. In a sense, the "signal-to-noise ratio" could be considered to have been improved. Such an organized non-random discharge from the area of the dominant focus might well be expected to dominate the pattern of efferent outflow from the otherwise loosely organized region.

Changes in the ratio of coherent to incoherent activity in a region might be achieved either by local excitatory or inhibitory influences. Increased local excitability might augment the number of neurons in a region which would respond to a particular afferent input above the normal density. At the same time, neural responsiveness to all excitatory processes would rise. Both coherent response to the relevant input and incoherent background activity would therefore be altered, and the over-all ratio might not be markedly improved. Additionally, the extent to which local increases in excitability might serve to organize a region so as to display a more uniform reaction to input is limited. Neurons could escape from membership in an excitable population by discharging and entering the refractory phase, which would become more likely as excitability increased. In contrast, it would seem as though inhibitory influences might exert a relatively more pronounced organizing effect. Thresholds would be increased, incoherent background activity would lessen, and escape from organizing influences would be made more difficult. When input excitation finally exceeded the raised threshold, unusually high coherence levels should be displayed under these conditions. Therefore, although the distribution of excitabilities in a region can be altered either by excitatory or inhibitory influences, it seems probable that inhibitory influences could achieve a more markedly nonrandom response from the neuronal aggregate.

It seems reasonable to suggest that the phenomena of functional transformation described earlier, attributed by Ukhtomski to the establishment of a dominant focus, may be manifestations of local postexcitatory facilitation analogous to posttetanic potentiation. In its original usage, posttetanic potentiation referred to an increased postsynaptic discharge elicited homosynaptically because of heightened presynaptic action. The term has also been used in a broader sense to refer to a

183

long-lasting increased responsiveness which has been observed not only from neuromuscular preparations, but in sympathetic ganglia, spinal cord, subcortical nuclei, and the visual, auditory, and olfactory systems. Residual postexcitatory increases in responsiveness lasting for minutes or even hours seem to be a generalized phenomenon found at many levels of the nervous system, possibly mediated by changes in the extraneuronal concentration of potassium and/or acetylcholine (Hughes, 1958). Data relevant to such changes were discussed earlier in this book.

C. Effects of anodal polarization

Whatever the nature of the chemical processes which produce short-term changes of excitability in a dominant focus and the long-term preservation of such altered excitability, it seems important to explore further the evidence which is available about the achievement of functional relationships between regions of the brain as a consequence of the sharing of activity. In the early 1950's, some characteristics of an electrically established dominant focus were reported by Rusinov (1953). Using the conscious restrained rabbit, this worker placed an electrode on a region of motor cortex, which, if cathodally stimulated, gave forelimb flexion. An anodal current, from 5 to 8 μamp, was applied through this electrode.* While this current flow was maintained, some strong

---

* Ostensibly, the consequence of an anodal polarization should be to raise the threshold of the subjacent cortex. A slight inhibitory influence of this sort would serve to diminish variations in excitability within the region. One might expect a somewhat raised threshold and more massive response to characterize this region. It is possible, however, that the distribution of current flow with these particular current parameters is such that, although thresholds may be raised in superficial regions of the cortex (axodendritic synapses), thresholds are actually lowered in deeper regions (axosomatic synapses), or even at the terminal ramification of axons projecting from these cortical cells to subcortical structures. The effect may occur at the unknown location of some virtual cathode. Note that essentially the same effect which Rusinov achieved by imposing anodal polarization on a region of motor cortex was also achieved by Zal'manson by placing strychnine on a region of motor cortex. Bishop and O'Leary (1950) compared the effects of cortical strychninization and anodal polarization and concluded that strychnine acted much like surface-positive polarization. Their results indicated that anodal polarization raises the threshold, increases the amplitude and duration of discharge, and decreases the absolutely refractory period. Surface cathodal polarization lowered the threshold and increased the amplitude of response, but to a lesser extent. It is of interest that they observed that surface-positive currents induced

sensory stimulus such as a touch, a sound, or a light was presented repeatedly. After a number of these presentations, the occurrence of the sensory stimulus alone elicited forelimb flexion for about a half an hour and was then no longer effective. However, during the period when the "conditioned stimulus" was effective, the presentation of novel stimuli

---

paroxysmal discharge at much lower current values than surface-negative currents. They concluded that any slowly developing biological potential should be looked upon as a factor influencing the excitability of neurons upon which it acts.

Arduini (1958) observed that surface-negative potential shifts, accompanied by EEG arousal, occurred in certain cortical areas after reticular formation stimulation, after midline thalamic nuclear stimulation, and after sensory stimulation. Low concentrations of strychnine, applied to cortex, strongly augmented the amplitude of such potential shifts, as did surface-positive (anodal) polarization of cortex. Similar findings have been reported by Brookhart and his co-workers (1958).

Jung reported changes in reactivity of cells in visual cortex during stimulation of the mesencephalic reticular formation and the nonspecific intralaminar thalamic nuclei. Such stimulation was accompanied by a surface-negative cortical wave, resembling a polarization of the cortex (1958). *During such stimulation of the nonspecific system, the number of neurons of the visual cortex responding to retinal afferents increased. His evidence indicated that convergence and complex interactions of specific and nonspecific impulses occur on the neurons of the visual cortex.* The discharge patterns of cortical neurons influenced and modified the effects of the nonspecific inflow, and *vice versa.* These interactions can be such as to facilitate or to inhibit cortical neurons.

Evidence is additionally cited by Purpura that stimulation of midline brain-stem reticular regions can cause late prolonged surface-positive responses in certain cortical regions, with a marked facilitation of dendritic synapses during this positivity (1958). It seems possible that surface-positive polarization with a subsequent enhancement of surface-negative effects (that is, axodendritic discharges) of subcortical stimuli, may occur in a number of different ways, reflecting the site and frequency of stimulation. Therefore, surface-positive polarization, which seems to facilitate the establishment of a dominant focus, may enhance the effects of stimulation of various structures. The consequences of such local enhancement may be to facilitate the convergence and interaction of specific and nonspecific impulses, such that corticofugal discharge occurs most readily from a surface-positive polarized region when specific systems are stimulated.

The work of Caspers may also be cited in this regard (1959). Caspers showed that the effects of mesencephalic or thalamic reticular formation stimulation on the spontaneous EEG could be simulated by applying dc polarization of a magnitude comparable to that which accompanies stimulation of these reticular systems. Finally, the work of Bindman, Lippold, and Redfearn should also be noted (1962a). These workers have described long-lasting changes in the amplitude of evoked potentials or in the discharge rate of cortical units, resulting after the repeated application of brief periods of anodal polarization to the region whose response was subsequently studied. Although initially ineffective, currents as low as 0.1 μamp were observed to increase the rate of unit discharge for periods of hours, following *several* brief applications of such polarization.

occasionally also elicited flexion, indicating that some generalized increase in excitability attended this phenomenon. It was also found that if foreleg flexion were conditioned to some particular stimulus, and the conditioned response then extinguished, establishment of a dominant focus at the forelimb region in motor cortex disinhibited the extinguished response and restored the action of the conditioned stimulus.

Furthermore, the establishment of a dominant focus in an animal, which had been previously conditioned to make a response involving other central nervous system regions than the site of the dominant focus, resulted in the suppression of the previously elaborated conditioned reflex. When the conditioned stimulus was then presented, the animal displayed responses reflecting activation of the polarized region. Apparently, establishment of a dominant focus was not compatible with performance of the previously established conditioned response. This suggests that the information propagated in the central nervous system by the presentation of the conditioned stimulus, instead of activating the processes established by the learning experience, was somehow rerouted or shunted by the imposed dominant focus. Implicit in this interpretation is the inference that a representational system, comparable to a set of dominant foci built during conditioning, normally directs the activity propagated in the central nervous system by the conditioned stimulus.

D. Effects of tetanization

Some evidence that the characteristic configuration of excitability necessary to establish a dominant focus can arise from processes related to the responses of neural tissue to stimuli, as well as from externally imposed and sustained anodal polarization, is afforded by the work of Roytbak (1955, 1956). This worker observed that tetanization of a critical region A was followed by a period of slow hypersynchronous activity of varying frequency. Stimulation of other cortical regions B was found to have no pronounced effect on region A previous to *tetanization*. If, however, as the tetanizing stimulation of region A stopped, cortical regions B were stimulated at some specific frequency $F1$, the subsequent hypersynchrony of region A displayed that frequency $F1$. This phenomenon was observed for many different cortical regions. Thus, the state of a cortical region after a tetanizing stimulation appears to be such that many other regions of cortex can control its pattern of discharge, although normally such influence is not apparent. Chow and Dewson (1963) have provided direct evidence that tetanization induces a surface positive shift at the stimulated site. The functional similarities between sustained anodal polarization and the aftereffects of tetanizing stimulation are of interest and raise questions as to possible mediating mechanisms which may be common to both phenomena.

In the experiments of Rusinov, one region of the nervous system is stimulated with light, while a second region which normally causes flexion is polarized. When these two influences have coexisted for a period of time, the light subsequently influences the discharge of the polarized region and can cause flexion to occur. Analogously, in the work of Roytbak a new functional relationship is established between two regions so that stimulation of one causes new electrical responses to appear in the second following tetanization.

E. Effects of contiguity between sensory stimuli

1. Cortical Conditioning

Investigations of sensory conditioning, the so-called "cortical conditioning," which have been conducted by Morrell with Jasper (1956), and with others (Morrell, 1957b, 1958; Morrell, Naquet, and Gastaut, 1957; Morrell, Roberts, and Jasper, 1956), Yoshii and his co-workers (Yoshii et al., 1957b; Yoshii and Hockaday, 1958), show that similar functional relationships between two regions of the nervous system can be established as the result of the paired action of peripheral stimuli, with no such artificial manipulation as polarization or tetanization.

In the paradigm of cortical conditioning a steady tone is presented for several seconds and then paired for an additional few seconds with a low-frequency flickering light. After a number of such paired presentations separated by random time intervals, changes occur in the electrophysiological responses to the stimuli. Upon the onset of the steady tone and *before* the onset of the flicker, the *visual* cortex displays rhythmic electrical activity which approximately corresponds to the frequency of the not-yet-presented flicker. This suggests that the presentation of flicker induced a dominant focus in the visual system so that it became susceptible to the influence of auditory stimuli.

2. Frequency-Specific Responses

Some controversy has taken place as to whether or not the "frequency-specific" discharge which occurs in the so-called "phase II" of cortical conditioning actually is frequency specific. Studies by Morrell, Barlow, and Brazier (1960) using digital computer analysis of such data indicate appreciable correspondence between the flicker frequency and the frequency of the rhythms observed in visual cortex in response to steady tone alone during "phase II." However, it seems unreasonable to insist that such rhythmic discharges in the visual cortex must be precisely at the flicker frequency if they derive from prior flicker experience. It is well known that an animal who has been behaviorally conditioned using a flickering conditioned stimulus displays a wide generalization gradient, performing the conditioned response to flickering stimuli over a range of frequencies that differ markedly from the stimulus used during the original training. There seems, therefore, no reason to expect accurate frequency representation under these circumstances.

According to Yoshii and his co-workers (1956), frequency-specific repetitive response can be observed in subcortical structures, including the mesencephalic reticular formation and the intralaminar nuclei, before it appears in visual cortex. Furthermore, Yoshii and Hockaday (1958) have reported evidence indicating that cortical conditioning can be blocked in animals with lesions of nucleus centre median. Thus, the intralaminar nuclei of the thalamus, the so-called nuclei of origin of the recruiting response, may occupy an essential position in the function of the system built during the procedure of cortical conditioning. However, relatively direct cortico-cortical interactions may also be involved.

Chow et al. (Chow, 1964; Chow and Dewson, 1964; Dewson, Chow, and Engel, 1964) have recently investigated the effects of tetanization and of polarization on the responsiveness of a region, and have found that these two diverse manipulations have essentially equivalent results. They explored the effects of these maneuvers on the responsiveness of some region A on a slab of isolated cortex to electrical stimulation delivered to a distant point B on the same slab. Not only did tetanization or polarization alter the response of region A to stimulation of point B, but, perhaps more interesting, if stimulation at point B was changed to frequency 2 following a period of excitation at frequency 1, *region A displayed a response that contained components at both frequency 1 and frequency 2.*

3. Temporal patterns of neuronal discharge

Morrell has demonstrated an analogous property at the level of the single neuron (1961b), recording with microelectrodes from units of the visual cortex. Examination of normal neuronal activity showed that certain units were not readily "driven" by rhythmic peripheral light flashes. However, if the cortex above the recorded unit were anodally polarized, the unit responses to the rhythmic flicker would become very rhythmic and reproducible, with similar pulse patterns elicited by each flash of light. Paired polarization and flicker continued for several minutes and polarization was then terminated while the flicker persisted. Under these conditions, the unit continued to display orderly response to each flash of light. If polarization and flicker were terminated together, subsequent presentation of a single light flash resulted in rhythmic bursts of neuronal discharge at the previous flicker frequency. Each burst seemed to possess the previously characteristic pulse pattern. The probability that these rhythmic bursts of response would be elicited by a single light flash decayed exponentially as a function of time after the termination of polarization and flicker, reaching the baseline about 20 minutes later. In subsequent work, Morrell (1965) has obtained analogous results using *syncopated* pattern of light flashes instead of light flickering at some fixed frequency. Unit discharges can reproduce the syncopated pattern when a single test flash is delivered after a period of syncopated stimulation during polarization.

The appearance of rhythmic electrical activity at frequencies corresponding to previously experienced stimulation, in these various experiments, indicates that when neural networks are active with a particular temporal pattern during the imposition of a dominant focus, they may acquire a propensity for the release of discharge with that pattern when activated later by input with different temporal characteristics. The possible functional significance of such released temporal patterns will be discussed later in the chapter on representational systems.

F. Conditionability of dc shifts

In a number of the previous experiments, it has been shown that the application of dc polarization serves to facilitate the establishment of functional relationships between brain regions. In an exceedingly interesting experiment Morrell has demonstrated that a dc shift itself may be conditioned (1960). He stimulated centre median in the cat, which normally causes a localized dc shift on the cortex, depending on the particular area of centre median stimulated and the parameters of stimulation. The initial presentation of tone to these animals did not result in a corresponding dc shift in that region. Repetitive pairing of tone with centre median stimulation eventually established the capacity of tone alone to produce a localized dc shift in cortex like that which had previously been elicited by centre median stimulation alone.

Gumnit and Grossman have shown that various auditory stimuli possess the intrinsic capacity to produce surface-*negative* dc shifts localized to the auditory cortex (1961). Rowland (1963) has studied the changes in this response which occur when auditory stimuli are systematically paired with an unconditioned stimulus, the taking of food, which produced a very stable and marked positive dc shift. After systematic pairing of click with food reward, click elicited a surface-*positive* shift on auditory cortex. However, no such shifts were observed when indifferent auditory or visual stimuli were presented. When crossover training occurred, with extinction of the click response and reinforcement of light flashes, the configuration of dc shifts was reversed. Thus, it not only would appear that application of dc polarization to a region of the brain facilitates the establishment of effective influences upon that region by other structures, but also that sensory stimuli can acquire an altered capacity to produce dc shifts in cortical regions as a consequence of conditioning procedures.

Some of the experiments related to consolidation which were mentioned earlier in this book provide an indication that dc shifts may occur in conventional conditioning situations and may be relevant to the consolidation process. The experiments of Albert (1966b) showed that surface cathodal cortical polarization blocked consolidation while surface anodal polarization seemed to facilitate storage. Similar results had earlier been provided by Morrell and Naitoh (1962), who showed that surface-cathodal polarization of the cortical regions responsive to the conditioned stimulus seemed to prevent registration of the learning experience while surface-anodal polarization resulted in subsequently enhanced performance.

Using a variety of visual discriminations, Kupferman (1965) has reported inability to observe differential effects of anodal and cathodal cortical polarization and has suggested that Morrell's data might have been due to the effects of distraction on an unstable CR. Although it is difficult to envisage how the proposed distraction effects could have been differential, this apparent contradiction indicates the necessity for further study of the behavioral effects of polarization.

G. Differential effects of contiguity

Morrell has provided evidence that the facilitation accomplished by establishment of a dominant focus is not to be attributed merely to sensitization, but represents a more specific effect (1961b). He presented two different signals, tone 1 and tone 2, to a cat. Initially, presentation of these tones elicited no overt movement from the cat. A region of the motor cortex was then subjected to a surface anodal polarization. That region, if cathodally stimulated, produced flexion of a limb. While the cortical polarization was maintained continuously, tone 1 was presented at random intervals. After a number of such presentations, tone 1 acquired the capacity to elicit flexion of the limb. If tone 2 was then presented while cortical polarization was maintained, it also elicited limb flexion. However, if the cortical polarization was terminated, presentation of tone 1 continued to elicit limb flexion, while tone 2 no longer had that property.

Thus, the functional influence of one brain region over another, established by stimulating that region while a dominant focus is maintained in the other, involves control which is *differential*. Stimuli which have been presented repeatedly during polarization retain their capacity to influence the polarized region after termination of current flow, while other stimuli do not possess that property.

Other data also suggest that contiguity may have differential effects. Chow and John have studied the effects of temporally contiguous activity on the functional relationships between different neural regions, without any introduction of polarization or tetanization (1965). In these experiments, three pairs of electrodes were placed on the suprasylvian gyrus. The electrodes were spaced approximately 1 cm between pairs, with the members of a pair separated by approximately 1 to 2 mm. The propagation of electrical stimuli was studied from each pair of electrodes to both other pairs. Using an average response computer, it was demonstrated that such propagation resulted in highly reproducible average response waveforms, when stimulus parameters and the number of stimulations were reproduced. Then, two of these electrode pairs were stimulated together intermittently, several times per minute over a period of 20 minutes. Following this interval of shared activity at two places in the monitored network, one of these pairs of electrodes was again stimulated by itself. It was frequently observed that the evoked potential propagating from the stimulated electrodes to the other two recording sites displayed differential enhancement. The average response recorded from the region which had shared activity with the stimulus site was markedly enhanced, whereas the average response computed from the other electrode pair remained essentially the same as before the pairing of stimulation.

In an analogous experiment, the effects of separate lateral geniculate stimulation and ventralis anterior stimulation were observed at the visual cortex, the suprasylvian cortex, and a number of other regions on cortex. After establishment of the characteristics of evoked potentials produced at these sites by stimulation of the two regions separately, lateral geniculate and ventralis anterior stimulation were presented simultaneously at irregular intervals over a 20-minute period. Following this paired experience, the effect of ventralis anterior stimulation alone was markedly enhanced on suprasylvian cortex. These studies suggest that the propagation of an electrical disturbance from an input site throughout a neuronal network may be differentially enhanced so that a portion of the network which has experienced shared activity with the stimulated region displays increased reactivity to events at the remote site, whereas such increased reactivity cannot be discerned elsewhere in the network.

H. Behavioral effects of contiguity

A number of workers have provided demonstrations that the contiguity of stimulation of two neural regions can produce behavioral response as well as new electrophysiological response. Nikolayeva presented a buzzer to dogs, at the same time that the region of the motor cortex causing leg flexion was electrically stimulated (1953). Repeated paired presentation of the buzzer with direct brain stimulation eventually resulted in performance of the flexion response upon presentation of the buzzer alone. Apparently, contiguous activity in the auditory system in response to the buzzer and in the motor cortex as a result of direct electrical stimulation eventually established a relationship between regions of the auditory system and the stimulated region of motor cortex. Presumably, the activity caused by the buzzer in the auditory system somehow effectuated discharge of the region of motor cortex with which it had previously shared activity.

The work of Sokolova indicates that similar behavioral responses can be established in an analogous paradigm and are concomitant with the appearance of new electrographic activity (1958). This worker polarized the motor cortex of rabbits with low levels of anodal current. The polarized region was one which, if cathodally stimulated, would cause leg flexion. While this dc polarization was maintained, flicker at frequency 1 was repeatedly presented to the animal. After a number of presentations, it was observed that, upon the presentation of flicker, flexion of the limb occurred. At the time that flicker acquired the capacity to elicit this movement, the EEG recordings from the polarized region of the motor cortex displayed rhythmic discharges at frequency 1 occurring in that structure.

It is possible to accomplish the establishment of new functional relationships using a paradigm opposite to that of Nikolayeva, namely one in which the direct electrical stimulation is delivered to a sensory region and the motor cortex is stimulated via peripheral influences.

In early work, Loucks reported the use of cortical stimulation through an implanted coil as a conditioned stimulus (1938). His results were initially ambiguous because of the possibility of concomitant vibratory stimulation. In subsequent studies, however, he successfully used direct central stimulation as a conditioned stimulus (Loucks, 1955, 1961). In more recent experiments (1956), Doty and his colleagues delivered direct electrical stimulation to the visual cortex which was accompanied by shock to the foot. After a number of pairings of cortical stimulation with foot shock, the presentation of electrical stimulation of the cortex alone elicited flexion of the paw. Extending this paradigm one step further (Giurgea, 1953; Doty and Giurgea, 1958), Giurgea demonstrated that

193

simultaneous electrical stimulation of a sensory region of the brain and a motor region of the brain, after a number of pairings, resulted in performance of the response normally elicited by stimulation of the motor region upon electrical stimulation of the sensory region alone. These studies provide what seems to be a demonstration that direct electrical stimulation of a less drastic sort than tetanization or dc polarization can well create the conditions required for the establishment of dominant foci and associated representational systems. Brief electrical stimulation of a region of motor cortex A which produced some definite motor response R was paired with electrical stimulation of some other region B of cortex. After a number of such paired stimuli, presentation of the electrical stimulus to region B elicited response R. According to these workers, a minimum of 3 minutes must intervene between trials. Failure of previous attempts to accomplish such direct central conditioning is probably to be attributed to insufficiently long intervals between paired presentations. The necessity of maintaining this interval between stimuli may reflect the period during which perturbations will disrupt some unfinished consolidation process.

It is noteworthy that the work of Giurgea and Doty essentially confirms, some 60 years later, the initial observations of Brown-Sequard and Baer. Feedback from the performance of R itself probably is not crucially involved in the establishment of this "central conditioning" since it has been shown not to be an essential component of more conventional procedures (Beck and Doty, 1957). It is noteworthy that no reinforcement is involved in the establishment of the centrally conditioned reflex. Although the two procedures differ in the parameters of electrical stimulation, the salient difference between the procedure of Roytbak and the procedure of Giurgea and Doty appears to be that, in the former procedure, an electrical response is the index of connection formation, while the latter procedure uses a motor response. The similarities between these procedures are sufficient to suggest that they share a common mediating mechanism and that brief intermittent stimulation of the motor cortex serves to establish a dominant focus.

It seems reasonable to suggest that the work of Doty, Rutledge, and Larsen (1956) can be interpreted as evidence that representational systems can be established in a somewhat more physiological fashion, although analogous to the work of Giurgea and Doty. In these experiments, the "conditioned stimulus" was still direct electrical stimulation of sensory cortex, now paired with shock to the foot. Neural activity in the motor system associated with the leg flexion caused by shock apparently sufficed to establish a dominant focus, so that subsequent stimulation of sensory cortex elicited performance of leg flexion.

I. Interactions between directly and naturally established systems

The basically physiological quality of the system built during the procedure of Doty and his colleagues is suggested by the fact that, if a conditioned response is established to direct electrical stimulation of a sensory region, subsequent acquisition of the same conditioned response to stimulation of the peripheral sense organs of the same modality may sometimes be facilitated. Similar saving of trials has been observed with the opposite sequence of learning. Generalization from peripheral to central stimulation and vice versa has also been obtained occasionally, suggesting that common mechanisms may be involved in mediation of responses in both situations. Additional evidence related to this question will be presented in subsequent chapters. Such results have also been achieved by Neff and his co-workers, Nieder and Osterreich (1959). These workers conditioned cats to perform avoidance responses to a series of clicks presented over a loudspeaker. Subsequent central electrical stimulation of auditory regions at the click frequency produced immediate performance of the conditioned avoidance response. The converse procedure, conditioning to electrical stimulation of auditory pathways and testing with clicks at the same frequency, also yielded positive results.

Livanov and Korolkova established a conditioned defensive reflex in rabbits to a flickering light (1951). Subsequent weak stimulation of the motor cortex with an electrical stimulus at that frequency caused performance of the conditioned response. The latency period of the motor response was minimal when the frequency of the electrical stimulus coincided with the flicker frequency used during conditioning.

These workers also reported that rhythmic electrical stimulation of the visual cortex, to which stimulation of the motor cortex at the same

195

frequency was added 10 seconds later, resulted in the appearance of a conditioned motor response to subsequent stimulation with flickering light at that frequency, without any electrical stimulation. Liberson *et al.* (1959, 1960) have obtained similar results with hippocampal stimulation, in a converse paradigm.

J. Anatomical extensiveness of representational systems

Such observations would seem to justify interpretation of the various experiments that will be described as providing information about the organization of representational systems during more conventional conditioning procedures.

When a flexion conditioned response has been established to a conditioned stimulus, consisting . of direct electrical stimulation of some cortical region A, transfer of this conditioned response to stimulation of other areas is possible. Apparently, cortical region A is not an essential part of this system, because ablation of region A does not severely impede subsequent transfer. Circumsection of the cortex around the site of stimulation does not abolish the established conditioned response. Transection of the corpus callosum does not effect the performance of a conditioned response established to a conditioned stimulus delivered to one hemisphere and an unconditioned stimulus delivered to the other hemisphere. These findings suggest that transcortical transmission is not essential in the mediation of the response. However, undercutting the site of cortical stimulation abolishes the conditioned response, indicating corticofugal pathways play an essential role. These conclusions correspond to those reported by Loucks. It is interesting that continued training enables the conditioned response to be reestablished to electrical stimulation of an undercut cortical region, indicating that transcortical transmission can contribute to mediation of the conditioned response under certain conditions. It would seem, therefore, that during conditioning to a direct central stimulus, a representational system is elaborated in which cortical regions that are responsive to the conditioned and unconditioned stimuli become functionally coupled via subcortical interactions. The failure of ablation of the cortical site of the conditioned stimulus to impede transfer suggests that activity resulting from the stimulation of other cortical regions may gain functional access to this representational system via subcortical regions.

196

K. Summary of experimental results

The various experimental results which have been described comprise a set of examples of basically the same phenomenon. In each of these instances some stimulus (S_1), which has been repeatedly associated with some other stimulus (S_2), ultimately seems to acquire the faculty of simulating the action of S_2. The examples which have been provided illustrate a process of "functional connection formation" resulting in what might be considered the establishment of equivalence for some aspect of the action of these stimuli. One can, of course, cast the classical conditioning procedures utilized by Pavlovian workers into the same framework. Stimulation of one brain region, which produces an unconditioned response, is initially accomplished by the unconditioned stimulus, while some other brain regions are affected by the conditioned stimulus. After pairing, the conditioned stimulus achieves the ability to elicit performance of the response which previously occurred as a consequence of unconditioned activation of a brain region to which the conditioned stimulus normally has difficult access. Thus, if we were to call S_1 the "conditioned stimulus" and S_2 the "unconditioned stimulus," we would emphasize the apparent similarity between the various phenomena described above and classical conditioning. The common features of the procedures that have been described and their broad generality are evident from an examination of Fig. IX-1.

Some of the effects of contiguity discussed previously are rather difficult to demonstrate, suggesting that rather special conditions are required for such interactions to take place. Yet, taken as a group, these various experiments indicate that under certain conditions *mere contiguity of activity in two neural regions suffices for the establishment of a functional relationship between them so that stimulation of one produces activation of the other.* The system established by contiguity of central stimuli seems to bear a similarity to those constructed with more conventional procedures since a physiologically natural stimulus can apparently gain functional access to it. The converse also seems to be true. Some of these data also suggest that systems built under these conditions may possess the capacity to reconstruct a previously experienced temporal pattern of electrical activity reflecting the time course of stimulation during their

197

IX. Effects of contiguity

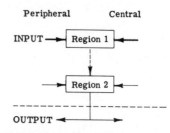

THE EXPERIMENTAL SUMMARIES BELOW ARE ARRANGED
ACCORDING TO THE GENERAL OUTLINE ABOVE

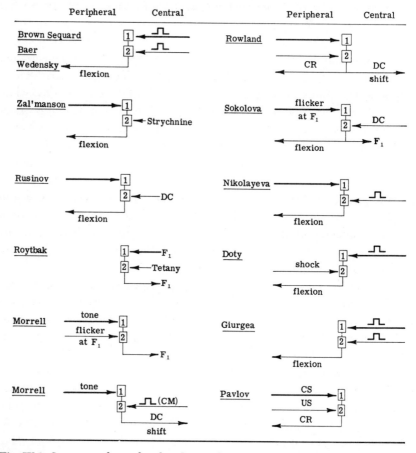

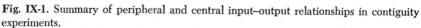

Fig. IX-1. Summary of peripheral and central input–output relationships in contiguity experiments.

establishment. Furthermore, the phenomena which have been described seem to reflect more than general sensitization since some evidence of differential specificity has been obtained.

L. Characteristics of dominant foci and representational systems

The evidence just summarized indicates that multiple regions of the nervous system in which sustained nonrandom neural activity occurs will become associated into an integrated system as a result of the temporal contiguity of activity. Such a system, linking together the different portions of the neural network in which nonrandom disturbances were caused by the various aspects of a stimulus complex, can be conceptualized as a *representation* of the total informational impact of the stimulus complex upon the brain. Memory of the occurrence of that stimulus complex would seem to require specification or storage of essential features of the spatio-temporal pattern of activity which characterizes the corresponding representational system. For these reasons, it is appropriate to introduce here a number of definitions about dominant foci, and some hypotheses related to the organization of representational neural systems based upon these processes:

(1) A *dominant focus* is an anatomically distributed neural aggregate which undergoes common fluctuations of excitability during some interval of time, increasing the probability that an adequate afferent input to the aggregate will cause the members of that subset of cells to display associated activity.

(2) When a group of neurons is repeatedly associated in discharge over a period of time, they become organized into a system characterized by a tendency for the constituent neurons to discharge in a coordinated fashion. The integrative consequences of associated activity may reflect the direct influence of induced dominant foci upon chemical processes related to information storage, or may arise secondarily as a result of achieving more coherent response in a neuronal population.

(3) If a particular temporal pattern has characterized the discharge of the group of neurons during their repeated association, the *mode of activity* displayed during subsequent activity involving a substantial proportion of that set of cells will tend to reproduce that temporal pattern.

(4) The *strength* of the coherent response tendency is the probability that the average activity of the group will correspond to the specified mode when some subgroup of member neurons discharge together. The strength of the coherent response tendency might be expected to reflect the frequency with which associated discharge has occurred in the past, and the time elapsed since such discharge, among other variables.

(5) The neural activity resulting from the discharge of a dominant focus in a characteristically organized mode constitutes afferent input to other brain regions with particular temporal sequences and spatial distributions. Two or more dominant foci active during the same period can interact via these propagated influences and constitute a reciprocally interlocked set or system of foci. This integrated system of foci contains the nonrandom or informationally significant patterns of neural activity resulting from the occurrence of a specified set of external and internal stimuli and will be referred to as a *representational system.*

(6) The interaction of a group of dominant foci, each displaying its individual mode of activity, will organize a representational system which displays a *common mode of activity,* compatible with the set of local modes.

(7) The discharge of some critical proportion of the set of neural aggregates comprising a representational system is the *significant level of activation.* When afferent inputs and the tonic levels of excitation in the system cause a significant level of activation, the propagation of the corresponding modes of neural activity from relevant regions of the nervous system results in the *coupling* of modes between the various representational subsets. The entire representational system consequently undergoes associated discharge, releasing its characteristic common mode of activity or oscillation.

M. A proposed mechanism for "connection formation"

From this viewpoint, the steps in formation of the functional stimulus equivalence described in this chapter would appear to be approximately as follows:

The effect of stimulation of region 1 with the conditioned stimulus S_1 is to initiate a mode of activity in the cells of that region and in responsive elements in more remote brain areas to which the effects of the sustained circulation in region 1 can propagate. This characteristic pattern of nonrandom activity impinging on distant populations is the signal that S_1 has occurred. While residual orderly activity from this patterned afferent input continues to circulate in some other region II, occurrence of the unconditioned stimulus S_2 causes coherent discharge of some portion of subgroup of cells in that population, producing some characteristic effect or response.

The set of cells initially sent into coherent discharge by S_2 regains reactivity to encounter a circulating pattern of activity which contains residuals with two different origins: (1) the persisting consequences of S_1 comprising one mode of oscillation in the network; (2) the consequences of S_2 causing a second mode of oscillation in the network. This coherent set of cells constitutes a dominant focus in this region. The pattern of activity impinging on this set of cells will tend to establish maximum involvement in a mode of oscillation common to the two residual circulating patterns. The set of cells which stabilize their response patterns to conform to this common mode will subsequently have a high probability of sharing coherent response in either of the two constituent modes.

Since the set of cells in region 2 which receive coherent afferent input from region 1 need not be capable of achieving coherent efferent effects elsewhere, the pattern of outflow from region 2 resulting from presentation of S_1 might well be random and ineffectual. However, the action of stimulus S_2 upon region 2 is more direct, and it seems reasonable to expect that in appropriate regions such unconditioned stimuli activate a subset of neurons which produce a coherent and effective outflow. The stabilization of responsiveness of a portion of this population to afferent input resulting from S_1 provides functional control over a set of neurons capable of coherent efferent outflow, thus achieving a nonrandom influence over a second population for the propagated effects of stimulation of the first population. This stabilization would presumably be mediated by chemical processes of the sort described in the first half of this volume. As the process was repeated, the specificity of control of coherent discharge in the second region would increase, due to fractionation and to the gradual diminution of response to random stimuli occurring sporadically during the period, analogous to inhibition.

Ultimately, presentation of the conditioned stimulus S_1 thus causes activation of a common mode of activity in the neural regions which initially displayed coherent response only to the unconditioned stimulus S_2. The selective coherence displayed by that subset of cells previously responsive to the unconditioned stimulus S_2 ultimately propagates to the set of effectors where it releases a variant of the earlier response, now considered to be a conditioned response. Thus, the functional influence of S_1 has been extended.

The hypothetical mechanism that has been described, although it does not specify the nature of the chemical process which is postulated to stabilize a mode of activity of the dominant focus so that a particular organization will be differentially elicited by particular stimuli, would seem adequate as a preliminary formulation of the possible mechanisms of connection formation, and, hence, stimulus substitution. These mechanisms comprise the essential ingredient for a description of simple classical or stimulus-controlled instrumental conditioning, wherein the response will occur if the stimulus is effective, or perceived—that is, *existential discrimination.*

From the viewpoint of the proposed mechanism, the difficulty of so-called "backward" conditioning can be straightforwardly explained. Since the conditioned response is considered to be a result of coherence caused by the conditioned stimulus in the system initially responsive to the unconditioned stimulus, it seems reasonable to compare the effects of forward and backward conditioning procedures on that system. First, we assume that the percentage, P_1, of neurons in that system which respond to the conditioned stimulus is smaller than the percentage, P_2, which respond to the unconditioned stimulus. Second, we assume that only those neurons which are still participating in the circulation of impulses derived from the presentation of the first stimulus can mediate the establishment of a common mode of oscillation to both stimuli. Both of these assumptions seem eminently reasonable and obvious. Then, from simple calculations, it can be seen that the ratio of the proportion of neurons responsive to the *first* stimulus which also respond to the *second* stimulus is P_2/P_1, when the effectiveness of the sequence $CS \rightarrow US$ is compared to the sequence $US \rightarrow CS$. Thus, backward conditioning should be very much more difficult to achieve although the total number of neurons affected by the separate stimuli are the same in both procedures.*

* In the case of simple classical conditioning in which the unconditioned stimulus elicits a response very similar to that which the conditioned stimulus will subsequently release, the mechanism just described seems sufficient to account for the effects of conditioning. Instrumental conditioning, in which presentation of the conditioned stimulus elicits a response which is arbitrarily selected as the prerequisite for delivery

N. Representational systems: general and specific

A mechanism of this sort, however, is inadequate to explain performance of *differential* responses requiring discrimination between stimuli. This is particularly true of discriminations between stimuli which cannot be based on instantaneous stimulus characteristics. A

---

of reinforcement, requires a more involved explanation. First, it is necessary to assume that an animal possesses a number of motivational systems which generate "drives" when homeostatic imbalance occurs. High.drive states generate pain or discomfort and can be considered to possess negative valence. Low drive states minimize discomfort and are therefore of positive valence. Although appreciable periods of time may ensue between the consummation of a behavior which will lower a high drive state and the reduction of discomfort, an animal learns during its lifetime that certain consummatory acts are followed by the reduction of previously high drive states, and such acts acquire positive valence by contiguity. Performance of these acts can now serve as secondary reinforcers of certain types of behavior by activating the appropriate valence systems.

Consider the rat learning to bar press for food in the presence of a visual cue. Early in life, the animal experienced hunger which was satiated following the ingestion of food, although many other randomly emitted behaviors failed to lessen the discomfort. A first order system was gradually built, associating the dominant foci activated by seeing and eating food with the dominant foci established by the reduction of a high drive state. Thus, eating acquired positive valence, and became more probable when the animal was hungry. Subsequently, in random exploration while hungry, the animal discovers that a bar pressing behavior produces food which can be eaten. Seeing and pressing the bar constitutes a complex visual-motor stimulus. The set of dominant foci activated by this stimulus is associated with the first order system activated by seeing and eating the food produced by the bar press. Consequently, a second order representational system is established; bar pressing acquires positive valence and becomes more probable when the animal is hungry. Once the bar pressing habit has been established, food delivery is made contingent upon the presence of some sensory cue serving as a discriminative stimulus. In the absence of the cue, bar pressing fails to elicit food and is accompanied by coherent activity in regions of the nervous system activated by high drive states and possessing negative valence. The contiguous activity of these processes establishes a new second order system, so that bar pressing in the absence of the cue acquires negative valence, leading to response inhibition. Conversely, the contiguity of the coherent response during presentation of the discriminative stimulus with the second order system activated by bar pressing and eating leads to establishment of a third order representational system, so that the cue acquires positive valence and bar pressing becomes more probable when the cue is present.

Thus, we envisage a process whereby the lower order systems activated by sensory stimuli, responses, and drive states become integrated into superordinate systems by chaining and contiguity. The activation of a lower order system is assumed to entail a characteristic mode of activity within an interlocked set of dominant foci, while the activation of higher order systems is assumed to involve establishment of a common mode of activity resulting from the coupling of modes between the constituent lower order systems.

single tone or a chord cannot serve to identify a symphony. A flash of light of specified intensity and duration occurring ten times a second cannot be distinguished from an *identical* flash occurring six times a second on the mere basis of the number and spatial distribution of retinal elements excited per flash. Discrimination between sequential series of stimuli, *composed of nonunique components,* would seem to necessitate internalization of the time sequence of events and comparison with representations of the temporal patterns of previously experienced sequences of stimuli, in order to achieve identification. This problem is closely related to the problem of serial order in behavior, which has been discussed so lucidly by Lashley (1951).

When an animal experiences stimuli in a learning situation, some configuration of activity of the viscera, endocrine system, hypothalamus, reticular formation, and rhinencephalon reflects what we might call the "affective and vegetative state" of the organism. In different CNS regions, at the time of peripheral stimulation, certain sets of neurons are nonrandomly associated in ongoing activity. (A basic dichotomy may exist between the configurations of activity in such structures during appetitive behavior and aversive behavior.) The afferent stimuli impinging on this network are themselves transmitted centrally along two relatively distinct pathways, one of which is the appropriate specific sensory pathway, the other of which is the ascending nonsensory specific system. We postulate that a *general representational system* is built as a consequence of

---

The reader may be somewhat distressed by the introduction of apparently anthropomorphic concepts such as drive and valence in the foregoing discussion. Yet, ample literature exists which demonstrates that various anatomical regions are strongly implicated in the motivation of different classes of behavior. The categorization of ergotrophic and trophotrophic regions of the diencephalon by Hess (1954), the elucidation of various drive-relevant systems by Olds (1956), and the demonstration of "push" and "pull" mechanisms by Grastyán et al. (1956, 1965) should constitute adequate examples. Nonrandom activity levels in portions of these systems generate what we have called drives, and incorporation of such active regions into representational systems attaches valence to them. The general features of instrumental conditioning, then, are assumed to correspond to the essential aspects of classical conditioning, except that sequential chaining of responses appears to be fundamentally involved in instrumental conditioning. The reason why the introduction of reinforcement (the attachment of valence to a response because of its relationship to drive reduction) facilitates learning is obscure although it is clear that such facilitation occurs. Perhaps the neural systems responsive to changes in the balance of intrinsic homeostatic mechanisms possess exceptional capacity to influence chemical reactions or coherence levels in other brain regions when they become activated, because of intrinsically massive and coherent effects upon the directly relevant regions. Such coherence may be influenced by dc shifts resulting from reinforcement (see p. 212).

repeated experiences of this sort, which might be called the "memory trace" or "engram" of that experience. This system lies in structures which do not belong to any specific sensory system. Regions of the reticular formation, the intralaminar and association nuclei of the thalamus, the hypothalamus, and the rhinencephalon, which are in a sustained nonrandom state of activity during the stimulus or which are activated by the stimulus, become associated in the general representational system.

The temporal and spatial pattern of afferent input in the various portions of the general representational system causes the activity of the corresponding neural populations to deviate from randomness in characteristic sequences. The resulting fluctuations in local excitability affect the temporal distribution of efferent outflow from neurons in this region, propagating to other regions of the nervous system. It has been shown that neurons in this system essentially change their functional connectivity as a result of the particular configuration of activity to which they are subjected (Scheibel and Scheibel, 1965). The interaction of these local patterns of excitability fluctuating in time, and the propagating reflection of these local patterns as variations in discharge frequency of axonal influences on other regions, is envisaged as producing a set of phased oscillations in a system of loosely coupled structures with a characteristic common mode determined by the specifications of the initial afferent stimulation. Persistence of these oscillatory modes for a sufficient time is assumed to accomplish a critical shift in the fortuitously selected set of cells engaged in such activity. The probability that the common mode of response will be coherently displayed by these neuronal populations is thereby enhanced, as outlined in earlier chapters. At the same time, and in an analogous fashion, a *specific representational system* becomes established between structures in the specific sensory system which are activated by the stimulus. As these two representational systems are elaborated, a set of associated links is established, whereby phase-locked activity in the two systems interacts. Depending upon parameters of stimulus and state, such patterns of phase-locked activity might develop with great rapidity or in gradual increments, and the resulting interaction might be inhibitory or facilitatory.

We assume that a mature animal has in nonspecific structures a large number of established general representational systems. The nonspecific systems of the animal are not a globally acting reticulum, but seem to be made up of a set of specifically sensitive subsystems, reciprocally antagonistic, with roughly equated global effects, but different patterns of inhibition, and excitation. The relative levels of activation of these various systems at any time are affected by the state of the animal. Those general systems largely including the regions of reticular formation, hypothalamus, and rhinencephalon, which immediately reflect the *present state,* will tend to dominate those general systems which do not include such representation of the "set" of the moment. Thus, the relative activation of the various general representational systems will vary during time, as the condition of the organism changes.

O. Interaction between specific and general representational systems

When a stimulus impinges on the organism, it is propagated centrally along the appropriate specific sensory system. This propagation is accompanied by activation of the *specific representational system* in accordance with the constraints of excitability imposed on that system by the presence of modulating inflows along links with the *general representational system* which is dominant at that moment. The temporal pattern of activity in the specific sensory system and the appropriate specific representational system tends to be *stimulus-bound,* that is, the characteristics of this pattern are largely determined by the characteristics of the stimulus although they can be modulated as a consequence of interaction with the *general representational system* most dominant at the moment.

Simultaneously, the stimulus, probably via collaterals to lateral regions of the reticular formation, has activated certain regions in the brain-stem. The general representational system, in nonspecific structures, which maximally includes the various neural regions activated by the total stimulus complex, including interoceptive as well as exteroceptive stimuli, plus those regions which reflect the preset "mood and motivation" of the animal will become fully activated in all its constituent parts with a shared mode of oscillation reflecting local excitability. Other general representational systems may be excited at the same time, but less fully. The activity pattern in this general representational system, while arising as a consequence of the afferent stimulus, need not be determined by that stimulus. Rather, it represents *release* of the configuration that is most compatible with the combination of excitatory effects of that stimulus in the presence of the configuration of excitability that reflects both the prior internal state and past experience. Thus, the characteristics of the temporal and spatial pattern evoked by the stimulus in the nonspecific structures comprising the extent of the general representational system are determined by *stimulus in the context of state.*

Finally, we postulate that, if a sufficient correspondence exists between the temporal pattern of activity in the neural ensembles comprising the *general* and the *specific* representational systems, there must be a significant departure from baseline in the activity of some central nervous system region, serving essentially as a coincidence-detector. As a result of the presumed outflow of activity from such a discharging coincidence-detector, the coherence of activity in related regions changes' and the configuration of dominant foci shifts. Thereby, a pattern of motor system discharge is initiated, which corresponds to that pattern previously most often associated with such coherent afferent barrages. On the other hand, if such coincidence does not exist, no coherent outflow occurs, and no particular motor discharge ensues.

P. A possible comparator mechanism

Clearly, some mechanism involving comparison of the patterns of activity in the general and specific representational systems must be assumed to perform the postulated coincidence-detection process. In the preceding speculations, the structures and constituent pathways of the specific sensory systems have been conceptualized as primarily involved in the representation of "reality," while activity in nonsensory specific structures reflecting past experience and the state of the organism was suggested to generate representations of "memory." The diffuse thalamic projection system would seem to provide a ready-made mechanism for displaying the dominant pattern of the memory system over large regions of cortex. We propose that the dominant temporal pattern activated by a stimulus in reticular formation and other associated nonspecific regions, reflecting the tonic influences of the moment from structures reporting the state and "set" of the organism, is propagated upward to the intralaminar nuclei of the thalamus, then to the association nuclei, and then to association areas of the cortex. From the association areas, this pattern might project to the specific sensory areas of cortex, via *axodendritic* synapses. Information arriving along the classical sensory pathways would activate *axosomatic* synapses. Proper phasing of patterns of axosomatic and axodendritic impulses, impinging on cortical neurons, might drastically alter the probability of consequent efferent discharge from the cortex. That such interactions actually can occur has been shown by the work of Jung (1958).

Chang has discussed some possible functional contributions of axosomatic synapses (pericorpuscular) and axodendritic synapses (paradendritic) of the cortex to elaboration of conditioned responses, concluding, "the importance of the thalamoreticular system in the formation of conditioned reactions is that the subcortical structures are the source of subliminal excitations for the cortical dendrites. The final integrating function is affected not by the reticular formation alone but by the cerebral cortex" (Chang, 1959). He considers paradendritic synapses as mechanisms for modulating the state of excitability of cortical neurons and pericorpuscular synapses as mechanisms to evoke activity. Jasper has described differences in the effects on cortical neurons of impulses arriving there from stimulation of specific and nonspecific thalamic nuclei, and has discussed the possibility of such a modulatory function of the nonspecific projection system (Jasper, 1954; Jasper et al., 1958). Alternative sites for the postulated interaction between patterns of activity of specific and nonspecific origin must be conceded to exist at a number of other cortical and subcortical structures than those which have been suggested.

Whatever the location of this interaction, its most crucial feature is that a marked nonrandomness of activity arises in the coincidence detector when congruence occurs between the temporal patterns of excitation arriving from the two different sources of input which have been hypothesized. With this congruence, "memory" and "reality" come into correspondence. The current input is related to patterns retrieved from "memory." This would appear to constitute a crucial step in the process of analyzing sensory input to achieve adaptive differentiated response. Once a configuration of sensory input was "identified" by sufficient congruence with the representation of past experience, response might occur by a mechanism analogous to that described for classical conditioned reflexes earlier in this chapter. Corticothalamic or cortico-reticular projections from the cortical area in which congruence becomes established might result in activation of those response system patterns which were previously associated in their activity with that general representational system which was dominant at the moment of congruence.

A possible mechanism for this influence of the corticofugal discharge may be analogous to one described by Hugelin and Bonvallet (1957). These workers, investigating a facilitation of motor discharge originating from cortex as a consequence of reticular formation stimulation, concluded that the cortical excitation, which resulted from action of the ascending reticular activating system, produced a secondary corticofugal inhibitory discharge which controlled the motor facilitation. They proposed a reticulo-cortico-reticular circuit, such that the ascending reticular activating system causes the discharge of diffuse interneuronal cortical ensembles. This corticofugal discharge arrests the reticular activation controlling the motor facilitation. This permits differentiation of motor excitability as a function of the configuration of activity in cortex and reticular formation.

A diagram of the proposed system is presented in Fig. IX-2.

Q. Comparison with scansion theories

The characteristics of the mechanism proposed here for readout of information stored in "memory" seem to differ in an essential way from the processes usually proposed. Many theorists, for example, Pitts and McCulloch (1947) and Walter (1953), have suggested that the stores of information in memory, registered in some unstipulated way, are "scanned" until a counterpart of the incoming information is found. In view of the vast amount of information presumably stored in an adult central nervous system and the remarkable speed of access, a "parallel" rather than a "serial" scan has been suggested by some.

Note that, in the present scheme, no "scan" of memory occurs. Memory, rather than consisting of a set of registers in which information lies passively, with location of the relevant items based on random search, is considered to be a dynamic process. As the state of the animal and the configuration of his environment alter, a continual fluctuation ensues in the levels of excitation of the numerous general representational systems which have been established by experience, with a related shift in the probability of particular modes of nonrandom oscillation. Those general systems that subsume nonspecific regions which reflect most closely the present state of the animal, as affected by the environment, become most excitable. Those which only slightly involve presently active

209

regions are less excitable. As a consequence, memory patterns become ordered in accordance with their correspondence to the present configuration of the relevant central nervous system parameters. The organism need not scan a vast number of equally probable patterns in order to identify an input. Rather, the most probable temporal and spatial pattern in terms of over-all resemblance to the present animal-

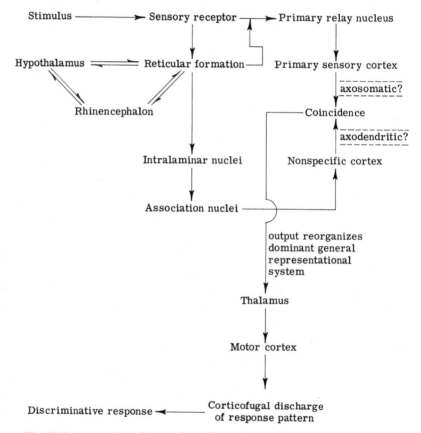

Fig. IX-2. Proposed mechanism for differential response (From John, 1962).

environment complex will be the one with easiest access, that is, the lowest threshold for significant levels of activation, and the remainder of memory will be hierarchically ordered in terms of similarity to the dominant configuration.

Thus, a stimulus complex activating some specific representational system will impinge on an animal in which the most relevant *general* representational systems, most closely corresponding to the internal state of the organism as well as the exteroceptive stimulus complex, are already being selected and ranked.

R. Salient features of the proposed representational mechanism

It may be worthwhile to recapitulate some of the major propositions set forth during this discussion. The informational effects of a stimulus upon a brain region were proposed to be the resulting deviation of the average activity of that neural ensemble from the normal baseline, over a period of time. These patterns of coherence in various structures reflected the total informational impact of the stimulus on the system. As a result of the temporal contiguity of activity in these dispersed regions, reciprocal relationships were postulated to integrate them into representational systems. Specific representational systems were considered to be largely stimulus-bound in their activity, while general representational systems displayed patterns of activity reflecting the past experience and present state of the organism. Excitation of an adequate proportion of a general representational system was considered sufficient to activate the entire system. When the entire system was activated, it displayed patterns of neural activity corresponding to the configuration of stimuli which initially established the system. Recognition or identification of a stimulus input was postulated to require a comparator mechanism, evaluating the similarity between the essential features of incoming information as reflected by spatiotemporal patterns of activity in specific representational systems and the patterns released from storage depots established during prior experience, manifested as the activity in general representational systems. Although the hypothesized comparison may take place *within* rather than *between* structures, it seems to constitute a logically necessary function.

Psychological data and theory, particularly the learning theories of Estes (1955), Bush and Mosteller (1955), and Hull (1943), might be hoped to describe the rate of organization of a general representational system, and the precision with which coincidence between general and specific representational systems must be achieved in order for properly discriminated response to occur.

At this juncture, there is little experimental evidence which, in the opinion of the writer, accounts for the apparent stabilization of a general representational system by reinforcement, whether positive or negative, or for the varying effectiveness of different schedules of reinforcement. Konorski (1950) has suggested that reinforcement may produce a rapid rate of change of activity in certain neural regions, and that such rapid changes may exert a "stamping-in" effect. The addition of reinforcement to a system in which stimuli are contiguously presented may establish a dc shift in some area, upon which convergence of influences occurs from neural regions directly responsive to the stimuli, thus facilitating the establishment of functional relationships.

This problem has been studied by Wurtz (1966), who has examined the steady potential correlates of reinforcing intracranial stimulation delivered to electrodes implanted in posterior diencephalic and anterior mesencephalic regions of rat brain known to produce self-stimulation or escape. High self-stimulation rates were accompanied by surface negative potential shifts in some cortical regions, while stimulation of escape points produced surface positive potential shifts. Thus, aversive and positively reinforcing intracranial stimuli produced opposite effects on the dc levels of cortical regions. However, the polarity of the dc shift caused by a specific stimulus varied from region to region of cortex. These findings raise the possibility that the facilitating effect of reinforcement on the establishment of conditioned responses may involve the action of local dc shifts in a manner analogous to the examples provided earlier in this chapter.

The model affords some conceptual utility in attempts to account for certain behavioral phenomena. Generalization gradients, for example, may reflect the extent to which new stimuli cause significant activity in the comparator mechanism. Contributions to achievement of adequate coincidence may arise from general environmental features or from activation of a particular central state due to arousal or drive levels. Hallucinations, fixations, delusions, and associations between memories may similarly reflect the heightened activity of a particular general representational system.

The discouraging failure of workers like Lashley to demonstrate localization of an engram for particular visual memories might become more understandable if we abandon the notion that the cortical mantle is a screen onto which pictures are flashed to be viewed by a popcorn-munching homunculus. Spatial relations in the visual field may not be isomorphically preserved as a topological array on the visual cortex. Spatial localization might be reflected in latency and amplitude differences between cortical regions, preserving some retinal-cortical correspondence. Separate spatial features may be extracted and coded as temporal sequences diffusely projected over broad areas of the cortex, there producing a typical mode of oscillation representing interactions between ensembles of feature extractors. So long as sufficient sensory cortex remained to respond to this temporal pattern of input from the peripheral receptors with the appropriate mode, it could effectively represent the arrival of information, coincidence detection could occur, and corticofugal discharge in the common mode could ensue. If the nonrandomness of such discharge were sufficient to affect the nonspecific regions from which the general representational system response mode had been released, adaptive behaviors might survive substantial damage to the structure.

Electrophysiological studies of neural activity during the elaboration and performance of conditioned responses might be expected to provide evidence bearing upon particular features which representational systems have been postulated to possess. In the remainder of this book, evidence will be presented for the existence of various phenomena which are compatible with these formulations. The changes in neural activity which accompany conditioning are extensively distributed throughout widespread regions of the brain. Neural systems built by experience apparently retain a specified spatiotemporal pattern or mode of activity, which can be released. Under certain circumstances, the release of these stored patterns of activity is accompanied by behavioral performance suggesting a functional role for the patterned discharge. Evidence will be presented that various neural regions display a common mode of activity during correct but not incorrect discriminative behavior, and that the temporal pattern of average activity in a region may be related to the processing of particular information.

Certain theoretical analyses by Lashley seem particularly relevant to the mechanisms under discussion and will be presented in some detail. Current knowledge and theory about electrophysiological processes in the brain, particularly with respect to changes observed during conditioning, will then be summarized. These background materials will comprise the next two chapters and should provide a useful context for the evaluation of the detailed experimental observations to be discussed in the remainder of this book.

CHAPTER X

THE STATISTICAL APPROACH: (2) LASHLEY AND TEMPORAL PATTERNS

A number of quotations from the work of Lashley, interpreting the results of his extensive ablation studies, are extremely relevant to a consideration of the material to be presented in the remainder of this book. The first reference I wish to quote is from the summary of Lashley's magnificent paper entitled "In search of the Engram." Reprinted in "The Neuropsychology of Lashley."*

> This series of experiments has yielded a good bit of information about what and where the memory trace is not. It has discovered nothing directly of the real nature of the engram. I sometimes feel, in reviewing the evidence on the localization of the memory trace, that the necessary conclusion is that learning just is not possible. It is difficult to conceive of a mechanism which can satisfy the conditions set for it. Nevertheless, in spite of such evidence against it, learning does sometimes occur. Although the negative data do not provide a clear picture of the nature of the engram, they do establish limits within which concepts of its nature must be confined, and thus indirectly define somewhat more clearly the nature of the nervous mechanisms which must be responsible for learning and retention. Some general conclusions are, I believe, justified by the evidence.

A. Characteristics of the engram

(1) It seems certain that the theory of well-defined conditioned reflex paths from sense organ via association areas to the motor cortex is false. The motor areas are not necessary for the retention of sensory-motor habits or even of skilled manipulative patterns.

* By Beach, Hebb, Morgan, and Nissen. Copyright © by McGraw-Hill, Inc. Used by permission of McGraw-Hill Book Company, pp. 478–505.

(2) It is not possible to demonstrate the isolated localization of a memory trace anywhere within the nervous system. Limited regions may be essential for learning or retention of a particular activity, but within such regions the parts are functionally equivalent. The engram is represented throughout the region.

(3) The so-called associative areas are not storehouses for specific memories. They seem to be concerned with modes of organization and with general facilitation or maintenance of the level of vigilance. The defects which occur after their destruction are not amnesias but difficulties in the performance of tasks which involve abstraction and generalization, or conflict of purposes. It is not possible as yet to describe these defects in the present psychological terminology. Goldstein (1940) has expressed them in part as a shift from the abstract to the concrete attitude, but this characterization is too vague and general to give a picture of the functional disturbance. For our present purpose the important point is that the defects are not fundamentally of memory.

(4) The trace of any activity is not an isolated connection between sensory and motor elements. It is tied in with the whole complex of spatial and temporal axes of nervous activity which forms a constant substratum of behavior. Each association is oriented with respect to space and time. Only by long practice under varying conditions does it become generalized or dissociated from these specific coordinates. The space and time coordinates in orientation can, I believe, only be maintained by some sort of polarization of activity and by rhythmic discharges which pervade the entire brain, influencing the organization of activity everywhere. The position and direction of motion in the visual field, for example, continuously modify the spinal postural adjustments, but, a fact that is more frequently overlooked, the postural adjustments also determine the orientation of the visual field, so that upright objects continue to appear upright, in spite of changes in the inclination of the head. This substratum of postural and tonic activity is constantly present and is integrated with the memory trace (Lashley, 1951).

I have mentioned briefly evidence that new associations are tied in spontaneously with a great mass of related associations. This conception is fundamental to the problems of attention and interest. There are no neurological data bearing directly upon these problems, but a good guess is that the phenomena which we designate as attention and interest are the result of partial, subthreshold activation of systems of related associations which have a mutual facilitative action. It seems impossible to account for many of the characters of organic amnesias except in such general terms as reduced vigilance or reduced facilitation.

(5) The equivalence of different regions of the cortex for retention of memories points to multiple representation. Somehow, equivalent traces are established throughout the functional area. Analysis of the sensory and motor aspects of habits shows that they are reducible only to relations among components which have no constant position with respect to structural elements. This means, I believe, that within a functional area the cells throughout the area acquire the capacity to react in certain definite patterns, which may have any distribution within the area. I have elsewhere proposed a possible mechanism to account for this multiple representation. Briefly, the characteristics of the nervous network are such that, when it is

subject to any pattern of excitation, *it may develop a pattern of activity, reduplicated throughout an entire functional area by spread of excitations, much as the surface of a liquid develops an interference pattern of spreading waves when it is disturbed at several points* (Lashley, 1942). *This means that, within a functional area, the neurons must be sensitized to react in certain combinations, perhaps in complex patterns of reverberatory circuits reduplicated throughout the area* [italics, E. R. John].

(6) Consideration of the numerical relations of sensory and other cells in the brain makes it certain, I believe, that all of the cells of the brain must be in almost constant activity, either firing or actively inhibited. There is no great excess of cells which can be reserved as the seat of special memories. The complexity of the functions involved in reproductive memory implies that every instance of recall requires the activity of literally millions of neurons. The same neurons which retain the memory traces of one experience must also participate in countless other activities.

Recall involves the synergic action of some sort of resonance among a very large number of neurons. The learning process must consist of the attunement of the elements of a complex system in such a way that a particular combination or pattern of cells responds more readily than before the experience. The particular mechanism by which this is brought about remains unknown. From the numerical relations involved, I believe that even the reservation of individual synapses for special associative reactions is impossible. The alternative is, perhaps, that the dendrites and cell body may be locally modified in such a manner that the cell responds differentially, at least in the timing of its firing, according to the pattern of combination of axon feet from which excitation is received.

B. Memory as trace systems

The last quotation from Lashley which is relevant to the topic of this book comes from one of his final papers, "Cerebral Organization and Behavior,"* published in 1958.

> Of the multitude of things which might be in consciousness, only a limited number are present at any one moment. It is held that this isolation has no parallel in the physical world and that energy changes, since they form a continuum, could not effect such isolation. This category of mental activity involves many problems, such as attention and dissociation, selective memory, and directed action. I can deal with them most readily by sketching the theory of cerebral organization that I have dreamed up in the course of years. It involves several postulates about integrative mechanisms.
>
> (1) The billions of neurons in the cerebral network are organized into a large number of systems. Each system consists of the traces of a number of habits or memories. Knowledge of the moves and games of chess would constitute one such system; memories of neuroanatomy another; and so on through all of the individual's varied interests. The traces or engramata in any system are more closely connected with one another than with other

* From "The Neuropsychology of Lashley," pp. 529–543, by Beach, Hebb, Morgan, and Nissen. Copyright © 1960 by McGraw-Hill, Inc. Used by permission of McGraw-Hill Book Company.

systems. The systems are not anatomically separate, and the same neurons, in different permutations, may participate in many systems. For brevity I shall call these 'trace systems.'

(2) Such a trace system may be thrown into a state of tonic activity by an external stimulus which activates one set of traces within it. In the tonic state the traces of the system are readily excitable and available to recall. Other systems are in abeyance. Thus when one plays chess, the Evans gambit or Philador's defense may be readily recalled. But if the player is interrupted by the question, 'Who won the pennant last year?,' he will take some time to 'collect his thoughts'; that is, to organize the baseball trace system. Such a general tonic activation seems a plausible explanation of concentration upon a particular subject, limiting associations to that subject. Questions of preparatory adjustment, organization of purposive activities, and the like can be formulated in such terms. An activated trace system would limit associations of the flow of ideas to the topics included in that group of traces. As I have stressed elsewhere (1951), grammatical structure and other ordered activities imply some sorting or arranging mechanism, active before the words reach overt speech or silent thought. The relations in thought structure are antecedent to consciousness. The tonic background might provide the basis for this preorganization. This leads to the problem of the neurology of logic, of which a bit more, later.

(3) A system in tonic activity dominates the brain field, limiting the organization of other systems. It is relatively impervious to unrelated excitations. An intense stimulus, or an emotionally charged one, such as the sound of one's name, may break in, but the great mass of afferent excitations is excluded. This blocking might be either an active inhibition or the preemption of neurons which might otherwise be included in the blocked system. The phenomena of attention demand some such hypothesis.

(4) The neurons in a trace system, under tonic activation, exert some mutual facilitation. The tonic state of the whole system is thus built up and maintained. This was the only sort of explanation that I could find for the reduction in efficiency of behavior in the proportion to the extent of brain damage. The assumption is consistent with Woodworth's notion (1918) that long practiced habits may be transformed into drives; that activities which have acquired many associations may become obsessive.

(5) The level of tonus in the partially activated system may vary. Circuits which have just been fully activated may retain a high level of subthreshold activity and thus contribute to the temporal organization evident in the memory span.

(6) Fixation in memory is generally possible only when the remembered material forms part of such a dominant system. Learning has been classified in two types: mechanical, produced by repetition; and rational, which is not dependent on repetition. We remember the content of a book, not in the author's words but in meanings which fit into previous knowledge of the subject. During the reading the meanings are not necessarily formulated clearly in verbal or other thought forms, but they may be so formulated later. That is, associations may be formed during reading with traces in the system which are not activated above tonic levels during learning.

This assumption would provide an explanation of some types of confusion in which the patient may show disconnected activities or disordered thinking, with no later memory of what occurred during the state.

Such a system of low level tonic excitation in a system of memory traces would provide a basis for many of the characteristics of mental organization. The circuits of the trace system which are actively firing at levels sufficient to excite other traces would constitute the content of experience, limited and changing from moment to moment. The background of tonic activity would determine the direction of attention and of the flow of thought, restricting it to related associations. It would provide the binding force that holds together the temporal sequences through memory span and more permanent associations. Reduction in the tonic level of the system, as in sleep or under anesthetics, or violent invasion, as in a convulsive seizure, would destroy the organization necessary for memory and the continuity of the conscious state. Partial incomplete disorganization in sleep would permit interaction of different partial systems with the bizarre contaminations that occur in dreams.

These assumptions concerning cerebral organization are, of course, purely speculative and mainly inferences from psychological events. There is no present direct evidence from physiology in support of them. However, they are not inconsistent with what is now known of the physiology of the brain, and I believe that some such mechanism is implied by our present knowledge of the structure and activities of the cerebral cortex [italics, E. R. John].

As I emphasized at a previous meeting of the association (Lashley, 1952), it is probable that every neuron in the cerebral cortex, and indeed in the whole nervous system, is subject to a continuous bombardment by nerve impulses. This follows from consideration of cell number, of frequency of sensory input, and of the continuity of the cerebral network. The observations of Gray Walter (1953) on synchronous firing of many areas of the cortex with driven alpha rhythms show how widespread the excitations may be.

Not all and perhaps not even a large proportion of the neurons are fired by the bombardment. It requires at least two and perhaps many more impulses from end buds to fire the cell. But partial depolarization with increase in excitability may result from subthreshold volleys and because of decremental conduction in the cell membrane, may be selected for special connections. When one set of circuits is actively fired, it should be expected that some neurons in associative connection with it would receive too few impulses to fire them, but sufficient to prime them for response to impulses from other circuits. Sherrington's studies of overlap in motor pools revealed a condition of increased excitatory state which could provide a mechanism for the tonic state of associated neurons at higher levels. This would result in a sort of priming of an entire associative or trace system.

I believe that what is known of the learning process justifies these assumptions concerning the role of the tonic background in the formation of associations. The importance of repetition in learning has been greatly exaggerated. Thorndike, who was the most eminent American student of learning and for many years an advocate of the theory of learning by repetition, finally denied its importance. He substituted for repetition a somewhat vague concept of 'belongingness' which implies, so far as I can interpret it, some unconscious relational structure or unconscious associations.

An organization of associated neurons excited at subthreshold levels seems not only a reasonable but an almost necessary consequence of the structure and known physiological properties of the cerebral cortex. As I have indicated, the interplay of such systems would provide a mechanism for a large proportion of the selective activities of mind.

By the extensive quotations from Hebb and Lashley, I have intended not only to express admiration for the cogency of the thinking of these two psychologists about memory, but to present, specifically, that portion of their hypotheses which bears most directly upon the evidence to be presented in the remainder of this volume. Many features of the mechanisms proposed in this book bear marked resemblance to processes envisaged by these earlier workers although much of the evidence which is cited was not available to them. That evidence, in the judgment of this writer, provides considerable physiological substantiation for the positions expressed in the quotations.

Formulations such as those which have just been presented, and the evaluation of accumulated results of ablation experiments, provided a stimulus for the development of new methods to study these problems. This stimulus has resulted in three particularly promising new lines of approach:

(1) The use of electrophysiological recording methods in conjunction with chronically implanted electrodes to study changes in the electrical responses of brain regions during the acquisition and performance of conditioned responses;

(2) The establishment of conditioned responses using direct electrical stimulation of brain regions as the conditioned stimulus, the unconditioned stimulus, or both;

(3) The application of electrical stimulation to various brain regions in order to disrupt learning or performance.

These methods have begun to provide new information about the processes which mediate learning and subsequent performance. Detailed reviews of the results of these studies have recently been published by Morrell (1961c) and by John (1961) and will not be duplicated in this book although a general summary of the results will be provided.

Before that summary is presented, it should be stated that, in my opinion, studies of changes in electrographic response during learning represent a more technically sophisticated variant of ablation studies, in the sense that information is obtained about the detailed changes of activity in specific anatomical regions. Although this does provide a more intimate and detailed picture of the participation of various brain areas in the conditioned response, the functional role of such involvement remains obscure. These studies show that many, if not most, brain regions display altered electrical response during learning. As conditioned responses are established, the pattern of electrical reaction to the conditioned stimuli shifts, which suggests that the participation of particular anatomical regions varies at different stages of the formation of the response. Although the regions which show. changed response are, thereby, potentially implicated in mediation of the behavior, our present understanding of electrophysiological phenomena limits the unequivocal interpretation of many such changes in terms of neuronal events. In later chapters, selected portions of these data will be presented, which, in the opinion of the author, permit some reasonable inferences to be made about the functional characteristics of the underlying mechanisms. At this point it seems appropriate to present a discussion of current understanding of various electrophysiological phenomena and then a summary of the changes which have been observed in the electrical activity of the brain during learning.

CHAPTER XI

BRAIN POTENTIALS: SOME INTER-RELATION-
SHIPS AND BEHAVIORAL CORRELATES

I. Brain Potentials

The preponderance of the evidence which will be adduced in the remainder of this book comes from electrophysiological studies conducted on animals during the acquisition and performance of various kinds of conditioned responses. Most of the data consist of electroencephalographic (EEG) or macropotential phenomena recorded from relatively large chronically implanted electrodes, although some microelectrode studies have yielded information about the activity of single neurons in conditioning situations. Our understanding of the mechanisms responsible for generation of macropotentials is still incomplete. It is difficult to specify the relationship between EEG or evoked potential observations and the activity of the cellular elements in the monitored regions. Yet, although macropotentials and unit activity represent two different levels of phenomena, both arise in neural tissue and it is important to examine the possible inferences which can be plausibly drawn from phenomena on one level about processes on the other level. A brief review of various kinds of electrical phenomena which can be observed in the brain, some of the current views about the origins and interactions of these processes, and a summary of some electrophysiological findings from conditioning studies may be useful for those readers who are unfamiliar with this field. In order to provide an overview of this research area, a number of studies will be mentioned in this chapter which are treated in more detail elsewhere in this book, even though this entails some repetition.

A. Evoked potentials

1. *Origin of slow waves*

The electrical potentials recorded from the brain using macroelectrodes represent the complex interaction of patterns of largely asynchronous activity arising from peripheral and central structures. Cortical recordings frequently display rather large and conspicuous rhythmic macropotentials, while relatively fast, low level activity is usually recorded from other sites (Bureš, Petráň, and Zachar, 1960b).

Upon afferent stimulation, these characteristic patterns of "ongoing" activity are usually replaced by low voltage fast potentials, while rhythmic potentials may be recorded from the hippocampus. The synchronous volley of impulses produced by the stimulus gives rise to macropotentials time-locked to the stimulus in both cortical and subcortical structures. Some of these "evoked" potentials may be rather distinct while others may be obscured by the ongoing background activity and require averaging techniques to detect them.

The physiological origins of the macropotentials, particularly those observed on the cortex, have been the subject of a large number of investigations. Early attempts to explain these electrical brain waves suggested that they were the "envelope" resulting from summation of the spike discharges of individual neurons, firing with some dispersion in time (Adrian and Matthews, 1934). Later formulations suggested that the slow waves were generated by summation of afterpotentials of longer duration than the brief action potentials. These proposals were based upon the belief that the *firing* of cells somehow produced the locally recorded slow potentials and could not be reconciled with subsequent evidence that under certain experimental conditions spikes could be abolished without the disappearance of slow waves. In order to account for the decoupling of spike and slow wave activity, it was suggested that slow waves arose from the summation of postsynaptic potentials, representing the interaction of hyperpolarizing and depolarizing shifts of the neuronal membrane, principally in dendritic regions of the cell, as a result of the action of transmitter substances released from presynaptic terminals (Purpura, 1959). These shifts in the resting potential could occur without accompaniment by firing of the postsynaptic cell. Direct measure-

224

ment of dendritic potentials has been achieved by Hild and Tasaki by microelectrode recordings from tissue culture (1962).

Due to the morphological and functional complexity of the dendritic fields, it has been difficult to attach a unique interpretation to the details of macropotential wave shapes. Positive potential shifts are often considered to reflect hyperpolarization due to inhibitory postsynaptic potentials, while negative shifts are attributed to depolarization due to excitatory postsynaptic potentials. It has been proposed that potentials recorded from the surface of the cerebral cortex, negative with respect to a distant reference electrode, are due to the depolarizing postsynaptic potentials generated in apical dendrites. The apical dendrites act as sinks to deeper lying somatic and basilar dendritic sources. Surface positive potentials have sometimes been attributed to depolarization of deeper regions, which then act as current sinks to apical dendrite sources (Purpura, 1959; Amassian, 1961).

There are considerable data from depth analysis of cortical regions with fairly orderly anatomical structure which seem consistent with source-sink descriptions. Components of evoked responses which are of given electrical sign when recorded from the cortical surface are often observed with opposite polarity when recorded in the cortical depths. However, some of the positive components of surface waves may be due to a dominance of hyperpolarizing activity in the apical dendrites rather than to deep sinks. It is particularly difficult to interpret potentials recorded from deeper neural regions which possess less orderly architectonic characteristics.

2. Central synaptic transmission

For many years, there was disagreement among neurophysiologists as to whether synaptic transmission in the central nervous system was mediated by a chemical or an electrical mechanism. With the advent of intracellular recording techniques, it became generally accepted that chemical transmission mediated most of the communication from nerve cell to nerve cell in the central nervous system, although electrical interactions may play a significant role in the synchronization of rhythmic responses. It is believed that most excitatory and inhibitory synaptic influences in the central nervous system are mediated by specific transmitter substances released by the presynaptic terminal, acting on special receptor sites on the postsynaptic membrane (Eccles, 1964). The usual candidates for the role of excitatory transmitter substances in the central nervous system are acetylcholine, noradrenaline, and 5-hydroxytryptamine, although evidence exists that these substances are involved in only a small proportion of synaptic actions. Among the other substances currently under consideration as excitatory transmitters are certain negatively charged amino acids. There is very little evidence relating to the nature of inhibitory transmitter substances in the central nervous system. It was suggested that γ-aminobutyric acid (GABA) might be such a substance. However, these proposals seem to have been based upon a general depressant action exerted by this compound on all postsynaptic neuronal responses, rather than upon a hyperpolarization of nerve cells resembling the action of inhibitory synapses. Curtis has examined a large number of compounds for this action, relying largely upon electrophoretic injection through coaxial micropipettes, and concluded that none of the substances studied met his criteria for an inhibitory transmitter (Curtis, 1963). No definitive compendium of the set of chemical substances which mediate excitatory and inhibitory transmission in the vertebrate central nervous system has yet been provided. Kandel *et al.* (1966) have recently presented evidence that two branches of an interneuron could differ in their synaptic action, one causing an inhibitory and the other an excitatory postsynaptic potential. Both actions were blocked by curare, suggesting that ACh may be released by both branches. Thus, the postsynaptic membrane may be critical in determining the response of a neuron to arrival of a synaptic transmitter, rather than only the nature of the impinging transmitter substance.

B. Steady potentials

The dc potential of the cortical surface is usually a few millivolts negative when measured against either a ventricular or remote extracortical reference electrode. Under these circumstances, evoked potentials contain a prominent surface negative component. A relatively moderate surface positive polarization leads to an increase in the height of the negative dendritic response. Conversely, moderate surface negative polarization leads to a decrease in the height of the negative dendritic response, while for stronger negative polarizations the dendritic response reverses to a pronounced positive potential. At an intermediate level of applied negative polarization, it is almost possible to abolish evidence of the dendritic response (Caspers, 1959).

Topical application of GABA to the cortical surface, which blocks postsynaptic responses in apical dendrites, has an effect similar to that of relatively strong negative polarization (Caspers, 1959). The dc potential of the treated region becomes more negative and the surface evoked responses shift toward the positive direction. Moderate anodal polarization will reduce the height of the GABA-induced positive evoked potentials, while stronger anodal polarization will restore the negative evoked potential component attributed to apical dendritic activity. Similarly, "spreading depression" is accompanied by a marked surface negative dc shift, and some of the ensuing functional impairment can be reversed by applied surface anodal polarization. Evidence of this sort suggests that the local dc potential may reflect a dynamic balance between the hyperpolarizing and depolarizing influences to which neurons in that region are subjected. A positive or negative shift of the local dc level may change the average number of units in that region which will respond an input by a relative increase in depolarization or hyperpolarization, respectively. Thus, local shifts in steady potentials may be related to changes in the coherence of neural activity.

A number of workers have observed that changes in the transcortical potential gradient are often associated with changes in the pattern of neuronal activity (Morrell, 1963). Many of these experiments involved the imposition of steady potential shifts on neural tissue by direct polarization or by drug administration. However, various neural processes are also capable of accomplishing dc shifts of significant amplitude. Widespread surface-negative dc shifts, particularly prominent in anterior portions of the brain, can be caused by strong sensory stimuli which are startling or by electrical stimulation of the reticular formation, and may be related to the so-called arousal response. Other shifts, more limited in extent, have been produced by stimulation of various thalamic regions, particularly the midline areas. The form and distribution of the shift depended upon the locus and frequency of the stimulus. Quite local dc shifts can arise after sensory stimulation of moderate intensity (Gumnit and Grossman, 1961). Thus, it appears possible that neural activity arising from afferent stimulation may cause more or less extensive steady potential shifts which can result in changes in the amount or in the coherence of neural activity in particular brain regions.

C. Relationship between macropotentials and unit activity

A resting nerve cell displays an electrical potential across the cell membrane such that the inside of the cell is electrically negative with respect to the outside. These resting potentials are of electrochemical origin, arising from the maintenance of ionic gradients across the membrane, which is differentially permeable to certain electrolytes. When membrane depolarization reaches a critical level, the electrochemical gradients are altered, the membrane becomes highly permeable, and the cell fires. As is well known, the central nervous system neuron consists of a cell body, or soma, which sends off a large number of fine processes. One of these processes is the axon along which the unit discharge propagates. The remaining processes are receptive in nature, receiving synaptic contacts from the axones of other neurons, and are called dendrites. Synaptic contacts are also made directly upon the soma. A neuron may receive such synaptic inputs in vast numbers. The arrival of an impulse at a synapse is followed by transmission of the presynaptic excitation across to the postsynaptic cell, probably by the release of minute amounts of a chemical transmitter substance. This process causes a change in the polarization of the postsynaptic membrane, a so-called postsynaptic potential. Postsynaptic potentials may be excitatory (EPSP) or inhibitory (IPSP). These postsynaptic dendritic potentials do not propagate, possibly due to the fine diameter of the dendrites, but they decrease electrotonically within a short distance. However, they achieve redistribution of the ionic densities on the cell membrane, so that summation and interaction of these effects can occur. Similar events can also take place on the soma. The crucial events for discharge of the cell seem to relate to the level of depolarization of the axon hillock, the region on the cell body from which the axon arises.

As indicated earlier in this chapter, the relationship between neural firing and regional slow wave activity has received much attention. The early suggestion that slow waves represented the envelope of discharges in a population of neurons was rejected after demonstrations that unit activity could be suppressed while slow potentials persisted. Subsequently, many workers believed that macropotentials reflected integrated EPSP's and IPSP's of a large volume of cells. The enormous number of cells whose activity might contribute to the potentials recorded from the volumes monitored by large electrodes becomes evident from the fact that 1 cubic millimeter of cortex contains from 10,000 to 30,000 neurons. Since the postsynaptic potentials modulate the excitability of neurons, if macropotentials represented PSP's integrated from a volume of cells, they should be related to the over-all probability of neural discharge in that volume. However, slow waves can also be observed in white matter, composed largely of fiber tracts. This strongly suggests that the slow waves recorded from a region are a composite of excitatory and inhibitory PSP's, plus the afterpotentials of spike discharges in cell bodies as well as in afferent and efferent fibers coursing through that volume of tissue.

Numerous investigations have shown a direct relationship between peripheral stimuli and the firing of single neurons, but until recently, the relationship between unit firings and macropotentials remained obscure, with poor correlations generally reported between extracellular unit recordings and the potentials derived from large electrodes. Gradually, data have emerged which help to clarify the picture. Some findings which indirectly relate unit activity to slow waves and steady potentials were reported by Creutzfeldt et al. (1962, 1966b). Direct current polarization of the cortex surface of cats leads to a change in excitability of single units. Anodal polarization usually increases spontaneous neural discharge and facilitates firing in response to a stimulus, while cathodal polarization has the opposite effect. The authors were reluctant to attribute physiological significance to these results, since the polarizing currents were large, on the order of 200 μA, to 1000 μA. However, Bindman et al, using much lower currents, have obtained similar results from rats (1962b). They observed enhanced evoked potentials and facilitation of unit firing for anodal polarizing currents of the order of 0.1 μA to 0.5 μA in a small region of cortex. These long-lasting increases in firing rate were not accompanied by a prolonged residual depolarization of the region (Bindman, 1965). The results are relevant to attempts at interpretation of the various steady potential studies mentioned in the previous section.

Appreciable evidence exists that surface potentials correlate well with the transmembrane potentials recorded with intracellular electrodes. Recently, Klee et al. (1965) carried out cross-correlation analysis between EEG potentials and the transmembrane potentials of single cortical

229

neurons, obtaining time-series correlation coefficients as high as 0.7. These quantitative results confirm the qualitative conclusions reached by others including Kandel and Spencer observing hippocampal neurons during seizure (1961), Fujita and Sato in hippocampal neurons during theta activity (1964), Purpura et al. in thalamic and cortical neurons during recruiting (Purpura et al., 1964; Purpura and Schofer, 1964), Klee and Offenloch during augmenting responses (1964), Creutzfeldt et al. in visual cortex neurons during spontaneous activity (1966b), Calvet et al. from laminar EEG analysis (1964), and Stefanis in the motor cortex (1963). Klee et al. interpreted the observed correlations to mean that the electrical rhythms of the encephalogram reflect an integration of the fluctuation of membrane potentials in both cell bodies and dendrites of large numbers of neurons.

In more recent studies, Creutzfeldt et al. (1966a) have demonstrated clear temporal relations between evoked cortical potentials and the transmembranal potential changes of pyramidal cells. In general, surface positivity was correlated with an incoming afferent volley or an EPSP, while surface negativity tended to be associated with cellular IPSP's. Afferent and efferent volleys and axo-dendritic and axo-somatic inputs all seemed to cause characteristic effects on both slow waves and cellular potentials. Pollen and Sie (1964) have also presented evidence that the surface negative wave is associated with inhibitory postsynaptic potentials generated in deeper layers of the cortex.

Elul reached the conclusion that the EEG could not be explained as resulting from the summation of fast neuronal activity and proposed the existence of unitary generators of slow activity, on the basis of the observation of large slow potentials between pairs of microelectrodes with tips as close together as 30 μ (1962). In later work (unpublished observations, 1966b), this worker found that cortical neurons exhibit wave activity similar to the EEG but of much greater amplitude. The fact that these intracellular potentials probably originate in the neurons, rather than constituting a secondary reflection of some external wave process, was indicated by several findings. Cells with a high resting potential but no incidence of spike discharge, presumably glial cells, showed no oscillations of the resting membrane potential. Furthermore, extracellular wave activity displayed an amplitude only about 1% of that found inside nerve cells, suggesting that the EEG resulted from combination of extracellular fields of neuronal wave activity. Amplitude histograms of the EEG were found to follow a normal probability distribution, although neuronal wave activity did not do so. However, frequency analysis of EEG and neuronal waves showed close similarity. On the basis of these observations, Elul suggested that the wave form and frequency content of the EEG give an indication of the oscillations of membrane potential of neurons in the same region. The frequency of the gross record reflects the frequencies and wave forms of individual neurons, but phase relations are lost.

The expectation that good correlation might be found between unit discharges and slow wave activity in a region was partially based upon the belief that a linear relationship held between the level of membrane depolarization and initiation of a propagating action potential from the axon hillock. Recent studies with intracellular electrodes, for example those reported by Purpura (Purpura et al., 1964; Purpura and Schofer, 1964), show that the unit discharge does not always occur when the transmembrane potential reaches a critical value. Other factors, such as the rate of change of potential or the spatial distribution of charge on the nerve membrane, may also contribute to the release of a propagating discharge.

The nature of the correlation between neuronal transmembrane potentials and regional slow wave activity, together with the fact that neuronal discharge does not always occur at the same level of membrane depolarization, means that unit spike activity and macropotentials cannot be expected to show an immediately demonstrable and consistently predictable relationship. Macropotentials seem to represent the summated effects of slow transmembranal, postsynaptic, and afterpotentials over a field encompassing great numbers of neurons and fibers, and thereby may reflect the existence of coherent processes within the average volume. However, the spike activity of any *single* nerve cell impaled upon a microelectrode might bear a relationship to such summated waves which was markedly nonlinear and which could only be approximated by statistical evaluation. Systematic relationships between the distribution of unit activity in a population of cells and the macropotentials derived from that region may only become apparent if there is some degree of averaging, either through the *simultaneous sampling of more than one unit,* or by *sequential averaging over time.* Related information might be obtained from consideration of the unit discharge as frequency-modulated information, and an attempt to cross-correlate the demodulated unit discharge

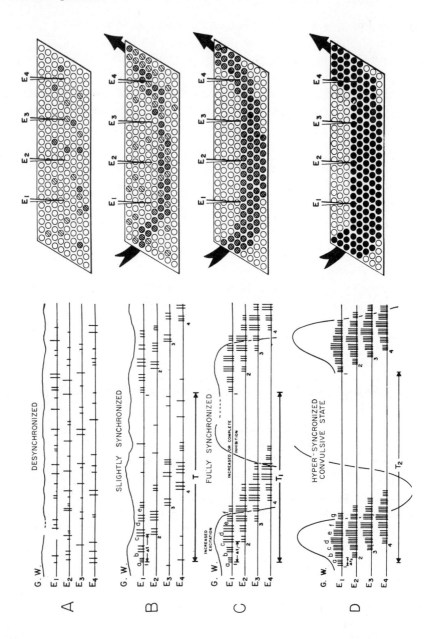

Fig. XI-1.—Relations between neuronal discharge, circulation of neuronal activity, and synchronization of the gross waves as they appear when recorded simultaneously with four microelectrodes with tips separated by 100 to 150 μ. Left: diagrammatic representation of oscilloscope tracings, showing the progressive changes that take

232

with macropotentials recorded from the region over a long epoch. These studies should reveal significant correlations if slow potentials influence the probability of nerve cell discharge.

Some work involving time averaging has been reported. Gerstein has obtained poststimulus histograms of unit firing and average response curves of slow potentials, both derived from the same microelectrode in the auditory cortex of lightly anesthetized cats (1961). Each record shows clear, stimulus time-locked components. To some extent there is a covariation of the average slow potential wave form with the poststimulus histogram. However, the author points out that uncertainty as to whether the particular local dendritic structure being recorded participates in modulation of activity of the monitored cell renders a definitive interpretation difficult.

Another example comes from reports by Green and his co-workers, who have shown a correlation between hippocampal theta rhythm and the firing patterns of single hippocampal units (1960). An ingenious vector-

---

place from the desynchronized to the hypersynchronized state. Right: diagrammatic two-dimensional representation of neuronal fields showing the neuronal activity corresponding to each successive state. E_1, E_2, E_3, E_4 represent the microelectrodes through which oscilloscope tracings E_1, E_2, E_3, E_4 (at left) would be obtained; the circles represent neurons in the field of the microelectrodes; the degree of darkness in each circle represents the degree of excitation of that particular neuron; the arrow represents the direction of the circulation of neuronal activity. A: Oscilloscope: infrequent clustering of the spikes, no circulation of neuronal activity, no synchronization of the gross waves. Neuronal field: scattered, sporadic neuronal activity, at low level of excitation; no circulation of neuronal activity. B: Oscilloscope: increased clustering of spikes; occurrence of neuronal activity in regular succession at each one of the tips of the microelectrodes indicating circulation through the neuronal network; decreased activity in the interval between successive passages of circulating activity through the network; gross waves slightly synchronized. Neuronal field: neuronal activity at higher level of excitation, concentrated mostly in the pathway of circulation (arrow); decreased activity outside this pathway. C: Oscilloscope: high degree of clustering of spikes; increase in the velocity of circulating activity ($\Delta^{t_1} < \Delta^t$); activity abolished in an increased interval between successive passages of circulating activity through the network; gross waves fully synchronized. Neuronal field: neuronal activity at high level of excitation in the pathway of circulation; no activity outside the pathway. D: Oscilloscope: extreme degree of clustering of spikes; high velocity of circulation ($\Delta^{t_2} < \Delta^{t_1}$); further increase in the interval between successive passages of circulating activity through the network; neuronal activity in this interval abolished; hypersynchronized gross waves of high amplitude. Neuronal field: neuronal activity at very high level of excitation concentrated exclusively in an enlarged, multilane pathway of circulation; completely abolished outside this pathway. (Data from Verzeano, 1963.) [See next page.]

oscillographic method was used to carry out the averaging. Positive relationships between single unit activity and slow potentials have also been reported by Robertson (1965), Vasilevs (1965), and Frost and Gol (1966).

Simultaneous sampling of the activity of appreciable numbers of units has been accomplished by Verzeano and his colleagues, with multiple microelectrodes (Verzeano and Negishi, 1960; Verzeano et al., 1965; Verzeano, 1963). Evidence has been provided of the circulation of activity through the neuronal networks, as indicated by the appearance of iterated patterns of unit discharge. These observations of circulating activity have been confirmed by Creutzfeldt and Jung (1961). Using a longitudinal array of microelectrodes with known tip spacings, the characteristics of the circulation of activity through the cortical and thalamic networks of the cat and the patterns of neuronal activity have been examined. Results show clearly that cellular discharge patterns are related to the degree of synchronization of the cortical or thalamic slow waves. Increasing synchronization of the gross waves corresponds to: a larger number of neurons involved in the pathway of circulation and an increased frequency and clustering of their spike discharges; an increasing apparent velocity of circulation; a lengthened period of silence between successive passages of circulating activity through the network; and a decrease in the activity of neurons located outside the pathway of circulation. These observations are depicted schematically in Fig. XI-1. (See previous page.)

The pathways of circulation follow a series of loops whose "locus" constantly displaces itself through the neuronal network. Particular wave shapes in the gross electrical activity correspond closely to the activity of neurons and groups of neurons discharging in sequence and in characteristic patterns. Whenever wave shapes change, the underlying discharge pattern also changes. However, *on any circulation through the network some neurons may drop out of the pattern and other neurons may enter it.* The relationship of the single unit discharge to the wave shape is therefore *statistical* in nature, occurring with greater or lesser reliability under various conditions.

Using appropriate amplifier time constants to observe both neuronal spikes and gross waves from each of a set of microelectrodes, recordings from monkey brain show this regular association between gross waves and spike discharges of a group of neurons. Different characteristics are displayed by the cells monitored by each electrode. This regularity of relationship is illustrated in Fig. XI-2 (p. 236). Results of spatiotemporal analysis using multiple microelectrodes suggest that increasing amplitude or synchronization of the gross electrical waves is related to the progressive coordination of regional neuronal networks until a resonance-like state is achieved.

Perhaps the most definite demonstration of the statistical relationship between the discharge of single neurons and evoked potentials in a region comes from the work of Fox and O'Brien (1965). The observed relationship is illustrated in Fig. XI-3 (p. 238). These workers compiled the frequency distribution of spikes from single cells in the visual cortex as a function of time after stimulation with light flashes, summating the responses obtained to several thousand flashes. These frequency distribution curves were then cross-correlated with the averaged evoked potentials recorded from the same region. Correlation coefficients ranged from 0.14 to 0.88, with 58% of the units studied showing a relationship between spike discharges and local slow waves which was significant at the .001 level. The range of observed correlations was probably much affected by nonlinear factors, such as the fact that in the case of considerable membrane hyperpolarization the probability of unit firing may be zero in spite of potential fluctuations which would normally be effective. The range of coefficients also suggested that cells in a given region can be differentially influenced by a stimulus in such a way that some are affected by the afferent input rather reliably while others are much less massively involved in response.

Since there is no reason to assume that the arbitrarily monitored units were atypical of the population as a whole, the implication of this study is that an equally good correlation would be obtained between the evoked potential and the average activity of the entire ensemble, if it were possible to monitor the discharge of thousands of neurons at the same time. This presumed ensemble correlation would arise not because the evoked potential was the envelope of unit discharges but rather because the evoked potential reflected the average discharge probability of neurons in the region due to modulations of excitability by shifts in transmembrane potentials.

D. The hypothetical origin of evoked response wave shapes

Considering these questions, Adey has suggested that within the population of neurons forming a cortical domain, intrinsic changes in

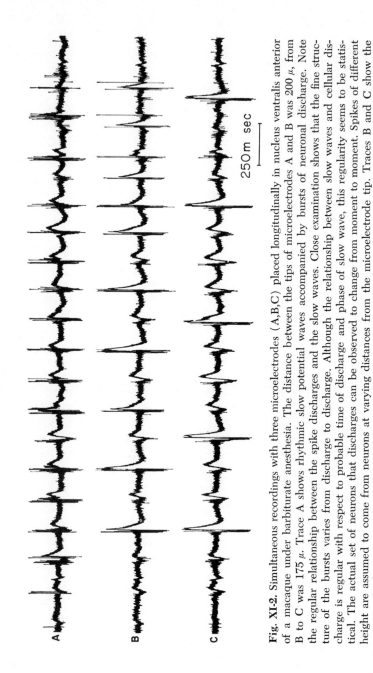

Fig. XI-2. Simultaneous recordings with three microelectrodes (A,B,C) placed longitudinally in nucleus ventralis anterior of a macaque under barbiturate anesthesia. The distance between the tips of microelectrodes A and B was 200 μ, from B to C was 175 μ. Trace A shows rhythmic slow potential waves accompanied by bursts of neuronal discharge. Note the regular relationship between the spike discharges and the slow waves. Close examination shows that the fine structure of the bursts varies from discharge to discharge. Although the relationship between slow waves and cellular discharge is regular with respect to probable time of discharge and phase of slow wave, this regularity seems to be statistical. The actual set of neurons that discharges can be observed to change from moment to moment. Spikes of different height are assumed to come from neurons at varying distances from the microelectrode tip. Traces B and C show the activity of other groups of neurons in the same general region which discharge at sub-multiples of the rhythmicity observed in trace A. [Based on data from Verzeano *et al.* (1965).]

neuronal excitability resulting from local phenomena may be expected to establish a basic pattern of neuronal firing having aspects of a random process. The arrival of a volley from a peripheral stimulus will superimpose aspects of a deterministic input, although the final relay of the afferent volley from thalamus to cortex may have some form of probabilistic organization. Although a particular cortical response may well reflect a spatiotemporal configuration related to the activation of specific neurons in an extensive volume of neural tissue, the informational specificity of that response presumably does not reside in the discharge of any one neuron or small set of neurons within that population. Rather, the output or efferent volley from the cortex, signaled by pulse-coded firing of a proportion of the neuronal population with a particular spatiotemporal configuration, can be achieved in essentially identical fashion to successive identical stimuli by the utilization of different neurons within the population (Adey, 1963).

Arguing the necessity for a probabilistic approach to cerebral cortical functions, Adey goes on to suggest that the integration of information at the cellular level may occur on the basis of wave processes. Such integration would be independent of the pulse-coded digital output which presumably serves to transfer information to distant nuclei. He proposes that the individual neuron may be viewed as a phase comparator sensing the spatiotemporal characteristics of wave patterns impinging on its surface, with the possibility that its responsiveness to a particular pattern may be influenced by previous participation in similar patterns. This writer has made similar suggestions on the basis of related but somewhat different considerations (John and Killam, 1960; John, 1963).

These formulations are relevant to the resistance of the central nervous system to functional disruption caused by the random perturbations of neural activity, to which it is continuously subjected. The inefficacy of these perturbations suggests the possibility that information in nuclear aggregates is processed in a statistical manner involving participation of large populations of neurons, with the relevant information specified by the *average* behavior of the ensemble.

Gersch (1966) has described a mathematical model which corresponds to the ensemble average over an unconnected set of statistically distributed linear elements. He has demonstrated that an arbitrary signal wave form can be duplicated by the behavior of the ensemble and can approximate the behavior of a highly nonlinear, intricately interconnected sys-

237

tem rather well with the set of linear elements. This stochastic model, based on ensemble averaging, has been applied to phenomena observed in studies of simulated neural nets and of evoked potentials.

The material presented thus far in this chapter seems to provide some basis for more detailed discussion of the relationship between evoked potential wave shape, activity in a neuronal ensemble, and the processing of information in that ensemble. Assume that a volume of neural tissue

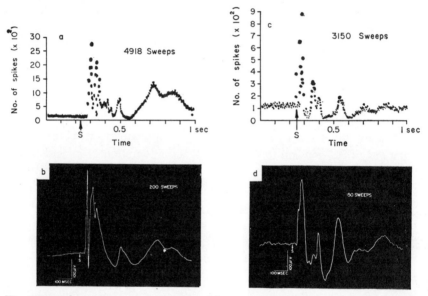

Fig. XI-3. Relation between probability of firing of a single cell and evoked potential waveform. (a) Frequency distribution of spikes from a single cell in the visual cortex of a cat after stimulation with 4918 flashes; (b) averaged evoked potential (200 oscilloscope sweeps) recorded from the same microelectrode, after cell death ($r = .60$; $p < .001$). Similarly, spike distribution for a single cell is shown in (c) (3150 sweeps) and the corresponding averaged evoked potential in (d) (150 sweeps) ($r = .51$; $p < .001$). Ordinate (for unit distributions): number of times the cell fired in response to light flash. Abscissa (for unit distributions): time, in 100-msec divisions. [Data from Fox and O'Brien (1965).]

contains a large number of neuronal circuits or *loops*, which are potentially reentrant and that a loop of given length requires a stipulated time to accomplish one circulation of impulses, corresponding to its period. That loop is capable of reverberation at the corresponding frequency. A cell in that loop will receive excitatory synaptic influences at that frequency when reverberation occurs. The EPSP's arising from such excitation will be of only brief duration, less than the interspike interval. Other cells in the population might receive IPSP's due to the circulating reverberation, and these might have a duration prolonged far beyond a single period. An electrode in a volume of cells containing a subset which were involved in reverberating loops of that length might detect electrical events at that frequency, with an amplitude proportional to the percentage of cells receiving EPSP's at that frequency. These events would be superimposed on a slower process of opposite sign, reflecting the appearance of sustained IPSP's in the ensemble. An additional slow electrical process might be expected to exist in the ensemble, related to the recovery and afterpotentials in cells and fibers after occurrence of spike discharges. The frequency correspondence between loop activity and slow waves would seem to depend upon the time course and shape of the membrane response, yet the observed similarity between the frequency distribution of EEG waves and transmembrane potentials suggests that the integrated activity reflects the frequency and wave shape of individual neural activity rather well. The amplitude of a particular frequency component would seem dependent upon whether some initiating event brought such activity into coherent phase. The occurrence of an afferent barrage might accomplish significant coherence, in addition to nonsynaptic (ephaptic) interactions between adjacent neurons and other physiological factors aiding synchronization.

The characteristic morphology of a region will determine the distribution of possible loop lengths, and thereby will define a set of possible frequencies which can be sustained by activity in a population. The circuits set into reverberation after an afferent barrage arrives in a region will be distributed among the various possible frequencies in such a way that a percentage (N_i) of the neurons involved will correspond to each frequency (F_i). Thus, the sum of the N_i equals the proportion of the total neural aggregate involved in sustained response to the afferent input. The sum of the various terms, $E(t) = \Sigma_i N_i \sin F_i t$, defines the oscillation which is the over-all sustained effect of the excitatory disturbance in the population, assuming phase-locking to the occurrence of the afferent barrage. The wave shape reflecting the accumulation of inhibitory processes in the population during this time interval, $I(t)$, must be added to the wave shape $E(t)$ reflecting these excitatory influences. The frequency composition of $I(t)$ is difficult to specify because it depends upon the time constant of decay of IPSP's, as well as the temporal pattern of inhibitory input. Yet, it seems probable that $I(t)$ would reflect the fundamental frequencies F_i and their subharmonics to some extent. Similarly, the process $D(t)$ representing the decay of afterpotentials should reflect the fundamental frequencies of excitation. The argument in the early chapters of this book asserted that the cells contributing to these oscillations must necessarily include those which will subsequently represent the event causing the disturbance. The complex phase-locked oscillation, $O(t) = E(t) + I(t) + D(t)$, just described, might approximately correspond to the shape of the evoked potential which would be sensed by an electrode in the volume of responding cells, sensitive to the time course of excitatory and inhibitory influences and afterpotentials in the whole population.

Were the above suggestion correct, how might the activity of a single neuron be related to the shape of the evoked potential? Since the duration of an evoked potential is much longer than a single unit discharge, the discharge of those neurons that are not influenced by the stimulus over an extended period cannot be expected to display any correlation with the evoked potential. In order for neurons to become involved in sustained activity as a consequence of the afferent input, they must be members of loops around which the recirculation of activity takes place. Suppose that a given neuron belongs only to one such loop. The activity resulting in that neuron because of events in that loop will occur at some frequency, F_i, corresponding to the length of that particular loop. The maximum correlation that could be expected between the activity of that neural unit and the macropotential recorded from the ensemble would be proportional to the relative contribution of the F_i component to the wave shape of the evoked potential. If F_i were the salient component of $O(t)$ the correlation might be rather high, whereas a low correlation would be expected if F_i were a minor component of the oscillation. Thus, non-nodal neurons, involved in representational activity in a single loop, should show a significant but low correlation to the total oscillatory pattern. Nodal neurons involved in a number of loops of different lengths corresponding to different frequencies might be expected to show a somewhat higher correlation, proportional to the amount of energy in the total oscillation contributed by components at these several frequencies. These speculations would be markedly affected by nonlinearities between neuronal firing rates and membrane potentials, and by the

240

amount of discharge by a particular cell related to engagement in other straight-chain circuits in addition to participation in reverberating loops. These would be among the variables expected to influence the factor of proportionality, thus determining the size of the sample of neural activity which would be required in order to demonstrate the existence of the correlation. This qualitative argument is intended to suggest the general nature of relationships expected between unit activity and evoked potentials.

The proposed formulation seems compatible with the data by Fox cited above. Observation of significant correlation between averaged evoked responses and the frequency distribution of spike discharges in a single neuron, summed across a large sample of repeated stimuli, suggests that the single evoked response recorded from a neural region reflects the EPSP's and IPSP's summed across the vast ensemble of neurons in that region, fluctuating from instant to instant as the sustained consequences of the afferent input reverberate through the network. It seems reasonable to suggest that the macropotentials recorded from a given region in some instances may describe the *probability* of unit discharge in the cells comprising the local neuronal population. The shape of that summed potential may reflect the distribution of that disturbance in paths of varying length and recirculation time, plus factors like the time constant of decay of shifts of membrane potentials and the rate of repolarization of membranes. Some of the neurons in the network are affected by the input only for a transient instant, others are involved in sustained participation in circulation of activity in a single loop, while others occupy a nodal position in several loops. If we assume that the informational representation of a stimulus in a neural population corresponds to the significant change in the neural firing patterns from the previous baseline of activity, then the average evoked potential wave shape would seem likely to reflect the probable time course of the over-all informational consequences of input to a neural network. If informational specificity indeed were reflected by the average activity of the ensemble rather than by the deterministic discharge of some specific neurons, evoked potentials elicited in certain regions by stimuli differing with respect to certain physical attributes but sharing common informational significance should display some invariant characteristics in common. These inferences are highly relevant to possible interpretations of some phenomena which will be presented later in this book.

II. Conditioning Methods and Terminology

Before proceeding to consideration of various sorts of electrophysiological studies of conditioning, a brief summary of conditioning methodology and terminology seems appropriate.

Classical conditioning can be considered as a procedure of achieving a degree of stimulus equivalence. By appropriately timed pairings, a previously neutral stimulus (conditioned stimulus, or CS) acquires the capacity to elicit a response (conditioned response, or CR) which closely resembles the relatively automatic reflex response (unconditioned response, or UR) to the unconditioned stimulus (US), with which it has been associated. For example, a mild shock to the leg will elicit a flexion response (UR). If this mild shock is systematically preceded by a tone (CS), which normally does not cause leg flexion, after a number of paired presentations the tone will elicit leg flexion (CR) without the necessity of shock. Variations of this basic paradigm exist, differing primarily with respect to the temporal arrangement and spacing of stimuli and their specific nature. In general, successful classical conditioning seems facilitated by the existence of an autonomic component to the unconditioned response. Conditioned responses are necessarily restricted to those variations in the activity pattern of the organism which are reliably caused by the US. *Sensory-sensory conditioning* is a special case of classical conditioning in which both CS and US are exteroceptive stimuli.

In contrast, *instrumental conditioning* is a procedure which will reliably increase the frequency of any behavior in the repertoire of an organism. Practically, the major constraint on successful instrumental conditioning is that the base rate of incidence (operant level) of the activity which is arbitrarily selected for manipulation be sufficiently high. The wide variety of instrumental conditioning techniques which have been developed have in common the feature that performance of the activity selected to become the conditioned response achieves a "reinforcing situation," which is usually either the termination of a noxious stimulus, such as shock, or the satisfaction of needs for food or water. Systematic reinforcement of the selected activity whenever it appears leads to a marked increase in rate of appearance. In these paradigms,

242

performance of the conditioned response alters the environment of the organism, hence is "instrumental." These behaviors can be brought under *stimulus control*, by utilizing the presence of a conditioned stimulus to signal a period in which performance of the CR will result in reinforcement not available in its absence.

Situations in which reinforcement is *contingent* upon the mere presence or absence of the CS when the CR is performed are sometimes referred to as *existential discriminations*. More complex procedures, in which one stimulus indicates the presence and another stimulus indicates the absence of some reinforcement contingency, or in which two different conditioned responses are simultaneously established under the control of two different conditioned stimuli, are sometimes referred to as *differential discriminations*.

In both classical and instrumental procedures, the stimuli need not be peripheral, but may be delivered centrally through implanted electrodes, as was discussed in previous chapters. Drugs and lesion effects have been utilized to disrupt acquisition or performance of these responses and thereby to facilitate further analysis.

III. Electrophysiological Studies of Conditioning

The techniques which have been used in electrophysiological studies of conditioning largely fall within the foregoing descriptions. The findings obtained from such studies can be categorized into a number of major classes: changes in levels of synchrony or intrinsic brain rhythms associated with presentation of the CS, with occurrence of the orientation response, or with "choice behavior"; phenomena related to steady potentials; and changes in evoked potentials or unit activity as conditioned responses are established to intermittent or rhythmic stimuli. Since the voluminous literature on these topics has been reviewed fairly recently (John, 1961; Morrell, 1961c), only a brief overview will be presented here.

A. Studies of changes in level of synchrony

The study of changes in the effects of stimuli on macropotentials as a function of conditioning or other experience dates back to Durup and

Fessard (1935). Since that time, alterations in the "ongoing" rhythmic cortical waves or the slow, synchronous hippocampal macropotentials have been observed during conditioning by numerous workers. When a CS, to which the animal has been previously habituated, is initially paired with the US, widespread changes from slow, high voltage alpha activity to relatively low, fast potentials occur in the surface electrocorticogram. As training proceeds and the CR becomes fully established, this activation pattern becomes limited to only a few "relevant" regions of the cortex (e.g., the motor cortex if the CR is a motor response or the visual cortex if the CS is light). During extinction, the patterns of electrical activity observed in the early stages of conditioning reappear in reverse order.

Usually, the changes in the "ongoing" activity associated with a given CR performance level occur prior to the appearance of the behavioral responses and, in extinction, persist beyond the disappearance of the behavioral responses. Many studies of this sort were focused on the sites of appearance of desynchronization. The results led to formulation of the idea that there was initial widespread irradiation of desynchronization over the cortex (adduced as evidence of involvement of the mesencephalic reticular formation in the early stages of conditioning), followed by consolidation or localized desynchronization, which was assumed by some to indicate a later shift to a dominant role for the thalamic reticular formation. Studies of the habituation of the arousal response led to concepts of phasic thalamic adjustment to iterated inconsequential events, followed by tonic mesencephalic adaptation resulting in diminution and disappearance of desynchronization. The cortical conditioning work of Morrell and Jasper (1956) in which a steady CS is paired with an intermittent US reveals a *Phase I* of widespread desynchronization, a *Phase II* of US-frequency-specific response to the steady CS in the US region, and a *Phase III* of localized desynchronization. These studies, while tending to support notions of shift from the mesencephalic to thalamic reticular formation similar to those arising from studies of conditioned alpha blocking, also provided early evidence of the ability of neural systems to represent the time sequence of previous stimulation in response to a new stimulus. These phenomena will be discussed in much more detail in subsequent chapters.

Such data clearly demonstrate a covariation between changes in "ongoing" and rhythmic macropotential activity and the behavioral changes during conditioning. However, it has been pointed out (Jasper et al., 1960) that changes in the spontaneous rhythmic activity need not necessarily reflect unique changes in the underlying neural processes.

A slow synchronous hippocampal response appears to ambiguous but significant stimuli early in conditioning, often in association with the orienting response (Grastyán et al., 1959; Lissák and Grastyán, 1960). This hippocampal response usually disappears in the later stages of conditioning, when the stimuli appear to take on an unambiguous meaning. Studies of changes in the hippocampal response have led to the suggestion that replacement of the dominance of mesencephalic reticular formation effects by those of the thalamic reticular formation may be due to hippocampal inhibition of the mesencephalic reticular formation.

Analysis of the slow hippocampal theta rhythms displayed by animals at choice points during conditioned visual discrimination for food (Adey et al., 1960) has revealed a change in phase relationship between entorhinal cortex, hippocampus, and the dentate gyrus which seems related to the appropriateness of the behavior. These data have been interpreted as evidence for a phase comparator mechanism in which phase relationship is dependent upon the similarity between present and previous input.

B. Steady potentials and conditioned responses

A body of evidence exists which suggests relationships between steady potentials and the neural activity involved in learning. The surface negative dc shift accompanying spreading depression has been correlated with deficit in acquisition of learned responses (Bureš et al., 1958). Chronic epileptogenic lesions are known to impair acquisition of conditioned behavioral or electrical responses when the discharging focus involves the cortical projection area responsive to the conditioned stimulus (Kraft et al., 1960; Morrell, 1957a), and a surface-negative shift seems to characterize these lesions (Ward and Malmke, 1960).

Many observations, summarized in Chapter IX, indicate that local dc polarization of a region may alter its responsiveness to previously ineffective stimuli and apparently facilitate the establishment of new functional relationships. Further studies of steady potentials suggest that they can disrupt performance of previously established conditioned responses, that local dc shifts can be conditioned, and that conditioning alters the dc effects caused by the conditioned stimulus.

Morrell has demonstrated that the prolonged aftereffects of polarization cannot be interpreted as mere sensitization, since muscular response can be differentially elicited by a tone which was repeatedly presented during polarization but not by a tone of another frequency (Morrell, 1961b). Additional study by Morrell has revealed that single cells in previously polarized tissue have a marked tendency to respond to single stimuli with bursts of discharges at the frequency of an intermittent rhythmic stimulation which was delivered during the earlier polarization period. Chow et al. (Dewson et al., 1964; Chow, 1964; Chow and Dewson, 1964) have demonstrated an analogous phenomenon in macropotential rhythms recorded from a chronically isolated slab, showing a marked tendency for electrical recordings from this preparation to display rhythms at the frequency of a previous stimulus applied during polarization, during subsequent stimulation at another frequency. Cathodal polarization seems to block registration of training experience, while anodal polarization may facilitate subsequent performance (Morrell and Naitoh, 1962). Recently, considerable interest has been aroused by the demonstration that the expectation of a meaningful event is attended in man by a pronounced dc shift (E-wave) that is detectable in recordings from certain scalp regions (Walter et al., 1964).

C. Studies using an intermittent "tracer" CS

Changes in amplitude and distribution of evoked potentials, as conditioned responses are elaborated to intermittent conditioned stimuli, provide, a further means of discerning changes in electrical activity associated with the conditioning process. In these studies, the intermittent signal is treated as a *"tracer" stimulus* and electrical responses at the stimulus frequency are considered as *"labeled" activity*. The appearance of labeled potentials in a structure is interpreted as sufficient but not necessary evidence of the influence of signal information on the structure. During conditioning, a widespread sequence of changes in labeled potentials has been reported.

1. Assimilation

Among the phenomena described by Livanov and Poliakov (1945), who first applied this technique, was that which they termed "assimilation of the rhythm." By this term, Livanov referred to the appearance of exceedingly marked hypersynchronous activity at the frequency of the intermittent CS, or harmonics thereof, which dominates the resting electrical activity observed during the intertrial interval. This activity increases during the sharply rising portion of the learning ogive and diminishes or disappears as criterion is reached. Assimilation provides additional evidence that the temporal sequence of previous stimulation can be represented by neural activity in the absence of the stimulus.

Yoshii and co-workers (1957b, 1960) conditioned frequency-specific potentials, originally elicited by a flicker or repetitive central stimulation used as the US, as the response to a CS consisting of steady tone or light. General desynchronization was seen early in conditioning, followed by hippocampal arousal. Subsequent to the subsiding of hippocampal arousal, frequency-specific responses were recorded from cortical, thalamic, and reticular formation sites. Yoshii noted further, at a later state of conditioning, that merely placing the animal in the experimental apparatus would elicit frequency-specific activity in various regions, and suggested that this activity might be a manifestation of a memory trace.

2. Simple conditioned responses

John and Killam (1959) studied the changes in amplitude and distribution of labeled responses during avoidance conditioning in the cat using flickering lights as the CS. Prior to conditioning, the animals were subjected to a prolonged familiarization procedure involving daily presentation of a number of periods of flicker stimulation. Early in the familiarization procedure, flicker presentation elicited labeled responses in widespread brain areas. As the animals became accustomed to this procedure, in which flicker was not accompanied by any reinforcement, there was a marked diminution of labeled responses, which eventually disappeared almost completely.

When avoidance conditioning began, with the introduction of electrical foot shock as reinforcement, the amount of labeled response in many structures increased dramatically. During the period in which the avoidance response was being elaborated, a complex sequence of changes in the distribution and form of labeled potentials was observed. New responses appeared in structures previously showing no frequency-specific activity, other structures revealed waxing and waning of labeled responses, while such activity disappeared from some regions in which it was initially displayed. In the fully trained animals, labeled responses were less marked than those observed during various stages of acquisition. This decrement of electrical response to the CS seems to be a characteristic feature of the electrophysiological activity accompanying the performance of a well-established simple conditioned response.

3. The effects of sensitization

The interpretation of the extent to which these changes in the electrical response of various brain regions to the tracer CS are indicative of changes in the processing of signal-derived information in these neural structures is extremely difficult. Alteration in labeled responses may reflect changes in local excitability due to unspecific features of the conditioning situation which bear no relationship to changes in information processing. Among these general influences might be the change in levels of synchronous activity due to arousal, the emotional reaction of the animal to the punishment or reward used as reinforcement, or the increased focus of attention on a particular sensory modality. This problem was investigated by McAdam (1962) in a careful series of experiments in which cats were trained to perform leg flexion in response to a flicker CS using a simple classical conditioning procedure. The changes in labeled responses displayed by the conditioned animals were compared with the electrical data obtained from a control group of cats subjected to a "pseudoconditioning" procedure, in which the CS and US were presented in random relationship so that no CR was established. This comparison revealed that most of the changes in electrical response which were observed in the trained animals also occurred in the pseudoconditioned animals. However, some of the structures monitored showed changes in labeled response only in the trained animals. These changes reflected neural processes related to acquisition of information about the CS, rather than the effects of sensitization. Yet these results emphasize the need for caution in interpretation of altered electrophysiological response and highlight the necessity to provide adequate controls for unspecific factors in studies of this sort.

4. Changes accompanying transfer

A number of plans have been devised to build controls into the procedures used with individual animals so that the relative contribution of changes reflecting altered information processing and those related to unspecific sensitization can be evaluated within the body of data obtained from each animal. These procedures permit more adequate evaluation of data from a single animal without the necessity of comparisons between experimental and control groups. One approach intended to permit this distinction to be drawn involves the initial training of animals to perform differentiated conditioned responses to stimuli such as steady tones of different pitch or steady lights in different positions. Following stable establishment of these behaviors, the differential conditioned responses are *transferred* to two new tracer conditioned stimuli differing in their repetition rate. The labeled responses elicited by the tracer stimuli before and after transfer are then compared. Since before transfer the animal is already fully conditioned to the steady CS's, factors which might be related to unspecific sensitization can be considered present. Animals which have been differentially trained to sensory cues of one modality are alert, attentive, and motivated throughout the transfer period. Therefore, if changes were observed in labeled responses after completion of transfer to an intermittent stimulus, whether in the same or a second modality, these changes would seem reasonably attributed to altered processing of information about the tracer CS.

Changes in the labeled responses evoked in various brain structures of previously trained cats following transfer of training to previously ineffective intermittent conditioned stimuli have been observed in a number of studies. Corley observed changes in labeled responses in some structures after transfer of differential avoidance responses to flicker after initial training with steady tones or lights (Corley, 1963). Similar results have been obtained after transfer of a differentiated flexion reflex to flicker after initial training with clicks (Majkowski and John, 1966), and after transfer of differentiated approach-avoidance responses to clicks after initial training with flicker (Shimokochi and John, 1965). It should be mentioned that transfer sometimes occurs very rapidly, with

249

behavioral responses to the new CS occurring after only a few reinforcements. Thus, changes in labeled responses accompanying behavioral transfer can sometimes be observed in a single training session. These results indicate that many of the changes in labeled response which accompany the attachment of cue value to a tracer stimulus cannot reasonably be attributed to unspecific general features of the conditioning situation, but seem to be related to altered neural response to the CS reflecting the processing of information.

5. Differential conditioning

It should also be mentioned that marked increase in the amount of labeled responses occurs in many structures as previously established instrumental responses are differentially brought under stimulus control. If a procedure is followed in which the significance of the *frequency* of a flicker CS is made more and more explicit and specific in a series of steps, the distribution and duration of labeled responses displayed by many structures increases progressively (John and Killam, 1960). Presentation of flicker with no cue value to a cat which is pressing a lever to obtain milk elicits very little if any labeled response. When this behavior is brought under control of the flicker CS so that lever-pressing occurs only after flicker presentation, labeled responses are displayed in a few structures. The frequency correspondence between the electrical rhythms and the tracer stimulus is only approximate and the periods of labeled response within a trial are of short duration. After discrimination training in which lever-pressing is rewarded during presentation of flicker at one frequency but not at a second frequency, the anatomical distribution of labeled responses becomes more widespread. In addition, the frequency correspondence between the electrical rhythms and the tracer stimuli becomes more exact and the periods of labeled response within a trial become much longer. When the tracer stimulus which was previously the negative cue for lever-pressing to obtain milk is made the aversive cue for performance of a different behavior to avoid shock, these changes are further accentuated and stabilized.

This increased labeled activity persists in a differentially trained animal, with no evidence of the diminution often seen following acquisition of a simple conditioned response. This difference may be due to the fact that information about the mere presence or onset of the conditioned stimulus provides sufficient basis for a decision to perform the simple response, while appropriate performance of differential response demands more specific analysis of the *quality* of the detected peripheral signal. The persistence of the widespread labeled response under these conditions argues against the assumption that processes mediating the analysis of information become focalized, an interpretation sometimes offered for the diminished distribution of labeled responses after simple conditioning.

6. Comparison of correct and erroneous behavioral responses

The establishment of differential conditioned responses to tracer stimuli differing in frequency made it possible to evaluate further the relationships between information processing and the distribution and form of labeled responses while controlling for unspecific effects which might reflect sensitization. Such hypothetical general factors can be considered present throughout a session in which an animal is required to perform differentially to a randomly mixed series of two conditioned stimuli. Comparison of labeled response characteristics from trials in which the performance was *correct* with those from trials in which *errors* occurred should provide insight into neural mechanisms involved in processing and evaluating signal-derived information. Sensitization effects should be equally present regardless of the behavioral accuracy and can therefore be partialed out. Furthermore, these comparisons might provide insight particularly into the more dynamic features of conditioned response mediation, as distinguished from processes primarily related to the relatively passive transmission of information between brain regions. The changes in anatomical distribution of labeled responses observed in various studies are numerous and difficult to interpret. No effort will be made to describe them in detail here since the interested reader can consult the original papers. Throughout the remainder of this volume, an effort will be made to focus upon those aspects of electrophysiological studies which seem to reflect mechanisms involved in information storage, retrieval, and evaluation.

It should be mentioned at this point that the changes in labeled response which occurred during the differential training described above were most marked in nonsensory-specific brain regions. When behavioral responses in the frequency-discrimination task were appropriate for the particular stimulus which was presented, the labeled electrical responses in both sensory-specific and nonmodality-specific structures were stable and congruent with the frequency of the tracer CS. However, when the performance was incorrect, this frequency correspondence became markedly less. Usually, the frequency observed in subcortical sensory specific structures such as the lateral geniculate body corresponded to the conditioned stimulus. However, recordings from sensory cortex often revealed labeled response at the stimulus frequency which waxed and waned almost as if amplitude modulated. Both the cortex and subcortical non-sensory-specific regions showed poor correspondence to the tracer frequency and had electrical patterns which often contained strong components approximately at the frequency of the other CS, *for which the behavioral response would have been appropriate.* These observations suggested that in certain brain regions the electrical activity elicited by a stimulus was largely *stimulus-bound,* and primarily reflected the peripheral input, while in other structures the mode of electrical activity reflected the *release* of temporal patterns which were related to previous experience. The behavioral outcome in discrimination situations seemed to involve interaction between these two systems.

7. *Electrical evidence for existence of representational systems*

Additional data provide support for the suggestion of a functional role for frequency specific potentials, and for the processes which produce such potentials in the absence of sensory stimulation at a corresponding frequency. In early stages of differential training, animals frequently perform a response learned to one conditioned stimulus upon the presentation of another stimulus. This behavior is often termed *generalization.* During generalization, potentials at the frequency of the intermittent CS used during training have been often observed in response to new stimuli of quite different frequencies. This activity has been most clearly discerned in nonmodality-specific subcortical structures and in visual cortex.

Data of this sort led to the suggestion that iterated stimulation builds a neural system capable of reflecting the temporal pattern of previous input (John and Killam, 1960; John, 1963). Data from assimilation, generalization, and differentiation studies, as well as from other types of experiments, provide evidence that nonmodality-specific structures participate extensively in such activity. The frequent observation of essentially synchronous temporal patterns in extensive brain regions suggested that such configurations may reflect activation of a *representational system*. Congruence between afferent input patterns and the output of such representational systems was proposed as a possible basis for stimulus identification and response selection. Some support for this hypothesis was obtained by applying techniques of multiple factor analysis to the study of large constellations of electrical wave shapes recorded simultaneously during behavioral performance. These studies showed that average evoked potential wave shapes in many brain structures became much more similar during conditioning, and could be described quantitatively as if they were composed by the interaction of a relatively small number of processes. However, the highly organized electrical patterns which seemed to characterize an anatomically extensive neural system during correct behavioral performance deteriorated when erroneous responses occurred.

These findings indicate that a quantitatively high synchronization between some components of complex electrical patterns occurs in an anatomically extensive system involving both sensory-specific and non-sensory-specific brain regions, when afferent input about a differential conditioned stimulus is correctly processed. This complex synchronization may reflect the influence of particular brain regions which modulate the excitability of other portions of this system, or may involve separate processes operating relatively independently within each part of the system.

D. Average response wave shape changes

The presence of frequency-specific potentials in the electrical activity of brain structures may implicate them in the mediation of conditioned responses. However, the details of the way in which these structures interact with one another to produce behavior remain unknown. Consideration of alterations in the wave shapes of the repetitively evoked macropotentials might shed further light upon this problem. Measurement difficulties arise, since evoked potentials recorded from unanesthetized animals are embedded in a background of "ongoing" activity. Average response computation can reduce the perturbing effect of the background activity which is not phase-locked to the CS, thereby facilitating a detailed study of evoked potential wave shapes.

The long latency, late components of the evoked potentials appear to be especially significant. These components have been noted to change during conditioning. The possible functional significance of these changes is suggested by the observation that disruption of late components by direct electrical stimulation of the cortex caused much more severe behavioral impairment than occurred when the same electrical input was used to disrupt the early components (John, 1963). Relatedly, averaged wave shapes computed during correct performance have been compared with those obtained during response failures and reveal that marked differences primarily occur in the late components (John and Ahn, 1966). Late components appear in the electrical responses evoked by novel stimuli when previously trained animals display behavioral generalization, but not if generalization fails to occur (John et al., 1965; Ruchkin and John, 1966a).

Evidence obtained from so-called "conflict" studies provides further indication of the importance of late components in information processing. In these studies, animals are simultaneously presented with two different tracer stimuli in two modalities, which have been previously established as the conditioned stimuli for two incompatible behavioral responses. Each conflict trial must be resolved by performing one of these responses. Since the two tracer stimuli differ with respect to frequency, it is possible to compute the average responses evoked in each neural structure separately for the two signals. In some brain regions, this analysis reveals that *the evoked potential which corresponds to the response of the structure to the "dominant" conditioned stimulus on that particular trial contains a marked late component.* However, *the late component in the response to that stimulus is absent if the conflict is resolved in favor of the alternative signal* (John and Shimokochi, 1966a). Since both signals are present in all conflict trials, and since the evoked responses being compared arise concurrently in the same neural volume, such studies provide continuous control for all possible unspecific influences and provide powerful support for the proposition that the late components of evoked response under discussion here are specifically related to neural mechanisms related to processing and evaluating information about the two signals.

Many of the phenomena summarized in the previous two sections will be discussed in greater detail in the remaining chapters.

E. Microelectrode studies

Some microelectrode studies have been carried out during conditioning and shed further light upon the macropotential data discussed previously.

Yoshii and Ogura (1960) studied the firing rates of units in the pontine reticular formation of cats immobilized by d-tubocurarine. Flicker, tone, and electroshock to the leg were used as stimuli. Units that were facilitated by the stimuli and units that were inhibited were both found. Effects of conditioning procedures were studied with respect to responsiveness of those units which were influenced by at least two of the three stimuli modalities. Flicker or shock provided the US, and tone or flicker provided the CS. Units that responded to all three modalities were most readily affected by conditioning, which was interpreted to suggest that "polyvalent" units might be particularly important in forming new neural interactions.

Morrell (1960) conducted a series of microelectrode studies of various brain structures during "cortical conditioning." His laminar analysis of the visual cortex suggested that early in conditioning new functional relationships first become apparent among the apical dendrites. Flicker was used as a US and tone as a CS. The discharge at US frequency, which was elicited in the visual cortex by the tone, first appeared in the surface layers and only appeared in the deep layers in the later stages of conditioning.

Morrell further studied changes in the firing of units in the visual cortex, nucleus ventralis anterior, mesencephalic reticular formation, and hippocampus during conditioning of cortical macropotentials. The US was either flicker or shock and the CS was steady tone.

Initial pairing of the CS with the US, following habituation, was accompanied by widespread desynchronization of the cortical macropotentials. Units in all these regions except nucleus ventralis anterior were markedly responsive. In the intermediate stage of conditioning the auditory CS evoked discharge at the US frequency in the visual cortex. Units in all regions were responsive to the CS at this stage. Subsequently, the macropotential desynchronization was limited to the visual cortex. Only units in the visual cortex and nucleus ventralis anterior responded to the CS at this stage. The similarities between these findings and some macropotential studies of behavioral conditioning (John and Killam, 1959) suggest good correlation between unit activity and macropotentials.

Jasper, Ricci, and Doane have studied the responses of neurons in various brain regions to flicker. Most of the units recorded during these experiments revealed no activity which seemed related to the specific effects of conditioning. However, some parietal neurons were observed which fired synchronously at the frequency of a flicker stimulus (Jasper *et al.*, 1960). This synchronous activity only occurred when the flicker frequency served as the cue for performance of a conditioned response to avoid shock. Flicker at other frequencies did not elicit unit synchrony. This finding suggests that *the correlation between unit discharge and macropotentials may be altered by conditioning* and differs in a fashion that reflects changes in coherence as stimuli become functionally relevant.

Morrell has shown that cortical units subjacent to an anodally polarized region will display temporal patterns of discharge resembling previously experienced sequences of visual stimuli when subsequently stimulated by single flashes of light (1961b). These observations indicate that neural systems are capable of reproducing previously experienced temporal patterns of activity. The patterned unit discharge probably reflects membership in such a system rather than indicating the capacity of the single cell to reproduce a specific firing pattern.

An extremely interesting and related experiment has been reported by Strumwasser and Rosenthal (1960). These workers explored the possibility that the spontaneous activity of a neuron could be reset as a result of a period of imposed patterned firing. Low-frequency extracellular stimulation through the recording microelectrode caused a transient increase in neural discharge followed by decrease in the probability of firing during the intervals between stimuli. This "entrainment" occurred more rapidly after a number of conditioning runs separated by rest periods and eventually appeared after only a few stimulus pulses. The extremely low current levels at which entrainment could be achieved seem to preclude direct stimulation of any significant number of cells in addition to the monitored unit. However, the results may reflect induction of a change in firing patterns in a small network of connected neurons, with negative feedback onto the excited cell or on cells driving it. The mechanism mediating the sustained inhibition is obscure. Working with tissue culture with cells from the isolated abdominal ganglion of *Aplysia*, Strumwasser and Bahr (1966) have studied the mechanism of entrainment of impulse patterns by the environmental photoperiod. Particular patterns of cellular activity have been maintained for as long as 3 weeks, indicating independence from sustained sensory input. Autoradiographic studies of other cells showed that tritiated leucine was incorporated into cytoplasmic protein and uridine into RNA in the nuclei of neurons. Different patterns of synthesis were observed in adjacent cells, suggesting that neurons can be in different states corresponding to the various electrical outputs.

Olds and Olds have demonstrated that the rate of discharge of arbitrarily selected units in certain brain regions can be greatly increased by application of conventional operant techniques, providing reinforcement upon the occurrence of the defined discharge (Olds and Olds, 1961; Olds, 1965a,b). Such evidence suggests that neural networks involving the relevant unit are selectively activated during the conditioning procedure, but does not justify the conclusion that the unit itself has been "conditioned" and is the site of some plastic change in response. It seems reasonable to suggest that some behavior in the "voluntary" repertoire of the animal, associated with discharge of the neuron, may have been reinforced by this procedure and occurs more frequently.

Recently, Bureš and Burešová have replicated and extended the results of Yoshii et al., showing changes in the response of units in the reticular formation of rats during conditioning (Bureš, 1965; Bureš and Burešová, 1965). At first, auditory stimulation alone caused no change in the activity pattern of the monitored units, while sciatic stimulation by itself caused a strong inhibition of activity. After pairing of sound with sciatic stimulation a number of times, sound alone caused marked diminution of unit activity. These workers also point out that these results do not imply that the monitored unit is the site of some plastic change but merely indicate that the unit participates in an affected network. It is interesting that the application of cortical spreading depression did not block the ability to obtain these effects. Changes in unit activity with conditioning have been reported by a number of other workers including Kamikawa et al. (1964), Buchwald et al. (1965a,b), Hori and Yoshii (1965), and Adam et al. (1966).

In a series of studies, Eccles and his collaborators (Eccles, 1964, 1965) have attempted to demonstrate changes in synaptic efficiency as a consequence of prolonged decrease or increase of synaptic use. These studies were predicated upon the assumption that the activation of

257

synapses increases their efficiency by causing an enduring change in their fine structure, perhaps involving the growth of synaptic spines or changes in the size of active synaptic zones. The theoretical formulation of memory underlying these experiments was that a given sensory input results in a uniquely patterned activation of central neurons; and that reoccurrence of the same input would be channeled along the same pathways because of residual increases in efficiency. Thus, remembering consists of discharge in this pathway. In order to produce prolonged total disuse of monosynaptic pathways, afferent nerves were severed just peripheral to the dorsal root ganglion. Some weeks later, it was possible to demonstrate a depression of monosynaptic reflexes relative to the control side. The depressed reflexes were more potentiated by high-frequency stimulation than normally, and exhibited relatively long-lasting residual effects. Intracellular recording from such a preparation shows that the monosynaptic excitatory action of the disused pathway is markedly reduced. The imposition of inactivity by surgical procedures has the disadvantage that some shrinkage of the dorsal root fibers occurs which may account for the diminished synaptic action. In order to rule out the possible contribution of this damage, muscle tendons were cut, which reduced the output from annulospiral receptors responsive to stretch applied through the tendon. Anomalously, after several weeks, volleys in the nerves of the tenotomized muscle had a more powerful monosynaptic action than was observed on the control side. Although these experiments showed plastic properties of monosynaptic reflexes, the evidence does not as yet permit the conclusion that the changes in synaptic effectiveness arose from altered use, since a variety of factors was possibly involved.

This group of workers also investigated the effects of prolonged excessive use on synaptic efficiency, by denervating all the muscles of a synergic group except one. It was assumed that the remaining muscle would be more utilized than its contralateral counterpart. Some animals thus treated were forced to walk on a treadmill for an extended period each day. The expected large increase in monosynaptic reflexes occurred for the residual muscle nerve when compared with the control side. However, exactly the same asymmetry was observed from those animals which were also subjected to immobilization by spinal transection, so that no stresses were placed on the residual muscles. As in the previously described experiments, these findings demonstrate a plastic increase in synaptic effectiveness, but do not permit the observed changes to be attributed to excessive synaptic usage.

The most convincing demonstration of changes in the response of a particular single nerve cell as a result of conditioning procedures has been provided in an elegant series of experiments by Kandel and Tauc. In their initial studies (Kandel and Tauc, 1963, 1964), these workers obtained intracellular recordings from single neurons in the isolated abdominal ganglion of *Aplysia*. Two separate afferent pathways exciting this neuron were identified and stimulus parameters were adjusted so that input to one pathway produced a relatively small excitatory effect (EPSP) while input to the other produced a burst of spikes. The two stimuli were paired for a prolonged period, with the less effective one preceding the more effective by a brief interval. In most cells, this pairing produced no changes in the effectiveness of the weaker input. However, in a particular group of cells in the ganglion, augmentation of the effect of the weaker input occurred during pairing, and persisted for some 20 minutes after termination of the pairing procedure. In some of the cells, these effects were apparently specific to the pairing procedure, since augmentation did not occur after repeated but unpaired stimulation of the stronger input. The demonstration of specificity would be somewhat more convincing if the effects of paired and randomized stimulation of the strong and weak inputs were compared.

In subsequent work (Kandel and Tauc, 1965a,b), these investigators have described a similar but less specific heterosynaptic facilitation consistently obtained from a particular identifiable cell in this ganglion. A procedure similar to the previous study was followed, but in this case the resulting facilitation was not dependent upon pairing of the stimuli but occurred after a series of unpaired presentations of the "priming" stimulus. In spite of the unspecificity of the observed effect, the analysis of the mediating mechanism carried out by these workers is of great interest, in view of the extremely long (10–40 minutes) duration of the facilitatory aftereffects.

The augmentation of the EPSP seemed to be unrelated to any changes in the properties of the postsynaptic cell. Participation of the spike-generation mechanism was excluded in a number of ways. A directly initiated train of action potentials could not serve as an effective priming stimulus. However, stimulation of the strong priming input produced facilitation even if the postsynaptic cell was hyperpolarized so that spike

259

discharge did not occur. Thus, the facilitation seems to arise from input to the postsynaptic cell rather than discharge by that cell. No change in postsynaptic membrane conductance was observed.

In view of these findings, the observed facilitation would seem to be due either to an increase in the intensity of excitatory input or a blockade of inhibitory components of the test pathway. Demonstration of facilitation while a major portion of the inhibitory processes in the ganglion were blocked by d-tubocurarine suggested that these effects were due to an increase in excitatory input. Detailed examination of the EPSP of the test stimulus suggested that the synaptic efficacy of elements mediating the test response had been increased. The data were consistent with the hypothesis that repetitive activity in the priming pathway may have increased the release of excitatory transmitter by terminals of the test pathway. Although these conclusions are tentative, they seem well-founded in that they are based upon a number of plausible assumptions. In further work, Kandel *et al.* (1965) have obtained evidence that the firing pattern of certain neurons can be influenced by a period of inhibitory input, with sustained aftereffects. Using an "instrumental" procedure, it was possible to produce changes in the frequency of the endogenous bursting rhythm and the occurrence of spontaneous inhibitory synaptic potentials. Response decrements which persisted for several hours could be produced by what seemed to be IPSP recruitment. These results suggest that the process of habituation might be mediated either by EPSP decrement or IPSP recruitment (Sokolov, 1965).

Results bearing directly on this question have been provided by Spencer *et al.* (1964, 1966), who showed that response decrement in the flexion reflex in acute spinal cord preparations during habituation was accompanied by a decrease in the amplitude of the EPSP. The intensity of phasic excitatory and inhibitory input diminished and was unaccompanied by any marked change in background synaptic bombardment or in membrane responsiveness. During dishabituation following a strong extrastimulus, the amplitude of PSP's generated by the test pathway temporarily increased. The reflex decrement might possibly be explained as the result either of inhibition or synaptic depression. A number of items of evidence against the inhibition hypothesis were presented, including the fact that reflex decrement persisted after reduction of presynaptic inhibition by picrotoxin or diminution of postsynaptic inhibition by strychnine. The mechanism mediating the sustained decrement remains obscure. These workers favor an explanation based on homosynaptic depression of interneuron synapses. Homosynaptic depression appears as a decreased PSP amplitude due to regularly repeated activation and is probably presynaptic in origin, perhaps reflecting transmitter depletion.

The various experiments summarized in this section, particularly the last group cited, offer promise of increased understanding of the mechanisms which mediate sustained alteration of the responsiveness of single nerve cells to specific inputs as a result of previous experience. This information has long been sought and is of exceptional interest and importance. These findings show that the responses of single nerve cells can be changed by conditioning procedures, and suggest that these changes are somehow mediated by the occurrence of presynaptic excitation rather than by the alteration of the postsynaptic cell.*

It is necessary to assume that memory involves some changes in the cells of which neural tissue is comprised. The storage of information in the brain must be mediated materialistically rather than magically. Perhaps the changes described in the preceding sections are the unitary elements of which memories are composed. What represents the information which is stored by systems built from these elements? The significance of these findings is in no way impugned by pointing out that the demonstration of changes in the responsiveness of specific nerve cells to certain inputs during the learning process is not equivalent to the demonstration that the memory of stored information is retrieved deterministically by the firing of those cells. The fundamental question devolves upon whether the retrieval which makes stored information functionally available to the nervous system is based upon deterministic discharge in a pathway constructed from facilitated or inhibited synaptic connections between specific cells, or upon the statistical assessment of the average pattern of activity in an ensemble of cells among which these changes are distributed. One of the primary purposes of this volume is to define these two alternatives clearly so that future analysis can be focused upon resolution of this question.

It is my opinion that our present state of knowledge is not sufficiently advanced for an unequivocal acceptance of *either* possibility. Much of the evidence to be examined in detail in the remainder of this volume suggests that even the performance of relatively simple conditioned responses is mediated by mechanisms involving widespread regions of

---

* One can look forward to most interesting results when these methods are applied to the learning phenomena displayed by insect nerve cords and isolated ganglia, so ingeniously studied by Eisenstein and Cohen (1964), Horridge (1962), and Hoyle (1965).

the central nervous system and is characterized by intricate interactions between complex processes arising in vast numbers of cells yet displaying relatively invariant features and posing severe difficulties for a deterministic formulation.

Is it plausible that the discrete discharge of a single neuron or neural pathway someplace in the nervous system might be *sufficient* to represent a particular item of information, either about a past or present event? For some, the credibility of this proposition has been markedly enhanced by the observations obtained in the elegant experiments by Hubel and Wiesel (Hubel, 1959; Hubel and Wiesel, 1962, 1963), who have studied the receptive fields of neurons at various levels of the visual system. Their results show that specific neurons in particular structures respond preferentially to discrete components of a stimulus complex. As one moves to successively higher levels of the central nervous system, the complexity of the stimuli which achieve maximal unit response becomes greater. Eventually, levels are reached wherein cells can be found which respond to extremely complex constellations of stimulus features, and might be considered as "feature extractors." These data may seem to provide support for formulations in which the deterministic response of specific cells "stands for" the occurrence of a particular complex peripheral event. Stabilization or facilitation of pathways achieving that deterministic response might reasonably comprise the memory of that event.

Unquestionably, these data do indicate appreciable processing of information in way stations of the visual system between the retina and the primary cortical projection area and progressively complex specification of the stimuli adequate to elicit maximum unit response at successive levels. This evidence indicates that particular cortical cells respond preferentially to organized features of the afferent input. Although this response is undoubtedly necessary for registration of the information, it does not necessarily follow that the discrete discharge of such a selective cell or set of cells is sufficient for representation of the peripheral event.

First of all, numerous cells are responsive to a particular stimulus feature and these cells have considerable anatomical distribution. The ease with which they can be found indicates that they exist in relative abundance and are diffusely distributed throughout cortical areas. Doty has shown that punctate photic stimulation of a restricted retinal area elicits evoked potentials over extremely widespread cortical areas, with latency differences between various regions (1958). These cells may also discharge spontaneously in the absence of the preferred peripheral stimulus, although less intensely than when optimally excited. Conversely, these cells may not respond identically to each occurrence of the appropriate stimulus. Furthermore, some of these cells may also show marked changes in discharge when other events occur. The suggestion that the same cells may represent a multiplicity of events receives strong support from such evidence as the continued performance of pattern discrimination by animals retaining only 2% of the fibers in the optic tract (Norton *et al.*, 1966). These considerations suggest that the occurrence of firing in a unique and selectively responsive cell constitutes neither a necessary nor a sufficient basis for the adequate representation of information about the presence of a unique peripheral event. Although selectively responsive cells provide the basis for considerable abstraction and integration of the various features of the stimulus field, it seems necessary to assess the behavior of the whole ensemble of cells in order to estimate the significance of particular neural events. Preferential response of groups of cells to characteristic configurations of the stimulus complex could constitute preprocessing of information and provide categories or dimensionality to the incoming excitation. The averaged activity of large ensembles, composed of subsets of cells corresponding to various features of the stimulus configuration, might constitute the basis for integration of the multitudinous and somewhat fortuitous responses of individual neurons into a reliable and coherent perception.

A number of experimental observations pose further difficulties for the deterministic view. Wiesel and Hubel have shown that the characteristics of cortical cells are not immutably wired in and reported that prolonged reduction or distortion of input to one eye immediately following birth causes a subsequent pronounced abnormality in the distribution of cortical fields contralateral to the previously occluded eye (1965a,b).

Previous events can also change the response of single units to specific stimuli. For example, Buchwald and Hull (1966) have shown that a conditioning procedure can result in sustained inhibition of the response of cortical units to stimulation of the lateral geniculate. Similarly, Morrell, Engel, and Bouris (1966) have demonstrated that the response of single units in the visual cortex to specified visual stimuli can be altered by conditioning procedures using a variety of unconditioned stimuli. A particularly interesting feature of some experiments is the fact that the response of the unit to the conditioned stimulus alone after pairing was essentially the *sum* of the responses elicited from the unit by presentation of the CS and US separately prior to pairing. These experiments were also noteworthy because of the specificity of the new response, indicated by the differential effects elicited by various stimuli. Some data from these experiments are summarized in Fig. XI-4.

Data of this sort show that the responses of single units to specific stimulation of a receptive field are labile and can be changed by conditioning procedures. In spite of such evidence, the proposition that information about the specific stimulus might nevertheless be represented deterministically by the discharge of a particular neuron or neurons may conceivably still be defended by the argument that the new unit response now uniquely stands for the stimulus contingencies which characterized the conditioning experience. This contention does not appear tenable in view of data showing that *the activity induced in cortical units depends not only upon the immediate afferent stimulus but also upon the configuration of ongoing activity elsewhere in the nervous system.* Spinelli *et al.* have shown that direct stimulation of many brain regions, auditory stimuli, or somatic stimulation can change the receptive fields of single units in the optic nerve, lateral geniculate body, and visual cortex. Changes in the shape of the receptive field as well as in the firing pattern of the unit were observed (Spinelli *et al.*, 1966; Spinelli and Weingarten, 1966; Weingarten *et al.*, 1966). Perhaps the strongest evidence against the deterministic model of information coding by specific discharge patterns of particular neurons is provided by the work of Lindsley *et al.* (1966; Chow *et al.*, 1966a). These workers have shown that the response patterns of single neurons in the lateral geniculate body to illumination of a spot on the retina of one eye can be altered by subsequent light stimulation of the other eye. This effect could be obtained even though the light stimulation of the second eye alone did not elicit any response from the recorded neuron. Furthermore, by means of a conditional training procedure they could obtain *one mode* of response from some units to illumination of the test spot in the presence of one conditional context (low level of background illumination) and a *different mode* of response from these units to the same test spot in the presence of the second conditional context (higher background level). No differential activity was elicited in these neurons by the conditional context levels alone. *The same specific stimulus could therefore elicit two alternative response patterns from the same neuron.*

264

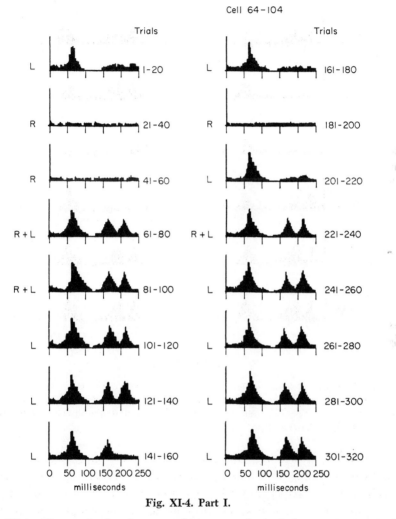

Fig. XI-4. Part I.

Fig. XI-4. All poststimulus frequency histograms obtained from units in visual cortex subjacent to 10 μA surface anodal polarization:

I. Change in response of cortical unit brought about by pairing test flash to left (L) and right (R) eyes, shown in poststimulus histograms. Note that after pairing of RL for 40 trials, L alone continues to elicit new response pattern for about 60 trials before resuming initial pattern. Repetition of pairing causes effect to persist from trials 240–320.

265

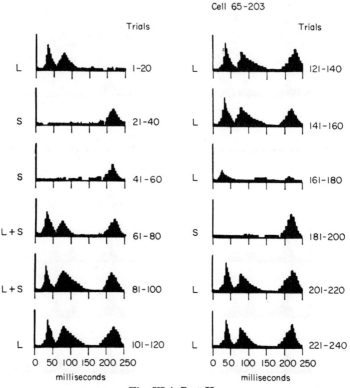

Fig. XI-4. Part II.

II. Response of unit to flash (L) plus mild shock (S) approximates sum of response to the two stimuli separately. After pairing, presentation of L alone produces response pattern resembling effect of L + S. Pattern gradually decays, but is restored by presentation of shock alone.

These reports suggest the possible generality and fundamental importance of suggestions such as those in the report by the Scheibels (Scheibel and Scheibel, 1965) that inputs to neurons in the reticular formation are flexible, possibly coupling and uncoupling the neuron from one or another system without any change in anatomical connectivity. Although single units can display reproducible response patterns to specific stimuli under certain conditions, it seems probable that such response patterns are seldom if ever invariant. Alteration of unit response patterns has been shown at several levels of the visual system: optic nerve, lateral geniculate, and visual cortex. Unit responses to a specified stimulus may

266

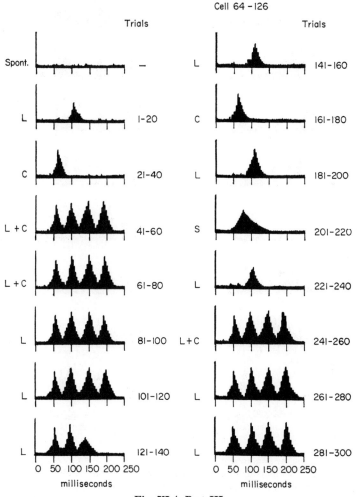

Cell 64 –126

Fig. XI-4. Part III.

III. Response of unit to light (L) plus click (C) is markedly different from effect of L or C alone. After pairing of L + C, presentation of L alone elicits new response pattern resembling L + C. After new response decays and L again elicits initial response pattern, presentation of shock (S) alone fails to alter response to L. Pairing of L + C restores new response pattern to L alone.

be changed as a function of the configuration of activity elsewhere in the nervous system at the time of information input to the receptors, by the sequence of events prior to that stimulus, or by the environmental context in which the stimulus occurs. In addition, spontaneous discharge of

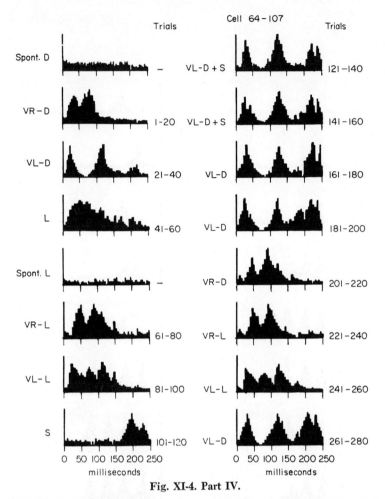

Fig. XI-4. Part IV.

IV. Unit displays spontaneous random activity in dim light (D). Presentation of a black bar on a white background in dim light elicits one response pattern when moving to the right (VR-D) and another pattern when moving to the left (VL-D). A flash of light (L) elicits a different response pattern, and the spontaneous activity in more intense light (Spont. L) is random but less than in dim light. When the bar is moved toward the right in intense light (VR-L) the response pattern is much the same as when the background illumination is dim. When the bar moves to the left in intense light (VL-L), the response is somewhat different. Shock (S) causes a different response pattern.

When shock is paired with bar movement to the left in dim light (VL − D + S), the response pattern resembles the sum of the separate effects of VL-D and S. After 40 paired presentations, VL-D alone elicits the new response pattern. *This effect is differential.* No change is seen in the patterns of response elicited by VR-D (Trials 201–220), VR-L (Trials 221–240), or VL-L (Trials 241–260). However, subsequent presentation of VL-D (Trials 261–280) shows that the new response pattern to that specific stimulus still persists. [Data from Morrell, Engel, and Bouris (1966).]

268

neurons occurs at an appreciable rate, as can be seen from the resting frequency histograms in Fig. XI-4. Furthermore, neurons often respond to a variety of stimuli, as is also obvious from that figure. Finally, a common feature of several of the studies discussed in this section is the surprisingly high percentage (8–10%) of the neurons studied which showed changes in response during conditioning. Since no unique properties can be attributed to the neurons fortuitously selected by an exploring microelectrode, it seems probable that a very large number of cells are altered by a learning experience, and every such cell must be influenced by many experiences.

The observed changes in unit response during conditioning look like changes in the temporal pattern of activity rather than the gating open of a new pathway. In view of the considerations above, it seems highly unlikely that the discharge of a given neuron or set of neurons can constitute either a necessary or a sufficient event for the deterministic representation of any specific item of peripheral information, within the central nervous system. It would seem impossible to infer the presence or absence of a particular feature in the environment on the basis of the discharge *per se* of any unique cell or set of cells in the nervous system of an unanesthetized and unrestrained animal. The informational significance of such neuronal discharge would seem to be contingent upon the recent history of the animal, the prior and present stimulus configuration, and the other ongoing activity in the ensemble. Assessment of the information contained in the activity of a neuronal ensemble would seem to necessitate some form of integration over the ensemble, in order to compensate for the contextual dependency and the relative rather than absolute nature of the neuronal response to a stimulus. Other evidence related to these problems will be discussed in subsequent chapters.

CHAPTER XII

REPRESENTATIONAL SYSTEMS

The logical arguments and experimental evidence presented in the first portion of this book were directed against a number of propositions: (1) learning involves the establishment of a pathway whereby specific neurons connect some input region to some output region of the brain; (2) memory of the experience is mediated by the connections between the neurons in that pathway; (3) remembering requires the deterministic discharge of the neurons in that pathway. The phenomena of consolidation and of alteration of the rate of learning were utilized to construct a number of propositions about the way in which the set of cells which will serve to mediate the representation of a particular experience might be selected. The essential feature of the mechanism that was proposed entailed the establishment of a characteristic mode of activity in a network of neurons in which the disturbance caused by some stimulus persisted for a period of time. A set of chemical reactions was then suggested as a possible way for these characteristic modes of oscillation to become stabilized. The postulated result of this stabilization process was to increase the probability that the neural ensemble would enter the specified mode when that stimulus recurred, although these associations of neural activity were initially fortuitous. It was proposed that the time course of the average activity of the ensemble would be reflected in the wave shape of the electrophysiological potentials recorded from the neural network.

In the latter part of this book, we have endeavored to marshall evidence that such characteristic modes of oscillation, reflecting *temporal patterns of average activity* in extensive networks, are in fact established during learning. We quoted extensively from the formulations of Hebb, who adopted a quasi-connectionistic position and suggested that cell assemblies and phase sequences were established statistically as a result of associated activity among neurons in a network. Whether or not the stabilization of these neuronal organizations requires the actual growth of synaptic connections, the electrophysiological reflections of the existence of these processes should be essentially identical with those expected to arise from a specified mode of oscillation in a network. Hebb relied on contiguity as the essential basis for establishment of such circuitry, although he felt that the argument should be constructed on primarily psychological bases in view of the deficiency of physiological evidence. In fact, abundant physiological evidence now exists and has been presented in some detail in the chapter on contiguity. The representational systems that were postulated in that chapter are essentially identical with phase sequences. A set of studies was reviewed which provided evidence that regions of the brain which participate in shared activity over a period of time become organized into a system and that subsequent discharge of a portion of the system causes discharge of the remainder. Although the experimental evidence which is available is limited to demonstration of new functional relationships between two or three brain regions, it seems reasonable to suggest that in more natural learning situations a much more extensive system might be established.

We suggested that when an animal experiences stimulation in a given environment, afferent input as a result of that stimulation enters many neuroanatomical regions. The neuronal activity in these regions is altered by the advent of the stimulus so as to produce some deviation from the normal baseline of average activity in the population of cells constituting that structure. The informational content of the activity of each structure with respect to that stimulus may be specified by the temporal course of this deviation from the baseline of average activity of the population. The set of deviations from baseline activity in the various anatomical regions of the brain are proposed to constitute the over-all information content of the brain as a consequence of the stimulus event.

This set of nonrandom patterns of activity might be expected on the basis of the mechanism apparent from the previous discussion to become functionally associated by contiguity. The resulting associative system of nonrandomly activated ensembles of neurons in the diverse anatomical regions was called a representational system, suggesting that the residual informational impact of the stimulus on the nervous system was largely mediated by the organized set of relationships.

The speculations of Lashley were cited to present his argument that conditioning must cause certain patterns of activity to become established and to reproduce themselves throughout additional brain areas. The relationship between Lashley's argument and that of Hebb seems logically quite close although derived from somewhat different lines of reasoning. Again, Lashley based his conclusions upon behavioral evidence, largely from lesion studies, stating his belief that neurophysiological support for these hypotheses was not yet available.

Our argument up to this point has been compounded from logical considerations, behavioral data, and the analysis of some neurochemical and physiological observations. In order to develop the position further, it is necessary to examine in detail certain phenomena, primarily of an electrophysiological nature, which have been observed both in our own laboratories and those of other workers. In the remaining chapters, we shall emphasize evidence gathered in studies of the electrical activity displayed by the brain during the acquisition and performance of conditioned responses. The complexity and diversity of electrical changes observed during these studies are at first bewildering to the experimenter in this area. Widespread regions of the brain show marked changes in response to the CS in the course of conditioning and subsequent performance, possibly indicative of extensive involvement of diverse anatomical regions in the elaboration and mediation of a new conditioned response. New electrical responses appear in some places in which little activity was initially elicited by the CS, while some regions display response initially and subsequently diminish in reactivity. Other regions display continued response throughout the conditioning procedure, sometimes revealing changes in the form of response. A portion of these changes may be related to unspecific factors not connected with the processing of information, while some changes may reflect the establishment of neural mechanisms which mediate the storage and retrieval of information directly relevant to the learning situation. It is extremely difficult to evaluate the functional significance that can be ascribed to the mere appearance or disappearance of some electrical response in a particular brain region, and we shall make little attempt to do so here. Rather than focusing on the anatomical distribution of activity, we shall emphasize certain features of the observed phenomena which seem to provide a particularly intimate insight into dynamic processes that may be related to the storage, retrieval, and processing of information in the brain. Phenomena of this sort are provided by studies in which intermittent conditioned stimuli are utilized. We shall attempt to demonstrate by means of this evidence that representational systems are built in the brain during conditioning, that these widespread systems are capable of discharging spontaneously with temporal patterns such as those experienced during prior stimulation, and that these temporal patterns of discharge have functional relevance to the performance of learned behaviors. Some of the evidence adduced has been mentioned previously in the context of other discussions and will be cited here once more to refresh the reader's recollection.

A. Tracer technique

Shortly after the advent of the electroencephalographic technique, Durup and Fessard (1935) showed that the so-called "arousal" response (desynchronization of the electrical rhythms of the brain causing low-voltage fast activity in response to certain stimuli) could be conditioned in a fashion quite parallel to the methods used for conventional conditioned motor responses. These observations led to a period of study which provided some relatively general indications of processes possibly involved in conditioning, as evidenced by changes in the electrical response of the brain. For some time these studies were largely restricted to the cortex. The nature of the response measure used in most of these studies, i.e. the occurrence of desynchronization in particular brain regions, was perhaps the most severe constraint on the insights provided by this method. As discussed in Chapter XI, studies of this sort revealed that the general desynchronization caused by a stimulus relatively early in training gave way to a more localized desynchronization as a conditioned response became fully established to that stimulus. These patterns of desynchronization corresponded to what was known to result from the activation of particular brain regions. Therefore, these observations were interpreted as suggesting that the mesencephalic reticular formation of the brain stem might be involved in the early mediation of response to a conditioned stimulus, and that later in conditioning, neural processes involving the thalamic reticular formation possibly replaced or subsumed the prior mesencephalic activity. The failure of this line of research to provide further significant insights into process may have been due primarily to the inability of the experimenters to stipulate specific features of the response of the brain for which to search. The detection of that portion of brain activity related to the processing of information about the environment in the presence of ongoing activity mediating numerous other functions was exceedingly difficult.

Two developments resulted in a marked improvement in the available plans of approach to this problem. The first was the advent of techniques for the chronic implantation of electrodes into subcortical as well as superficial regions of the brain, which enabled long-term detailed study of changes in the electrical activity of any brain region during the establishment and subsequent performance of conditioned responses. The second development was the use of intermittent stimuli as the conditioned stimuli in studies of this sort. The rationale for the use of intermittent stimuli is quite straightforward but nonetheless crucial for the solution of the problem of an unfavorable signal to noise ratio in experimental observations. Whatever the nature of the electrical response of the brain to a peripheral stimulus, as that stimulus becomes established as the adequate signal for the reliable performance of a conditioned response which necessarily involves the retrieval of stored information, it might come to elicit some reproducible electrical effects. If one specifies as a conditioned stimulus some event in the environment which occurs with a characteristic rate of repetition, *a tracer stimulus,* one may expect some portion of the response of the brain to that event to occur with the same frequency. This expectation must, of course, be qualified by the reservations that the repetition rate should be sufficiently low to minimize entrainment, and that certain brain regions may respond to the frequencies of afferent input by nonfrequency-specific transformations. Nonetheless, bearing these constraints in mind, there is reasonable justification to expect that some of the neural structures processing information about an intermittent stimulus will display oscillations which are phase-locked to that stimulus. Therefore, the search of the experimenter for the "signal" becomes immensely simplified. *Labeled responses* are defined as electrical potentials which occur in the brain at the frequency of the tracer stimulus or a harmonic thereof. The appearance of labeled responses in a structure is a *sufficient but not necessary* condition to conclude that the structure is affected *by presentation of a given tracer stimulus.*

Two basic applications of tracer technique can be discerned. In one method, intermittent stimuli are presented as "background" events in the environment. The appearance of labeled responses in anatomical regions is interpreted as evidence that these regions are "idling," and are therefore responsive to irrelevant inputs. Disappearance of labeled responses from a region when the system is challenged by some additional informational input is interpreted as evidence that the regions displaying diminution of labeled activity have become preempted by mediation of responses to the new input. Conversely, one can examine the distribution and characteristics of labeled responses throughout the various regions of the brain as functional significance is acquired by a tracer conditioned stimulus during the establishment of a conditioned response. Changes in the form and distribution of labeled responses potentially provide insight into brain mechanisms mediating the processing of information relevant to the tracer stimulus. The latter application of tracer technique is the one upon which we shall focus in this discussion.

When tracer technique is utilized in this fashion, it becomes evident that the response of the brain to a repetitive signal changes in many different regions as a conditioned response is established to that cue. As summarized in Chapter XI, much of the brain alters its response to such a signal during conditioning.

B. Pseudoconditioning and sensitization

Some of these changes are undoubtedly due to generalized factors, such as arousal and excitation related to the conditioning situation per se. Before we proceed further with a detailed examination of particularly interesting features of labeled responses observed in various circumstances, it may be worthwhile to provide a number of examples which demonstrate that many of the changes in labeled response distribution, amplitude or form which occur during conditioning cannot reasonably be attributed to sensitization or pseudoconditioning. Perhaps the best reassurance on this question comes from studies in which control over a previously learned response is *transferred* to another stimulus.

1. *Transfer of training from steady to intermittent conditioned stimuli*

The first example of such transfer is illustrated by Fig. XII-1, taken from the work of Corley (1963). The records on the left of this figure represent EEG recordings taken from the visual cortex at various stages in a sequential conditioning procedure. The wave shapes on the right portion of the figure represent average response computations derived from these EEG data. The *first* line of data was taken during the presentation of flicker to a naïve animal resting in the avoidance apparatus. There is no indication of frequency specific response in the EEG tracings,

FC-14 R VISUAL CORTEX m 4/SEC

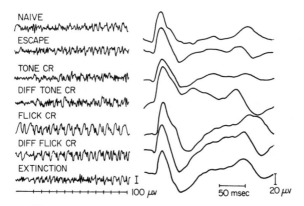

Fig. XII-1. Responses evoked from visual cortex (monopolar) of cat by 4-cps flicker at various stages of training. EEG recordings are on the left, averaged evoked responses on the right. *Naïve*—response to *flicker* before beginning of training; *Escape*—after establishment of hurdle jump to escape foot shock; *Tone CR*—after establishment of conditioned avoidance response to auditory conditioned stimulus; *Diff Tone CR*—after differential avoidance training to two tones; *Flick CR*—after transfer of conditioned avoidance response to flicker. This is first stage at which flicker acquires informational significance. Note the appearance of pronounced surface positive (downward) labeled response seen both in EEG and average response. *Diff Flick CR*—after establishment of differential avoidance response to two flicker frequencies. *Extinction*—after extinction of avoidance response. *Bottom Line*—tracer stimulus.

Note the essential similarity of the last three average response wave shapes although differences are discernible in the corresponding EEG. This suggests that in those instances a constant "signal" is imbedded in variable amounts of other activity, or "noise." [Based on data from Corley (1963).]

although average response computation shows some coherent activity. The animal was then trained to escape shock delivered to the feet through a grid in the floor by jumping a hurdle. Following this escape training, presentation of the flicker to the thoroughly aroused animal indicated no increase in the labeled responses in the EEG, nor was there any marked change in the average response wave shape, as shown on the *second* line of data.

277

A conditioned avoidance response (CAR) was then established to an auditory conditioned stimulus, the presentation of *a steady tone*. Presentation of the flicker, following the avoidance training to tone, comprises the data on the *third* line of the figure. No frequency-specific activity was elicited in the EEG recording by the flicker, nor did the average response computation show any change. The animal was then trained differentially, jumping a hurdle in one direction to one tone, and jumping a second hurdle in another direction to a second tone. Presentation of the flicker still elicited no clear labeled responses in the EEG records and no noteworthy changes of the evoked potential could be discerned in the average response computation, as seen in the *fourth* line.

The next set of recordings show that a marked increase in labeled responses took place after the CAR was transferred to control by the flickering stimulus. Examination of the EEG on the *fifth* line shows massive labeled potentials, and the average response computation shows marked new components. Frequency-specific response in the EEG was further enhanced after completion of differential training to two flicker frequencies: one eliciting jumps of the hurdle in one direction, the other requiring hurdle jump in the opposite direction. Slight modifications of the average response wave shape after differentiation can be observed on the *sixth* line of the figure. The final line of data illustrates that following behavioral extinction of the avoidance response, the flicker CS continued to elicit substantial although diminished responses, seen in both the electrographic recordings and the average response computation. This indicates that extinction is by no means a mere reversal of what takes place during conditioning. It seems more compatible with the data to interpret extinction as a dynamic inhibition upon performance.

Although this animal was thoroughly aroused and trained to two steady tones as discriminated cues for performance of differential avoidance responses, presentation of flicker in the training environment elicited minimal labeled responses in the visual cortex *until flicker was established as a cue controlling the conditioned performance* after transfer of training. Therefore, the appearance of frequency-specific activity in this structure cannot be attributed to sensitization or factors related to pseudoconditioning, but seems related to the acquisition of *informational significance* by the tracer stimulus.

It is noteworthy that in the first four lines of Fig. XII-1, clear average evoked responses were computed although little evidence of labeled

response appeared in the EEG itsèlf. Comparison with the fifth and sub-
• sequent lines of data shows that conditioning was accompanied by some
changes in average response wave shape but no significant increase in
amplitude, although an enormous increase occurred in the amount of
labeled response. If we consider the amplitude of the average response as
reflecting the integrated "strength" of phase-locked signals in the region,
no great increase seems to have occurred as transfer of training took
place. *The enhanced visibility of labeled response in the ongoing electrical activity may be related to a decrease in "noise" or unrelated events
in the region.* Altered amounts of labeled response in a region may or
may not be accompanied by changes in the intensity of phase-locked
signal. Average response computation alone does not provide a complete
description of changes in the effects of a stimulus on various brain
structures. Computation of the signal to noise ratio and study of the
"raw" EEG data are extremely informative.

2. *Transfer of training between tracer stimuli in two sensory modalities*

Additional evidence that many of the changes in labeled responses
during the acquisition of cue value by a tracer stimulus are not attributable to sensitization comes from studies in which differential performance
is transferred from intermittent stimuli in one sensory modality to intermittent stimuli in a second sensory modality. For example, cats have
been differentially trained to perform a lever-press to obtain food upon
presentation of flicker at one frequency, V_1, and to press another lever
to avoid shock in response to a second flicker frequency, V_2. Labeled
responses elicited by the corresponding frequencies of intermittent clicks,
A_1 and A_2, were then compared before and after transfer.

Figure XII-2 illustrates some increases in labeled responses which
were observed by Shimokochi and John (1966) upon such transfer
from flicker to click (I) to electrical stimulation of the lateral geniculate
body (II). Other examples from different animals are provided in Fig.
XII-3. The augmentation of *late components* of the labeled responses
after transfer is especially noteworthy.

Similar results have been observed by Majkowski and John (1966)
upon transfer from click to flicker. In some cases, conditioned responses
begin to be displayed after very few reinforced trials to the second
stimulus after transfer of training begins. Electrical changes such as those
illustrated can therefore be observed within a single training session,

279

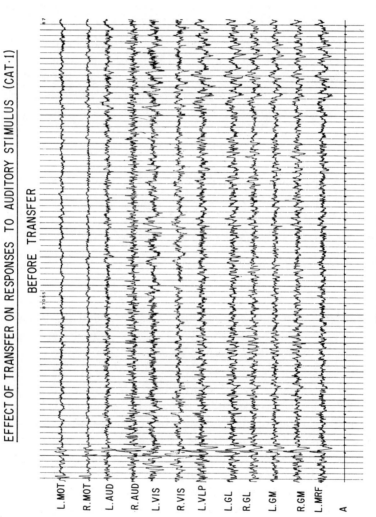

EFFECT OF TRANSFER ON RESPONSES TO AUDITORY STIMULUS (CAT·1)

BEFORE TRANSFER

L.MOT
R.MOT
L.AUD
R.AUD
L.VIS
R.VIS
L.VLP
L.GL
R.GL
L.GM
R.GM
L.MRF
A

Fig. XII-2. Part I. Top.

Top records: EEG tracings from a cat after completion of differential approach-avoidance training to two flicker frequencies (3.1 and 7.7 cps). These data illustrate the effect of *clicks* at the same frequency as the flicker signal for the avoidance response (3.1 cps), before clicks acquired cue value.

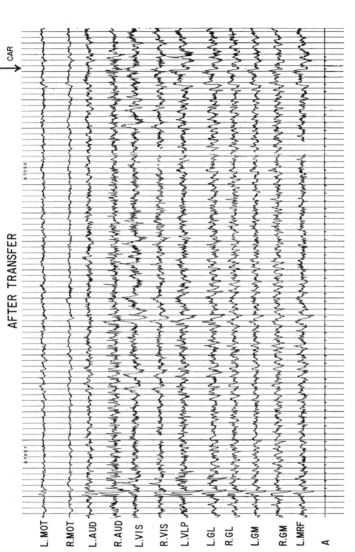

Fig. XII-2. Part I. Bottom.

Bottom records: Effects of clicks after *transfer* of conditioned avoidance response to the auditory signal. This record was obtained later in the same session from which the upper record was taken. Note the changes in wave shape and amount of labeled responses particularly in R. AUD., L. GL., R. GL., L. GM., R. GM., and L. MRF. All derivations are monopolar. MOT—motor cortex, AUD—auditory cortex, VIS—visual cortex, VLP—nucleus ventralis lateralis posterior, GL—lateral geniculate, GM—medial geniculate, MRF—mesencephalic reticular formation. L—left side, R—right side, A—clicks.

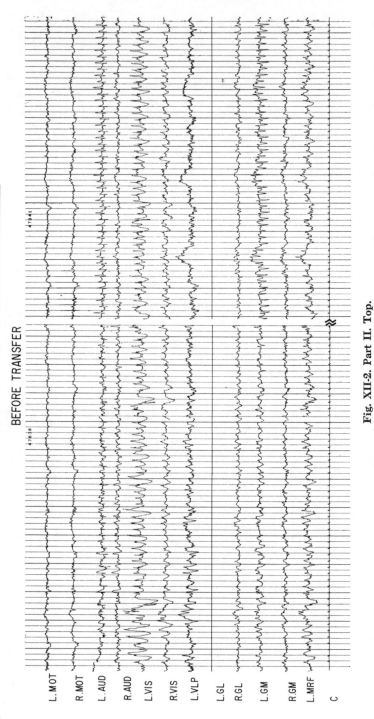

EFFECT OF TRANSFER ON RESPONSES TO ELECTRICAL STIMULUS OF GL (CAT·1)

BEFORE TRANSFER

L.MOT
R.MOT
L.AUD
R.AUD
L.VIS
R.VIS
L.VLP
L.GL
R.GL
L.GM
R.GM
L.MRF
C

Fig. XII-2. Part II. Top.

EEG tracings from same cat as in XII-2:I, illustrating the change in labeled response following transfer of the conditioned approach response to direct electrical stimulation, C, of the lateral geniculate nucleus.

282

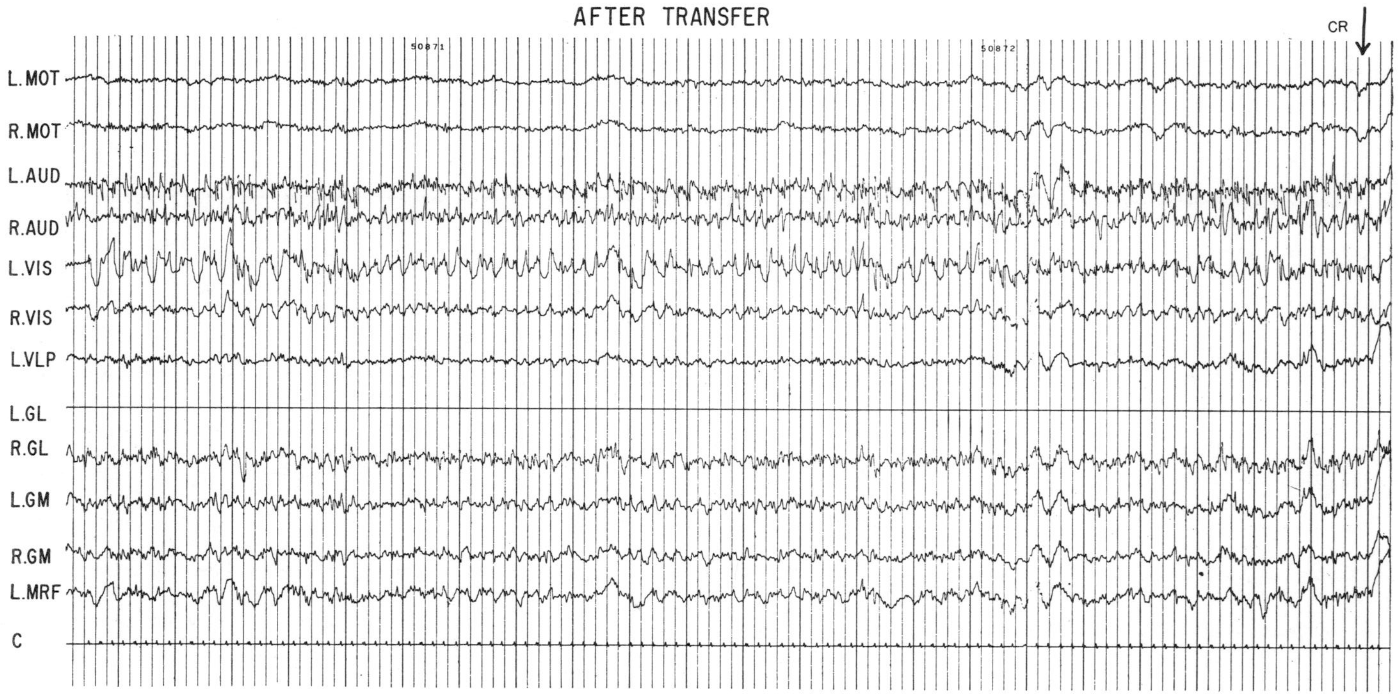

AFTER TRANSFER
CR
50871
50872
L.MOT
R.MOT
L.AUD
R.AUD
L.VIS
R.VIS
L.VLP
L.GL
R.GL
L.GM
R.GM
L.MRF
C

Fig. XII-2. Part II. Bottom.

Although some differences between the top and bottom records are apparent upon visual inspection, especially during the several seconds preceding the CR, changes during conditioning to central stimulation are much less marked than to peripheral stimuli. Average response computation is essential in order to demonstrate the changes clearly, as shown in the next section, B.3, p. 288. (Both records are from John and Shimokochi, 1966.)

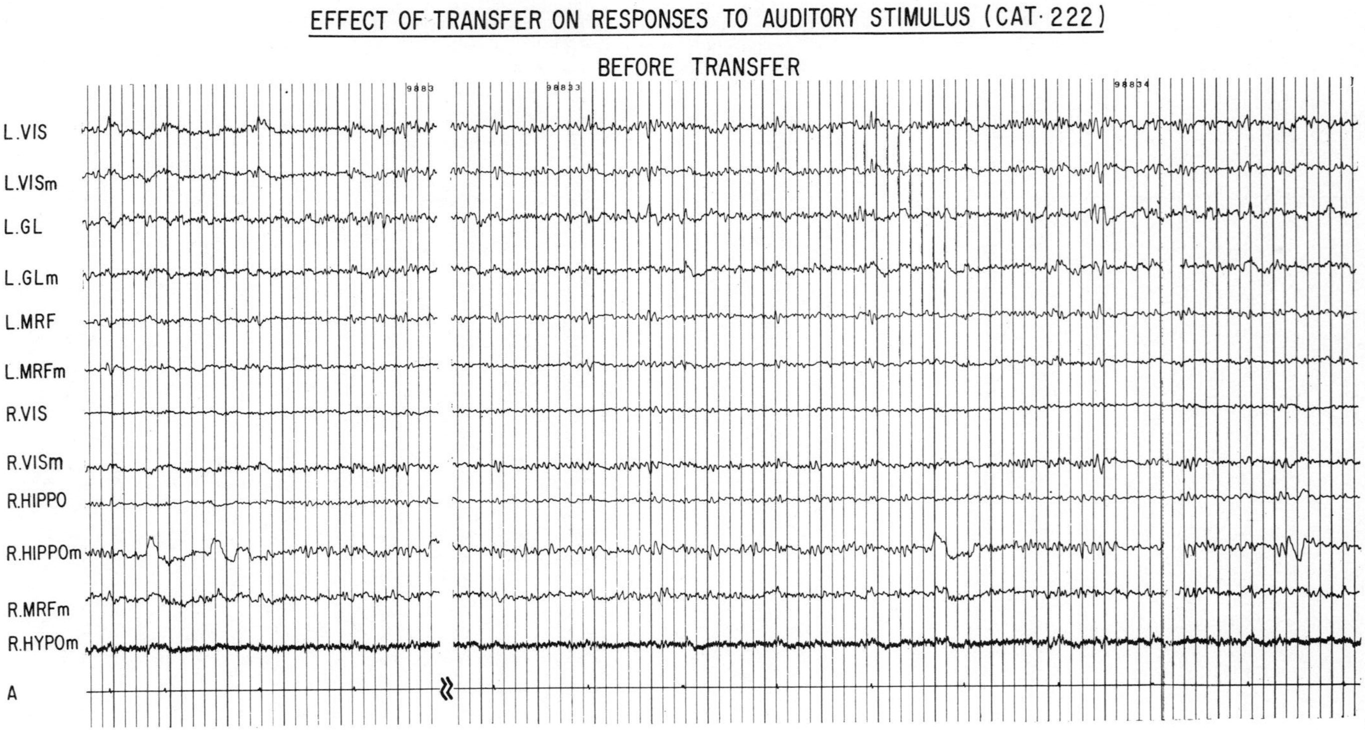

284

EFFECT OF TRANSFER ON RESPONSES TO AUDITORY STIMULUS (CAT·222)

BEFORE TRANSFER

L.VIS
L.VISm
L.GL
L.GLm
L.MRF
L.MRFm
R.VIS
R.VISm
R.HIPPO
R.HIPPOm
R.MRFm
R.HYPOm
A

Fig. XII-3. Part I. Top.

EEG tracings from cat after completion of differential approach-avoidance training to two flicker frequencies (1 and 2.5 cps). Examples of effect of 1-cps clicks before (top) and after (bottom) *transfer* of conditioned avoidance response previously established to 1-cps flicker CS. Transfer of training was accompanied by widespread alteration of response to click. Note marked

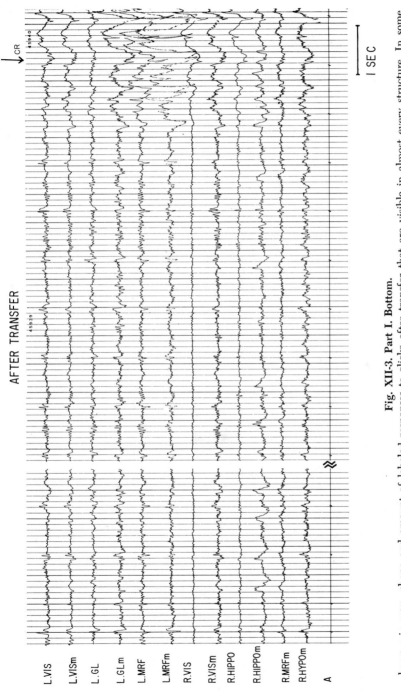

AFTER TRANSFER

CR

L.VIS
L.VISm
L.GL
L.GLm
L.MRF
L.MRFm
R.VIS
R.VISm
R.HIPPO
R.HIPPOm
R.MRFm
R.HYPOm
A

1 SEC

Fig. XII-3. Part I. Bottom.

changes in wave shape and amount of labeled responses to clicks after transfer that are visible in almost every structure. In some structures (e.g., MRF), the changes are as marked in bipolar as in monopolar recordings. Both top and bottom records were obtained in the same session. No changes in amplification were made.

285

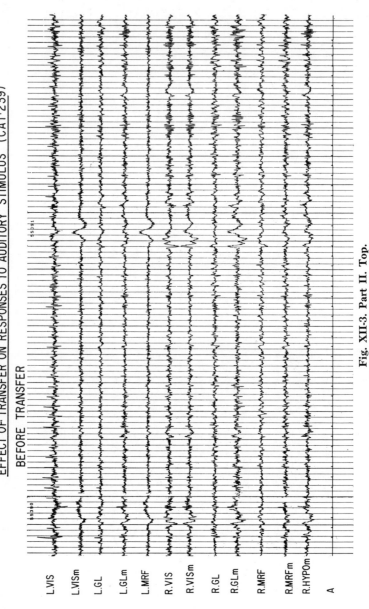

EFFECT OF TRANSFER ON RESPONSES TO AUDITORY STIMULUS (CAT-239)

BEFORE TRANSFER

L.VIS
L.VISm
L.GL
L.GLm
L.MRF
R.VIS
R.VISm
R.GL
R.GLm
R.MRF
R.MRFm
R.HYPOm
A

Fig. XII-3. Part II. Top.

Records from a third cat trained as above. These tracings illustrate the effect of 2.5-cps clicks before (top) and after (bottom) *transfer* of conditioned avoidance response previously established to 2.5-cps flicker CS. Note widespread changes in wave shape and amount of labeled responses to clicks after transfer, visible in almost every structure.

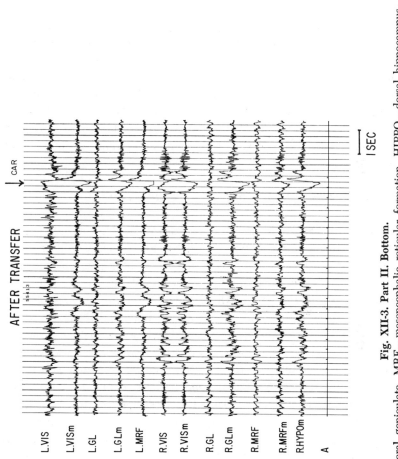

Fig. XII-3. Part II. Bottom.

VIS—visual cortex, GL—lateral geniculate, MRF—mesencephalic reticular formation, HIPPO—dorsal hippocampus, HYPO—posterior hypothalamus. L—left side, R—right side. Lower case m denotes monopolar derivations, others are bipolar. [From John and Shimokochi (1966).]

separated only by several minutes of conditioning. These changes indicate that the appearance of labeled responses under these conditions is related to the informational significance attached to the tracer stimuli by the transfer procedure. The extreme rapidity with which these changes often appear has relevance to a theoretical issue extensively discussed in this volume. *It seems highly unlikely that synaptic growth occurs during the few minutes sometimes sufficient for the transfer procedure to be completed.* The striking increase of labeled response during transfer is extremely difficult to reconcile with the Growth Hypothesis. There is little evidence for reverberatory activity during the transfer period, although reverberatory activity observed under training conditions will be described later.

3. *Transfer of training from peripheral to central stimuli*

Further evidence that some of the changes in labeled response cannot be attributed to sensitization but are related to the acquisition of informational significance by a stimulus comes from studies in which conditioned responses were established to intermittent electrical stimulation of various places in the brain. All of the illustrations provided in this section have been taken from the work of Leiman (1962). In these studies, a conditioned avoidance response (CAR) was initially established to a flicker CS. The propagation of evoked responses to various brain regions was then studied before and after transfer of training to direct electrical stimulation of the lateral geniculate body (LG), at the same repetition rate. This will be referred to as *central transfer I*. In some cases, the propagation of evoked responses was studied before and after the *further* transfer of training to direct electrical stimulation of the mesencephalic reticular formation (MRF), at the same repetition rate. This will be referred to as *central transfer II*. Only averaged evoked response computations will be presented here.

Figure XII-4 shows the good reproducibility of averaged responses evoked in various regions by the propagation of activity produced by local electrical stimulation with well-controlled stimulus parameters.

Figure XII-5 shows that large changes in amplitude and wave shape of evoked responses appeared in some brain regions when a CAR was established to a flicker CS.

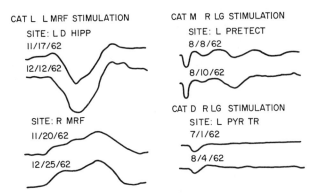

Fig. XII-4. Averaged responses evoked in various brain regions by direct electrical stimulation of MRF or LG. Data taken from three cats. Replication of wave shapes on different days illustrates reproducibility of response. MRF—mesencephalic reticular formation, LG—lateral geniculate, D HIPP—dorsal hippocampus, PRETECT—pretectal area, PYR TR—pyramidal tract. [Data from Leiman (1962).]

Many of the changes which are apparent on comparison of evoked responses before and after subsequent central transfers I and II seem to reflect the acquisition of cue value by the electrical stimuli delivered to particular brain regions. A number of examples of *enhanced* response will be provided. Figure XII-6 shows increase in the amplitude of re-

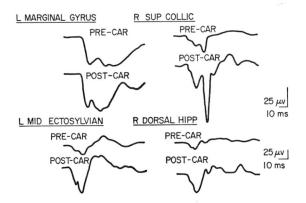

Fig. XII-5. Effect of avoidance training (cat G) on average response evoked by 10-cps flicker used as CS. MARGINAL GYRUS—visual cortex, SUP COLLIC—superior colliculus, MID ECTOSYLVIAN—auditory cortex, DORSAL HIPP—dorsal hippocampus. Pre-CAR—before avoidance training. Post-CAR—after avoidance training. [Data from Leiman (1962).]

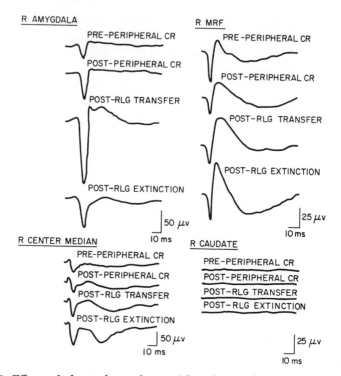

Fig. XII-6. Effects of electrical stimulation of lateral geniculate (10 pulses per second, 0.4 mA) before training (Pre-peripheral CR), after establishment of conditioned avoidance response to 10-cps flicker CS (Post-peripheral CR), after *transfer* of conditioned avoidance response to 10-cps right LG stimulation (Post-RLG transfer), and after extinction of conditioned response to LG but not to flicker CS (Post-RLG extinction).

Note marked changes in average response evoked by LG stimulation in amygdala and reticular formation (MRF) after LG transfer. Extinction causes decrement in response of amygdala, little change in MRF, and appearance of new component in center median wave shape. No effect of LG stimulation was detected in the caudate at any stage. These data not only illustrate the changes in evoked response that may accompany alteration in informational significance of a stimulus, but indicate the wide variety of changes that can be observed. [Data from Leiman (1962).]

sponses to LG stimulation evoked in the amygdala and the reticular formation following central transfer I.

Figure XII-7 shows the change in threshold intensity of MRF stimulation indicated by the appearance of evoked response on sigmoid cortex, following central transfer II. Notice the effects of 0.1 mA stimulation.

Figure XII-8 shows that the enhancement of evoked response in MRF after central transfer I is *differential*. This animal was trained to perform the CAR when the LG was electrically stimulated at 10 cps but not when stimulation was at 4 cps. The two intermittent stimuli were delivered with identical parameters for each electrical pulse. Note the marked difference in the amplitude of response to the S^D and S^Δ repetition rates. This observation provides further evidence for the inadequacy of a sensitization

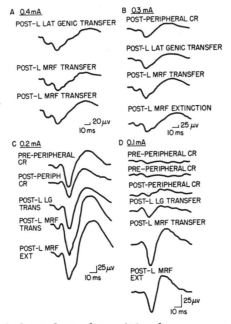

Fig. XII-7. Effects of electrical stimulation (10 pulses per second) of left mesencephalic reticular formation on activity of left anterior sigmoid gyrus (cat L) at various stages of training: Training procedures were the same as for the animal described in the previous figure, but after LG training, transfer to electrical stimulation of MRF was carried out. *Post-LMRF transfer*—after transfer of CAR to 10-cps electrical stimulation of left mesencephalic reticular formation; *Post-LMRF extinction* —after extinction of conditioned response to MRF stimulation only.

Although no major change in wave shape of average evoked response was apparent during this sequence of stages in training, marked enhancement of response occurred after transfer of CAR to reticular stimulation. This could be seen most clearly when stimulation intensity was reduced to 0.1 mA. [Data from Leiman (1962).]

interpretation. *Furthermore, it illustrates the ability of the nervous system to discriminate between two temporal patterns of identical pulses at the same place.*

The examples of changed response to direct electrical stimulation provided above consisted primarily of enhancement of response. Qualita-

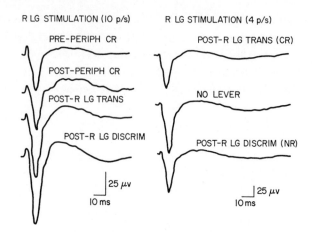

Fig. XII-8. Effect of electrical stimulation of right lateral geniculate on activity of right mesencephalic reticular formation at various stages of training (cat D): Procedures were similar to those used with animals described in the two preceding figures. However, after transfer of the CAR from 10-cps flicker to LG stimulation, frequency discrimination was established using *10-cps* electrical input to LG as the positive signal and *4-cps* stimulation as the negative signal. POST-R LG DISCRIM—average responses evoked by 10-cps stimulus after completion of differential training; POST-R LG TRANS (CR)—responses evoked by 4-cps stimulus during generalization at onset of differential training; NO LEVER—responses evoked by 4-cps stimulus while lever withdrawn to decrease lever pressing tendency; POST-R LG DISCRIM (NR)—responses evoked by 4-cps stimulus after completion of differential training.

Note markedly greater response to positive stimulus after differential training. [Data from Leiman (1962).]

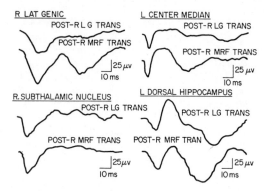

Fig. XII-9. Note appearance of new late component in averaged responses evoked from lateral geniculate (LG) and center median by electrical stimulation of MRF (mesencephalic reticular formation) *after transfer* (cat E). Some change can also be seen in response of dorsal hippocampus, while the response of the subthalamic nucleus appears unaltered. Procedures as in Fig. XII-7. [Data from Leiman (1962).]

292

tive changes in the effects of stimulation also occur as reflected by the appearance of *new evoked response wave shapes* in some structures after transfer. An example of such alteration in the form of response is provided in Fig. XII-9. Note the *second component* of the response evoked in the lateral geniculate, centre median, and the hippocampus by MRF stimulation after central transfer II.

Another example of changed evoked response wave shape is illustrated in Fig. XII-10, appearing to LG stimulation after central transfer I. Note the differential responsiveness implied by the change in response evoked in several regions while no change appears in records taken from MRF in this animal.

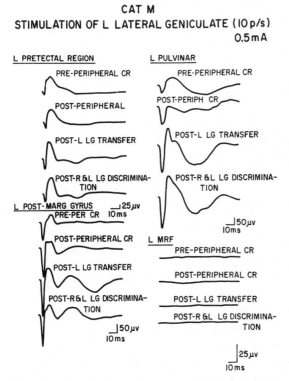

CAT M

STIMULATION OF L LATERAL GENICULATE (10 p/s)

0.5 mA

Fig. XII-10. Note appearance of new late component in averaged responses evoked from pretectal region, pulvinar, and marginal gyrus by electrical stimulation of left lateral geniculate (10 pulses per second, 0.5 mA) (cat M) *after transfer*. Procedures as in Fig. XII-8, except that discrimination was established between 10-cps electrical stimuli delivered to left (positive) and right (negative) lateral geniculate bodies. [Data from Leiman (1962).]

These illustrations constitute abundant demonstration from a number of animals in a variety of situations that *some* of the changes in labeled response which appear after conditioning to a tracer CS are related to the acquisition of "meaning" by the stimulus. These changes may reasonably be interpreted as reflecting alterations in information processing rather than mere sensitization. Having established the potential relevance of electrophysiological phenomena of this sort to the neural mechanisms involved in information processing, we can now turn to selected features of these data which may reflect dynamic processes related to the storage, retrieval, and evaluation of information in the brain. Insofar as possible, evidence will be provided that the various electrophysiological phenomena to be presented are differential in some regard, thereby giving continuing reassurance that the observations cannot be attributed to simple sensitization.

C. Assimilation of rhythms

The fact that changes occur in the response of the brain to a stimulus as information about the significance of that stimulus is acquired is not at all surprising. It would be surprising if such changes could not be demonstrated. The mere fact of change, while it reveals that certain brain regions are altering their response, tells lamentably little about the nature of the process of information storage and retrieval. Some of these changes in distribution, size, or shape of labeled responses may reflect changes in the level of excitation or in the focus of attention. These effects are usually subsumed under the rubric of sensitization. Those changes which are specifically related to the acquisition of informational significance by a stimulus may reflect a variety of processes: Altered appearance of labeled responses in a region after establishment of some conditioned response to a tracer stimulus may indicate the opening or closing of a transmission gate or shunt affecting the propagation of activity from structure to structure, the release of a pattern of activity as a result of the prior storage of information in the region, or the evaluation of arriving information in the context of the state and recent experience of the organism. Thus, labeled responses may be related to different functional processes in various brain regions and under various circumstances. We shall endeavor to provide some bases for distinguishing between these different possibilities. Furthermore, *the appearance of labeled responses may simply mean that the stimulus is important. Alternatively, the shape of the labeled response may relate to the appropriate behavior.* Would the wave forms of the labeled response change if the behavioral response were different? We shall return to this question in Chapter XIII.

Fortunately, certain aspects of the data acquired in these experiments seem to provide promising insights into the interpretation of this activity. Among such findings are some phenomena first observed by Livanov in the Soviet Union, who described what he called "assimilation of the rhythm" (Livanov and Poliakov, 1945). By this term Livanov wished to identify electrical activity which appeared in many regions of the brain, at the same frequency as an intermittent stimulus which was being used as the conditioned stimulus for the elaboration of a new behavioral response by the animal. Assimilated rhythms are sometimes at harmonics or subharmonics of the stimulus frequency. This activity appeared *during the intertrial intervals when the actual stimulus was absent.* As an animal acquires a conditioned response to an intermittent stimulus, electrical waves at the frequency of that stimulus gradually increase in amount during the intertrial intervals, eventually come to dominate the intertrial record, and then diminish as the conditioned response becomes fully elaborated. This rhythmic activity disappears while the animal is in his home cage but reappears when he is replaced in the conditioning apparatus. Furthermore, those rhythms return in force during the period immediately following performance of an erroneous response by the animal. Assimilated rhythms have been observed in the rat, rabbit, cat, dog, monkey, and man (John, 1961). They have been observed using a wide range of stimulus frequencies and in a wide variety of experimental situations. It seems highly probable that such rhythms are not idiosyncratic to a particular conditioning situation nor to a particular species but represent a general capacity of the central nervous system to reflect the temporal pattern of prior stimulation for a period of time following the cessation of that external event.

Similar observations were made by John and Killam, who used flickering light as the conditioned stimulus for the establishment of a conditioned avoidance response of shock in the cat (1959). In Fig. XII-11:I, a number of recordings from a cat learning an avoidance response to a

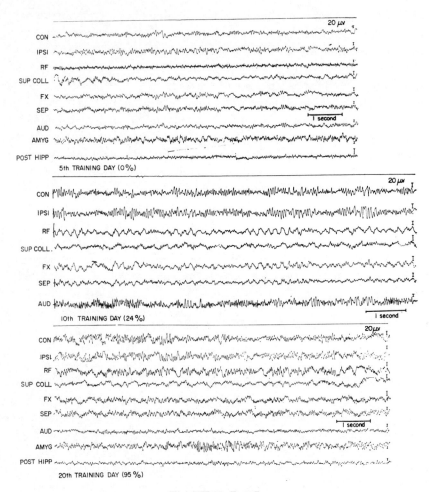

Fig. XII-11. Part I.

Fig. XII-11. I. Assimilated rhythms recorded from the same cat at three stages of training. Upper records show intertrial activity early during avoidance training using a 10-cps flicker conditioned stimulus; the middle set of records shows activity 5 days later at the 24% performance level; and the bottom records were obtained after the conditioned response was well established. Note the rhythmic activity in the middle records, which appears almost simultaneously in the reticular formation, fornix and septum. CON—bipolar visual derivation, one electrode on each marginal gyrus, IPSI —bipolar visual cortex, both electrodes on same gyrus, RF—mesencephalic reticular formation, SUP COLL—superior colliculus, FX—fornix, SEP—septum, AUD—auditory cortex, AMYG—amygdala, POST HIPP—dorsal hippocampus; all derivations are bipolar.

296

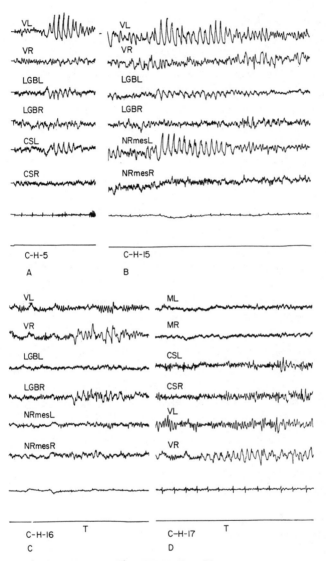

Fig. XII-11. Part II.

II. Assimilated rhythms recorded from both hemispheres of cat whose brain has been split, including section of corpus collosum, anterior commissure, posterior commissure, massa intermedia, and optic tectum. The tracings shown in portions A and B of this figure illustrate internal spontaneous rhythmic discharge at 5 cps. At this stage, the left eye and hemisphere were being trained to a conditioned defensive reflex using a 5-cps flicker CS. Note that *the frequency specific assimilated rhythm*

297

10-per-second flickering light are presented. These recordings are taken at successive stages of training. The upper set of records shows the intertrial activity recorded from a set of leads in an animal who has not yet performed the first correct avoidance response to a 10-per-second flicker. The middle set of recordings shows the intertrial activity after some days of training when the avoidance response performance is at about the 24% level. Note the rhythmic activity which appears almost simultaneously in the reticular formation, the fornix, and the septum. This activity is at a 5-per-second rhythm, in this instance one-half the tracer stimulus frequency. The lower set of recordings shows intertrial electrical activity after the conditioned response has been well established. Discussing these early observations, it was suggested that assimilated rhythms might perhaps be a manifestation of reverberatory activity persisting after the stimulus, during the period while consolidation was taking place. These data also indicate that during repeated experience with a rhythmic stimulus a system is elaborated involving a number of anatomical regions, which has the capacity of discharging spontaneously later with the temporal pattern of previous stimulation.

A particularly interesting example of assimilation of the rhythm has recently been provided by Majkowski (1966) and is illustrated in Fig. XII-11: II. These data show that assimilated rhythms are localized to the "learning" hemisphere of split-brain cats, but appear on the second side during transfer of the conditioned response to the previously untrained hemisphere. These differential observations strongly suggest that the spontaneous appearance of frequency-specific repetitive responses in various anatomical regions during training with a rhythmic stimulus reflects the establishment of a representational system mediating the storage of information about the stimulus rather than unspecific influences.

---

was confined to structures on the side of the brain which was being trained, but appears at about the same time in different regions.

Portions C and D of this figure illustrate the appearance of assimilated rhythms on the right side as transfer (T) of training was carried out using the right eye and hemisphere. All derivations are bipolar: VL—visual cortex (left side); VR—visual cortex (right side); LGBL—lateral geniculate body, left; LGBR—lateral geniculate body, right; CSL—superior colliculus, left; CSR—superior colliculus, right; NR mes L—mesencephalic reticular formation, left; NR mes R—mesencephalic reticular formation, right; ML—motor cortex, left; MR—motor cortex, right; unlabeled seventh channel shows EKG and EMG, eighth channel—stimulus artifact. [Data from Majkowski (1966).]

D. Cyclic conditioning

Phenomena apparently related to analogous mechanisms can be seen in a number of different experimental paradigms, some of which have been previously mentioned. The writer and his co-workers (John *et al.*, 1957), and Yoshii and Hockaday (1958), have observed that if intermittent stimuli are presented at regular intervals, that is, every 30 seconds, and are then occasionally withheld, a frequency-specific repetitive response will often be observed in the sensory cortex. These observations seem to provide evidence that the repeated regular experience with rhythmic stimulation has organized a representational system in some structures which, under appropriate circumstances, can reproduce the temporal pattern of activity which typically accompanied the events which established the system. These rhythms cannot be discerned during the intervening intervals. It is well known that behavioral responses can also be established by cyclic procedures.

E. Cortical conditioning

A similar phenomenon can be observed in "cortical conditioning." As described earlier, in this procedure a steady tone which normally elicits no frequency-specific electrical discharge of the brain is presented to the animal for several seconds, and then a flickering light is added to the auditory stimulus. After a number of periodic pairings of this sort, changes in response to the tone are observed, which have been classified into three phases. At first, the tone elicits a generalized desynchronization of widespread cortical areas. *In phase II, the tone elicits rhythmic discharge, at the approximate frequency of the flicker, in the visual cortex before the flicker is presented.* In phase III, presentation of the tone results only in a localized desynchronization of the visual cortical area. An example of the frequency-specific response during phase II is provided in Fig. XII-12, which is from the work of Morrell (1958).

During cortical conditioning, a representational system may be constructed which possesses the capacity to produce a fluctuation in the

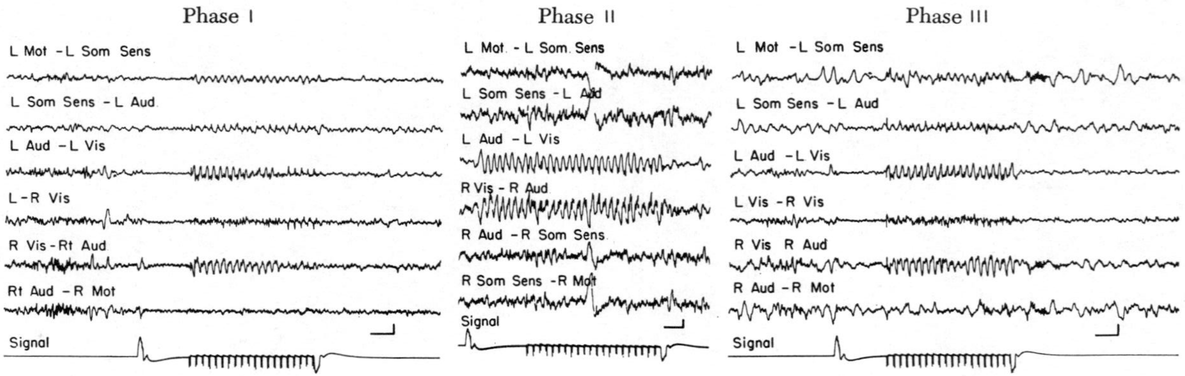

Fig. XII-12. Effects of cortical conditioning on response to steady tone. First upward deflection in Signal record indicates onset of steady tone. After two seconds of tone, flicker is presented at rate indicated by downward deflections of Signal artifact. Tone and flicker terminate together.

Phase I—Generalized desynchronization observed in all areas at onset of tone, early in conditioning.

Phase II—At onset of steady tone, frequency specific repetitive response appears in visual cortex, before flicker is presented.

Phase III—Steady tone elicits desynchronization localized to visual cortex. [Data from Morrell (1961d).]

potentials recorded from visual cortex corresponding to the activity induced by flicker. The steady tone, repeatedly present while this system was established, possibly activates a portion of this system. Subsequent presentation of steady tone, presumably by activation of that portion, seems to initiate discharge of the whole representational system. Consequently, there is appearance of frequency-specific repetitive response in the visual cortex, which has become functionally integrated into the representational system because it was repeatedly active while the system was built.

According to Yoshii and his co-workers (1957b), frequency-specific repetitive response appears in subcortical structures, including the mesencephalic reticular formation and the intralaminar nuclei, before it appears in visual cortex. Furthermore, Yoshii and Hockaday (1958) have reported preliminary evidence suggesting that cortical conditioning is blocked in animals with lesions of the centre median. Thus, the intralaminar nuclei of the thalamus, the so-called nuclei of origin of the recruiting response, may occupy an essential position in the function of the representational system built during the procedure of cortical conditioning.

Chow et al. (1966b) have analyzed this problem further, exploring the effects of various brain lesions on the development of conditioned cortical potentials. Their results indicate that transcortical connections are essential for the establishment of conditioned repetitive responses. Frequency-specific repetitive responses were obtained in cats with lesions in the rostral thalamus, midline dorsal thalamus, and midbrain reticular formation but were not obtained in cats with neocortical lesions between auditory and visual areas. The role of cortico-cortical connections was demonstrated by the fact that tones elicited repetitive responses in regions of visual cortex lying laterally but not medially to knife cuts in the visual areas. These results suggest that the repetitive response is produced locally within the neural network comprising the visual cortex, as a result of transcortical afferent input from the auditory cortex.

Assimilated rhythms were observed in most of the animals in this study, including those with subcortical lesions. This activity was not observed in cats with bilateral cortical lesions in auditory regions, although cats with knife cuts in visual cortex showed spontaneous rhythms at the flicker frequency. These findings suggest that the phenomenon of assimilation is not dependent upon subcortical mediation, but can be mediated by a set of cortical relationships.

Conditioned repetitive responses could be induced in cats with total destruction of the septal region, making it unlikely that such discharges represent conditioned hippocampal theta waves reaching the cortex. Of the many lesions studied, only total ablation of rostral thalamus blocked the appearance of localized desynchronization (phase III). The appearance of local desynchronization in animals which do not show conditioned repetitive responses indicates that the various phases of cortical conditioning involve independent brain structures. These results further support the proposition that extensive regions and vast numbers of cells are involved in mediation of even such simple conditioned responses as these.

In an extremely interesting variation of cortical conditioning, Rosen and Stamm (1966) studied the effects of pairing a CS at one frequency (clicks or flashes) with a US at a second frequency (flashes or clicks). After conditioning, the CS caused a surface-*negative* shift in the cortex of the US modality, accompanied by rhythmic activity *at the US frequency*. A surface-*positive* shift occurred in the cortex of the CS modality at a latency corresponding to the CS-US interval. No systematic changes in other cortical regions were observed.

F. Isolated cortical slab

Evidence that the brain can reproduce a previously experienced temporal pattern of discharge is available from the work of Chow and Dewson, who have studied the isolated cortical slab (Chow and Dewson, 1963; Chow, 1964). This is a region of cortex which has been undercut and circumscribed so that it retains no neural connection with the rest of the brain, although its blood supply is left intact. On such a slab, three pairs of electrodes are positioned: two for stimulating and two for recording, separated by a pair through which a weak dc polarizing current can flow. If tetanizing stimulation or cathodal polarizing current of several microamps is applied to these intermediate electrodes, it is possible to observe the following: Direct electrical stimulation of the first pair of electrodes at frequency *one* results in recording of electrical activity dominated by frequency *one* at the recording electrodes. If, after a period of stimulation at frequency *one,* the frequency applied to the stimulating electrodes is abruptly changed to frequency *two,* the recordings which are obtained include a component at frequency *one.* The effects are illustrated in Fig. XII-13.

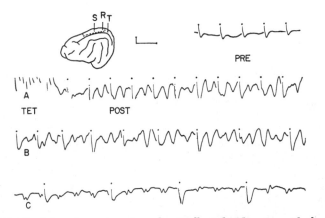

Fig. XII-13. The induced responses in a chronically isolated cortex with the tetanizing shocks outside the isolated area. Record taken from an anesthetized cat (BC-51). The interrupted lines on the brain map indicate the isolated area. The isolation was performed 4 months earlier. R, monopolar recording electrode; S, bipolar stimulating electrodes; T, bipolar tetanizing electrodes; Pre, low-frequency stimulation (9/sec, 20 V); A: Tet, high-frequency tetanization (50/sec, 30 V); Post, 9/sec stimulation immediately after tetanization; B: during the process of changing the stimulus frequency; C: 3/sec stimulation. The dots indicate the low-frequency stimulation. Calibration, 100 μV and 100 msec. Note that response during 3/sec stimulation shows persistent rhythm at frequency of previous 9/sec stimulus. [Data from Chow and Dewson (1964).]

G. Single cortical cells

Related evidence at the level of electrical discharge of single nerve cells in the cortex has been reported by Morrell (1960). It is possible to find cells in the visual cortex which are spontaneously active and which do not display any consistent change in such activity as a consequence of the presentation of a flash of light to the eye. If a weak dc field is applied to the cortex over such a cell, the response of this cell becomes much more reliably "driven" by the peripheral flash of light. While polarization is maintained, if such a cell is driven for several minutes at

303

a particular frequency, for example 3 cps, a most interesting aftereffect can be observed. Presentation of a single flash of light after such rhythmic stimulation results in rhythmic discharge of this cell at a 3-cps burst frequency, and the number of spikes in the burst is the same as that which characterized the cell's response to the rhythmic flash of light. The probability that this frequency-specific response will be elicited by a single flash of light decays in a smooth exponential curve and reaches the base line at about 20 minutes. This phenomenon is illustrated in Fig. XII-14:I.

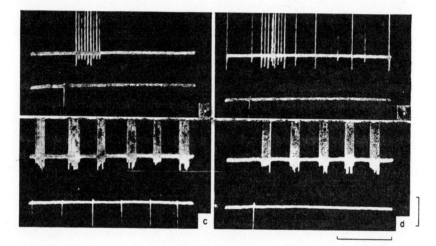

Fig. XII-14. Part I.
Conditioning of a rhythmic burst response to a single flash. Anodal polarization was applied to the visual receiving area. Single flash elicited a single burst in a quiescent (a) and in a randomly firing cell (b). Three-per-second stroboscopic stimulation (c) produced driving of unit discharge at that frequency. A single flash (d) delivered 30 sec after termination of the rhythmic stimulus resulted in repetitive unit discharge at about 3/sec. Unit potentials are seen in the upper channel of the oscilloscope, stimulus artifacts in the lower channel. Amplitude calibration: 2 mV. Time calibration: 500 msec. (a and b) and 1 sec. (c and d). [Data from Morrell (1961d).]

Another example of the retention of frequency-specific response patterns by the activity of a single unit is shown in Fig. XII-14:II. As can be seen by inspection of the poststimulus frequency histograms, repeated presentation of 10-cps flicker gradually established a regular "driven" response from a single neuron subjacent to polarized visual cortex. When the stimulus frequency was changed to 1 cps, the unit responded to each flash of light with the same pattern of response displayed to the previous

10-cps stimulus. *Notice that the cell does not fire rigorously 10 times per second under either condition. Rather, the firing rate is such that the periods when discharge is most probable are separated by about 100 msec.* The *level of probability* of unit discharge fluctuates 10 times per second.

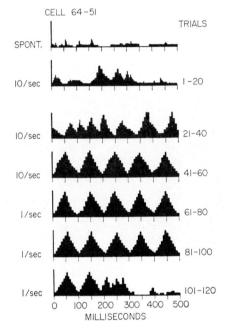

Fig. XII-14. Part II.

Poststimulus frequency histograms from single neuron in visual cortex subjacent to 10 μampere surface positive polarization. Current flow was maintained throughout the interval. Top record shows spontaneous firing pattern. Notice how "driven" response of unit improves from first to third block of 20 trials in response to 10-cps flicker. Stimulus frequency was then changed to 1 cps. Poststimulus frequency histogram shows that unit continued to display a 10/sec response pattern which dominated activity during next 40 trials, gradually lessening by 120th trial, as seen in last histogram. [Data from Morrell, Engel, and Bouris (1966).]

This persistent representation of the temporal pattern of stimulation experienced for an extended period is not due to activation of an intrinsic rhythm of corresponding frequency nor is it probable that it represents reverberation sustained throughout the entire duration of the experiment. This is shown by Fig. XII-14:III. If paired flashes of light are used, separated by a brief interval and repeated for some period at a character-

305

istic rate, each double flash will come to elicit paired bursts of discharge from single neurons, at the repetition frequency. If stimulation is then shifted to a train of single flashes, the neuron continues to respond with a double pulse pattern. When stimulation is interrupted, the cell continues to fire briefly with the previous pattern, pauses for a time, and then resumes sporadic firing at random intervals. Resumption of stimulation by single flashes of light restores the double response pattern momentarily, but the cell soon reverts to a single pulse response mode.

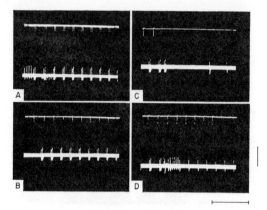

Fig. XII-14. Part III.

Procedure as in I, but light flashes delivered in pairs. Cell 63-774. Site: Anterior Lateral Gyrus Right. Depth 1.3 mm. Unanesthetized, flaxedil, artificial respiration, surface anodal polarization—10 μamp/mm²; upper beam: stimulus pulse; lower beam: unit record. (A) Cell is responding in doublets to paired flash (duration 50 μsec, interval 70 msec). (B) Cell continues to give double response when stimulus changed to single flash. (C) Stimulus is stopped. Cell stops after slight afterdischarge and resumed random firing 1.5 sec later. (D) Resumption of rhythmic 4/sec single flash results in two doublets then brief rapid discharge, then synchronizes with externally delivered signal. Calibration: 10 mV, 1 sec. [Data from Morrell, Engel, and Bouris (1966).]

Figure XII-14:IV shows the poststimulus frequency histograms displayed by a typical unit during a procedure like that just described. Examination of the data shows clearly that the double response mode persisted for some time after single flash presentation was initiated, and subsequent double flash stimulation had to be maintained for an extended period before the double response mode was restored. As in Fig. XII-14:II, note that the unit response does not consist of one or two discharges to every flash, at precisely the interflash interval. Rather *the probability of unit discharge fluctuates* and displays one or two maxima in the period following each stimulus, and the interval between the maxima corresponds to the interval between the first and second members of the double flash.

Data of this sort indicate that the temporal pattern of previous stimulation can be approximated by the discharge patterns of single

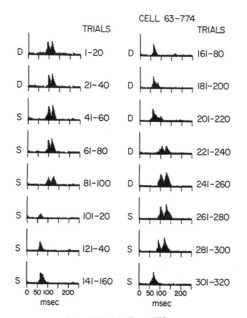

Fig. XII-14. Part IV.

IV. Post stimulus histogram. Cell 63-774. Computed analysis of all trials, same as in Fig. XII-14:III. D = double flash (both eyes) S = single flash (both eyes). Binwidth = 1 msec, analysis time = 220 msec. Each histogram represents an average of 20 trials. Note the persistence of double response pattern to single flash in trials 41–100, gradually giving way to single response pattern in trials 141–160. When double flash is reintroduced, a single response pattern dominates unit activity. Double response pattern reestablished by trials 221–260. When a single flash is reintroduced, a double response pattern again persisted for some time. [Data from Morrell, Engel, and Bouris (1966).]

neurons subsequently released by different stimuli. Although these findings provide evidence that the single cell can participate in assimilation processes, they should not be interpreted as meaning that the process itself is stored in the individual monitored cell. No uniqueness can be claimed for the cell fortuitously selected by the questing microelectrode.

More reasonably, this evidence indicates the involvement of many cells in a representational system capable of reproducing the previously experienced temporal pattern of input. These changes in cellular activity indicate alterations in firing pattern rather than the opening of new pathways and are easier to reconcile with the Mode Hypothesis than with the Growth or Shunt Hypotheses. The probabilistic relationship observed between the stimulus frequency and the incidence of unit discharge is compatible with the suggestion that the representation of stimulus frequency may be mediated by the statistical characteristics of the activity of a neuronal ensemble.

H. Trace conditioning

The phenomena observed by Stern, Ulett, and Sines (1960) during trace conditioning may be related, although these phenomena probably reflect a reverberatory process more than those cited above. These workers studied the electrical activity in various brain regions during a delay period which intervened between termination of a tracer stimulus and the opportunity for an animal to perform a conditioned response. Wave analyzer evaluation of brain potentials during this interval revealed persistence of rhythms at the stimulus frequency.

I. Functional role of assimilated rhythms

Does this property of nervous tissue have functional significance? Does assimilation of the rhythm, in the various forms which have been described, reflect the existence of a representational process in the brain? The remainder of this chapter will emphasize other phenomena in support of the view that such activity serves a functional, representational purpose. Some indication of this is provided by the observation that spontaneous performance of conditioned responses is often preceded by the appearance of assimilated rhythms at the frequency of the conditioned stimulus (Yoshii, 1962).

Perhaps the earliest experimental approach to this question was made by Livanov and his colleagues (Livanov and Korolkova, 1951). After observing the spread of labeled responses to the motor cortex during conditioning, as well as the appearance of assimilated rhythms, they explored the effects of electrical stimulation of the motor cortex of trained animals at various frequencies. They observed that performance of the conditioned response could be elicited most readily and with the shortest latency when the cortical stimulus was delivered at the tracer frequency.

A few years later, Chow, Dement, and John (1957) devised a somewhat more direct approach to evaluating the functional role of endogenously generated rhythms. Cats were conditioned first to perform hurdle jumps to avoid shock within 15 seconds after presentation of a flickering light. Following acquisition of this behavior, steady tone and flicker were paired in a cortical conditioning paradigm carried out in a different apparatus. When phase II of cortical conditioning had been achieved, and tone successfully elicited rhythms at the flicker frequency in the visual cortex, the animals were returned to the avoidance apparatus. When tone alone was presented, labeled responses at the flicker tracer frequency appeared in the visual cortex, but the animals did not perform the avoidance response which had been established using flicker. Presentation of flicker, however, resulted in avoidance response with short latency. These authors concluded that the release of assimilated rhythms alone was not sufficient for release of a learned pattern of behavior. It was felt that a definitive evaluation of the functional role of such rhythms required additional behavioral measures, particularly related to savings during transfer of avoidance training to tone after cortical conditioning.

More recently, Schuckman and Battersby (1965) undertook a reexamination of this problem using a paradigm in which the cortical conditioning procedure did not constitute an extinction period for the CAR. Their experimental design differed from that used in the study just cited, in that cortical conditioning occurred *first* and avoidance training to flicker *second* in the experimental sequence. On subsequent presentation of *steady tone* to the animals in the avoidance apparatus, performance of the conditioned avoidance response was elicited as much as 40% of the time and was often accompanied by electrical rhythms at the tracer flicker frequency in the visual cortex. Although these rhythms were not always observed when the CAR was elicited by tone and sometimes occurred without behavioral performance, the data suggest that this release of assimilated rhythms might reflect the activation of a representational system with some functional significance. However, activation of the representational system in these experiments appeared to be

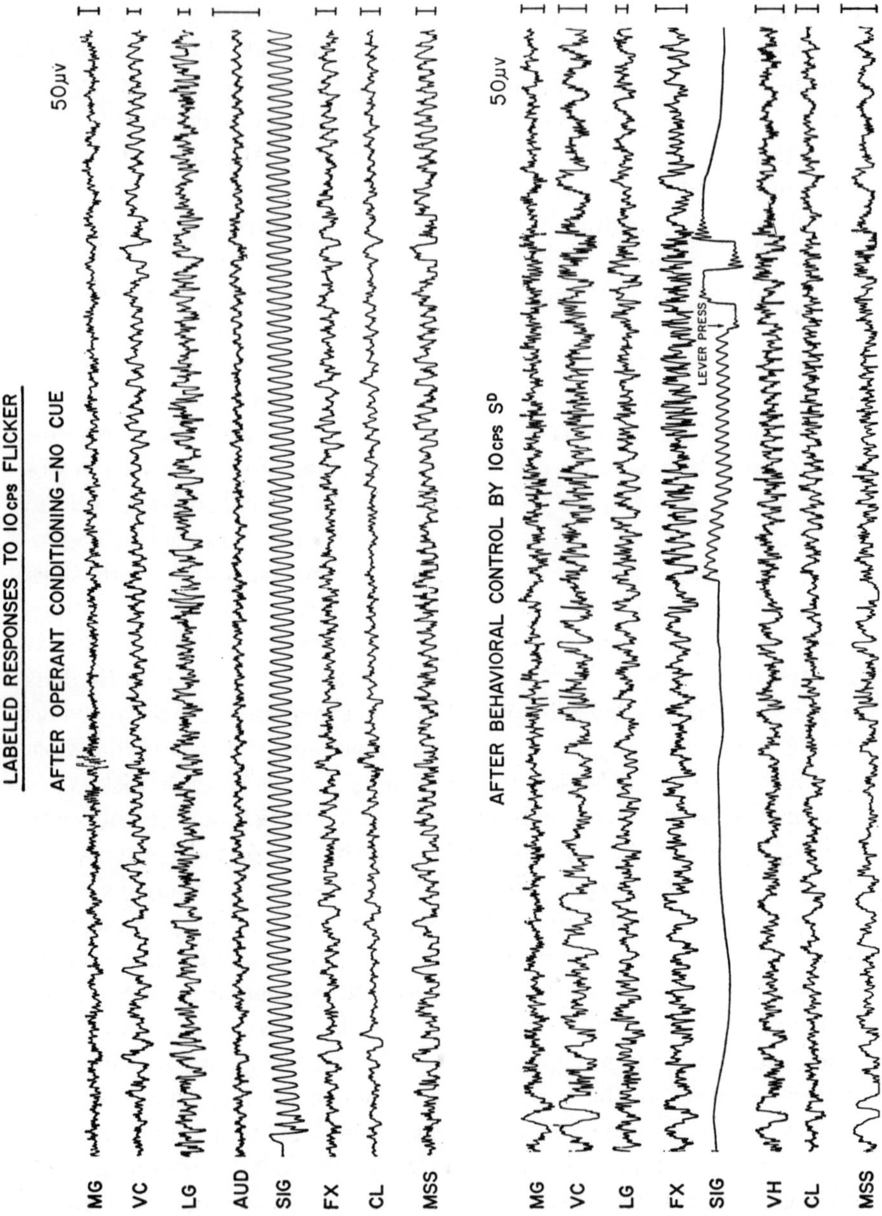

310

LABELED RESPONSES TO 10cps FLICKER

AFTER OPERANT CONDITIONING—NO CUE

50μν

MG
VC
LG
AUD
SIG
FX
CL
MSS

AFTER BEHAVIORAL CONTROL BY 10cps S^D

50μν

MG
VC
LG
FX
SIG
VH
CL
MSS

LEVER PRESS

Fig. XII-15.

neither necessary nor sufficient for the behavioral response to occur. Some additional critical factors seem to have been involved.

J. Differential approach-avoidance

During studies of discriminative approach and avoidance behavior in the cat, controlled by flicker stimuli of two different frequencies, John and Killam made further observations which seem highly relevant to this question (1960). Cats were trained first to press a lever for milk ad libitum. Recordings obtained from such an animal are shown by Fig. XII-15. The upper set of data were gathered after the animal had learned to press a lever to get milk, which was provided as reinforcement for *each* depression of the lever. The occurrence of 10-cps flicker in the apparatus while the cat was working to get milk resulted in the electrical activity illustrated in the upper tracings. Next, the animal was taught that milk would be provided *only* if the lever were pressed during the 10-cps flickering light. Subsequent to such conditioning, a marked enhancement of the response of a number of regions was observed, especially in the fornix (at the junction with the dorsal hippocampus) and N. centralis lateralis, as shown in the lower set of records in Fig. XII-15.

The animal was then taught that lever pressing during 10-cps flicker would still be reinforced with milk, while lever pressing during 6-cps flicker would not only fail to bring about the delivery of milk, but would *delay* the subsequent presentation of 10-cps flicker. Studying the elec-

---

Fig. XII-15. *Upper records:* Effect of 10-cps flicker presentation to a cat which had learned to get milk whenever it pressed a lever. Flicker had no signal significance at this stage. Note the paucity of labeled electrical rhythms at the flicker frequency.

Bottom records: Effect of 10-cps flicker presentation after cat had learned that milk could be obtained only if the lever were pressed during the flicker. The arrow indicates when the lever was pressed. Flicker was the conditioned stimulus at this stage. Note that the marked labeled potentials at the signal frequency are greatly increased in comparison to the upper records. MG—medial geniculate, VC—visual cortex, LG—lateral geniculate, AUD—auditory cortex, SIG—flicker artifact, FX—fornix, VH—ventral hippocampus, CL—nucleus centralis lateralis, MSS—medial suprasylvian cortex. Calibration—50 μV. All records bipolar.

trical activity from various brain regions during this discrimination behavior, interesting differences were observed between correct and erroneous responses to both stimuli. During correct behavioral responses to 10-cps flicker, clear frequency-specific potentials appeared in the visual

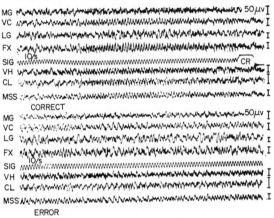

Fig. XII-16. Effect of 10-cps flicker presentation to same cat as illustrated in Fig. XII-15, but after elaboration of frequency discrimination, in which 10 cps was the positive stimulus and 6 cps was the negative stimulus. The cat obtained milk if lever was pressed during 10-cps flicker, but was punished by long delay before next trial if lever was pressed during 6-cps flicker.

Upper records: Labeled responses during correct response to 10-cps flicker. Lever was pressed at time indicated by the arrow. Notice that regularity and duration of frequency-specific waves is much enhanced after differential training. Note correspondence of rhythmic potentials to signal frequency.

Bottom records: Labeled response during *error of omission* in which cat failed to press lever during positive 10-cps signal. Notice deterioration of frequency-specific response. Note particularly the pronounced slow activity at about 6 cps, which is seen most clearly in nucleus centralis lateralis. Structures as in Figure XII-15.

cortex, the fornix, and N. centralis lateralis, as can be seen in the top portion of Fig. XII-16. There was, in general, much more labeled response than had been apparent at the previous stage of training.

The *bottom* portion of Fig. XII-16 shows recordings typical of those obtained during the *error of omission*. Although a 10-cps flicker was presented, the cat failed to press the lever. Since this was a hungry animal who could get food only by working in this situation, such errors of omission were attributed to inaccurate perception of the signal rather than to lack of motivation. Note that the labeled potentials at the tracer frequency are much less dominant in the lower set of recordings than in those above. A slower rhythm is apparent in certain portions of the record in the visual cortex, the fornix and N. centralis lateralis. Those rhythms were approximately at the frequency of the negative stimulus.

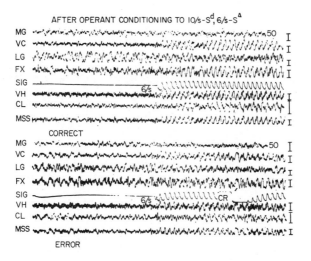

Fig. XII-17. Response to 6-cps flicker CS after differential training. *Top:* electrical activity during correct inhibition of lever press to 6-cps negative stimulus.

Bottom: electrical activity during *error of commission* in which lever press was performed during 6-cps flicker, at time indicated by arrow. Note diminution of labeled responses in some structures during error and sustained fast rhythms in CL after stimulus onset.

The converse case is illustrated in Fig. XII-17. The upper records show the electrical activity elicited during correct behavior, which consisted of withholding the lever press throughout the presentation of the 6-cps flicker. Note the clear labeled potentials at the tracer frequency in the visual cortex, fornix, and N. centralis lateralis. The lower set of records illustrates the electrical activity which occurred during an *error of commission.* Labeled responses were diminished. Notice the fast ac-

313

tivity which appeared in the fornix and N. centralis lateralis at the onset of the stimulus. That activity approximately corresponded with the frequency of the positive stimulus. These data may be further clarified by an examination of Fig. XII-18.

The animal, previously differentiated to lever-press for milk in response to a 10-cps flicker but not to a 6-cps flicker, was subsequently taught to perform an avoidance response upon presentation of the 6-cps flicker. The records in Fig. XII-18 illustrate the prototypic response to 10-cps flicker which was displayed by this animal *after* avoidance train-

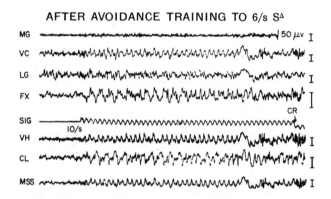

Fig. XII-18. Records obtained during lever press to 10-cps flicker after avoidance training to the 6-cps flicker. Arrow indicates conditioned response.

ing to 6-cps flicker. Upon presentation of the 10-cps tracer signal, the initial response in the fornix and N. centralis lateralis was a slow wave at approximately 6 cps, while the dominant activity of the visual cortex was at the actual stimulus frequency, 10 cps. Careful inspection of the tracings reveals a faster activity; this is readily visible as a modulation on the upper aspect of the slower waves. This faster activity gradually emerges, toward the end of the illustrated example, as a 10-cps rhythm in both the fornix and N. centralis lateralis. Shortly thereafter, a change in wave form appears in the visual cortex, the fornix, and N. centralis lateralis and is soon followed by the performance of the appropriate conditioned response. This sequence of electrical events was sufficiently reproducible to serve as a reasonably good basis for predicting whether or not the cat would perform the appropriate behavioral response upon presentation of the two tracer signals in a randomized series of trials.

These observations suggested that the 6-cps rhythms observed in Fig. XII-18 upon presentation of the 10-cps appetitive stimulus were actually a *representation* of the aversive stimulus. In order to test this interpretation, reserpine was administered to the animal in sufficient dosage to block *performance* of the avoidance response to the 6-cps flicker and leave unimpaired the performance of the lever pressing response for food during 10-cps flicker.

As can be seen from Fig. XII-19A, after medication with reserpine so that performance of the avoidance response to the 6-cps stimulus was abolished, presentation of the 10-cps flicker no longer elicited the dominant slow wave so characteristic of the response of the animal under normal conditions, as seen in the previous figure. These structures now displayed labeled responses corresponding to the 10-cps flicker which was actually present. As the reserpine wore off and *performance* of the avoidance response reappeared to the 6-cps flicker, presentation of 10-cps flicker again caused the reappearance of slow activity in the fornix and N. centralis lateralis. Conversely, if the animal were satiated with food which remained available in a dish inside the apparatus, presentation of the 10-cps appetitive stimulus elicited even stronger 6-cps activity in nonsensory-specific structures, as can be seen in Fig. XII-19B.

The effects of medication and satiation which have just been described seem to provide evidence that representational systems can be *biased* by changes in drive level, indicating that motivational processes must influence representational systems. The state of the animal is an important determinant of the mode of activity released in such systems.

Another illustration of related phenomena is provided in the records contained in Fig. XII-20, which were obtained from a different cat. The *upper* set of data were recorded after the establishment of a lever-pressing behavior to obtain milk. At this stage of training, flicker had no cue value. Note the disappearance of labeled responses from the lateral geniculate lead after the lever-press indicated by the arrow, although the presentation of flickering light continued. Little labeled response at the frequency of the 6-cps tracer stimulus can be seen in other regions.

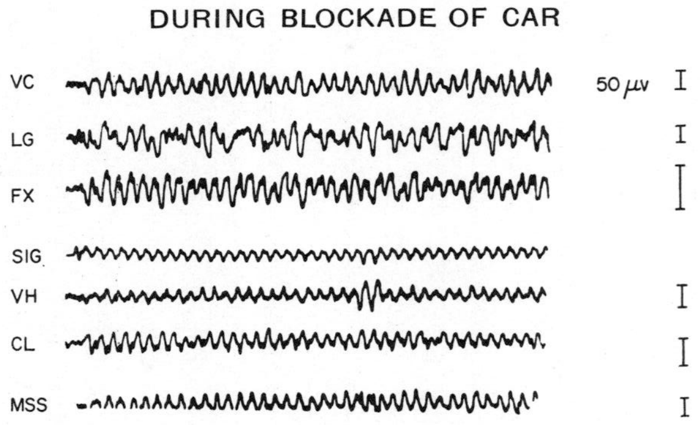

DURING BLOCKADE OF CAR

VC

LG

FX

SIG

VH

CL

MSS

50 μν

Fig. XII-19. A.

Labeled responses to food stimulus (10 cps) during blockade of CAR after administration of reserpine. Note that activity in fornix and centralis lateralis is now accurately at the frequency of the 10-cps tracer stimulus. The slow rhythm at about 6 cps previously seen in those structures was absent while the capability of the 6-cps aversive stimulus to elicit the CAR was blocked. [Data in Figs. XII-16 to XII-19A from John and Killam (1960). Figs. XII-15 and XII-19B from John and Killam, unpublished data.]

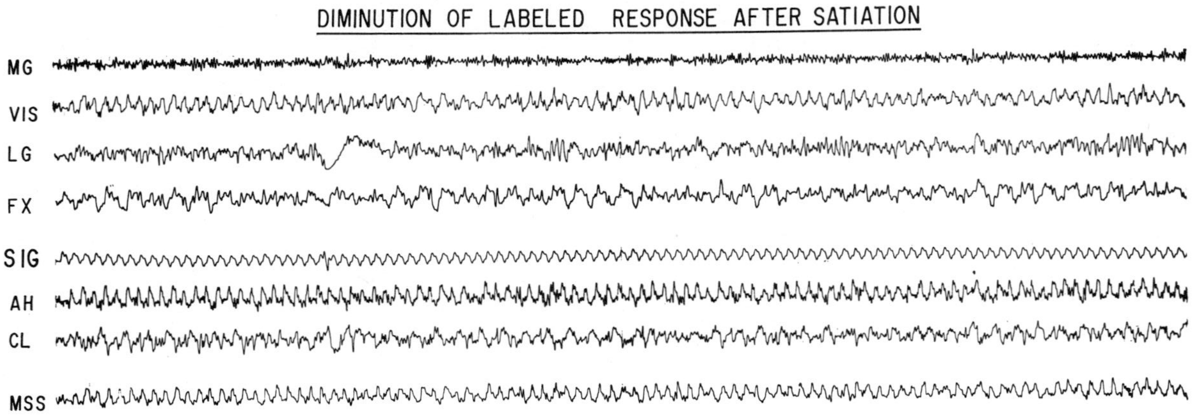

DIMINUTION OF LABELED RESPONSE AFTER SATIATION

Fig. XII-19. B.

Labeled responses to food stimulus (10 cps) following ad lib eating to complete satiation, so that conditioned approach response was not performed. Full food dish remained in the apparatus throughout this recording session. Note that activity in fornix and centralis lateralis is now dominated by a slow rhythm at approximately 6 cps, such as the activity seen during errors of omission (Fig. XII-16) or after avoidance training (Fig. XII-18).

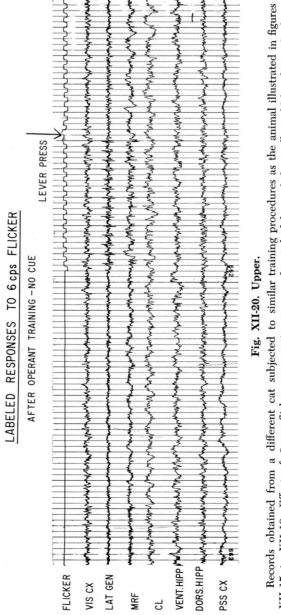

Fig. XII-20. Upper.

Records obtained from a different cat subjected to similar training procedures as the animal illustrated in figures XII-15 to XII-19. Effect of 6-cps flicker presentation to cat after it had learned that milk could be obtained whenever a lever was pressed. Flicker had no signal value at this stage. Notice how little labeled activity was elicited by the flicker except in the lateral geniculate. Note disappearance of response in lateral geniculate due to internal inhibition, as cat presses lever and waits for milk.

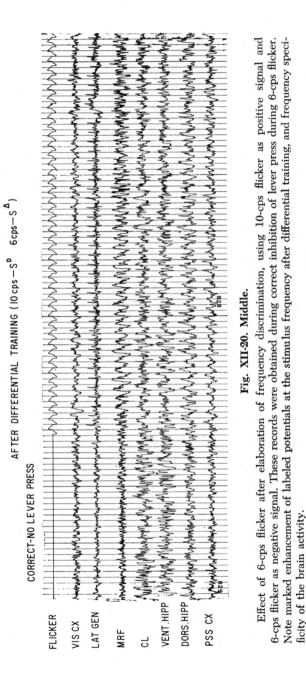

Fig. XII-20. Middle.

Effect of 6-cps flicker after elaboration of frequency discrimination, using 10-cps flicker as positive signal and 6-cps flicker as negative signal. These records were obtained during correct inhibition of lever press during 6-cps flicker. Note marked enhancement of labeled potentials at the stimulus frequency after differential training, and frequency specificity of the brain activity.

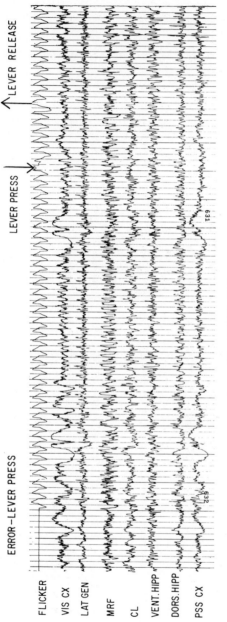

Fig. XII-20. Bottom.

Effect of 6-cps flicker during an *error of commission,* in which the cat pressed the lever during the inhibitory 6-cps signal. At stimulus onset the cat moves restlessly, causing movement artifacts which can be seen in first part of the tracing. As the animal settles down, clear potentials at the 6-cps flicker frequency can be seen in the lateral geniculate. However, in other structures little activity corresponding to the signal frequency can be seen. In the visual cortex, mesencephalic reticular formation, and dorsal hippocampus, marked 10-cps electrical rhythms appear and are followed by performance of the lever pressing behavior which would be appropriate to a 10-cps signal. Note the disappearance of 6-cps activity in the lateral geniculate while the animal holds down the lever and looks in the dish for milk to appear. The 10-cps reticular activity continues during this interval. Finally, the animal releases the lever, 6-cps activity reappears in the lateral geniculate, and then the mesencephalic reticular formation begins to show activity corresponding to the actual stimulus frequency. This rhythm then appears in dorsal hippocampus and in the visual cortex. FLICKER—stimulus artifact, VIS. CX.—visual cortex, LAT. GEN.—lateral geniculate, MRF—mesencephalic reticular formation, CL—nucleus centralis lateralis, VENT. HIPP.—ventral hippocampus, DORS. HIPP.—dorsal hippocampus, PSS. CX.—posterior suprasylvian cortex.

The other data contained in this figure were obtained after differential conditioning, in which 10-cps flicker served as the positive stimulus and 6-cps flicker was negative. The *middle* set of recordings shows the configuration of labeled responses during a correct behavioral response to the 6-cps S$^\Delta$, consisting of inhibition of the lever press. Marked labeled responses at the stimulus frequency now dominate the activity of many of the monitored structures. In contrast, the *bottom* set of tracings were obtained during an *error of commission,* in which the cat pressed the lever while 6-cps flicker was presented. Note the pronounced fast activity which appeared in the visual cortex, reticular formation, and dorsal hippocampus during the period before the first arrow, which indicates the occurrence of the erroneous lever press. The 6-cps labeled response in the lateral geniculate disappeared at the lever press, while the cat stared at the food dish. When no milk appeared in the dish, the cat released the lever, shown by the second arrow. Labeled response at the 6-cps stimulus frequency reappeared in the lateral geniculate. Shortly thereafter, a strong labeled response emerged in the reticular formation and the dorsal hippocampus. However, the labeled response in these structures now corresponded to the actual stimulus frequency.

In these and subsequent studies (John and Shimokochi, 1966), we have repeatedly observed the performance of spontaneous approach or avoidance responses. Examination of records made while animals display such behavior in the absence of any peripheral conditioned stimulus shows that marked electrical waves at about the frequency of the appropriate signal often arise in various structures just before the animal acts. These spontaneous rhythms have been most commonly observed in regions like the dorsal hippocampus, the mesencephalic reticular formation, or the intralaminar nuclei of the thalamus.

K. The coincidence detector hypothesis

Observing configurations of electrical patterns like those which have been illustrated in the preceding section, John and Killam (1960) interpreted them to mean that in the sensory-specific pathways, the effect of the tracer stimulus was to produce stimulus-bound labeled responses at the signal frequency. In almost all instances, labeled responses appearing in the lateral geniculate body corresponded to the actual repetition rate of the physical event. However, in nonsensory-specific brain structures, the presentation of the tracer conditioned stimulus elicited a mode of response which did not appear to be similarly stimulus-bound. Rather, the temporal patterns in these regions seemed to be strongly influenced by the momentary state and the previous experience of the animal, although they were *released* by the afferent influx from the stimulus. These systems seemed to exert a profound influence upon the sensory cortex. Sometimes the cortex displayed activity as if the labeled responses to the actual stimulus were amplitude-modulated by the patterns released in these nonsensory-specific regions, and occasionally cortical response seemed to reflect primarily such patterns, with minimal activity discernible at the real signal frequency.

When these two systems corresponded with respect to their temporal patterns of electrical activity, the ensuing behavior was usually appropriate to the stimulus. When the two systems did not correspond, behavior was generally inappropriate to the actual peripheral stimulus but *would have been appropriate* for that stimulus whose frequency was *closest* to the temporal pattern of discharge released in the nonsensory-specific structures. On the basis of such evidence, we suggested the existence of a comparator system which estimated the degree of correspondence or congruence between the temporal patterns of activity *elicited* by a peripheral stimulus and the temporal pattern *released* from nonsensory-specific systems which were triggered by the action of that stimulus.

According to this Coincidence Detection Hypothesis, the real stimuli impinging on the organism produced an *exogenous* temporal rhythm, which was conducted centrally via the specific sensory pathways appropriate to that modality. Simultaneously, the regions of the brain where assimilated rhythms appeared first, were most marked, and persisted longest, the so-called nonspecific regions of the brain, were activated by the stimulus. However, they developed an *endogenous* mode of activity which seemed to be released by the action of the stimulus, in the context of the past experience and the present state of the animal, and sometimes resulted in electrical rhythms which were inappropriate to the actual physical stimulus. These two pathways were envisaged as projecting to a comparator which evaluated the similarity of temporal patterns between impulses arriving via these various pathways. The hypothesized comparator function might be subserved by the sensory cortex, or by some region to which impulses from the sensory cortex propagate. When the "fit" between the two classes of input to the comparator was adequate, the response of regions including the cortex seemed to undergo a change and the conditioned behavior emerged. The proposed mechanism seemed to accomplish "identification" of an afferent stimulus via reference to a released representation of previously stored information. This was the essential feature of the hypothesis.

L. Effects of differential electrical interference

It has been difficult to devise experiments which provide an appropriate test of the Coincidence Detector Hypothesis. The results of one exploratory attempt are summarized in Fig. XII-21. We reasoned that it

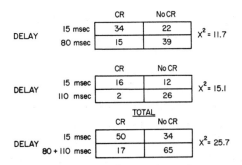

Fig. XII-21. Effects of electrical stimulation of visual cortex at various delays after presentation of 4-cps flash from peripheral tracer conditioned stimulus. (2.8 mA, 100 cps, biphasic, 2 msec pulse width, 25 msec pulse train duration).

might be possible to evaluate this hypothesis by examining the effects of applying bilateral electrical perturbations to the visual cortex at various times following the peripheral presentation of a conditioned stimulus. Perturbations timed so as to coincide with the early component of the evoked potential were considered as interfering primarily with the sensory-specific afferent impulses to the visual cortex, via the lateral geniculate body. Later perturbations would coincide with the arrival of afferent impulses at the visual cortex from the more slowly conducting multisynaptic nonsensory-specific system.

We therefore constructed compound stimuli consisting of a peripheral flicker plus a central electrical stimulation applied bilaterally to the visual cortex. Two different delays separated the peripheral and central components. In one case, the electrical stimulation was delivered 15 msec after the peripheral flash, which we termed *early*. In the other case, the electrical disturbance was delayed until 80–100 msec after the peripheral flash, and this relationship we called *late*. Current parameters of the electrical stimuli were identical in all cases, independent of the delay involved. A counter-balanced stimulus sequence was then constructed as follows: flicker alone, flicker plus *early*, flicker plus *late*, flicker alone, flicker plus *late*, flicker plus *early*, flicker alone. This balanced sequence was then repeatedly applied during experimental sessions. Data obtained during presentation of such compound stimuli were discarded if either or both of the bracketing trials to "flicker alone" were not perfectly performed, within the acceptable response latency. The results show that interference with the early component caused markedly less disruption of behavior than interference with the late component of the evoked response.

These data suggest that information processing about a peripheral event does not take place homogenously through time in the visual cortex. There may be particular time intervals after a peripheral stimulus which are especially crucial for the processing of information about that stimulus. These critical periods of time seem to correspond to the expected time of arrival of influences from the nonsensory-specific system. However, other plausible explanations for these findings can be provided. It is possible that the early electrical disturbance effectively merges with the arrival of peripheral influences, while the late disturbance creates a new signal which does not fuse with the afferent input from the periphery. Alternatively, the late components may be suggested to relate to motivational processes. The described experiment does not permit such explanations to be excluded.*

M. Evidence from central conditioning studies

The experiments by Leiman (1962), mentioned earlier in this chapter, also provided information bearing upon the possible role of the mesen-

* Part of the difficulty in interpretation of these results arises because differential responses were not utilized. The ambiguity might be resolved by establishing two different responses to 5-cps and 10-cps tracer stimuli. Presentation of *alternating* peripheral and central stimuli at 5 cps, spaced 100 msec apart, would help clarify this question. If no response ensued, the central stimulus would seem capable of "blanking" the effects of the peripheral input. If response occurred appropriate to 10-cps input, this would indicate that the two signals did not fuse.

cephalic reticular formation and other nonsensory structures in the processing of information. The reader may recall that in those studies animals were initially trained to perform an avoidance response (CAR) to a flicker cue. That behavioral response was subsequently transferred, first to direct electrical stimulation of the lateral geniculate body *on one side* (central transfer I), and then to direct stimulation of the mesencephalic reticular formation (central transfer II).

Each animal was chronically implanted with 34 electrodes inserted into a wide variety of brain regions. After completion of initial flicker training, all implanted regions were electrically stimulated at the flicker frequency. Structures were tested one at a time, in trials interspersed between flicker presentations. The CAR previously established to the flicker CS could not be elicited by direct electrical stimulation of any of the brain regions tested. All such tests were conducted without shock reinforcement, under extinction conditions, although flicker presentations continued to be reinforced.

Central transfer I was then carried out, stimulating the lateral geniculate body with a 10-cps electrical pulse. A substantial number of trials were required to establish transfer I, almost as many as the initial flicker training. There was little evidence of savings. After completion of transfer I, all other implanted regions were electrically stimulated one at a time, using 10-cps pulses. These test trials were interspersed between presentations of central and peripheral conditioned stimuli. Visual cortex stimulation on the side ipsilateral with the trained lateral geniculate body occasionally elicited performance of the CAR. This effect was not produced by stimulation of other brain regions, at this stage of training.

In particular, 10-cps stimulation of the mesencephalic reticular formation failed to elicit CAR performance. However, when reticular stimulation was reinforced, central transfer II occurred rapidly, requiring only a small number of trials to reach criterion levels of performance. After completion of transfer II, all other regions were again stimulated as before. Test trials were interspersed between presentations of the various conditioned stimuli but were never reinforced. In contrast to the negative results previously obtained, 10-cps electrical stimulation of numerous structures now regularly elicited performance of the CAR. Among the regions in which stimulation was now found to be effective were the intralaminar nuclei of the thalamus, the substantia nigra, nucleus ruber, and even the pyramidal tract. However, this capability was not universal;

interestingly enough, one of the structures in which 10-cps stimulation was ineffective was the *untrained* lateral geniculate body.

In Fig. XII-22, learning curves are shown which describe the rate at which these successive conditioned behaviors were established in a typical cat. The left graph shows the rate of acquisition of the conditioned avoidance response to 10-cps flicker. The middle graph shows the speed of transfer I using 10-cps electrical stimulation of the right lateral genicu-

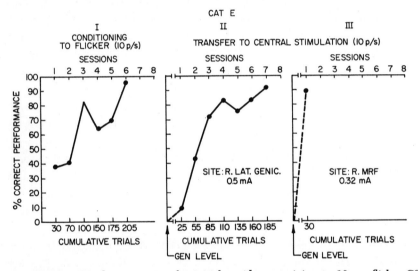

Fig. XII-22. I. Trials to criterion for initial avoidance training to 10-cps flicker CS. After completion of training, 10-cps electrical stimulation delivered to numerous brain structures did not result in performance of conditioned response.

II. Learning curve illustrating transfer of CAR to 10-cps electrical stimulation of right lateral geniculate. After LG transfer, 10-cps electrical stimulation elicited CAR when applied to right visual cortex. No behavioral response could be elicited from other structures. GEN. LEVEL—amount of generalization to LG stimulation before transfer.

III. Learning curve illustrating transfer of CAR to 10-cps stimulation of right mesencephalic reticular formation. After MRF transfer, 10-cps electrical stimulation elicited CAR when applied to many different brain regions (see text for further explanation). [Data from Leiman (1962).]

late body. The third graph shows the progress of transfer II using 10-cps electrical stimulation of the right mesencephalic reticular formation.

Apparently, the mechanism elaborated for the mediation of the conditioned response to geniculate stimulation was relatively discrete since only the ipsilateral visual cortex could achieve effective access to that mechanism. The fact that stimulation of numerous brain regions was effective following reticular training cannot be interpreted as reflecting merely a generally increased response tendency or a "set" for generalization after transfer II since not all regions were effective stimulus sites for such generalization. The fact that substantial reinforcement was required subsequently to transfer control over this behavior to electrical stimulation of the untrained *left* lateral geniculate not only illustrates this point but provides further indication of the discrete nature of the response established earlier to right lateral geniculate input.

The effects described may relate in part to the diffuse connectivity of the reticular formation. Further studies of this sort, involving analysis of evoked potentials and stimulation of other regions in balanced sequences, would be extremely interesting. Yet the relative ease of transfer of conditioned response to reticular formation stimulation, as well as the widespread distribution of sites in which electrical stimulation could elicit performance after completion of reticular formation training, suggest that the nonsensory-specific structures may play an intimate role in the representation of past experience and in the mediation of information processing in the brain.

This suggestion is compatible with some other aspects of the data cited in this chapter: assimilated rhythms arise earliest, are most marked, and persist longest in nonsensory-specific structures. It is in these regions of the brain that the most marked changes in labeled responses are displayed during conditioning. Endogenous activity with similar features seems to be released from such regions under various circumstances. Direct cortical stimulation studies suggest that critical stages in information processing may occur at the time when influences from nonsensory-specific structures reach the cortex. Such observations suggest that these regions may be involved in the processing of information as well as in the more generalized functions which they are believed to mediate.

N. Extensive nature of the general representational system

The data adduced thus far provide evidence that the changes in electrical activity during conditioning occur in widespread regions of the brain, and that many of these changes are related to the processing of information rather than to unspecific consequences of sensitization. Part of the activity observed when a conditioned stimulus is presented to a trained animal consists of stimulus-bound response to the peripheral signal. However, part of the electrical activity seen under such circumstances is released rather than evoked by the signal. The form of the released activity is influenced by the context of the situation and the state of the animal, as well as its previous experience, and the temporal pattern of the released activity can reflect such attributes of previous stimulus configurations as the timing of afferent input.

The released activity presumably arises from the representational systems which have been postulated to be formed during conditioning. In addition to the widespread appearance of released patterns, various data lend support to the idea that extensive anatomical regions may be included in representational systems. Much evidence has been provided that regions in nonspecific structures can become susceptible to the action of particular stimuli during conditioning. Pavlygina (1956) has shown that a hypothalamic dominant focus can be made responsive to sensory stimuli. Segundo *et al.* (1959) have shown that exteroceptive stimuli can elicit conditioned responses corresponding to the effects of localized stimulation of the reticular formation. Olds (1959) reported the appearance of electrical responses to a photic CS for food in hypothalamic regions where self-stimulation rates covaried with food deprivation. Liberson and Ellen (1960; Liberson *et al.*, 1959) showed that stimulation of hippocampal regions can elicit performance of a conditioned response, presumably activating a portion of a representational system. Other workers found that direct electrical stimulation of a number of rhinencephalic, hypothalamic, and mesencephalic regions can elicit well-coordinated performance of approach or avoidance responses previously established to peripheral stimuli (Grastyán *et al.*, 1956; Wyrwicka *et al.*, 1959, 1960; Lissák and Grastyán, 1957; Andersson and Wyrwicka, 1957).

The work of Gavlichek provides electrographic evidence that aspects of the experimental environment can acquire signal significance during conditioning, serving to activate response systems established to conditioned stimuli which have been presented in that environment (1958). Similarly, it has been mentioned previously that animals repeatedly exposed to a specific frequency of flickering light in an experimental room show spontaneous electrocortical activity at that frequency, in the absence of flicker, when brought into the room (Yoshii, Matsumoto, and Hori, 1957a). These findings, together with numerous behavioral examples

328

of "secondary reinforcement," might be interpreted as indicating that stimulation of a region which was part of a general representational system established during conditioning can cause activation of the complete representational system, thereby producing a well-integrated and complex sequence of behavior.

Although the data indicate that representational systems mediating a conditioned response can be established by contiguity, without drive reduction or "reinforcement," regions relevant to motivation can be included in these representational systems. The effects of tranquilizing drugs and satiation described earlier in this chapter indicate the relevance of state to the ability of stimuli to achieve activation of a representational system. The work of Nielson and his collaborators provides evidence which suggests that a neural region related to motivation can be incorporated into a representational system by conditioning (1958). They report that when a region, initially not negatively reinforcing for self-stimulation, is directly stimulated to provide the *conditioned stimulus* for an avoidance response, subsequent evaluation of that region using the self-stimulation procedure shows it to be negatively reinforcing. Thus, the "motivational" aspects of central stimulation of certain regions seem to be susceptible to change with experience.

Grastyán, Lissák, and Kékesi have provided evidence that, in the mesencephalon, approach responses and avoidance responses seem to be differentially mediated by two separate systems roughly lying side by side (1956). A similar distinction may exist for dorsal versus ventral hippocampal regions. It would seem reasonable to expect that during approach conditioning certain hypothalamic areas including the so-called trophotropic areas of Hess would be active to a greater extent than the so-called ergotropic areas. During avoidance conditioning, one might expect approximately the opposite configuration of activity. Thus, there might be differential incorporation of these areas, among others, into the respective representational systems established during these various conditioning procedures or by life experiences associated with approach toward or avoidance of certain stimuli. Activation of these systems might account for an approach or avoidance tendency toward the stimulus which caused such activation. These considerations seem relevant to the interpretation of certain results obtained in so-called "self-stimulation" experiments. Thus, Grastyán *et al.* have described the "push" and "pull" properties belonging to certain types of stimulation (1965). Also, feedback from an instrumental response, simultaneous with afferent input related to presentation of a conditioned stimulus, may involve regions mediating motor responses in such a fashion as to cause their incorporation into representational systems. Perhaps it should be pointed out explicitly that representational systems may exert inhibitory influences, as evidenced by data showing differential habituation, for example. Taken as a whole, these data indicate that stimulation of a portion of a representational system may result in the activation of the entire system and performance of a previously learned response.

The evidence which has been discussed provides a basis of justifying the contention that representational systems are anatomically extensive. Additional evidence comes from the quantitative analysis of electrophysiological patterns observed in various brain regions which were obtained in order to evaluate the extent to which such phenomena seem to arise from a coordinated system. The next chapter will present the results of quantitative studies of this problem.

CHAPTER XIII

ESTABLISHMENT OF COMMON RESPONSE MODES DURING CONDITIONING

The theoretical formulations presented earlier in this volume attribute informational significance to the modes of average activity displayed by neuronal ensembles. Anatomically extensive representational systems have been postulated to exist that can release particular patterns of activity when appropriately stimulated. Comparison of the temporal pattern of discharge produced by afferent input with the patterns of released activity has been proposed as a critical step in the identification of signals and the selection of appropriate response. A body of data has been summarized which, upon qualitative examination, seems to provide support for these propositions. Quantitative methods have been developed to permit more precise evaluation of whether common modes of activity in various sensory-specific and nonsensory-specific brain regions are actually displayed after establishment of conditioned responses. The results of these studies will be summarized since they are of extreme importance for evaluation of the theoretical model.

In some of our early studies of electrophysiological changes during conditioning, we were surprised to note that certain brain regions sometimes acquired striking similarities in electrical activity during and after conditioning even though these relationships were not previously displayed (John and Killam, 1959). Other workers have seen and commented upon similar phenomena. Galambos and Sheatz, for example, in a study of neural responses evoked by auditory stimuli in conditioned animals, drew attention to the emergent similarity between wave shapes in many diverse anatomical regions (1962).

Yoshii, Pruvot, and Gastaut have noted the following during conditioning (1957b):

> In cat Number 2 the tracings from the cortex and those from the subcortical structures recorded during the first few days were clearly different from each other, yet towards the fifth day, there appeared an evident relationship between the electrical activity of the occipital cortex and that of the reticular formation. The relationships of phase, form, and amplitude between the bursts and other electrographic elements of the tracings recorded in these two locations became increasingly more marked until, on certain occasions, they almost reached identity.

Glivenko *et al.* have commented (1962):

> During investigation of the bioelectrical manifestations accompanying the formation of the temporary connection, increasing attention is being paid to the fact that the waves obtained from different points in the brain are similar.

SIMILAR AVERAGE RESPONSE WAVE SHAPES IN
DIFFERENT BRAIN REGIONS OF TRAINED CAT

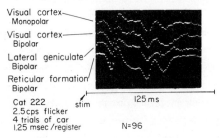

Visual cortex
Monopolar

Visual cortex
Bipolar

Lateral geniculate
Bipolar

Reticular formation
Bipolar

Cat 222
2.5 cps flicker
4 trials of car
1.25 msec /register

stim

125 ms

N=96

Fig. XIII-1. Average response wave shapes recorded from different derivations in a trained cat. Note the marked similarity of the potentials in different brain regions.

An illustration of this phenomenon from our recent studies is provided in Fig. XIII-1. These average responses were computed from different regions during four behavioral trials, in which a trained cat correctly performed conditioned avoidance responses to a 2.5-cps flicker CS. Notice the remarkable similarity of the average response wave shapes recorded from bipolar derivations in the reticular formation, lateral geniculate, and visual cortex, as well as from a monopolar visual cortex derivation versus a frontal reference. The extreme similarity between regions illustrated here appears between some but not all structures of the brain, and has been observed this dramatically only in highly overtrained animals.

As such observations accumulated, it gradually became apparent that quantitative methods must be used to evaluate whether the similarity in electrical activity recorded from various brain regions actually increased during conditioning. This chapter will describe the methods we have developed for these purposes and some of the results of applying them to data from conditioning studies.

A complete exposition of these methods and findings would require an extensive discussion of work published in previous papers and, therefore, only the salient features of this work will be summarized here.

A. Signal analysis methods

1. Brief review of other methods

The analysis of macropotential recordings has elicited considerable interest for several years. Techniques have been sought which offer substantial data reduction and which afford insight into the nature of the potentials.

Filtering schemes of various types have been developed. Some detect activity at and very near to individual frequencies of interest. Other schemes subdivide the potentials into relatively broad bands which then may be analyzed individually. Auto-correlation, cross-correlation, and average response techniques have come into increasing use as computers have become more available. A variety of amplitude histogram and pattern recognition schemes has also been implemented.

For a detailed review of the above-mentioned techniques, it is suggested that the reader consult Kozhevnikov (1958), Burch (1959), Brazier (1961), and Siebert et al. (1959); both detailed discussion and an extensive bibliography of data analysis methods may be found in these references.

2. General considerations

In the techniques under discussion here, EEG signals were recorded from cats with chronically implanted electrodes in response to repeated presentation of a peripheral stimulus under carefully specified conditions. These wave forms were processed on line by an Average Response

Computer (CAT 400) or were tape recorded for subsequent digital analysis on a high speed computer (CDC 1604). The "phase locked" average response wave forms to the stimulus were computed. These average response wave forms constituted the raw data for subsequent analysis.

The theory of average response computation (ARC) has been described in detail by others (Siebert *et al.*, 1959). Use of ARC implies that the EEG signals recorded during repetitive stimulation can be roughly described as repetitive evoked potentials, of the same periodicity as the stimulus, plus incoherent "ongoing" activity. The averaging process suppresses the incoherent signal and the result is a detailed description of the time course of the coherent portions of the potentials evoked by the iterated stimuli.

Average response computation in itself constitutes a considerable degree of data reduction. The responses characteristically evoked from a large number of sites can be studied in detail. This study raises further questions and possibilities. For example, using a multiple channel ARC, one can frequently observe similarities between wave forms recorded from different regions. Further inspection of these simultaneously obtained averages suggests that covariation occurs between certain components of one wave form and aspects of other wave forms.

For example, during correct performance of a CAR to flicker, the average response computations from visual cortex, lateral geniculate, and centralis lateralis might appear as shown in Fig. XIII-2a. During erroneous performance, the average responses might change to the form of Fig. XIII-2b.

These patterns of covariation imply that these changes might be functionally related and might provide impetus for attempts to develop objective descriptions of the relationships between wave shapes. The need for such objective description is increased by the large volume of data to be evaluated since the number of wave shapes in a given sample may be forty or fifty. The apparent resemblance between particular components of average response wave shapes from different structures suggested the possibility of further data reduction by treating a large number of wave shapes as if they represented different combinations of a smaller set of basic components. The covariation observed between corresponding components of different wave shapes suggested that this might reflect the existence of functional physiological relationships between various anatomical regions, which change in a way that might be related to the behavioral observations.

334

The analysis to be described attempted to extend data reduction methods in these directions and to organize the data so as to facilitate the study of the covariation in components of wave shapes. Particular atten-

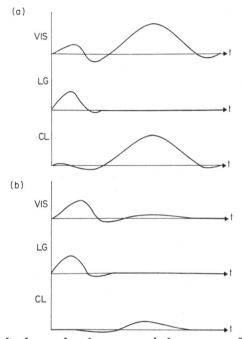

Fig. XIII-2. Idealized examples of average evoked response configurations sometimes seen in behavioral situations. During correct response to a visual conditioned stimulus one might observe potentials such as those illustrated in the upper half of the figure (a): The complex response of the visual cortex to a flash of light contains an early and late portion. The early portion often resembles the wave shape displayed by the lateral geniculate body, while the later portion is similar to the response observed in nucleus centralis lateralis or other thalamic intralaminar nuclei. During failure of behavioral response to the visual signal, shown in (b): The early component of the wave shape in the visual cortex appears unaltered as does the lateral geniculate activity. However, the late portion of the cortical response is often markedly attenuated, and this decrement also appears in nucleus centralis lateralis. Repeated observations of such covariation of certain components of the response of one brain region with activity in some but not other brain regions gradually suggest that this covariation reflects interactions which might be linear.

tion was given to changes occurring with alterations in the experimental conditions or in the behavioral performance of the animal.

It should be noted that the average response wave form confines the data analysis to the characteristic size and shape of the evoked potential. Information concerning the background "ongoing" activity and its relationship to the evoked potential is discarded. It is recognized that at least some of this discarded information may be relevant and it is also being evaluated.

3. Correlation coefficients

Any average response wave shape can be represented as a series of numbers which correspond to the amplitude of the wave shape at successive instants in time. The *correlation coefficient* between two such series, representing two digitized average response wave shapes, can be computed in the conventional fashion. This computation provides a quantitative measure of the similarity between the two wave shapes. The measurement can be made independent of the relative size of the two signals by normalization if this is desirable. If the original responses were of identical form, then the normalized correlation coefficient will be unity. If the two wave shapes have the same form, but one is of opposite polarity to the other, the correlation coefficient will be equal to -1. If the wave shapes have no components in common, then the coefficient will be 0.

Obviously, computation of the matrix of correlation coefficients, which defines the similarity of each average response wave shape recorded from a particular brain region to every other average response wave form simultaneously recorded from electrodes in other brain regions, provides a quantitative measure of the similarity in electrical processes in different parts of a complex neural system. Such a concise description is both extremely informative (because of the precise measures made available) and extremely bewildering (because of the abundance of detail which it provides). A major difficulty in interpretation of a set of correlation coefficients arises from the fact that wave shapes may contain multiple components with different patterns of covariation. The resulting complexity of relationships can be extremely hard to encompass.

4. Factor analysis

This abundance of detail, at first overwhelming, constitutes the basis for application of a method which provides enormous simplification and order to the set of phenomena under consideration. The set of similarities described by a correlation matrix defines a set of constraints on the properties of the original wave shapes. Separable components must exist in those wave shapes which permit these simultaneous constraints to be satisfied. Mathematical methods of signal analysis have been developed to deal with this problem. These methods make explicit the set of components which, combined in a specified way, can satisfy the constraints imposed by a correlation matrix. These methods are generically termed *factor analysis*.

Application of factor analysis methods to a correlation matrix provides two results. First, one obtains *a set of components* capable of linear combination in a specified fashion so as to reconstruct the wave shapes whose covariation was defined by the original correlation matrix. Second, one obtains the *specific coefficients* required to weight every component appropriately in order to reconstruct each of the original wave shapes precisely. Thus, the technique of factor analysis provides a method to decompose a set of wave shapes into a set of constituent components, and specifies the amount of each component contained in a given wave shape. In a sense, this method enables the relatively coarse information provided by a correlation matrix to be replaced by a much more detailed body of information describing the *relative* contribution of a set of specified components to each member of the initial set of measurements. In such a treatment, the initial set of data wave forms defines a *signal space,* each wave shape constitutes a *signal vector* in that space, the correlation coefficient between two wave shapes defines the *cosine of the angle* between the two corresponding signal vectors in the space, and the number of components required to reconstruct the constituent set of signals defines the *dimensionality* of the space. The greater the independence of the data wave forms and the less the coupling between electrical processes, the greater will be the dimensionality of the signal space (Shannon, 1949; Lerner, 1959).

In work described elsewhere in detail, such methods of signal analysis have been applied to sets of average evoked responses by the author and his colleagues (John, Ruchkin, and Villegas, 1963c, 1964). In early work, the method of *principal component analysis* was used (Harmon, 1960), which requires that the set of derived components meet certain mathematical criteria for independence and economy. The components identified by such treatment are physiologically meaningless and exist only as mathematical idealizations. In later work (Ruchkin, Villegas, and John, 1964) using methods of *linear regression* (Cramer, 1954), a set of

337

components has been constructed which corresponds to the activity of identifiable anatomical systems. The latter method has been termed *physiological factorization.*

B. Results of signal analysis

The results of application of the methods of signal analysis just described to electrophysiological data obtained in conditioning studies will be summarized briefly.

Computation of correlation coefficients between wave forms recorded from various brain structures clearly shows that *the similarity between electrical activity in certain brain regions increases as significance is attached to a peripheral stimulus by conditioning techniques.* These results are in agreement with those which have been reported by Livanov (1962). The reproducibility of average evoked wave shapes in many structures increases during conditioning, and can achieve high stability, as illustrated in Table XIII-I. It is interesting that the invariance of

TABLE XIII-I. *Correlation Coefficients between Average Evoked Wave Shapes Elicited in Various Brain Regions on Presentation of a Visual Conditioned Stimulus to a Trained Cat on 4 Days*

Comparison between wave form on sessions	Left visual cortex	Right visual cortex	Left auditory cortex	Right auditory cortex	Left lateral geniculate
1 versus 2	.949	.972	.833	.902	.719
1 versus 3	.948	.970	.791	.882	.727
1 versus 4	.880	.961	.984	.887	.686
2 versus 3	.974	.986	.971	.965	.673
2 versus 4	.919	.958	.824	.851	.625
3 versus 4	.854	.948	.774	.789	.559
Average	.921	.966	.863	.879	.665

cortical response to visual stimuli obtained from this trained animal cannot easily be attributed to constancy of the input from the lateral geniculate, which displays marked variability. This suggests that the visual cortex in this case computed an essentially invariant response in the face of a variable afferent input from the primary thalamic relay nucleus.

Application of principal component analysis revealed that during correct behavioral response, widespread anatomical regions showed close correspondence in the composition of their electrical activity. Regions involved in this highly organized system included the sensory cortex of the stimulus modality, portions of the thalamic and mesencephalic reticular systems, and certain rhinencephalic areas. The dimensionality of the signal space decreased, indicating enhanced coupling between the signals in various brain structures.

An illustration of the results of such analysis for one animal under various conditions is provided in Table XIII-II. In each condition, $H_1(t)$ refers to the first component of the electrical signals, $H_2(t)$ refers to the second component, and so forth. The numbers in each column define the percentage of the energy in each signal wave shape contributed by the corresponding component. Thus, in correct CAR performance to a 10-cps conditioned stimulus, Table XIII-IIA, 70% of the energy in the wave shape evoked by the flicker in the visual cortex was contributed by the first component, 23.3% by the second component, 1.9% by the third component, and 0.1% by the fourth component. The cumulative contribution of these components to the total energy of the signal space is indicated in the last row, as V_M. Note that four components accounted for 88% of the total energy in the system during correct response to the 10-cps signal.

The contribution of the major components to wave shapes in various structures can be observed to change under different conditions. Table XIII-IIB shows the configuration of activity during erroneous response to the 10-cps S^D. Table XIII-IIC shows the configuration of activity evoked by the S^D during CAR blockade following reserpine administration. Table XIII-IID shows the composition of activity evoked by the 4-cps S^Δ during correct CAR inhibition, and Table XIII-IIE shows the change in effects of the S^Δ after reserpine. Although these constellations of activity will not be discussed in detail here, it may be worthwhile to point out that Table XIII-IIA shows a widespread influence of the first component across visual, auditory, and medial suprasylvian cortex, as well as on the mesencephalic and thalamic reticular systems. The relationship of the primary visual relay, the lateral geniculate body, to this grouping is very slight. This suggests mediation of the first component by the nonsensory-specific diffuse projection system, since the influence is not limited to the visual cortex. Notice that this type of organization is not displayed in the various instances of response inhibition.

Physiological factorization suggests that the primary influence on most brain regions during stimulation with a novel input comes from the

TABLE XIII-II. *Coefficients of the Regression Equations which Reconstruct the Average Response Evoked in Various Brain Regions by Visual Stimuli under the Five Indicated Conditions*[a]

	A. SD—10/S—Correct				B. SD—Error				C. SD—Reserpine			
	$H_1(t)$	$H_2(t)$	$H_3(t)$	$H_4(t)$	$H_1(t)$	$H_2(t)$	$H_3(t)$	$H_4(t)$	$H_1(t)$	$H_2(t)$	$H_3(t)$	$H_4(t)$
L VIS	.700	.233	.019	.001	.054	.695	.151	.016	.894	.026	.009	.000
L AUD	.843	.013	.082	.023	.002	.846	.060	.009	.012	.923	.010	.008
L MSS	.908	.017	.000	.008	.450	.109	.138	.132	.091	.893	.001	.000
L LG$_B$	.003	.565	.122	.151	.636	.008	.021	.036	.573	.258	.057	.051
L CL$_B$	.012	.393	.009	.297	—	—	—	—	.391	.026	.566	.000
L CL$_M$	.023	.650	.001	.200	.006	.035	.742	.061	.748	.214	.007	.005
CM$_B$	.736	.214	.001	.005	—	—	—	—	.481	.030	.444	.034
MD$_B$	.022	.449	.484	.003	—	—	—	—	.406	.157	.033	.208
L RF$_B$	.706	.086	.009	.047	.681	.016	.001	.115	.205	.708	.016	.042
L RF$_M$	.127	.692	.051	.000	—	—	—	—	.862	.053	.012	.030
L-R RF	.091	.537	.000	.190	—	—	—	—	.412	.326	.007	.090
L DH$_B$	.002	.119	.708	.014	—	—	—	—	.768	.009	.034	.013
R DH$_B$	—	—	—	—	.805	.030	.001	.010	—	—	—	—
L VH$_B$	.183	.547	.076	.053	.805	.011	.092	.006	.827	.002	.031	.073
V_M =	.38	.70	.80	.88	.39	.60	.77	.86	.53	.81	.89	.94

D. S^A—4/S—Correct

	$H_1(t)$	$H_2(t)$	$H_3(t)$	$H_4(t)$	$H_5(t)$	$H_6(t)$
L VIS	.901	.003	.056	.010		
L AUD	.075	.780	.116	.012		
L MSS	.020	.865	.079	.006		
L LG$_B$	.001	.044	.024	.451	.182	.129
L Cl$_B$	.310	.623	.013	.018		
L CL$_M$	.605	.033	.249	.018		
CM$_B$	.712	.056	.012	.118		
MD$_B$	.002	.000	.003	.076	.671	.241
L RF$_B$	.008	.585	.175	.051		
L RF$_M$	.201	.007	.677	.063		
L-R RF	.620	.004	.129	.112		
L DH$_B$	.125	.001	.046	.313	.101	.213
R DH$_B$	—	—	—	—	—	—
L VH$_B$	.261	.263	.329	.008		
V_M =	.29	.51	.71	.80		

E. S^A—Reserpine

	$H_1(t)$	$H_2(t)$	$H_3(t)$	$H_4(t)$	$H_5(t)$	$H_6(t)$
L VIS	.061	.332	.203	.255		
L AUD	.666	.140	.039	.112		
L MSS	.706	.061	.202	.000		
L LG$_B$	.207	.253	.041	.254	.210	.000
L Cl$_B$	.117	.043	.400	.135	.183	.001
L CL$_M$	.339	.295	.173	.076		
CM$_B$	.198	.009	.633	.011		
MD$_B$	.077	.131	.397	.187		
L RF$_B$	.026	.142	.478	.094		
L RF$_M$	.360	.495	.069	.015		
L-R RF	.581	.372	.002	.002		
L DH$_B$	.557	.020	.014	.292		
R DH$_B$	—	—	—	—	—	—
L VH$_B$	.218	.432	.187	.001		
V_M =	.31	.56	.75	.87		

[a] The $H_i(t)$ represent factor wave shapes. Only the first four factors are included in this table. Weighting coefficients have been squared so that their sum across all factors equals unity. Each coefficient can therefore be considered to reflect the percentage of the energy in the original signal which was contributed by the corresponding factor.

An illustrative example may help the reader interpret data of this sort. During correct behavioral response to the 4/s flicker S^A, the average response wave form evoked in the bipolar derivation from nucleus centre median can be described by the equation:

$$CM_B = .712H_1(t) + .056H_2(t) + .012H_3(t) + .118H_4(t)$$

These four terms account for 89.8% of the energy of the average response. The terms V_M indicate the percentage of the total energy of the signal set which is contributed by summation of the successive factors.

primary sensory relay nucleus, while in the trained and correctly performing animal the dominant influence comes from nuclei of the non-sensory-specific system.

C. Conclusions

Application of correlation techniques and factor analysis to electrophysiological data obtained during studies of the acquisition and performance of conditioned responses provides quantitative confirmation that *specific modes of activity do in fact emerge during conditioning. Common modes of activity are characteristic of an extensive anatomical system during correct performance to a conditioned stimulus. The neural networks sustaining this common mode activity would seem to correspond to our hypothetical representational system.* It is possible that these common patterns of average activity in neuronal ensembles arise from processes within each of the separate anatomical regions comprising the system, or that the coordination of this organized configuration is accomplished by the action of some special regions that are responsible for the complex synchronization, perhaps the diffuse projection system. During incorrect behavioral response to a conditioned stimulus, certain anatomical regions depart from participation in common mode activity.

These findings indicate that the average electrical activity elicited from a neural population by a stimulus cannot be considered to be invariant, but is modified by experience associated with the occurrence of that event. A corresponding change in the time course of discharge in the neural units comprising these ensembles must accompany the observed changes in evoked potential shape. Since populations which initially display different modes of activity come to share common modes, the response of a neural population must be considered to contain, at least potentially, two components: one arises from the physical characteristics of the stimulus, and is appropriately classified as *exogenous,* or evoked, activity. The second is a consequence of prior stimulation of the neural network and is legitimately considered as *endogenous* in origin, but is released by the action of the afferent stimulus. The correspondence between the electrical processes in different anatomical regions, which is necessary for the achievement of a common mode of activity, must be attributed to establishment of equivalence between their exogenous plus endogenous components. These conclusions do not establish the validity of the postulated coincidence detector hypothesis, but must be considered as providing strong support for that formulation. The body of data which has been reviewed thus far shows considerable agreement with important features of the processes envisaged by Hebb and Lashley. Now that we have provided evidence that neural processes with these characteristics can be observed in the brain, it is necessary to examine data which bear upon whether these phenomena may possess functional significance for behavior.

CHAPTER XIV

THE FUNCTIONAL ROLE OF ENDOGENOUS
TEMPORAL PATTERNS

The proposition that the temporal sequence of events at a given place can serve as information for the brain is implicit in the argument which has been constructed up to this point. In evaluating the possible functional significance of the particular temporal patterns of electrical activity which have been evident in records such as those discussed thus far, the question inevitably arises: do these patterns directly reflect the local processing of information about the peripheral stimulus or do they merely indicate that the stimulus affects the structure? While that question is difficult to answer definitively, it is possible to ask whether the temporal patterns of activity at a specified place *can* serve as information for the brain.

A. Differential response to patterned brain stimulation

For this reason, we attempted to establish differential conditioned responses to patterned electrical stimulation of a particular electrode pair in the brain, *using pulse sequences equated for energy but differing in the temporal distribution of energy* (John, Leiman, and Sachs, 1961). We specified an electrical pulse 2 msec in duration, with a current of 1.8 mA. Two patterns were constructed from "bursts" of such pulses. The pulses within each burst were separated by 8 msec. One pattern consisted of 4 bursts per second of 12–13 pulses each—called the 4-cps pattern. The other sequence consisted of 10 bursts per second, of 5 pulses each—called the 10-cps pattern. In both of these sequences, the total number of pulses per second was 50. Whenever electrical current flowed into the stimulating electrodes the current per pulse was identical, regardless of which pattern was being delivered. Thus, these stimuli were equated for total energy, and for current per pulse, and differed only in the temporal distribution of pulses.

We investigated whether an animal could be taught to differentiate between these two electrical patterns, when delivered to the same pair of cortical electrodes. Figure XIV-1 illustrates the progress of such differ-

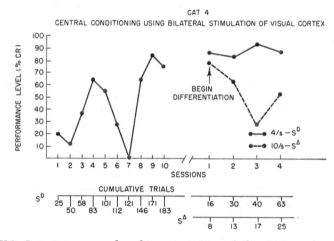

Fig. XIV-1. Learning curves describing acquisition of the CAR to direct cortical stimulation. Left side of graph shows growth of conditioned response to 4-cps stimulation. Right portion of graph shows establishment of differential response to two temporal patterns of electrical input.

entiation. The first portion of the figure shows the rate of establishment of a lever-pressing response to avoid foot shock, upon stimulation of electrodes on the visual cortex with the 4-cps pattern. After achievement of a reasonably high level of performance to the 4-cps pattern, differentiation training began. The animal was punished for *performing* to the 10-cps pattern, and also punished for *failure* to perform to the 4-cps pattern. The remainder of this graph illustrates the development of differentiation in the behavioral responses displayed to these two stimuli. It is quite clear that an animal can readily learn to differentiate between these two temporal patterns of electrical activity that are equated for energy

346

and delivered as identical pulses to the *same* place in the brain. These results have been confirmed by Schuckman and Battersby (1966), and Doty has reported comparable results in the monkey (1965). Differential responses were successfully established to electrical stimulation of a pair of cortical electrodes at two different frequencies. (These animals could also discriminate between identical electrical stimuli delivered to electrodes 1.0 to 3.0 mm apart.) Thus, *temporal patterns of activity at a place may serve as functional information,* enabling discriminated behavior to occur. While the results do not establish the informational significance of the temporal patterns of activity observed in electrographic recordings obtained during performance to peripheral intermittent stimuli, this evidence is compatible with the suggestion that such activity plays a functional role.

TABLE XIV-I. *Generalization of Differentiated Response to Central Stimulation of Other Electrode Placements—Cat 10[a]*

	10 cps		4 cps	
	CR	NR	CR	NR
Right visual + other cortical sites	10	7	0	11
Left visual + other cortical sites	1	18	2	4
Subcortical sites	0	15		

[a] After establishment of conditioned response to electrical stimuli delivered to two cortical electrodes, the effects of stimulating each training electrode in conjunction with every other electrode were tested. Stimulation involving right visual cortex electrode was much more effective than left, but only in conjunction with other cortical sites. Stimulation between subcortical sites and right visual cortex electrode was ineffective.

It is of interest that the mediation of the behavior by the regions underlying the two stimulated electrodes is not identical. Table XIV-I illustrates this with data from another animal. This animal was similarly trained to respond to electrical stimuli delivered to a pair of electrodes. One member of the electrode pair was on the left visual cortex, and the other electrode was on the corresponding point of the right visual cortex. After completion of training, when the *right* visual electrode was stimulated in combination with other cortical sites, differential performance was observed. In contrast, stimulation of the *left* visual electrode in such combinations failed to provide any evidence of performance. This is corroborative of the report of Loucks (1955, 1961), who used three electrodes placed on the cortex at approximately the vertices of an equilateral

347

triangle, A, B, and C. After establishment of conditioned response to bipolar stimulation of A versus B, he then tested to see the effects of stimulating A versus C, and B versus C. He found that A versus C *always* elicited performance of the conditioned response, while stimulation of B versus C *never* elicited such performance. These data show that similar brain regions receiving equivalent excitation may become very differently involved in the mediation of behavioral responses.*

B. Facilitation of transfer by common temporal pattern

Some evidence which indirectly suggests the functional relevance of temporal patterns comes from behavioral studies of the effect of temporal patterning on the transfer of training between stimuli in different sensory modalities (John, Killam, Wenzel, and Mass, 1958c). A group of cats was trained to perform an avoidance response to a steady visual stimulus. These animals displayed moderate savings on transfer of training in subsequent conditioning to a steady tone. A second group of cats was trained in the reverse order, and showed essentially no savings upon transfer to a second stimulus.

Other cats, conditioned using either a pulsed sound or pulsed light as the first conditioned stimulus, showed essentially *complete* transfer of training in one to ten trials in subsequent conditioning with light or sound *pulsed at the same frequency as the first conditioned stimulus*. In one of these animals, conditioned first to 10-cps flicker and second to 10-cps click, it was observed that following the transfer of training, which required four trials, the auditory stimulus elicited potentials in visual structures resembling those which were evoked by the visual conditioned

---

* It may be worthwhile to point out that these data show that a pair of electrodes in a given brain area constitutes an information input channel. Information consists not only of the presence or absence of activity in the stimulated region, but the spatiotemporal pattern of that activity. The potential information handling capacity of such a channel depends upon the minimum change in stimulus parameters, such as temporal pattern and intensity, which can be successfully discriminated at the same input point, as well as the minimum distance between two points which is required to discriminate between identical electrical events in the two places. Evaluation of the informational capacity of such input channels should be performed, with potential applications to such problems as the design of sensory prosthetic devices, to assess the possibility that implanted electrode arrays might enable appreciable information to be delivered to the brain.

stimulus. All groups required about the same number of trials for the initial training. These findings must be considered as merely suggestive, since the data are based upon three or four animals in each group. Unfortunately, a systematic study of transfer under these different conditions has not been carried out. However, in recent conditioning work related to our electrophysiological studies, we have been struck by the speed of transfer between stimuli of the same repetition rate but different sensory modalities. This rapid transfer was observed both in approach and avoidance responses in a different behavioral situation than the previous observations.

These data suggest that, in contrast to the situation when steady stimuli were used, the second *pulsatile* stimulus may have ready access to the general representational system presumably established during prior conditioning with another stimulus pulsed at the same frequency, even though the two stimuli are of different sensory modalities. The fact that marked transfer occurred from flicker training to subsequent click training, and vice versa, indicated the probable independence of this phenomenon from processes unique to a particular sensory modality, and suggested mediation of nonspecific structures in the representation of the temporal pattern of stimulation common to the two stimuli.

C. Generalization

Perhaps the most direct evidence that the release of endogenous temporal patterns is of functional significance comes from studies of generalization, in which an animal performs a previously acquired conditioned response upon the presentation of a new stimulus which resembles the conditioned stimulus used during training.

In Fig. XIV-2, recordings are presented that were obtained when a cat, which had previously been trained to perform an avoidance response to a 4-cps flicker, was presented with a 10-cps flicker for the first time. At the first arrow in the figure, the 10-cps flicker was presented. It can be seen that labeled responses at the tracer frequency appear in the lateral geniculate body, the primary thalamic relay nucleus for vision, and in the visual cortex. At the next arrow, the cortical activity can be seen to change to a much slower rhythm, approximately 4 cps. Shortly after the onset of this rhythm, the animal (which was previously sitting in the apparatus) displayed a marked behavioral startle response and stood up.

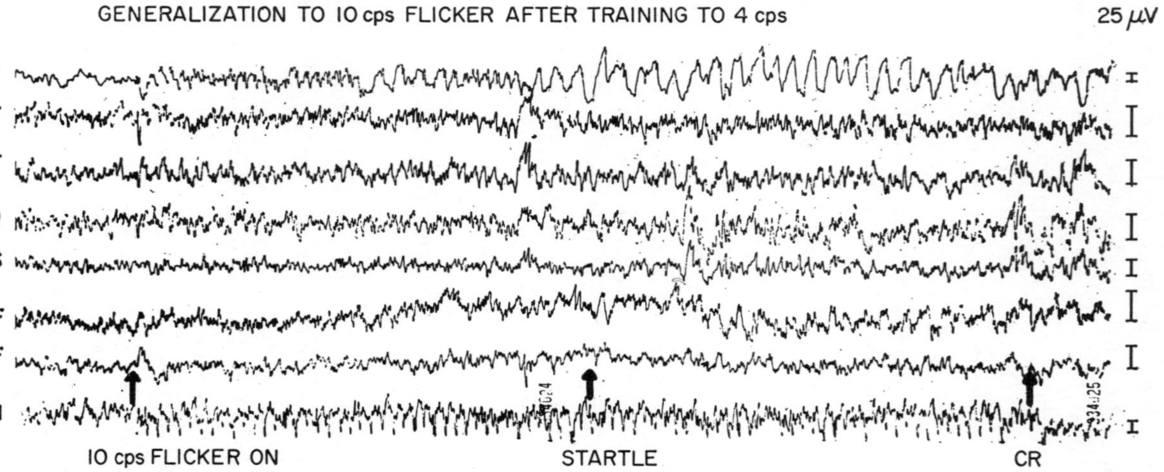

Fig. XIV-2. This recording was obtained during generalization. It illustrates the effects of presentation of a 10-cps flicker to a cat after completion of avoidance training in which a 4-cps flicker was used as the conditioned stimulus. Upon presentation of the novel 10-cps signal, the lateral geniculate and visual cortex display clear frequency-specific responses at the stimulus frequency. After several seconds, a slow wave at about 4 cps appears in the visual cortex and the animal displays a startle response at the second arrow. The animal then walked slowly across the cage and performed the conditioned avoidance response, pressing the lever at the third arrow. Throughout this interval, the visual cortex and reticular formation were dominated by slow activity at about the frequency of the 4-cps aversive stimulus, while the lateral geniculate continued to display a 10-cps discharge corresponding to the actual stimulus frequency. (VIS CX—visual cortex, CENT LAT—nucleus centralis lateralis, CENT MED—nucleus centre median, MED DORS—nucleus medialis dorsalis, RF—mesencephalic reticular formation, LAT GEN—lateral geniculate, L—left side, R—right side. No stimulus artifact is shown on this record.)

During the ensuing period, it walked slowly across the cage to the far wall in which a lever was located. The cat then pressed the lever, performing the previously acquired avoidance response at the last arrow. Notice that throughout this period the visual cortex displays a dominant slow activity, while the lateral geniculate continues to respond to the actual flicker frequency. Repeated observations of this phenomenon suggested that the occurrence of a novel event which resembled a familiar stimulus could activate a neural system previously established in a trained animal by repeated presentations of the conditioned stimulus. When activated by the novel event, that neural circuit discharged with the temporal pattern characteristic of its response to the conditioned stimulus. This discharge was often accompanied by performance of the conditioned response. It may well be that the presence of the environmental context in which the conditioned stimulus has so often been experienced serves a "priming" function and biases the representational system so as to facilitate the release of the corresponding mode of activity by stimuli with general features similar to the CS.

These observations correspond closely to the findings of Majkowski (1958). A defensive reflex is established by pairing a rhythmic CS with foot shock at the same frequency. After the defensive flexion response has been established, a novel stimulus is presented in the same sensory modality but at a different repetition rate than the CS. Generalization usually occurs, and the previously established conditioned response is performed to the new stimulus. In such circumstances, some sensory structures may show labeled responses at the frequency of the novel stimulus, while other regions show marked rhythmic activity at the frequency of the CS used during training. Figure XIV-3 shows a particularly interesting body of data of this sort, obtained during generalization from a split-brain cat when a novel stimulus was presented first to the initially trained side and later to the second side following transfer of training (Majkowski, 1966).

These findings seem related to the report by Podsossenaia (1958). The foot of a rabbit was stimulated with electric shocks occurring 12 times per second. Following systematic variation in shock intensity, it was observed that subsequently a defensive reflex of the limb occurred on the presentation of previously indifferent sensory stimuli. These continuous stimuli elicited rhythmic foot movements occurring 12 times per second.

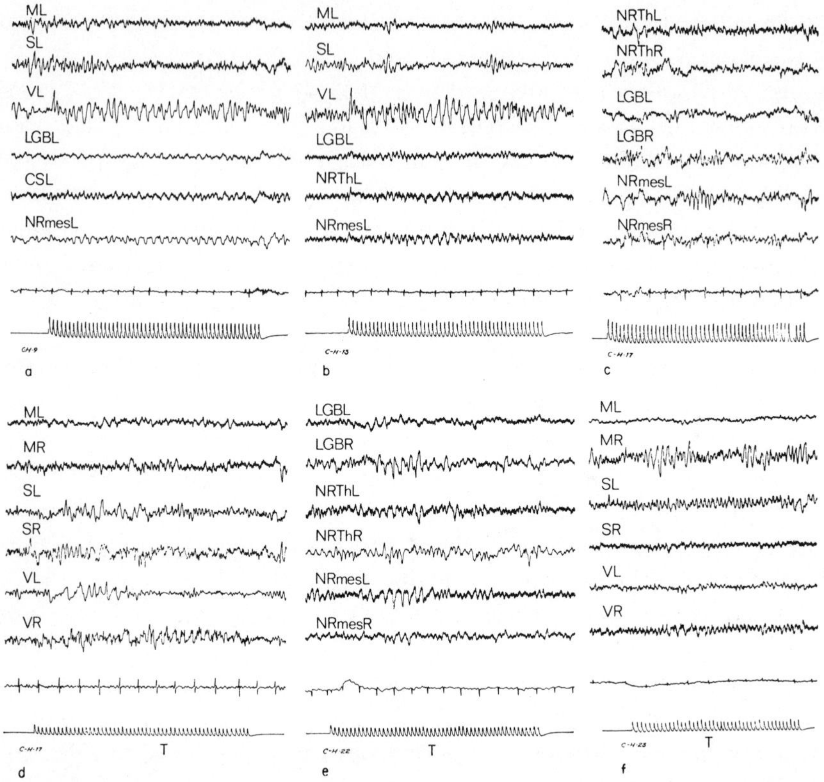

Fig. XIV-3. Electrophysiological correlates of generalization and differentiation, observed in a "split-brain" cat. Portions a, b, and c were recorded after the *left eye and hemisphere* had been trained to perform a conditioned defensive reflex to a 5-cps flicker CS. *After left side training:* (a) Recordings obtained during *generalization* of conditioned response upon initial presentation of novel 12-cps flicker, following establishment of CR to the 5-cps CS. Note marked labeled responses at 5 cps released in visual cortex (VL), superior colliculus (CSL), and mesencephalic reticular formation (NR mes L) on the left side. Seventh channel shows EKG and EMG and indicates that flexion CR was performed at the end of trial. (b) As differential training was carried out, performance of the CR to the unreinforced 12-cps signal gradually dropped out. These recordings were obtained during an early nonperformance trial. Note that the 12-cps signal still elicited marked 5 cps, clearly visible in the visual cortex, mesencephalic reticular formation, and nucleus reticularis of the thalamus (NR Th L). (c) Records obtained after completion of differentiation. Note that the 12-cps signal now elicits labeled responses corresponding to the stimulus frequency, particularly marked on the left side.

After transfer of training to right side: (d) Recordings obtained during generalization to novel 12-cps flicker presented to right eye and hemisphere after completion of transfer (T) of the CR to the 5-cps flicker CS to the right side. Note the 5-cps labeled responses which appear in some right side structures (R). (e) As differentia-

352

These experiments all indicate that an exteroceptive stimulus seems to trigger release of the characteristic pattern of activity in a representational system, accompanied by performance of a conditioned response. This release can also take place without presentation of a peripheral stimulus and has been observed by a number of workers preceding noncued performance of conditioned responses. Yoshii, Matsumoto, and Hori (1957a; Yoshii, 1962) have described the spontaneous appearance of rhythmic waves at the CS frequency accompanied by performance of conditioned avoidance responses in the absence of the CS.

Like other evidence presented earlier, these findings suggested that part of the electrical activity recorded from the brain of a previously trained animal might be endogenously generated as a consequence of past experience, while some electrical responses were the consequence of the immediate exogenous stimulation. In an attempt to differentiate between these two kinds of activity, we devised the so-called "*limp*" technique, in which an animal previously trained with a continuous flickering light was tested with a flickering light *from which flashes were periodically deleted*. Evoked responses which appeared during this period of flash deletion could be interpreted as responses to light which "should have occurred," on the basis of the prior experience. Responses of this sort, occurring in the absence of stimuli, are reasonably attributed to endogenous origin. Interesting data were gathered by Weiss, who conducted a study using this technique (1962).

The next figure shows the electrical activity recorded from a cat originally trained to perform a CAR to a 4-cps flicker. This recording was obtained during presentation of a 10-cps flicker from which each *tenth* flash was deleted, as can be seen from the stimulus artifact. This cat generalized reliably in response to the 10-cps flicker, pressing the lever in the wall each time this frequency was presented. The records in the

---

tion proceeds, generalization is still occasionally displayed. These records were taken from a trial in which behavioral response was displayed. Note that the marked 5-cps labeled activity in some structures, visible on the right as well as on the left side. (f) After completion of differentiation. Notice the clear 12-cps responses now elicited by the 12-cps signal.

All derivations are bipolar: L denotes left side, R denotes right side. M—motor cortex, S—sensorimotor cortex, V—visual cortex, LGB—lateral geniculate body, CS— superior colliculus, NR mes—mesencephalic reticular formation, NR Th—nucleus reticularis of thalamus, seventh channel of all sets indicates EKG and forepaw EMG, eighth channel indicates flicker artifact. [Data from Majkowski (1966).]

top section of Fig. XIV-4 were taken during such generalization. Notice that the lateral geniculate body responds reliably to each flash of light, while both visual cortices and the reticular formation show a clear slow rhythm, which seems to be about 4 cps, clearly *not* at the frequency of the physically present 10-cps flicker.

First of all, it is interesting to examine these records from the viewpoint of the utility of the limp technique. Inspection of these records shows that deflections which resemble evoked responses occur on several occasions in various structures at a time when the flash was deleted, suggesting possible endogenous origin. Haider, Spong, and Lindsley (1964) and Barlow *et al.* (1965) have reported similar findings.* After repeated presentations of stimulus trains with a characteristic temporal pattern, these workers observed that an "evoked" potential appeared at the *expected* time when stimuli were deleted from the pattern. The data in the upper part of Fig. XIV-4 warrant more careful scrutiny. Note that the response of the visual cortex seems to be a composite of two processes which act with opposite sign. There is a marked slow component at about 4 cps which can be seen most clearly as a *downward* deflection, and a faster component at 10 cps which manifests itself as an *upward* deflection. Although the over-all wave shape seems to resemble an interference pattern between these two processes, separate examination of the upper and lower portions of the tracings from visual derivations clearly reveals this dichotomy. These are monopolar cortical derivations that are negative upward. It appears that the surface *negative* processes may primarily reflect exogenous stimulation while the surface *positive* processes may be more responsive to endogenous patterns. The slow wave in the reticular formation suggests that it may be the origin of these endogenous influences. These observations possibly indicate a different anatomical origin for the two rhythms and provide support for the suggestion that the outflow of specific sensory pathways and nonspecific representational systems may converge upon the cortex, as proposed in the comparator hypothesis. The fact that generalization occurred in spite of the obvious discrepancy between the two temporal patterns suggests that undifferentiated behaviors do not require very precise congruence between the two incident patterns of activity.

The lower section of Fig. XIV-4 shows the response of this same animal after differential conditioning has been completed. Performance

---

* See also Rusinov (1959) and Sutton *et al.* (1967) discussed in Chapter XV.

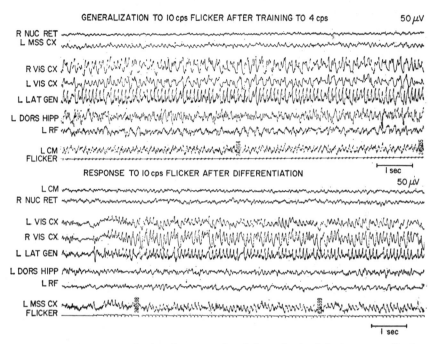

GENERALIZATION TO 10 cps FLICKER AFTER TRAINING TO 4 cps   50 μV

R NUC RET
L MSS CX

R VIS CX
L VIS CX
L LAT GEN

L DORS HIPP
L RF

L CM
FLICKER

RESPONSE TO 10 cps FLICKER AFTER DIFFERENTIATION   I sec
                                                           50 μV
L CM
R NUC RET

L VIS CX
R VIS CX
L LAT GEN

L DORS HIPP
L RF

L MSS CX
FLICKER

                                                          I sec

Fig. XIV-4. *Upper records:* Another example of data obtained during generalization
from a different cat. These records show the electrical activity elicited by a 10-cps
novel stimulus presented to a cat after completion of avoidance training in which a
4-cps flicker was the conditioned stimulus. Note the clear labeled potentials at the
actual 10-cps stimulus frequency in the lateral geniculate, while the visual cortex on
both sides and the reticular formation show marked slow activity at about the frequency of the 4-cps stimulus used in previous training.

Bottom records: Records obtained from the same animal after completion of frequency discrimination training in which the animal was punished if it pressed the
lever during 10-cps flicker. Note that the activity in the visual leads and the reticular
formation no longer contains the previous slow rhythms, but corresponds well to the
actual stimulus frequency. (NUC RET—nucleus reticularis, MSS CX—medial suprasylvian cortex, VIS CX—visual cortex, LAT GEN—lateral geniculate, DORS HIPP—
dorsal hippocampus, RF—mesencephalic reticular formation, CM—nucleus centre
median, FLICKER—stimulus artifact.)

of the avoidance response to the 10-cps flicker is now punished with
electrical shock, while performance of the avoidance response to the 4-cps
flicker avoids that shock. Notice that this animal, which now accurately
differentiates between the two flicker frequencies, shows a predominantly
10-cps electrical response to 10-cps flicker in both visual cortical derivations and the reticular formation where previously slow rhythms were
dominant. More quantitative confirmation of these observations can be

355

obtained from the average response computations which were obtained simultaneously with the EEG recordings during these experimental sessions.

D. Average response wave shapes in generalization

The average response computer was triggered by the pulse which deleted each tenth flash of light, in an attempt to see whether endogenously generated activity reliably appeared at the time that the flash was deleted. In order to contrast that activity with evoked potentials elicited

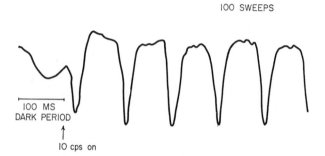

100 SWEEPS

100 MS
DARK PERIOD

10 cps on

Fig. XIV-5. Average evoked response computed from lateral geniculate body of cat illustrated in previous figure, during repeated performance of generalization on presentation of novel 10-cps flicker after training to 4-cps. Computer was triggered at onset of 100-msec dark period following every tenth flash. Analysis epoch was 625 msec. Computation is the average of 100 stimulus sequences. These data show regular evoked potentials at 100-msec intervals and accurately reflect the stimulus frequency.

by actually presented stimuli, the averaging epoch of the computer was extended to 625 msec. In these averages, then, the first 100 msec represents the activity of the structure in the dark period during the deleted flash, and the rest of the interval represents the averaged response to the subsequent flashes of light. All averages which are presented are based on 100 superpositions of response sequences; we have found averages from samples of this size to be reproducible. The samples were obtained from numerous behavioral trials.

Figure XIV-5 illustrates the response of the lateral geniculate body of the cat, whose EEG was presented in Fig. XIV-4, during generalization of conditioned response to a 10-cps flicker. Notice that the wave shape recorded from the lateral geniculate body is a rhythmic potential with a periodicity of 100 msec, a 10-cps response.

356

Figure XIV-6 contains three wave shapes recorded at various times. The *first* is the average response of the visual cortex to the 4-cps flash of light which was used as the tracer conditioned stimulus, after completion of avoidance training. The *second* illustrates the average response of the visual cortex during repeated generalization of the conditioned response to a 10-cps flicker. Notice that this wave shape does not display a periodicity at 100 msec, although a sharp spike can be discerned at such intervals. This wave shape resembles a complex interference pattern between the 10-cps stimulus and a slower process at about 4 cps. The *third* wave shape represents the average response of the visual cortex to the 10-cps flicker after differentiation, when performance of the avoidance response during presentation of the 10-cps flicker had been inhibited. Notice that now the response of the visual cortex to the 10-cps flicker displays a clear periodicity every 100 msec.

The first wave shape in this figure, then, illustrates the response of the visual cortex to the stimulus which was actually used during conditioning. The second wave shape illustrates the response of the cortex to a new stimulus being treated like the old stimulus. The third wave shape represents the response of the cortex to that new stimulus after training, when it had been informationally differentiated from the old stimulus. When a new stimulus is treated as if it had been previously experienced, does the response of the brain include a component which resembles the response to the previously experienced stimulus? The apparent interference pattern which is discernible in the second wave shape is presented as tentative evidence for interaction between neural responses to the physically present 10-cps flash and the released *memory* of the familiar 4-cps conditioned stimulus.

Figure XIV-7 indicates that quite the same phenomena can be observed in the mesencephalic reticular formation during generalization of the conditioned response. The first wave shape shows the effect of the 4-cps conditioned stimulus when training has been completed. The second wave shape shows the average response to the novel 10-cps flicker during generalization. This complex response is not periodic at 100 msec, but again resembles an interference pattern. The third wave shape shows the response to the 10-cps flicker after completion of discrimination training. The wave shape is now periodic at the actual stimulus frequency. Several other brain regions which were monitored in this animal did not respond in this fashion but, in the same manner as the lateral geniculate

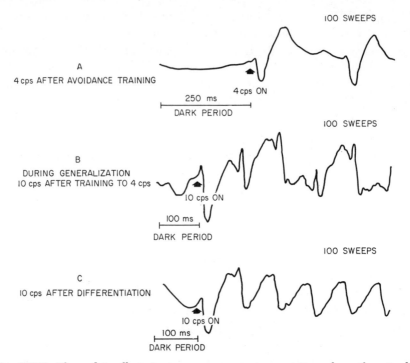

100 SWEEPS

A
4 cps AFTER AVOIDANCE TRAINING

4 cps ON

250 ms

DARK PERIOD

100 SWEEPS

B
DURING GENERALIZATION
10 cps AFTER TRAINING TO 4 cps

10 cps ON

100 ms

DARK PERIOD

100 SWEEPS

C
10 cps AFTER DIFFERENTIATION

10 cps ON

100 ms

DARK PERIOD

Fig. XIV-6. These data illustrate average response computations from the visual cortex of the animal discussed in Figs. XIV-4 and XIV-5 under various conditions. Again, each average was based on 100 repetitions, the analysis epoch was 625 msec, and the computer was triggered at the onset of a dark interval preceding stimulus delivery.

A. Average response of the visual cortex to the 4-cps flicker actually used as the conditioned stimulus during avoidance training.

B. Average response of the visual cortex to the novel 10-cps flicker during repeated performance of generalization. Note that the evoked response wave shape is not periodic at 100 msec, although a 10-cps spike is visible on the upper contour of the wave shape, as if modulating a slower rhythm.

C. Average response of the visual cortex to the 10-cps flicker after completion of differential frequency training. Note that the evoked response wave shape is now regular and periodic at the actual stimulus frequency.

body, reflected the frequency of the peripheral stimulus quite accurately. Whether or not other brain regions may be involved, there seems to be an interaction between the visual cortex and the reticular formation when a behavior occurs which requires readout from memory. Average responses computed during generalization suggest the appearance of a released potential during the initial "limp" interval, particularly noticeable in the cortical response shown in line B of Fig. XIV-6.

The data provide support for the contention that during generalization to a new stimulus, the electrical activity which appears in the visual cortex and the reticular formation contains two components. One component is apparently derived from the physical stimulus presented to the eye. The other resembles the effect of the stimulus actually used during conditioning. This component must arise as a consequence of the activation of a representational system, and there is a release of a mode of oscillation similar to that previously established by the conditioned stimulus.

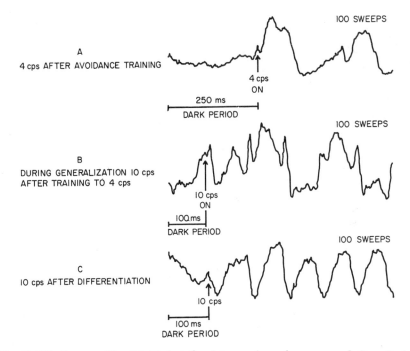

Fig. XIV-7. Same as Fig. XIV-6, but the data are from the mesencephalic reticular formation.

It seems logically justifiable to invoke "readout" from memory in order to account for generalization. It is difficult to explain the performance of so unnatural a response as pressing a lever mounted in the wall whenever a novel 10-cps flicker appears, without assuming mediation by response processes and systems which were established during the prior training experiences. The novel stimulus must suffice to trigger the release of activity in a population of cells, which resembles (in some critical ways) the past action of the conditioned stimulus itself. The most intriguing

359

feature of these data is the suggestion that the retrieval of stored information may actually be symmetrical with the "readin" so that the resulting electrical activity literally reconstructs the process which accompanied registration of the experience. Whatever the nature of the chemical mechanisms mediating the long-term storage of information in the brain, these mechanisms may possess the capacity to reconstruct complex patterns of electrical activity in populations consisting of very large numbers of neurons. It appears unlikely that such extensive macropotential phenomena could be observed if memories were stored in a specific set of cells, whose discharge represented particular past experiences. It seems highly improbable that such discharge could be detected by the methods used in these experiments. If it could be conclusively established that retrieval reconstructed the salient features of the average electrical activity in neural ensembles caused by the original influence of the stored information, this would constitute rather compelling evidence that remembering was not accomplished by the deterministic discharge of specific cells. Rather, it would seem related to the achievement of a particular mode of oscillation, common to certain anatomical regions. This requires the postulation of mediation processes which involve large populations of cells in which the time sequence of states has been specified by the storage mechanism.

E. Further analysis of generalization wave shapes

Additional data on electrophysiological events during generalization were obtained from the animals which were initially trained by Leiman in the research described in Chapter XII. At the end of his studies, all animals were subjected to experimental extinction of the full set of behavioral responses which had been established. Subsequently, we retrained these animals step by step, tape recording all electrophysiological responses to the conditioned and test stimuli at each stage of the procedure.*

Particular attention will be paid to data obtained from those animals during generalization tests to a 7.7-cps neutral flicker, following reestablishment of the conditioned avoidance response to the 10-cps flicker which had originally been utilized as the tracer conditioned stimulus.

* These data were intensively analyzed by Hansook Ahn in our laboratories.

These data were obtained from four animals. Although the results illustrated here came primarily from one of these cats, the other three cats displayed basically similar phenomena. The processes to be discussed may be somewhat peculiar to particular animals and details may vary from individual to individual.

The data of special interest were obtained from a total of 30 generalization trials using a 7.7-cps flicker interspersed throughout a long session in which the majority of the stimuli presented were the 10-cps flicker used during training. Although 10-cps flicker was usually reinforced during this session, all 7.7-cps flicker presentations were unreinforced by shock. If the animal failed to perform within 30 seconds after onset of the 7.7-cps test flicker, the stimulus was terminated. However, performance of the conditioned avoidance response to the neutral stimulus *also resulted in flicker termination.* One might argue that this constituted appreciable reinforcement, but the test trials were spaced at sufficiently long intervals so that we consider the behavioral response to be based primarily upon the tendency to generalize.

The 30 trials selected for intensive analysis all occurred while the same set of recording derivations was being used. In this set of trials, the animal was very cooperative, in that the generalization responses were performed with latencies ranging from 2 to 5 seconds evenly distributed into four groups. A group of control trials with comparable latencies was selected in which the actual 10-cps flicker CS was used. These data were selected for particularly detailed analysis because they provided stepwise increments in performance latencies occurring in random sequence.

Figure XIV-8 illustrates sets of average response wave forms computed from the activity evoked in the lateral geniculate body by the neutral 7.7-cps stimulus, during the 30 generalization trials just described. These data were analyzed separately for five groups containing 6 trials each: CR_1 refers to those trials in which generalization occurred after 2 seconds of photic stimulation; CR_2 refers to trials with a 3-second latency; CR_3 refers to a 4-second latency; CR_4 refers to a 5-second latency; and NR refers to trials in which generalization failed to occur within 30 seconds. Data from each of these groups are in a separate *row* of Fig. XIV-8. Six average response wave shapes were then computed for each of these groups at successive times, and are arranged in six *columns* in the figure.

The first column represents averages of the initial evoked potentials in each of the six trials of each group. The sample size is therefore six.

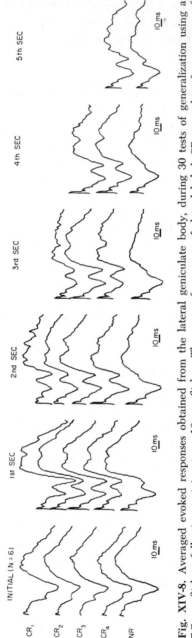

Fig. XIV-8. Averaged evoked responses obtained from the lateral geniculate body, during 30 tests of generalization using a 7.7-cps flicker, following training to a 10-cps flicker. The upper four rows of data labeled CR are taken from groups of trials resulting in generalization (see text). The bottom row, labeled NR, comes from a group of trials in which no performance occurred. The first column of wave shapes represents the average of the initial evoked response in each of six trials. The other columns represent second-by-second averages, each based upon 48 evoked potentials. The total analysis epoch is 125 msec. [From Ruchkin and John (1966a).]

The successive columns respectively represent averages of the evoked potentials during the first, second, third, fourth, and fifth seconds of stimulation. Each of these averages is based on 48 evoked potentials.

Unless Lashley's "response-set" explanation for generalization is to be accepted, one would expect that the initial effect of the stimulus should be the same in all trials whether or not the conditioned behavior is subsequently performed. Note that all wave shapes in the first column are essentially identical. However, by the end of the first second, *a marked second component is discernible in each of the averages obtained from trials resulting in generalization.* That second component seems to be characteristic of all the subsequent averages from CR_1, CR_2, CR_3, and CR_4, with no striking differences corresponding to latencies of performance. The absence of correlation between the time at which the second component appears and the latency of the behavioral response shows that the change in wave form is not a consequence of movement related to the performance. The average of the first second of NR trials shows a small second component which diminishes and disappears in subsequent averages of this group. Note the high consistency of double-peaked wave shapes in the averages computed from trials resulting in generalization and the single-peaked shape obtained in trials in which generalization failed to occur.

In Fig. XIV-9, average evoked responses are presented that were computed from the lateral geniculate body and nucleus reticularis of the thalamus under a number of different conditions. Each of these averages is based upon 42 samples. The upper wave shape in each column illustrates the evoked potential produced in these structures by presentation of the 10-cps conditioned stimulus during a number of trials resulting in correct performance of the conditioned response. The middle wave shape illustrates the evoked response elicited by the 7.7-cps test stimulus during a group of trials resulting in generalization. The lower wave shape shows the average responses evoked by the same test stimulus during trials in which no behavioral performance occurred. The samples used in these computations were carefully equated with respect to the time after stimulus onset at which they were computed.

These averages show that the evoked response in these structures contains three positive components (I, II, III) which are clearly seen in the top and middle wave shapes. Components II and III are absent when generalization fails to occur. The variance of amplitudes in the sample

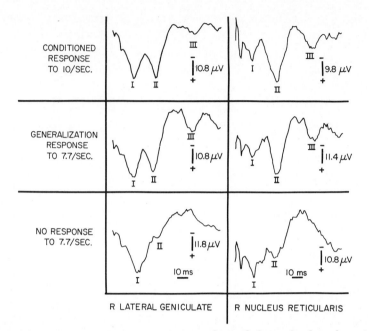

Fig. XIV-9. Average response computations obtained from the lateral geniculate nucleus and nucleus reticularis of the cat under various conditions during the same experimental session. All averages in this illustration are based upon 42 stimulus repetitions from a number of behavioral trials. Analysis epoch was 62.5 msec.

Upper records: Average responses evoked in structures by the 10-cps conditioned stimulus (flicker) actually used in training, during repeated correct behavioral performances.

Middle records: Average responses evoked by a novel 7.7-cps flicker, during repeated generalization behavior. Test trials with the 7.7-cps stimulus were interspersed among trials with the actual 10-cps conditioned stimulus, and were never reinforced.

Bottom records: Average responses evoked by the 7.7-cps flicker on presentations when no generalization behavior was elicited. Note the similarity of the wave shape elicited by the actual conditioned stimulus to the response evoked by the novel stimulus during generalization. Notice the absence of the second positive component in the evoked potential when generalization failed to occur. [From Ruchkin and John (1966a).]

populations from which these averages were constructed was computed, and the significance of the differences observed in these components was calculated. As can be seen from Table XIV-II, the absence of component II during failure of the test stimulus to elicit generalization was significant at the 0.001 level in both structures, and the absence of III was significant in one.

However, no significant difference between the various conditions exists for component I. These results were interpreted to mean that

364

Table XIV-II. *Significance of Differences between Average Evoked Potentials from Generalization and No Response Trials. Evaluated by the Two-Tailed t-Test[a]*

	Latency (msec)	σ_{cr}	σ_{nr}	t	P (%)
Right lateral geniculate					
Component I	18	13.9	20.0	.856	50
Component II	35	18.0	20.0	5.11	.1
Component III	67	16.6	22.5	2.10	5
Right nucleus reticularis					
Component I	16	16.8	28.0	1.08	50
Component II	34	23.5	24.8	3.86	.1
Component III	67	20.3	28.0	3.38	.1

[a] Degrees of freedom = 82; σ_{cr} and σ_{nr} are the standard deviations in μV for the generalization and no response cases, respectively.

$$ t = \frac{|\overline{CR} - \overline{NR}|\ \sqrt{N}}{\sqrt{\sigma_{CR}^2 + \sigma_{NR}^2}} $$

CR is the amplitude of the average response wave form for the generalization case at the time that the particular component is at its maximum deflection. NR is the amplitude of the no response average at the corresponding instant of time. The baseline from which the amplitudes are measured is the time average of the wave form, computed over the full 130-msec interstimulus interval. (All recordings were made through ac coupled amplifiers.) σ^2 is the unbiased estimate of the variance. N is the number of evoked potentials used to compute the average response wave forms.

Since the differing late components did not appear until the third evoked potential, the first two evoked potentials were excluded from all averages. N was 42 for all averages. To ensure that the background noise was uncorrelated, the averages were computed by taking every other evoked potential from a trial, thereby making the minimum time between any two samples equal to 260 msec. Estimates of the noise correlation function indicated that this was adequate. Boneau (1960) has demonstrated that the assumptions of normality and equality of variance may be relaxed without affecting the validity of the two tailed t-test or as long as the number of samples in each average are the same. From Ruchkin and John (1966a).]

component I was related to the *registration* of the afferent stimulus upon the structure, while component II (and perhaps III) comprised a *reaction* of the neural ensemble to that input, possibly related to the retrieval of stored information. Marked wave shape differences when generalization occurred were seen in the other three animals in this group. Two of those animals showed definite appearance of a process with the shape and latency of component II in one or more monitored brain structures during generalization.

In previous discussions, we commented upon late components which appeared in responses evoked by the CS in various brain regions as the stimulus acquired cue value. The data of Killam and Hance (1965) similarly showed the appearance of new second components in various structures of the cat brain as pattern discriminations were established. In this work, *impressively accurate predictions of choice behavior* were made on the basis of cross-correlating ongoing electrical activity (recorded from the brain of a cat in the discrimination apparatus) against "stencils" constructed from average response wave forms previously observed during correct and incorrect choices. Such prediction suggests the informational relevance of these wave shapes. Asratyan (1965) has described a new surface negative cortical component which he has observed after conditioning. Sakhuilina and Merzhanova have reported that after elaboration of a conditioned food reflex in response to stimulation of midline thalamic nuclei, an additional surface negative component appeared in the cortical projection area of the responding forelimb but not in adjacent cortical regions (1966). The altered shape of the recruiting response is attributed to dendritic postsynaptic potentials generated by the interaction of interneurons. The new component was also observed when the skin of the working forelimb was stimulated, but was absent during sleep.

It is interesting to note the remarkable correspondence shown in Fig. XIV-9 between the wave shape elicited by the actual 10-cps CS during correct performance of the conditioned response and the wave shape displayed when presentation of the 7.7-cps test stimulus resulted in the occurrence of generalization. The similarity between the wave shapes under these two conditions is rather extraordinary. Since it is clear that the generalization wave shape cannot be interpreted as a simple evoked response, this constitutes further evidence that the process *released* from storage during readout approximately reproduces the electrical effects of the previously experienced event. In subsequent studies (John and Ahn, 1966), animals have been trained to perform differential approach and avoidance responses to two stimuli differing in frequency. Generalization tests were then conducted using a novel stimulus of intermediate frequency. *The shape of the evoked potential during generalization differed, depending on which behavioral response was performed.*

F. Estimation of the readout process by the "difference" method

Component II reflects a process which is markedly evident when a neutral stimulus causes the activation of a memory about previous experience, which is operationally defined by the performance of a behavioral response acquired by training to a different stimulus. This process is activated less, or not at all, when readout fails to occur. Similar processes have been observed in approach situations and indicate appreciable generality for this phenomenon. Preliminary experiments using computer pattern recognition techniques suggest that the appearance of these wave shape components may be of utility for the prediction of generalization behavior. One might conceptualize the wave shape during generalization as one which reflects *input* plus *readout,* while the wave shape when generalization fails to occur reflects *input alone.* Differences in wave shape can be observed in many structures under these two conditions. Reasoning thus, it seemed reasonable to subtract the average response wave shape obtained during nonperformance trials from the wave shapes observed during generalization. This operation subtracts the process mediating input alone from the processes mediating input plus readout. *The resulting "difference wave shape" provides an estimate of the characteristics of the neural process mediating readout of previously stored information.*

G. Difference wave shapes in several cats

The data shown in Fig XIV-10 were obtained in the following way: A sample of 200 potentials was taken during generalization to the 7.7-cps stimulus. From that average, we then subtracted an average of 200 potentials obtained during nonresponse to the same stimulus, to construct a *difference wave shape.* This provides an estimate of the process which occurs in the structure during generalization but not during nonperformance. This figure illustrates the shape of the difference process computed in each of the four cats, using only data from the visual cortex and the reticular formation.

Note that there is a *rough* similarity in the difference process observed at corresponding placements in the four cats under comparable circumstances. These animals were all trained the same way and were all tested with the same neutral stimulus, and they all display comparable tendencies toward generalization. These data not only reveal marked difference processes in each of these animals, but surprising correspondence in certain features of the response observed in different animals.

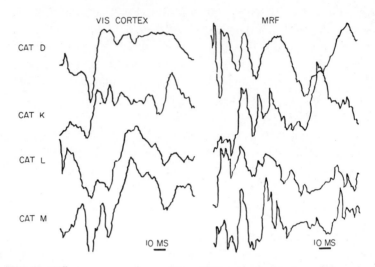

Fig. XIV-10. Difference wave shapes ($N = 200$) computed in four different cats. All animals had been subjected to the same training procedures and were tested for generalization as in the data presented in Fig. XIV-9. Average responses obtained during "no response" trials to the novel 7.7-cps stimulus were subtracted from averages obtained during generalization. All constituent averages were based on 200 evoked responses. (VIS CORTEX—visual cortex, MRF—mesencephalic reticular formation.)

H. Latency and form of difference wave shape in various structures

Computation of difference wave shapes across a large number of anatomical structures in the same animal during a common set of stimulus presentations enables several important questions to be answered. If the hypothesis is accepted that the difference wave shape provides an estimate of the readout of stored information, then such readout must occur earliest from the anatomical region where the engram is stored. *Measurement of differential latencies for the difference process should identify the engram-containing region, if this does in fact exist, as the region with shortest latency.* The details of the difference wave shape should provide information about the various anatomical regions involved in remembering, and the characteristic activity displayed during mediation of this process by different brain structures.

Figure XIV-11 presents a set of difference processes, computed by *subtracting* averages obtained during nonperformance to the stimulus from averages obtained during generalization. These differences were computed on the same set of 30 generalization tests described for Fig. XIV-8. The generalization data were selected equally from each of the four generalization (CR) groups. The nonperformance data were selected from the NR trials, carefully equating features of the sample such as time after onset of stimulus. Each constituent average was based on a sample of 200 evoked potentials. The structures listed in the figure are those which were simultaneously recorded during this full set of trials. They are arranged in order of the increasing latency of two salient components of the difference process, as indicated by the small arrows on each wave shape. (Note: the wave shapes displayed in Fig. XIV-11 begin 10 msec after stimulus onset, and end 52.5 msec later.)

Examination of Fig. XIV-11 reveals an unexpected and intriguing fact. Within the limits of time resolution available with the computer parameters used in analysis of this data, *the release of the difference wave shape occurs with approximate simultaneity* (within less than 1 msec) in the visual cortex, the posterior suprasylvian gyrus, nucleus ventralis lateralis in the thalamus, and the mesencephalic reticular formation. The distances between these various anatomical regions are so great as to preclude the possibility of propagated conduction between them in so short a period. Furthermore, the wave shape of the difference process in these different structures is highly similar. The system comprising these regions then seems to influence a set of other structures, in which the difference process appears successively later, with the most delayed appearance discernible in the lateral geniculate body. Thus, the readout process seems to propagate back to the thalamic nucleus responsible for the afferent input of information about the presence of the stimulus in the environment.

In later studies, we have computed difference wave shapes between correct responses and errors in a differential approach-avoidance situation requiring cats to discriminate between 1-cps and 2.5-cps flicker (John and Shimokochi, 1966). These animals were much less overtrained than those described above. Difference wave shapes have been repeatedly computed from *bipolar* cortical, thalamic, and mesencephalic placements, revealing *essentially identical form and latency* to the difference process which was released in these various structures. These findings are illustrated in Fig. XIV-12. Thus, evidence for simultaneous release of activity,

369

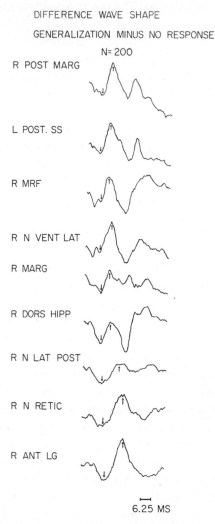

DIFFERENCE WAVE SHAPE

GENERALIZATION MINUS NO RESPONSE

N= 200

R POST MARG

L POST. SS

R MRF

R N VENT LAT

R MARG

R DORS HIPP

R N LAT POST

R N RETIC

R ANT LG

6.25 MS

↓ TIME OF FIRST DIFFERENCE COMPONENT

↑ TIME OF SECOND DIFFERENCE COMPONENT

Fig. XIV-11. "Difference" wave shapes constructed by subtraction of averaged re-sponses evoked by 7.7-cps test stimulus during trials resulting in no behavioral per-formance from averaged responses evoked by the same stimulus when generalization occurred. Each of the original averages was based on 200 evoked potentials providing a sample from 5 behavioral trials. Analysis epoch was 52.5 msec. The onset and maximum of the difference wave has been marked by two arrows on each wave shape. The structures have been arranged from top to bottom in rank order with respect to latency of the difference wave. Note that the latency and shape of the initial com-

analogous to that just presented, has been obtained in other cats performing in a different behavioral situation and stimulated in a much lower frequency range. It is interesting that difference wave shapes computed in these animals *immediately* following acquisition of a new conditioned response, after transfer, reveal that the process *then* has shortest latency in the MRF.

Reverting to the problem of the localization of the engram, we seem to be forced to an unexpected conclusion. If the premises presented above were acceptable, the region in which the difference process appeared earliest would reasonably be the site to which engram storage must be attributed. Unless these premises are invalid, since the evidence in Figs. XIV-11 and XIV-12 indicates simultaneous emergence of the readout process in cortical, thalamic, and mesencephalic regions, the tentative conclusion must be that *the representational system comprising the memory of a previous experience involves all of these structures.* In addition, the similarity in the wave shape of the released process suggests that *the readout establishes a common mode of activity in these various ensembles of neurons.*

A number of alternative interpretations of these data exist. The first possibility is that this set of similar modes of activity arises independently in each of the structures in which it is observed and represents the simultaneous activation of portions of a representational system according to the speculations presented earlier. A second possibility is that the observed synchronous pattern arises in these different brain regions because of the phasing influence of some "pacemaker" system, perhaps the intralaminar thalamic nuclei of the diffuse projection system. The known capacity for achievement of widespread synchrony possessed by this system may also provide an explanation for the greater organization and simpler structure of the signal space after conditioning, which has been revealed by our factor analysis studies. Further experiments will be necessary to evaluate these alternatives.

---

ponent of the difference wave is extremely similar in the first four structures, and then appears progressively later in the remaining regions. (POST MARG—posterior marginal gyrus, POST SS—posterior suprasylvian gyrus, MRF—mesencephalic reticular formation, N VENT LAT—nucleus ventralis lateralis, MARG—marginal gyrus, DORS HIPP—dorsal hippocampus, N LAT POST—nucleus lateralis posterior, N RETIC—nucleus reticularis, ANT LG—anterior lateral geniculate, R—right side, L—left side.)

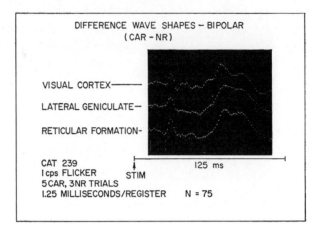

Fig. XIV-12. Part I.

Difference wave shapes obtained by subtracting average responses computed during three trials resulting in no performance (NR) from average responses computed during five trials resulting in correct performance of the conditioned avoidance response (CAR). All recordings were *bipolar,* and 75 evoked potentials were used in each of the constituent averages. Note the correspondence in latency and wave shape of the difference process in these various regions.

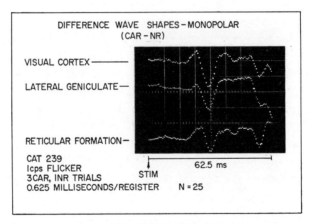

Fig. XIV-12. Part II.

These data were obtained from the same animal as those in Part I of this figure. However, these results were computed in different trials and illustrate the difference wave shapes from *monopolar* derivations. Twenty-five evoked potentials were used in each constituent average and were taken from three CAR and one NR trials. The onset, first negative peak, and first positive peak in these three structures show remarkable correspondence with respect to latency. Note that the resolution is 0.625 msec per register (spot) in the average response computer.

372

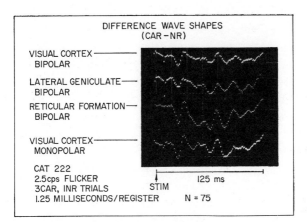

Fig. XIV-12. Part III.

Difference wave shapes from another animal. Seventy-five evoked potentials were.used in each constituent average and were taken from three CAR and one NR trials. Note the similarity in the latency and form of the difference wave shape in the three bipolar derivations from reticular formation, lateral geniculate, and visual cortex, as well as the correspondence between the process observed in monopolar and bipolar derivations from the visual cortex.

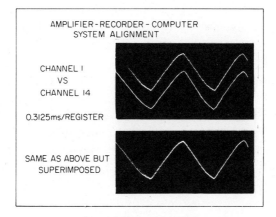

Fig. XIV-12. Part IV.

Results of system calibration to check timing accuracy. A sawtooth signal was simultaneously impressed upon the two inputs between which timing errors would be most evident. The amplifier outputs were recorded, retrieved, and averaged using the same equipment as in other parts of this figure. Note that resolution is 0.3125 msec per register. These results indicate that the temporal relationships observed between the difference wave shapes computed in various brain regions reflect the actual timing of physiological processes, with minimal timing error introduced by the measuring apparatus.

373

I. Evidence from conflict studies

Evidence has also been obtained that the late wave shape components under discussion here cannot be attributed to unspecific factors of the sort which would merely increase the general excitability of any given brain region. In these experiments (John and Shimokochi, 1966), we have conditioned cats to perform a lever response to obtain food upon the presentation of a flicker CS at frequency 1 (V_1). An avoidance response was next established to flicker at frequency 2 (V_2). These two conditioned responses were then transferred to two intermittent auditory stimuli at the corresponding repetition rates, A_1 and A_2.

The animals trained in this way would reliably perform one conditioned response for food on presentation of *either* A_1 or V_1, and a second conditioned response to avoid shock on presentation of A_2 or V_2. After these animals had been highly overtrained, so that they performed essentially without error for very long periods, we carried out what we called the *conflict* experiment. After presentation of a series of the visual and auditory stimuli in random sequence to get the animals working steadily, stimuli were presented simultaneously in *both* modalities. If the frequencies corresponded, so that ($A_1 + V_1$) or ($A_2 + V_2$) were presented together, the trial was designated as *concordant*. If the two frequencies disagreed, so that either ($A_1 + V_2$) or ($V_1 + A_2$) were presented together, the trial was classed as *conflict*. Obviously, the conflict caused by simultaneous presentation of a given stimulus pair could be resolved by performance of *either* the approach *or* the avoidance response. Thus, the member of the conflict stimulus pair which *controlled* the behavior successfully when conflict was resolved by one response *failed to control* the behavior when conflict was resolved by the other response. Comparison of the electrophysiological responses to the members of a conflict pair in trials which were resolved differently enables the effects of factors such as arousal and movement to be controlled completely. Since these influences will be precisely the same in a given volume of tissue insofar as neural response to both of the simultaneous incoming signals is concerned, *differential characteristics of electrical activity in conflict trials which are differently resolved* must necessarily be attributed to different processing of information in the two instances. *It is clear from examination of data from concordant and corflict trials that the late components which have been discussed in the previous section are related to informational rather than unspecific factors.*

In Fig. XIV-13:I and II (pp. 376–379), data are presented from four trials with concordant stimulation. In both examples, the upper records were obtained during a trial in which correct performance appropriate to the frequency shared by the two stimuli took place. The lower records were obtained during a presentation of the same pair of stimuli which failed to elicit any behavioral performance. The presence of late components in the responses evoked in a number of structures in the upper records is apparent on visual inspection of the data, while these components are substantially absent in the lower records.

In Fig. XIV-14 (pp. 380–383), data are illustrated from four conflict trials. Although the pair of stimuli presented to the animal were the same in all instances, in the upper case the conflict was resolved in favor of the visual member of the pair, while in the bottom case the auditory stimulus prevailed. Examination of the data obtained in the four cases clearly shows that the late components in the evoked responses of various structures to the visual stimulus are much more pronounced in the cases in which it controls the behavioral outcome, in the top records, than when it does not, as in the bottom examples. Therefore, since the animal is aroused and performing *some* conditioned response in *all* cases, the late components cannot be assumed to arise from unspecific features of the situation. Note the basic similarity between the activity illustrated in Fig. XIV-14, and that shown in Fig. XIV-13.

In view of considerations similar to those presented, we have suggested that component I relates to the registration of afferent input on the structure, and component II (and perhaps III) reflects the processes mediating retrieval of stored information relevant to that input. How might that second component arise? The occurrence of component I may be envisaged as an "interrogation pulse" sent into a neural network, while component II represents an affirmative reply to the interrogation. Readout or decoding of the retrieved information might be accomplished by evaluation of the local sign and temporal pattern of the initial interrogation pulse, assigning specific content to the event identified as familiar by the second pulse. It should be pointed out that *the electrophysiological phenomena which have been described correspond well to those which would reasonably be expected from the hypotheses of Robinson,* described earlier in this book (Robinson, 1965).

J. Transmission, storage, and evaluation functions

Analysis of the various functions which the system is logically required to perform, and evaluation of additional data, may permit the tentative allocation of different functional roles to various anatomical regions. No

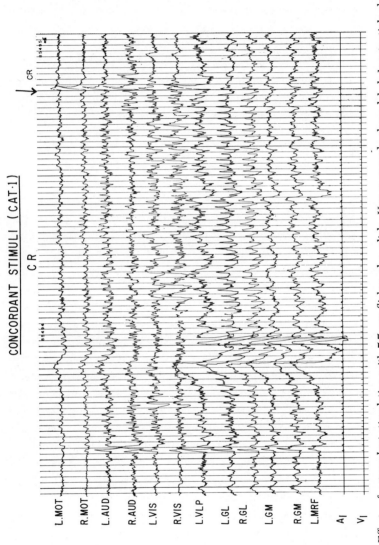

Fig. XIV-13. I. Effects of *concordant* stimulation with 7.7-cps flicker plus click. Upper records show labeled potentials during correct performance of approach response. Lower records were obtained during the same session, but the cat sat motionless throughout stimulus presentation. The form and distribution of labeled responses differ markedly in these two cases.

Notice the regular labeled responses at the stimulus frequency in the motor cortex (MOT) in the upper records. Perhaps more relevant to the subsequent figures is a comparison of the details of wave shape in most of the structures under the two conditions. A

N R

L.MOT
R.MOT
L.AUD
R.AUD
L.VIS
R.VIS
L.VLP
L.GL
R.GL
L.GM
R.GM
L.MRF
A₁
V₁

I SEC

careful examination of the labeled responses shows that in trials in which conditioned response was performed, the late components of the evoked potential contain a fine structure which is discernible as a relatively high-frequency process. During trials resulting in failure to perform, these high-frequency components are absent. Labeled response waves contain only the fundamental frequency of the tracer stimulus and are so "clean" as to appear almost sinusoidal. Monopolar derivations as in Fig. XII-2.

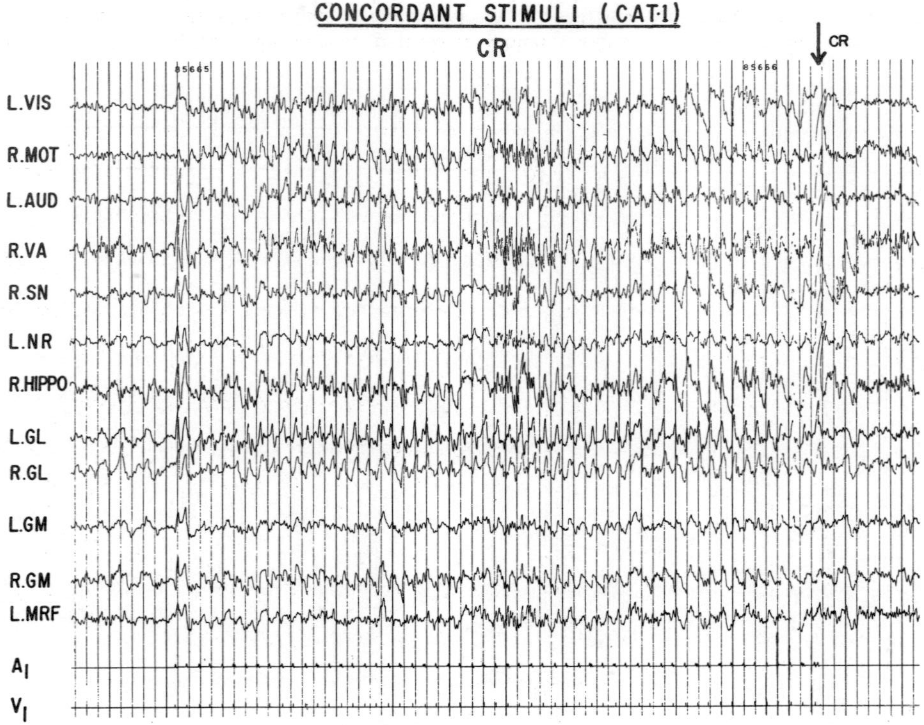
CONCORDANT STIMULI (CAT·1)
CR
CR
85665
85666
L.VIS
R.MOT
L.AUD
R.VA
R.SN
L.NR
R.HIPPO
L.GL
R.GL
L.GM
R.GM
L.MRF
A1
V1

Fig. XIV-13. Part II. Top.

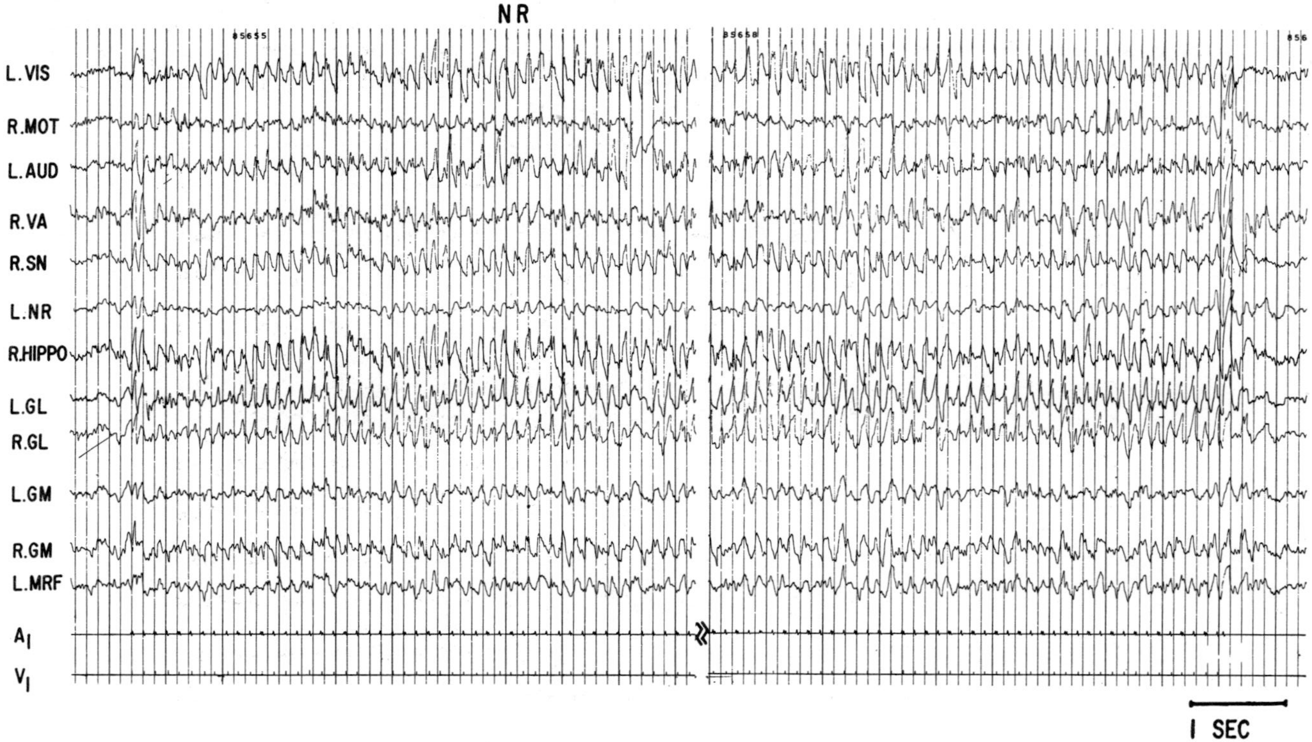

Fig. XIV-13. Part II. Bottom.

II. Another example of wave shape differences between trials with concordant stimuli resulting in correct performance (CR) and failure (NR). Derivations are the same as in Fig. XII-2, I and II from the same animal. [Data from John and Shimokochi (1966).]

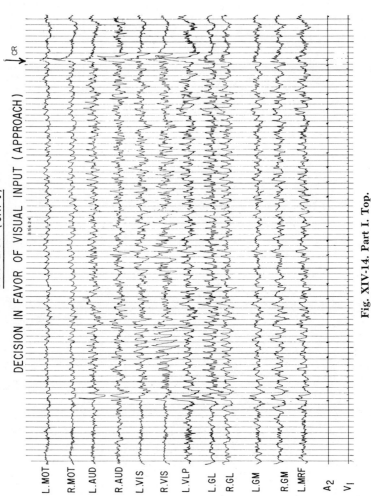

Fig. XIV-14. Part I. Top.

Examples of conflict resolution: I. Effects *of conflict* stimulation in which the 3.1-cps click avoidance stimulus was presented simultaneously with the 7.7-cps flicker approach stimulus. Records on top illustrate the electrical activity displayed when this conflict was resolved in favor of the *visual* input. The bottom records show activity displayed when conflict was resolved in favor of the *auditory* input. Note that when the visual stimulus *prevails* in the conflict trial, the late components of the labeled responses at the flicker frequency contain a fine structure that is absent when the visual stimulus *loses*. Comparison of these data with Part I of the previous figure

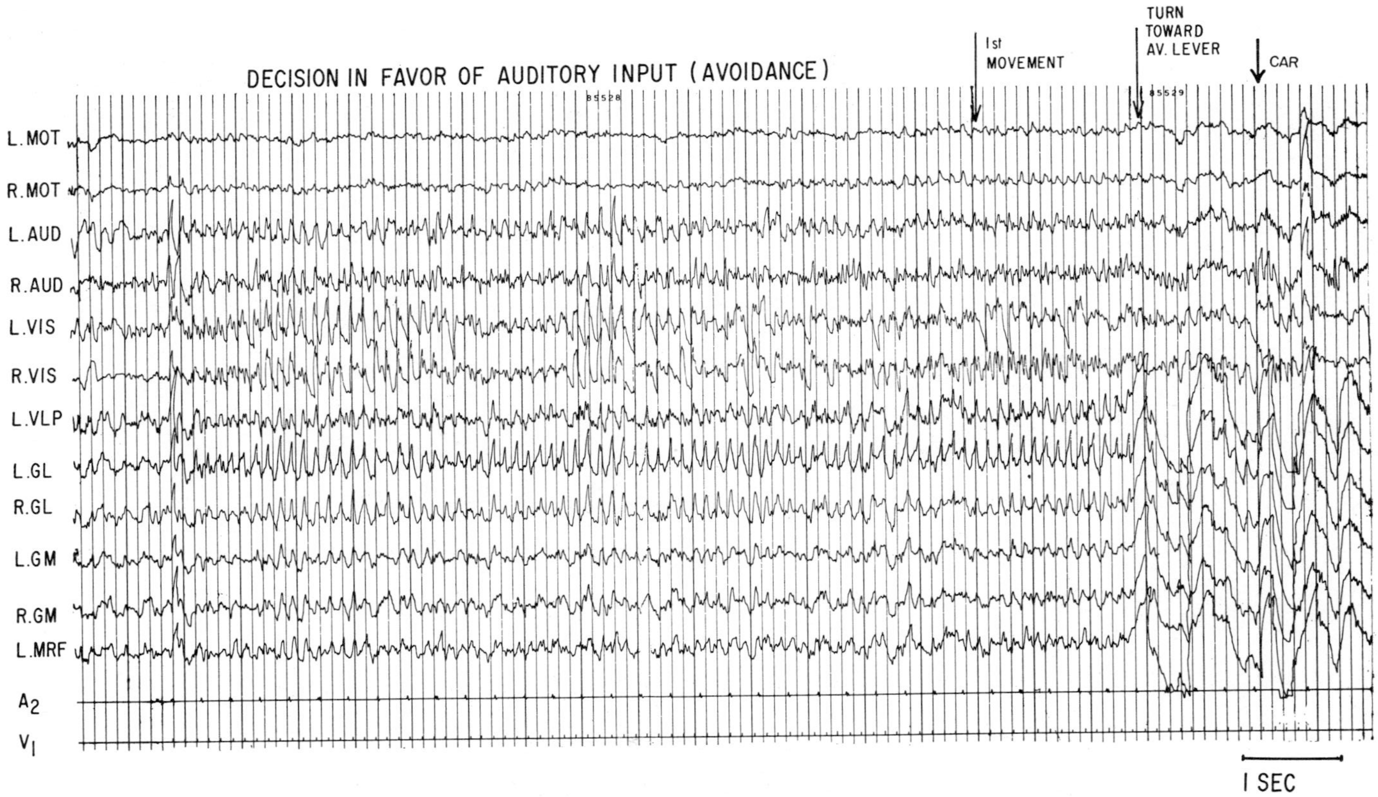

DECISION IN FAVOR OF AUDITORY INPUT (AVOIDANCE)

L.MOT
R.MOT
L.AUD
R.AUD
L.VIS
R.VIS
L.VLP
L.GL
R.GL
L.GM
R.GM
L.MRF
A₂
V₁

1st MOVEMENT

TURN TOWARD AV. LEVER

CAR

I SEC

Fig. XIV-14. Part I. Bottom.

381

shows that they are essentially identical. Yet, the bottom records of Fig. XIV-13.I were obtained from an animal which sat motionless throughout the concurrent stimulus presentation while the bottom records shown in this figure were obtained from an animal which was performing a conditioned avoidance response appropriate to the click CS.

These results suggest that the presence of the fine structure of labeled responses in the upper but not the lower records cannot be

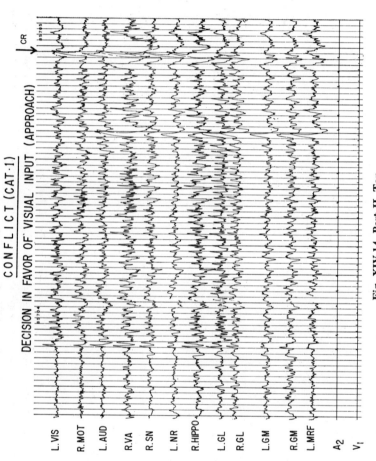

Fig. XIV-14. Part II. Top.

attributed to differences in arousal level, drive level, attention, or movement. All such unspecific factors were equally present in the two cases from which the data of this figure were taken. The differences in fine structure would seem to relate to the processing of information about the stimuli. (Monopolar derivations from the same animal as Fig. XII-2; VA—nucleus ventralis anterior, SN—substantia nigra, NR—nucleus ruber.)

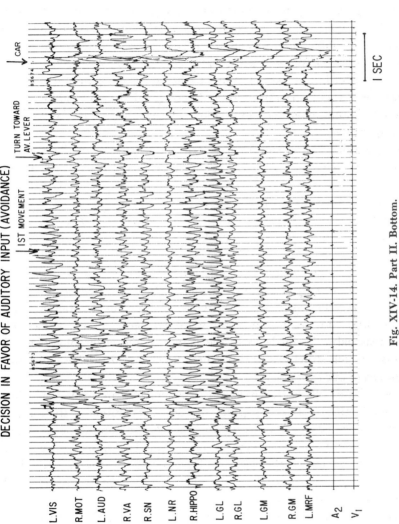

Fig. XIV-14. Part II. Bottom.

II. Another example of wave shape changes with different resolutions of conflict. Same animal and conditions as I, but second recording configuration. Monopolar derivations, leads as in Fig. XII-2. [All data from John and Shimokochi (1966).]

matter how the system may be organized, processes must exist which correspond to the performance of three basic functions: First, information about peripheral events must be encoded and transmitted centrally, propagating from region to region as it is processed. We will call this the *transmission function*, "T". Second, mechanisms must exist to store incoming information and somehow to interrogate the depots of previously stored information. We will call this the *storage and interrogation function*, "S". Third, the system must evaluate incoming information together with what is retrieved from interrogated depots, and organize responses based upon that evaluation. We will call this the *readout and response function*, "R".

Suppose that the organization of the brain is such that these three functions are relatively localized, in the sense that particular groups of structures are primarily involved in the mediation of one or another function. We postulate three types of structure: *Type T* plays the role of transmission line. The transmission function may become established by experience, that is, learning may "gate" open a previously closed transmission process. All type T structures need not function as throughputs before training. *Type S* structures function as data storage depots, or mediate interrogation of information stores. *Type R* structures are concerned with evaluating information retrieved after interrogation of type S structures and organizing appropriate response. What predictions might reasonably be made as to the nature of the electrophysiological processes which structures of these three types would display under the conditions of our experiments?

Four classes of electrophysiological phenomena are available, using behavioral criteria: In trials using the actual conditioned stimulus, a stimulus impinges on the brain which is in fact the same stimulus which previously established a memory in that system. That input is responded to correctly in one class (CR) and incorrectly in the second class (ERROR). In test trials, the same animal is presented with a novel stimulus which he has never seen before. In the third class (GEN), he retrieves from his memory a past experience which did not in fact correspond to this present event, and reacts to the new input as if it actually corresponded to the previous event. In the fourth class (NR), this process does not occur. How might these *four classes of phenomena* be expected to differ in *the three types of structures* which have been hypothesized to mediate transmission, storage and interrogation, and readout?

In the case in which the real conditioned stimulus is being processed, it seems reasonable to expect that the effects of the stimulus impinging on the nervous system should propagate through transmission lines to the region where the hypothetical storage depots exist. Although failure of transmission or incorrect peripheral encoding might conceivably occur under abnormal circumstances, these seem unlikely in the normal animal. Under usual conditions, one must assume fairly reliable encoding and transmission of a stimulus in a fashion primarily determined by the physical characteristics of the stimulus itself. One would expect, therefore, that the responses evoked in type T structures by the actual conditioned stimulus should be essentially the same, whether or not the correct behavior is performed after subsequent processing. However, the response of type T structures to the conditioned stimulus should be *different* from response to the test stimulus. The response evoked by the test stimulus should also be independent of outcome. Therefore, it seems reasonable to argue that *the response, "A", of type T structures during events in class CR should be the same as in class ERROR, and different from the response, "B", to class GEN, which should be the same as class NR.*

In contrast to the determination of the response mode of type T primarily by *stimulus characteristics,* the previous discussion has argued that the response mode of type S structures is also influenced by the *state* of the animal. Information about a peripheral event reaching type S structures might conceivably fail to read-in appropriately because of the influences of other neural processes related to attention, context, or motivation. Conversely, it is possible that the interference resulting from incompatible state occurs at the level of interrogation and readout. This is equivalent to the statement that malfunction might occur either at the interface between type T and type S processes, or at the interface between type S and type R processes.

In order to choose between these alternatives, one is forced temporarily to rely upon intuitive judgment. The remarkable reliability of the memory mechanism can be offered as an indication that access to storage depots and interrogation thereof is primarily determined by the physical characteristics of the stimulus. That is, the physical characteristics of the stimulus might be the parameters which guarantee ready access to the appropriate storage depots for an afferent input. Reasoning in this manner, it is plausible to predict that the invariant physical characteristics of the conditioned stimulus suffice to accomplish reliable access to and interrogation of the storage depot containing information about prior experience with the stimulus. However, one is hard put to explain the occurrence of generalization to a neutral stimulus without assuming that it succeeded, although inappropriately, in gaining access to the storage depot. This access must be attributed to the fact that its physical characteristics were sufficiently similar to those of the conditioned stimulus, in the presence of the momentary state provided by attention, context, and motivation. The influence of the neutral stimulus upon the storage depot effectively reproduces what takes place when the real stimulus arrives there. This assumption fits well with the data previously presented, indicating release of a characteristic stored mode of oscillation during generalization. When generalization fails to occur upon presentation of a test stimulus, it seems likely that the storage and interrogation depots functioned more precisely, denying access to an inappropriate input configuration. This argument, although admittedly tenuous, leads to the prediction that *the processes, "C", observed in type S structures during events in class CR will be the same as those during class ERROR and also during class GEN, but will differ from those, "D", in class NR.* In making this prediction, we have taken the position that the malfunction in the system during response failures to the presentation of the conditioned stimulus probably occurs at the interface between type S and type R structures, whereas the malfunction during generalization to a neutral stimulus probably occurs at the interface between type T and type S structures.

No matter at what level the malfunctions just discussed actually occur, there is little ambiguity in the nature of the processes expected in type R structures. *When the results of the evaluation process are affirmative,* whether they lead to correct performance in response to presentation of the conditioned stimulus (CR) or to inaccurate generalization after presentation of the test stimulus (GEN), *the activity, "E", in Type R structures should be the same. This activity should differ from the process, "F", which occurs when the conditioned stimulus fails to elicit correct performance (ERROR), or the activity "G" displayed when no generalization occurs upon presentation of the test stimulus (NR).* Thus, Type R structures would be expected to show a similar process during events in class CR or class GEN. A different process should appear during events in class ERROR or class NR, which may or may not have similar features.

These various predictions are summarized in Fig. XIV-15.

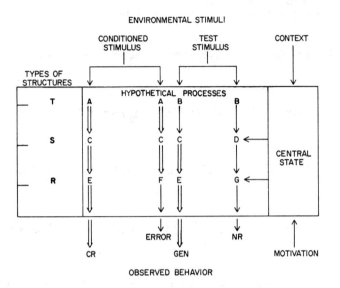

Fig. XIV-15. Hypothetical processes expected in brain structures mediating various classes of functions under four different behavioral conditions: T—structures concerned with transmission; S—structures concerned with storage of information; R—structures concerned with evaluation and readout.

K. Comparison of responses to conditioned and neutral stimuli

Figure XIV-16 provides the data necessary to evaluate the differences in response of various structures under the four conditions. All averages are based on samples of 90 evoked potentials, carefully equated with respect to distribution among trials and time since onset of stimulus. The *first column* presents the average wave shapes elicited by the 10-cps conditioned stimulus actually used in training, during CR trials culminating in correct performance (solid line) and ERROR trials in which the animal failed to perform (dotted line). The *second column* presents the average wave shapes evoked by the 7.7-cps neutral stimulus during GEN trials resulting in generalization (solid line) and NR trials in which no performance was elicited (dotted line). The *third column* compares the average wave shapes observed when correct performance occurred during 10-cps flicker (dotted line) and when generalization occurred dur-

387

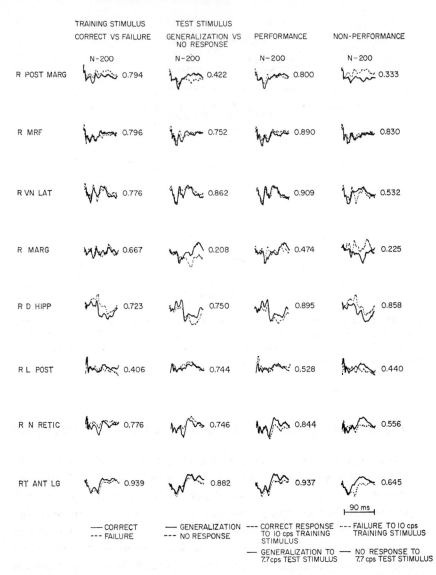

Fig. XIV-16. Comparison of averaged evoked responses to the 10-cps training CS and the 7-cps test stimulus during performance and nonperformance for a number of brain areas. The significance of each wave shape is indicated in the legend under each column. Every average response is based upon 200 evoked potentials obtained from a number of behavioral trials, using a 62.5-msec analysis epoch.

The numbers to the right of each pair of averaged responses are the Pearson product moment correlation coefficients between the two wave shapes. Structures are the same as in Fig. XIV-11.

ing 7.7-cps flicker (solid line). The *fourth column* compares the average wave shapes during errors to the 10-cps CS (dotted line) and during nonperformance to the 7.7-cps test stimulus (solid line). The correlation coefficient between each pair of wave shapes has been computed digitally, using the methods discussed earlier, and is presented next to the data to which it is relevant.

L. Factor analysis of the types of structure

It is now possible to utilize factor analysis to classify structures according to their type. A correlation matrix can be constructed for each structure, consisting of the intercorrelations between the response wave shapes obtained in these four conditions. Type T structures should be characterized by a high loading on one factor during CR and ERROR trials, and a high loading on a second factor during GEN and NR trials. Type S structures should be characterized by a high loading on one factor during CR, ERROR, and GEN trials, and a high loading on another factor during NR trials. Type R structures should display a high loading on one factor for CR and GEN trials, and another loading configuration for ERROR and NR trials. These predictions follow from Fig. XIV-15, if one considers the response processes A–F as components or factors contained in evoked responses.

Factor analyses of these data have been carried out, and a tentative classification of some structures according to the foregoing criteria has been obtained (Ruchkin and John, 1966b). No structures met the criteria for classification as type T structures. The marginal and posterior marginal gyrus correspond to the configuration expected for type S structures. The lateral geniculate body and nucleus ventralis lateralis strongly resemble the configuration predicted for type R structures, while nucleus reticularis and the mesencephalic reticular formation do so somewhat less clearly.

It is not possible to evaluate the significance of these preliminary studies without knowledge of the variance of these responses. The results are presented here to indicate the possibility of using such methods for functional analysis. Perhaps the most interesting aspect of the findings is the striking correspondence in the CR and GEN wave shapes in many structures. This indicates that the neutral stimulus elicits a neuronal

389

process during generalization very similar to that caused by the actual conditioned stimulus during correct performance of the learned response.

M. Factor analysis of the four classes of data

The data just presented indicate that certain structures show differences in the size but not the shape of the processes elicited under these various conditions, while other structures show marked differences in response wave shape with or without concomitant changes in amplitude. We have here assumed that the process underlying two responses of similar wave shape but different size is essentially the same process, activated to a differing quantitative level. Processes underlying two responses of different wave shape have been assumed to differ qualitatively. The foregoing analysis has emphasized the importance of qualitative rather than quantitative differences. The legitimacy of this choice cannot be established at this time. It is, however, a necessary consequence of the lines of argument previously constructed.

Factor analysis of the set of 32 wave forms computed in these eight structures under the four conditions has been carried out. It was found that the signal space containing these average response wave shapes was such that 97.2% of the energy could be accounted for by ten components. Thus, a relatively high level of coupling or dependence must exist between the processes manifested in some of these instances. Because of the complexity and abundance of data made available from a complete analysis of this sort, only the relative contributions to these signals made by the three major components will be presented. These components accounted for 71% of the variance in the full signal set. The weighting coefficients representing the percentage of each of the original signals attributable to the three components are shown in Table XIV-III.

Inspection of the data in this table reveals that a number of anatomical regions share particular configurations of weighting coefficients. During correct performance to the 10-cps CS, the lateral geniculate body and the mesencephalic reticular formation are dominated by the influence of the first component, which is also the major constituent of the activity in the dorsal hippocampus and nucleus reticularis, and contributes importantly to the lateral posterior thalamic nucleus. A second cluster can be discerned, containing a part of the visual cortex and the ventrolateral nucleus of the thalamus, strongly influenced by the second component.

TABLE XIV-III. *Weighting Coefficients*[a]

	10 cps								7.7 cps							
	CR				ERROR				GEN				NR			
Component:	1	2	3	Total	1	2	3	Total	1	2	3	Total	1	2	3	Total
Structure																
R MARG	.02	.54	.11	.67	.01	.45	.04	.50	.21	.60	.00	.81	.18	.06	.41	.65
R P MARG	.19	.18	.36	.73	.17	.16	.10	.43	.47	.33	.06	.86	.00	.03	.78	.81
R LG	.90	.01	.00	.91	.73	.06	.01	.80	.84	.00	.11	.95	.75	.01	.04	.80
R D HIPP	.61	.05	.24	.90	.50	.28	.02	.80	.58	.01	.09	.68	.44	.27	.22	.93
R MRF	.82	.01	.06	.89	.44	.00	.27	.71	.73	.01	.00	.74	.48	.02	.08	.58
R V LAT	.26	.62	.02	.90	.30	.42	.03	.75	.37	.42	.00	.79	.40	.19	.00	.59
R N RET	.47	.05	.04	.56	.38	.01	.00	.39	.74	.02	.03	.79	.72	.02	.06	.80
R L POST	.24	.07	.26	.57	.04	.29	.11	.44	.46	.04	.00	.50	.19	.14	.18	.51

[a] Weighting coefficients for first three factors of regression equations which reconstruct the average response wave shapes evoked in various brain structures by the 10-cps conditioned stimulus during correct and erroneous performance and by the 7.7-cps test stimulus during generalization and no response. Structures are the same as in Fig. XIV-1I.

When errors occur upon presentation of the CS, these constellations are altered. The most striking change is the pronounced decoupling of activity in the reticular formation from that in the lateral geniculate. Dorsal hippocampus, nucleus reticularis, and lateralis posterior also become more independent of the first component. Although the two structures in the second cluster continue to be dominated by the second component, it exerts a decreased amount of control.

During generalization to the 7.7-cps test stimulus, the configuration of factor loadings is markedly similar to that observed during appropriate conditioned response to the CS. The activity of the reticular formation and the lateral geniculate body are strongly coupled to the first component, which also dominates the hippocampus, nucleus reticularis, and lateralis posterior. Posterior regions of the visual cortex are also influenced by this component. The more anterior portion of the visual cortex and nucleus ventralis lateralis comprise a second cluster markedly coupled to the second component.

Note the great contrast which is provided by the pattern of factor loadings when the test stimulus fails to elicit generalization. The lateral geniculate and the reticular formation are less strongly coupled, the latter structure responding much less to the influence of the first component. The hippocampus and lateralis posterior substantially depart from the cluster to which they previously belonged, as does the posterior visual cortex. Furthermore, the association of anterior visual cortex with ventralis lateralis also decomposes; both regions shift away from the second component.

Therefore, detailed consideration of the factor analysis of this body of data seems to show that during conditioned response performance to the CS, these various brain structures are highly organized into two clusters. The structures within a cluster show similar responsiveness to particular influences in the system. The organization observed during conditioned response is characterized by the association of extensive sensory-specific and nonsensory-specific regions into a system which displays a common mode of activity. During errors, the nonsensory-specific structures depart from the common mode and no longer display activity which corresponds to the effect of the sensory stimulus on the primary relay nucleus. In these data, the monitored cortical regions do not seem to conform to the mode of activity displayed either by the reticular formation or by the lateral geniculate, in contrast to most of our comparable previous analyses. The reason for this discrepancy is not understood. Although the data show marked correspondence in composition between multiple nonsensory-specific regions and the lateral geniculate, they do not provide support for the suggestion that the hypothesized comparator function is located at the cortical level.

During generalization, it is clear that the test stimulus accomplished an organization of these neural regions into clusters like the constellations observed when the CS elicited correct performance of the conditioned response. Furthermore, these constellations displayed the same common mode of activity during the test stimulus as that which characterized the response to the CS.

These various data, then, seem to constitute substantial evidence that a representational system involving extensive regions in both sensory specific and nonsensory-specific brain areas is established during conditioning, and that this system can release a common mode of activity stored during previous experience, when activated by an appropriate afferent input. Release of this common mode of activity by the representational system is accompanied by performance of a previously learned behavior, as though readout of memory had occurred.

CHAPTER XV

WAVE SHAPES AND INFORMATION

When we first described our use of the tracer technique, Killam and I proposed that the appearance of labeled potentials in a given brain region was sufficient basis to conclude that the activity of that structure was *influenced* by the presentation of the intermittent peripheral stimulus. Gradually, as evidence accumulated about the release of frequency-specific patterns of activity in such phenomena as those observed during assimilation, cortical conditioning, generalization, or erroneous performance after discrimination, it began to seem as though the temporal patterns of electrical activity observed in certain circumstances might be related to the *representation* of information about intermittent stimuli which were at corresponding frequencies. It was possible that the apparent correlation between the functional significance of an intermittent stimulus and the frequency patterns which it elicited in the electrical activity of the brain was essentially a laboratory curiosity, relevant *only* to the artificial situation in which the informational significance of a stimulus was confined to its rate of repetition. The coding of more natural stimuli might not involve characteristic temporal patterns of activity. Acceptance of this proposition entailed acceptance of the notion that various kinds of information were coded in different ways. The difficulty resulting from this assumption arises from the necessity of reconciling many different codes in order to achieve integration of the several attributes of a stimulus. The requirement of simultaneous translation of multiple codes seems like a severe burden to inflict upon a conceptual nervous system if it can be avoided. The alternative is to assume that the representation of tracer stimuli by the temporal patterns of labeled response is not an exceptional case, but rather reflects a general mechanism by which the nervous system codes information as temporal patterns.

If we consider the data on average response wave shapes which have been presented, it seems possible that wave shape may reflect informational significance. It must be made clear that the *wave shape* of average evoked potentials is not the same as the *rhythm* of labeled responses. These characteristic temporal patterns do not necessarily depend only on the rate at which the input is reiterated. The occurrence of temporally ordered activity in a neuronal population otherwise characterized by random or baseline activity might represent the information being processed by the cellular aggregate. This organized sequence of coherence would be reflected in measures of the ensemble average as a temporal pattern or wave shape phase-locked to the time of afferent input to the system. Restated, *it is proposed that the information contained in the activity of a specified neuronal aggregate is represented by the temporal pattern of decreases in entropy of the ensemble* (Shannon and Weaver, 1949).

A. Relationship between wave shape and site of stimulation

We have studied the relationship between the *shape* of evoked potentials recorded in different brain regions and the *site* at which electrical stimulation is delivered to the brain. The data to be discussed were obtained from one of the previously mentioned animals in which 10-cps stimulation produced performance of the conditioned avoidance response whether applied as flicker or as direct electrical input to various regions of the brain. Evoked potentials were recorded from ten different brain regions as behavioral response was elicited by five different kinds of stimuli at 10 cps: one stimulus was the flicker CS, and the others were electrical stimulation of the lateral geniculate, reticular formation, nucleus ruber, or pyramidal tract. Thus, an array of averaged evoked potentials was obtained consisting of the responses recorded from ten different anatomical regions to five different kinds of stimuli.

These data were divided into two groups, each comprised of the wave shapes displayed by five different structures. In each array, the responses of a given structure to five different stimuli constituted a *row* of averaged evoked potentials, while the effects of a given stimulus on five different structures constituted a *column*. Each wave shape in a row was then correlated with every other wave shape in that row, yielding a *row matrix*. Similarly, each wave shape in a column was then correlated with every other wave shape in that column, yielding a *column matrix*. The resulting ten row matrices and ten column matrices were then subjected to factor analysis (Ruchkin and John, 1966b).

The *factor analysis of column matrices* permits evaluation of whether a specified neural disturbance produces similar effects in different anatomical regions. *The factor analysis of row matrices* provides information about the extent to which the responses evoked in a given brain region by a variety of stimuli display features characteristic to that region. Restated, *the comparison of factor analyses of column and row matrices indicates whether an evoked response is more characteristic of the region from which it is recorded or the stimulus by which it is evoked.* Figure XV-1 shows the results of the factor analysis of these data, carried out on two sets of five different structures. The graphs show the partial communality, V_M, versus the number of factors, for both row and column matrices. These graphs can be interpreted as reflecting the extent to which different evoked potentials contain common components. The greater the amount of signal energy in common components, the higher will be the V_M curve. These data show at about the .01 significance level that *the shape of an evoked potential is determined more by the region from which a propagated disturbance arises than by the region from which the response is recorded.*

Two factors may have contributed to the higher similarity within columns than within rows. First, possible stimulus artifact in early portions of the wave shape might have spuriously enhanced similarity. An attempt was made to rule out this possibility by repeating the same analysis on the full set of wave shapes after deletion of the initial 10 msec of response. Basically the same results were obtained as before, although the V_M curves for rows and columns now showed some overlap. Second, it must be kept in mind that row data were obtained sequentially while column data were obtained simultaneously. Although the stability of average response wave shapes on repeated stimulation has been found to be quite high, these conclusions must be considered tentative until further studies of this sort have been done with control for sequence. Keeping these reservations in mind, these preliminary findings raise the definite possibility that information propagating through the brain as a result of nonrandom excitation in some particular structures carries the *local sign* of the originally stimulated structure in its wave shape. That is, the temporal pattern of response to a given stimulus may include the key signature of the region which was initially stimulated.

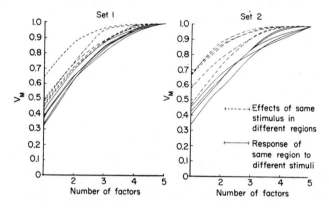

Fig. XV-1. V_M curves for factor analyses of correlation coefficients between wave shapes of: (a) averaged responses evoked in five different brain regions by the same stimulus (dotted lines); or (b) averaged responses evoked in the same brain region by five different stimuli (solid lines). Data presented on the left are for five stimuli (10-cps flicker, 10-cps electrical stimulation of right lateral geniculate, left pyramidal tract, right nucleus entopeduncularis, or right nucleus ruber) and five structures (right visual cortex, left motor cortex, left medial suprasylvian cortex, right mesencephalic reticular formation, and left nucleus ventralis anterior). Data presented on the right are for the same five stimuli, but the set of five structures included right visual cortex, right putamen, right caudate nucleus, left globus pallidus, and the left caudate nucleus.

Note that the dotted curves lie above the solid curves. This means that there is greater similarity between the wave shapes evoked in five different brain regions by the same stimulus than between the wave shapes evoked in the same brain region by five different stimuli.

B. Integration of information by linear interaction

The fact that regression equations constructed from the results of factor analysis can account for the bulk of the signal energy, as well as other results to be cited later in this chapter, provides support for the proposition that a substantial portion of the electrophysiological transactions of the brain can be treated as linear interactions. The results presented in the preceding section suggest that information about nonrandom or *significant* disturbances in particular brain regions may propagate to many other brain regions as a temporal pattern with characteristic features. Presumably, the specification of this pattern is contained in the temporal distribution of impulses in the afferent barrage impinging on the recipient regions. If the momentary barrage of stimuli on receptors is assumed to produce an anatomically distributed set of nonrandom disturbances in the corresponding projection areas, the propagation of perturbations with the appropriate key signatures to other brain regions might constitute the distribution of information about these events to many other regions of the brain. If we conceive of linear interaction of the propagating disturbances, we can envisage a mechanism of informational integration whereby the set of stimuli that are significant at any moment are represented in many regions of the brain by characteristic patterns of activity in the ensemble average. If significant integration of the informational content of regional activity were accomplished by means of such a mechanism, it seems essential that the average activity of ensembles comprising a particular receptive region reflects not only the occurrence of some event but the unique characteristics of that event in the resulting temporal pattern.

C. Coding of specific information as wave shapes in human beings

In view of the propositions just presented, it is necessary to evaluate whether the specific informational content of the stimuli (which produce excitation of a particular anatomical region) is reflected by the wave shape evoked in that structure. Studies of sensory evoked responses in man are particularly relevant to this question because of the relative ease by which attitudinal sets can be established with verbal instructions. Since the introduction of averaging techniques (Dawson, 1947), numerous experiments have explored the relationship between electrophysiological, and psychophysiological measurements. The logic underlying these attempts has been discussed in two articles by Rosner (1962) and Uttal (1965). These studies formed a substantial portion of the work presented in a recent symposium on sensory evoked responses in man (Whipple, 1964). This chapter will include only a few examples of this work and is not to be considered as a thorough survey.

The possibility that evoked potentials recorded from the scalp might contain major components of muscular origin was suggested by the work

399

of Bickford *et al.* (1964). Rémond *et al.* (1965) have shown that a relationship exists between components of the lambda complex and eye movements. They found that the number of components of averaged responses obtained during visual exploration, as well as the latency, topography, and amplitude of the various electrophysiological components, changed with the complexity of the visual field being explored. Gilden *et al.* (1965) averaged backward from voluntary movements and found that a characteristic motor potential could be recorded from certain scalp regions prior to movement. Although these findings indicate the necessity for caution and appropriate controls in evoked response studies, a comparison of recordings taken from the scalp and the cortical surface on an unanesthetized man shows essential similarity (Domino *et al.*, 1964; Vaughan, 1965). The scalp recording reflects the configuration of evoked responses on the underlying cortex in detail, and little contribution is made by extracerebral activity, particularly in recordings taken from posterior head regions.

Our interest in human evoked response studies arises from the proposition that the detailed wave shape of an evoked response may be related to the informational content or "meaning" of the stimulus. An evaluation of this suggestion is complicated by several considerations. Before changes or differences between the averaged responses elicited by two different stimuli or under two different conditions can be attributed to variations in the meaning of the stimuli, it is necessary to control or separate unspecific effects which might be due to changes in state (such as attention or arousal) as well as differences due to the physical parameters of the stimuli. Evidence exists that many of these factors can contribute to the evoked potential wave shape. In attempting to partial out these factors, it may be possible to utilize procedures involving summation or subtraction of evoked potentials, in view of a set of findings which suggest that evoked potential interactions are approximately linear (John *et al.*, 1964; Sutton *et al.*, 1965b; Van Hof, 1960a; Donchin and Lindsley, 1965; Clynes, 1965; Vaughan, 1965).

D. Effects of attention on evoked potentials

A large number of human studies have provided evidence that the focus of attention upon a stimulus alters the shape of the potential which that stimulus evokes. Most of these studies have been concerned primarily with the amplitude of averaged evoked responses. Haider *et al.* (1964) have reported enhancement of evoked potentials by requiring increased attention to visual stimuli in a detection task. Responses to correctly identified stimuli were greater than to stimuli which were incorrectly identified. Garcia-Austt *et al.* (1964) found that mental calculation decreased the amplitude of visually evoked potentials, while counting the stimuli increased response amplitude. Gross *et al.* (1965b) obtained essentially identical results with auditory stimuli. Davis (1964) has shown that in a task requiring loudness discrimination between the second and third tones in a four-tone sequence, the average evoked response was larger for the stimuli relevant to the decision. Callaway *et al.* (1965) found that evoked potentials elicited by two tones were closely similar in wave shape until one tone was systematically paired with light, whereupon differences in the wave shapes evoked by the two tones became appreciable. Interestingly, schizophrenic patients who might be expected to display preoccupation with trivial distinctions showed reduced similarity between wave shapes elicited by two tones. These results were based on digital computation of correlation coefficients between wave shapes.

E. Relation between perception and evoked potentials

A number of studies have examined the relationship between the evoked potential and various parameters of sensory stimuli that are sometimes correlated with psychophysical judgments. Some of these experiments have been surveyed by Uttal (1965), who believes that the psychophysical results obtained thus far from central evoked potential measurements are inconclusive. However, systematic relationships between certain evoked potential characteristics and various stimulus parameters have been reported. For example, stimulus intensity, area, spectral composition, and retinal location have been shown to influence the visual evoked response (Vaughan, 1965). Among these, the reports that the shape of cortical evoked potentials changes as different colors are presented, except in color blind subjects, are particularly interesting (Shipley, Jones, and Fry, 1965; Clynes, 1965). These results suggest a relationship between the processes generating evoked potentials and subjective experience. That suggestion receives further support from a number of perceptual studies.

One of the first attempts to correlate averaged evoked responses with psychophysical measurements was conducted by Geisler *et al.* (1958), who showed that an evoked potential produced by a click stimulus appeared in the response averaged from scalp at about the same stimulus intensity as that at which the subject first detected the stimulus. Similar results have been reported by Rapin (1964). Lansing (1965) has examined the electrophysiological correlates of binocular rivalry with separate and competing visual fields, one steady and one flickering. He found that, under appropriate circumstances, electrical responses paralleled the perceptual judgment of dominance in such binocular rivalry.

It has been known for some time that the perception of some characteristic contained in a brief test flash (TF), such as the form of a visual pattern, can be influenced by subsequent presentation of a second and brighter flash (BF). At brief interflash intervals, TF can be masked or blanked by BF, while at longer intervals the perception of TF can be enhanced. Electrophysiological correlates of the perceptual masking and enhancement phenomena were studied by Donchin and Lindsley (1965). Average evoked responses were computed to paired flashes separated by different intervals and also to the TF and BF alone. The averaged response to BF alone was subtracted from the response to the combined stimuli TF + BF, with appropriate correction for the interflash interval. The resulting difference wave shape was assumed to be the contribution of TF to the response. In all cases, the subjective perceptual experience of brightness enhancement was associated with overlap or summation of the evoked potential patterns of the two stimuli. Potentials in the enhancement range resembled neither the response to TF nor to BF alone, suggesting occurrence of interaction. However, in the blanking range, the averaged response evoked by the two combined stimuli resembled that elicited by the BF alone. In this study, synthesized compound evoked potentials were constructed by summation in a digital computer and compared with the actual evoked potentials elicited by particular combinations of TF plus BF. When no perceptual interaction took place, the actual and synthetic evoked potential corresponded closely. However, when masking or enhancement occurred, the experimental and calculated wave shapes showed marked discrepancies. The authors interpreted these results as suggesting that evoked potentials were intimately related to the information processing activity of the cortex and they covaried with the perception of stimuli and with the arousal and attentive state of the subject.

402

Earlier studies by these workers with Wicke *et al.* (1964) established a correlation between the evoked potential and subjective brightness of a flash. The apparent brightness of a flash depends on the total luminous energy, that is, on the product of luminance and duration. This relationship is sometimes referred to as the Bunsen-Roscoe law. Although evoked potential wave shape and amplitude are known to change as the luminance of a visual stimulus is varied, these experiments showed that when luminance and duration were varied reciprocally so that their product remained constant, no change appeared in the evoked potential. Thus, evoked potential wave shape and amplitude depend on total luminous energy, as does apparent brightness. These results have been confirmed by Vaughan (1965). In additional studies, Vaughan has observed that the ability of a subject to resolve a pair of stimuli as a double event increased with the interstimulus interval and correlated well with the appearance of an early component of the response to the *second* flash. Latency changes observed in some experiments by this worker may relate to the fact that if stimulus intensity is held constant while duration is increased, apparent brightness reaches a maximum at some duration and then decreases if the stimulus is lengthened further. This is sometimes called the Broca-Sulzer effect.

F. Relation between meaning and evoked potentials

Although the human experiments cited in this chapter thus far clearly indicate that evoked potentials change as a function of alteration in stimulus parameters or with the subjective focus of attention, and that they correlate with aspects of subjective experience or psychophysical judgment, these results do not demonstrate a relationship between the meaning or significance of a stimulus and the evoked potential. Some results relating more directly to these questions have been obtained. Begleiter *et al.* (1965) have shown that affective meaning can significantly alter the response evoked by a visual stimulus. Three orientations of a flashing line figure were systematically associated with pleasant, neutral, and unpleasant word lists. Although subjects seemed unaware of any conditioning experience, subsequent presentation of the line figure in the three orientations elicited three characteristically different wave shapes.

Considerable interest has been aroused by the observation by Walter and his colleagues (1964) of a prolonged surface-negative response,

403

which seems to be related to the contingencies of an experimental situation and ends when an expected event occurs. This contingent negative variation (CNV) drops abruptly at the usual time of an expected event, even if it is withheld. These workers later reported (Walter *et al.*, 1965) that CNV appears with associated stimuli with constant energy if they are informationally significant. The responses to semantic experiences were different from those evoked by energetic physiological stimuli in latency, distribution, and form. Sutton *et al.* (1965b) have shown the appearance of pronounced components in the evoked potential is related to uncertainty about the nature of the forthcoming stimulus.

Van Hof (1960b) has studied the effects of projecting a wire figure of negligible area with respect to the window in which it appears. The evoked potential elicited by a flash of light when the window was empty was markedly different from the response when the figure was present. Similar results were obtained by Chapman and Bragdon (1964). Subjects were instructed to solve simple numerical problems that required perception of numerical visual stimuli presented in sequence and were interspersed with other visual stimuli which were irrelevant. Differences in evoked potentials were found that were not attributable to the physical energy of the stimulus but were related to meaningfulness in the sense of task relevance. The measurements were made over a 2000:1 range of luminance. The amplitude of response to numbers did not decrease appreciably until the recognition threshold was reached, but the size of responses to blank flashes decreased rapidly with diminished luminance. At the same time, no differences were observed in electroretinogram amplitudes, suggesting that peripheral mechanisms were not responsible for the observed effects. In these studies, the *wave shapes* elicited by meaningful stimuli differed from those evoked by nonmeaningful stimuli.

Further evidence for the relation between information about the stimulus and details of contour of the evoked potential wave shape has recently been obtained. Spehlman has shown that presentation of a checkerboard pattern in the visual field causes change in the evoked response wave shape from that usually seen with stimulation by an empty visual field (1965). However, if the subject wears glasses which distort the pattern into a blur, the evoked potential reverts to that elicited by an empty field. This finding is illustrated in Fig. XV-2.

Changes in the size of the squares comprising the checkerboard pattern with no change in over-all black-white ratio resulted in changes in evoked potential wave shape. The results illustrated in Fig. XV-2 make it unlikely that the wave shape change was due to the "greyness" of the pattern.

In recent work, Sutton *et al.* (1965a) have utilized the linearity of interaction of evoked potentials to identify components related to the perceptual, emotional, and cognitive components of response to a stimu-

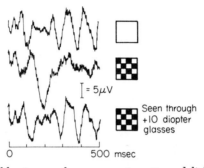

Fig. XV-2. Effect of blurring on the response to patterned light. Each tracing is an average of 100 responses. The subject wears a frame for interchangeable lenses. The first tracing shows the response to diffuse light; the second tracing, the response to patterned light. Note that the wave shape of response to patterned light is markedly different from the response evoked by diffuse light. The third tracing was obtained after lenses of +10 diopters had been interposed so that the pattern could not be perceived. Note the similarity of this with the response to diffuse light. The similarity between the third and first tracing suggests that the presence of pattern or contrast rather than the change in total luminance was the major cause of the wave shape changes seen in the second tracing. [Data from Spehlman (1965).]

lus. Subjects were presented with sequences consisting of single or double clicks in random order. After each stimulus, the subject guessed the nature of the next stimulus, wagering a small amount of money on each guess. Equations of averaged evoked potentials were then constructed to partial out the different components. For example, the average response to "single stimulus guessed right" was subtracted from "single stimulus guessed wrong." This is equivalent to the difference between the *expectancy* of a double and a single stimulus. The resulting wave shape is the response evoked by a click which did *not* occur.

Figure XV-3 shows the results of this operation on three sets of data from the same subject. The first sample was gathered using a random sequence in which the double clicks included an interval of 180 msec between the first and second members of the pair. In the second set, the interval separating the members of a pair was 280 msec, and in the third

405

set it was 380 msec. Note that the difference equation produced 3 wave shapes of identical form, but the latency of the major component successively displaced an amount corresponding to the double click interval. This finding suggests that the brain constructs a facsimile of an expected event at the expected time of occurrence (Sutton *et al.*, 1965b, 1967).

The accuracy of these algebraic manipulations of averaged potentials is shown by Fig. XV-4. These data, from several subjects, permit comparison of derived wave shapes with those obtained more directly. The solid curves were computed as follows: averaged responses evoked by

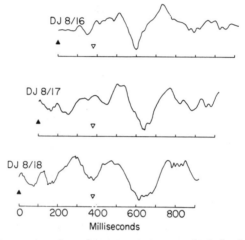

Fig. XV-3. Difference curves from three experiments in which the double click latency was varied. These wave forms were constructed by subtracting the averaged response evoked by a "single click guessed right" from the response to "single click guessed wrong" (i.e., double click was expected). The closed triangle indicates the time at which the first click stimulus occurred; the open triangles indicate the time at which the expected second click did *not* occur. Monopolar recordings, C 3 to left earlobe, 10–20 system. [Data from Sutton, Braren, Zubin and John (1965b).]

"double click guessed right" were added to those evoked by "double click guessed wrong." From this sum the averaged responses to "single clicks guessed right" plus "single clicks guessed wrong" were subtracted. It should be noted that the four constituent averaged responses in this equation were markedly different with respect to wave shape. The dotted curves were obtained by presenting a series of single and double clicks in perfect alternation, thus eliminating effects of uncertainty and error. These results show that derived wave shapes correspond well to more direct measurements.

The experiments which have been described thus far in this section show clearly that affective connotation, contingency, or expectancy influence evoked responses. Changes in the significance of stimuli also alter the evoked potentials. However, these results may relate to significance in the sense of "task-relevance" rather than in the sense of specific meaning. We have conducted a series of experiments investigating the relationship between evoked potential wave shape and the informational content or

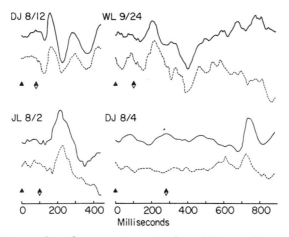

Fig. XV-4. Data are from four experiments in three different subjects. *Solid lines* are wave forms computed by *addition* of averaged responses evoked by "double clicks guessed right" to responses evoked by "double clicks guessed wrong," followed by *subtraction* of "single clicks guessed right" plus "single clicks guessed wrong." The *dotted lines* are difference curves computed by subtracting the responses evoked by single clicks from those evoked by double clicks when both stimuli were presented in regular alternation. Triangles and diamonds indicate the time of occurrence of the first and second clicks. Monopolar recordings, C 3 to left earlobe, 10–20 system. [Data from Sutton *et al.* (1965a).]

meaning of stimuli equated for physical energy. In earlier work we noted that the evoked potential caused by light flashes presented to cats seemed to vary in shape as a function of the content in the visual field of the animal (John and Lowy, 1962). These data were difficult to evaluate with proper psychophysical controls. More recently, we have carried out a series of experiments in human subjects with appropriate controls included (John, Herrington, and Sutton, 1967). In many of these experiments, recordings of eye movement potentials were obtained throughout.

Averaged eye movement potentials revealed no systematic differences which might account for the observations to be described. These observations were not significantly altered when subjects were tested using an artificial pupil following full dilatation with atropine. To rule out possible contributions from movements of the speech musculature related to subverbal or unconscious vocalization, subjects were asked to count the number of stimuli aloud. The use of these precautions did not change the data obtained. In view of these controls, the findings to be reported must be attributed to central mechanisms. The results of these experiments are extremely relevant to this discussion and will be presented in some detail.

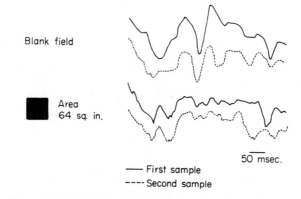

Fig. XV-5. Comparison of averaged responses evoked by weak flash illuminating a blank, white visual field or the same field containing a black square which was 64 square inches in area. Stimuli were presented in blocks of 25, arranged in a Latin square sequence so as to provide two replications for each sample. Each replication consisted of 50 repetitions of the stimulus. In this and subsequent figures, the data were obtained from scalp recordings, monopolar derivation, 3 cm above the inion versus earlobe reference. Analysis epoch was 500 msec.

Figure XV-5 shows the difference between the potentials evoked at a scalp electrode 3 cm above the inion in man by two different stimuli, one consisting of a flash illuminating a blank visual field and the second illuminating a black figure located in the center of the field. In this and all subsequent examples which will be presented, stimuli were presented in a Latin square design so that the response to *each* stimulus was replicated in the same session. This procedure provides an estimate of reproducibility and offers control of factors such as type, recency of stimulation, fatigue, and accommodation.

Figure XV-6 shows the difference between the evoked potentials elicited by a square and a circle, equated for area. The differences in wave shape are obvious.

The stimuli used in the previous figure are physically different, and one might question whether they were really equivalent with respect to

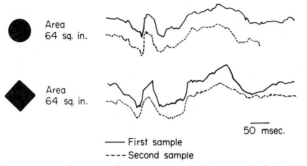

50 msec.

—— First sample
- - - - Second sample

Fig. XV-6. Comparison of averaged response evoked by weak flash illuminating a white visual field containing either a black square or a circle, *equated for area.* Details as in Fig. XV-5 but averages based on 100 repetitions each.

reflectance, area, etc., although the utmost care was exerted to see that this was the case. These questions are unequivocally ruled out by the data shown in Fig. XV-7. These data were elicited by comparing the response

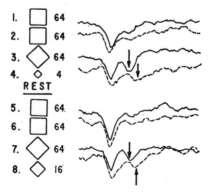

Fig. XV-7. Averaged responses from two sessions with the same subject, separated by 30 minutes. All averages based upon 100 repetitions of the stimulus, and a 500-millisecond analysis epoch. Negative upward. Responses 1, 2, 5, and 6 were to squares with an area of 64 square inches, responses 3 and 7 to diamonds 64 square inches in area, response 4 to a diamond of 4 square inches, and response 8 to a diamond of 16 square inches. Note the new components, marked by the arrows, which appeared in 3 and 7 when the square was rotated 45°. (Data from John, Herrington, and Sutton, 1967).

to a square with the response evoked by *the same stimulus rotated 45° to represent a diamond.* The differences in wave shape caused by the same stimulus in two different perceptual orientations are clear.

Since these data indicated that different wave shapes were evoked by stimuli of different form, the question arose as to whether *particular forms might elicit characteristic evoked response wave shapes.* Figure XV-8 shows the wave shapes produced by two squares of different size, presented in Latin square sequence with two circular stimuli with an area equal to the larger square. The responses to the circle are reproducible and different from the responses to the squares, but *the two squares of different size elicit evoked responses of essentially identical wave shape.*

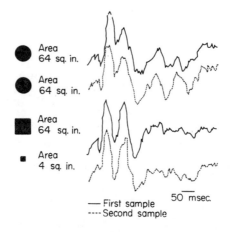

Area 64 sq. in.
Area 64 sq. in.
Area 64 sq. in.
Area 4 sq. in.

50 msec.

— First sample
---- Second sample

Fig. XV-8. Comparison of averaged responses evoked by weak flash illuminating a blank visual field containing either a square or a circle. Stimulus sequence was *large* circle, *large* square, *large* circle, *small* square. Note similarity of response to large and small squares. Each average based upon 200 repetitions.

These data suggest that the visual evoked response caused by a geometric figure may depend upon the form of the figure. These findings are corroborated by the similarity in wave shapes evoked by large and small diamonds in Fig. XV-7. In unpublished work, Herrington and Schneidau (1966) and Ruchkin *et al.* (1966) have observed that the wave shapes resembling those normally evoked by presentation of a particular geometric form can be obtained in response to illumination of an empty visual field *if the subject imagines that the same form is present in the field.*

These results also suggested that the wave shape might be related to the meaning of the stimulus. Therefore, stimuli were constructed consisting of the words "square" and "circle," printed in block letters equated for area to each other and to the area of the corresponding form. Figure XV-9 shows that these two psychophysically equivalent verbal stimuli produce clearly different evoked response wave shapes. It will be extremely interesting to see whether subsequent investigations can successfully demonstrate an invariant aspect to the wave shape of responses evoked in some brain region by presentation of two informationally equivalent visual stimuli, one consisting of a *geometric form* and the other consist-

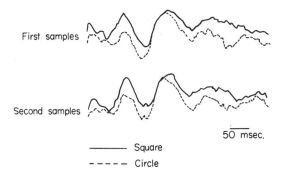

Fig. XV-9. Comparison of averaged responses evoked by weak flash illuminating the word "SQUARE" or "CIRCLE," printed in block letters. Total black area of both words was made equal. Note reproducibility of difference between responses to first samples (top), and second samples (bottom). Each average based upon 100 repetitions.

ing of the *name* for that form. Such invariance should theoretically be demonstrable.

These findings have been repeatedly obtained in twelve subjects. Although the phenomena described are rather labile and vary with the attention and mood of the subject, they are the general rather than the exceptional result of these procedures. The data seem to establish unequivocally that the relationship between wave shape and perceptual content of the stimulus is to be found generally and cannot be considered as a mere laboratory curiosity arising from the peculiar properties of tracer stimuli and frequency labeled rhythms.

The findings discussed in this chapter provide evidence that the processes involved in representation of information by neural systems, reflected in the temporal patterns of recorded electrical activity, are not restricted to information about repetition rates of rhythmic stimuli but may be relevant to other kinds of information as well. These results are compatible with the suggestion that the information content of the activity of a neural ensemble may be specified by the time course of decrease in entropy, and may be reflected in the temporal pattern of the average activity of the ensemble, approximately described by the averaged evoked response.

CHAPTER XVI

CONCLUSIONS

In the first chapter of this book, a set of objections was raised against the proposition that memory consisted of the establishment of a pathway by which specific cells linked brain regions that are receptive to certain inputs and responsible for certain outputs in such a fashion that discharge of the cells in this pathway constituted remembering. We undertook to provide evidence indicating the plausibility of an alternative viewpoint; now that the argument has been constructed, let us summarize its major features.

The initial discussion centers around the problem of the way in which a subset of cells is selected for mediation of the memory of an event from the vast number of neurons which respond to the occurrence of a stimulus. The answer proposed is derived from consolidation phenomena, which indicate that time is required to achieve permanent registration of an experience. Since this period is orders of magnitude longer than the duration of a single response sequence in a neuron, those neurons whose reactivity and connectivity enabled them to maintain an altered discharge rate over a prolonged period following a stimulus were postulated thereby to represent the event.

Maintenance of adequately altered rate for a sufficient time was assumed to effect a shift in the concentration of a critical substance in such a way as to achieve activation of a chemical reaction. The product of that reaction was proposed to act as an effector, which inactivates a repressor substance. In turn, that repressor substance released a previously repressed operator, and nuclear DNA produced a new mRNA. The new mRNA entered the cytoplasm where a new protein was synthesized in consequence. This new protein was postulated as having two modes of

413

action. One function was to assume the role initially played by the effector substance, thus establishing a feedback loop which would thereafter maintain the synthetic cycle. The second function assigned to the new protein was to alter the responsiveness of the cell membrane to particular temporal sequences, possibly by altering ionic mobility.

Characteristic features were predicted for the sustained participation of the representational subset of neurons in the circulation of activity during the consolidation period. These features, determined by the fortuitous distribution of available reentrant path lengths in the network, provided the basis for arguing that the average activity over the whole ensemble should be an oscillation with a characteristic wave shape. The chemical changes during the consolidation period were assumed to alter the participating population so as to achieve an increase in the probability that the ensemble might subsequently enter the same mode of oscillation.

Present knowledge suggests that the pattern of electrical oscillation recorded from a region corresponds to the integrated membrane potentials of vast numbers of neurons. These potentials do not correspond to spike discharges; rather, they influence the probability of spike discharge. The shape of a pattern of oscillation then reflects the probable time course of fluctuation of the average activity in an ensemble of nerve cells. If the population over which the activity is averaged remains of constant size, an increase in the amplitude reflects a probable increase in the coherence of the ensemble. We argued that only departures from baseline coherence levels constituted information for the brain, thus compensating for the unreliability of its components. Stabilization of a particular time sequence of coherence by the processes taking place during consolidation, so that the population is subsequently more likely to enter that mode of oscillation, thus achieves the representation of past information which affected the ensemble.

A salient feature of these various hypotheses, constructed in the first half of this volume, was the expectation that the electrical characteristics of readout of stored information from memory would literally reproduce the wave shape displayed by the responsive neural population during the actual experience. In the second half of this book, a body of psychological and electrophysiological evidence has been presented in order to evaluate the propositions formulated in the first half.

Numerous examples were provided that the occurrence of local coherence in several anatomical regions which were contiguously active sufficed to organize a neuronal system coordinating the subsequent activity of both regions. Studies of the changes in electrical activity of the brain during conditioning were cited to indicate that these changes occurred in widespread anatomical regions. Examination of the details of these changes, both by visual scrutiny of recordings and by mathematical analysis, established evidence that the temporal pattern of coherent activity in various brain regions was initially variable and acquired strikingly similar features in diverse structures as informational significance became attached to the stimulus. Such evidence demonstrates that the shape of local electrical oscillations is not solely determined by local morphology, which indicates that it also reflects a process —the time course of coherent activity in the population.

If the set of active cells at any instant defines the instantaneous state of the network, the time sequence of states after afferent input is a stochastic process describing the propagation of the resulting disturbance in the neural population. A particular wave shape corresponds to a set of transition probabilities for the representational stochastic process. The observation that wave shapes elicited in various brain regions by a conditioned stimulus after informational significance has been achieved become essentially identical is equivalent to the statement that the transition probabilities of the stochastic processes in each of the respective neural populations now follow a common rule. The details of the unitary neuronal processes underlying these similar ensemble modes must differ greatly from region to region.

Viewed in this way, the function which defines the transition probabilities is the information about the event. Therefore, storage of memory about that information consists of storage of the rules determining transition probabilities in the population. Remembering the stored information requires that the population enter a mode of oscillation in which the temporal sequence of states adheres to the specified transition rules.

Studies of the configuration of electrical activity during differential approach-avoidance performance revealed that when discriminative responses were correctly performed, there was a correspondence between the electrical patterns of activity observed in sensory-specific and non-sensory-specific regions. Conversely, when the performed behavior was inappropriate to the stimulus actually presented, this correspondence did not exist.

Data of this sort led to the formulation of a coincidence detector hypothesis and generated a series of attempts to evaluate the functional significance of such patterns of discharge. First of all, it was demonstrated that part of the electrical activity in the nonsensory-specific structures was not to be attributed to sensitization or pseudoconditioning but seemed to be a consequence of the acquisition of informational significance by a stimulus as it was established as the cue controlling adaptive behavior. Second, exploration of the time course of events in the visual cortex by electrical stimulation at various times after the peripheral presentation of information revealed that information processing does not seem to be homogeneously distributed through time. Events which occur relatively late in the evoked potential, at the time that influences from nonsensory-specific structures reach the cortex, appear to be more crucial for information processing than earlier events which arrive from the classical sensory-specific pathways.

The evidence summarized thus far generated the proposition that the temporal sequence of events at a place might comprise information for the brain. The adequacy of temporal patterns of discharge for informational significance was demonstrated by establishing differential performance to two patterns of electrical stimulation, which were constructed from identical pulses and equated for energy but differed in the temporal distribution of energy applied to the same electrodes in the brain. This indicated that the temporal sequence of events at a place could serve as information.

Electrophysiological studies of electrical activity during establishment of conditioned responses to intermittent stimuli using many different animal species, varied behavioral situations, and a wide range of frequencies have revealed that many regions of the brain display electrical rhythms related to the frequency of the tracer stimulus during intertrial intervals in the absence of the stimulus. Such assimilated rhythms are not discernible in the home cage of the animal but appear when he is placed in the training situation. Assimilated rhythms tend to appear in a number of anatomical regions with approximate simultaneity; they appear first, are most marked, and persist longest in nonsensory-specific structures.

Studies of conditioning to intermittent stimulation of the brain revealed that transfer from peripheral stimulation to electrical stimulation of specific sensory pathways of the same modality as the peripheral stimulus could be accomplished with some difficulty. Transfer to electrical stimulation of the mesencephalic reticular formation could be accomplished readily. Using the conditioned frequency, the effects of electrical stimulation of many brain regions were studied after peripheral training to flicker, again after lateral geniculate training, and finally after reticular formation training. These explorations showed little or no generalization after peripheral training, limited generalization confined to specific cortical regions corresponding to the modality of the stimulus after lateral geniculate training, and widespread generalization from many nonsensory-specific regions after reticular training. Generalization was not obtained at this stage by stimulation of other sensory-specific regions. These results indicated widespread participation or distribution of access to the representational system for these previous experiences after reticular training.

The specificity of these effects was demonstrated by the observation that propagation of evoked potentials resulting from electrical stimulation of a given brain structure altered markedly after such stimulation was established as an adequate cue for the performance of the conditioned response. The observed effects cannot be attributed to sensitization or pseudoconditioning, but rather to the informational significance of the stimulus.

Studies of the electrical events during generalization indicated that the electrical activity of various brain regions under those conditions consists of two components. One component can reasonably be attributed to the afferent input of information about the peripheral test stimulus. The second component arises from the release of a mode of oscillation which seems to constitute the readout from memory of the electrical effects of the stimulus which was used during the original training, but which is absent during generalization.

Differences in the polarity of these two components at the cortical level suggest two different anatomical origins for these processes. Further analysis indicates that the result of the joint action of these two processes is to approximate the over-all effect of the original training stimulus in some structures. Evaluation of differences in the characteristics of electrical events observed during correct and incorrect performance to the conditioned stimulus, and comparison with differences observed during generalization and nonresponse to neutral stimuli, indicated that various brain regions may subsume the general functions of transmission, storage, and evaluation of information. Detailed examina-

417

tion of the form and latency of the readout process activated during release of a previously acquired behavior by a neutral stimulus also showed that this process arises with approximate simultaneity and identical form in cortical, thalamic, and mesencephalic regions.

The theoretical discussion of many of the electrophysiological studies in the second half of this book drew inferences about the neural mechanisms involved in information processing from the frequency characteristics observed in the electrical waves recorded from various brain regions during conditioning to various intermittent stimuli. Many reservations might be expressed about the generality of such findings. Since information in the environment is not normally presented as a periodic train of stimuli, the usual processing of information in the brain might well not involve temporal patterns. However, the mathematical demonstration of the emergence of similar wave shapes in various anatomical regions after conditioning, the observation that evoked potential shapes are determined more by the transmitting than the receiving region, and the evidence that evoked potential shapes can reflect various attributes of peripheral stimuli indicate that these inferences may be more generally applicable. Temporal patterns of electrical activity in the brain are evidently relevant to other stimulus parameters than merely the repetition rate of tracer conditioned stimuli.

In the foregoing chapters, a mass of evidence from diverse kinds of experiments has been gathered, and a set of logical propositions has been formulated. In the face of this body of fact and logic, it seems reasonable to conclude that learned behaviors are mediated by systems which are anatomically extensive and involve many brain regions. In view of the widespread participation suggested by the evidence, it seems unlikely that any one structure, or set of neurons therein, is uniquely responsible for the storage of memory about a specific experience. The evidence argues against the proposition that memory is stored as a requirement that a specific set of cells must discharge when a familiar event occurs, or that remembering that event demands the deterministic discharge of a specific set of cells. It does not seem likely that the discharge of a given set of cells is either a necessary or sufficient condition for the activation of a particular memory.

One cannot insist that the conception of the engram as a discrete entity localized to specific cells has been decisively refuted by the arguments presented. The counter arguments involve several assumptions which remain incompletely validated, particularly the hypothesis that the

418

temporal pattern of electrical events in a region actually *represents* the processing of information rather than constitutes a nonfunctional correlate to the actual mechanisms of informational analysis. Although appreciable evidence has been cited to support this hypothesis, it cannot be accepted as conclusively established.

Yet the body of evidence gathered here is sufficiently substantial to warrant the assertion that a plausible alternative to the deterministic concept has been formulated. Numerous additional experiments will be required to establish the correctness of one or another of these alternatives. However, the methods affording the performance of these experiments have been fashioned and the answers will, in time, be forthcoming. Perhaps the correct formulation will involve features of both of these suggested conceptions.

The salient feature of the model suggested in this book is that information in the nervous system is conceived of, not as the deterministic discharge of certain coded cells which "stand for" an item of information, but as the spatiotemporal patterns of organization in enormous aggregates of neurons. The activity or absence of activity of any particular cell is of itself not informative. Information is the time course of coherence, or the time course of deviation from random or baseline activity in extensive neural populations. In this view, information is a statistical property of the neural aggregate. The information content of the neuronal masses of the brain at any moment is the full set of nonrandom coherent activities occurring in these multiple populations.

The fact that computed difference wave shapes appear simultaneously and with the same form in the cortical mantle, the thalamus, and the brain stem when memories are remembered is a remarkable observation. To which of these levels should we attribute the conscious experience of the remembered events? We assume that the generalizing or discriminating experimental animal subjectively experiences the memories whose readout we observe electrically. Even if we choose to attribute the consciousness of remembering to some one of the regions displaying simultaneous and identical readout processes, to what mechanism in that crucial experiencing region shall we ascribe the mediation of the subjective experience? Is it plausible to attribute the activity to an "ultimate pontifical neuron?"

The information content of the remembered event has been postulated to be represented by the time course of the decreases of entropy in the neuronal population. The contribution of any cell in the region is

419

presumed to be important only insofar as it contributes to the statistical occurrence of coherence. Furthermore, the content of the remembered experience is not stipulated by the state of the population at any instant, but by the particular temporal sequence of states defined by the relevant transition probabilities. Since the information content of the brain during a given time interval is viewed as the sequence of organized states, the content of subjective awareness during that time, derived from the information content, must be specified by the same sequence of order or nonrandomness in the constituent neural populations. Since the activity of any single cell is of informational significance presumably only insofar as it contributes to these statistical processes, one cannot reasonably ascribe awareness of the statistical processes to any cell.

If one accepts these statistical propositions about information processing in the brain, the conclusion seems inescapable that the experiential content of subjective consciousness also arises from the appearance of organized sequences of state in huge populations. Restated, subjective experience would appear to be a consequence of the emergence of order in the organization of the activity of vast neural aggregates. Subjective experience cannot be attributed to the activity of particular cells whose function is to mediate the content of consciousness, but must be a property of the organized aggregates themselves.

In this view, the experienced constancy of the self, the apparent simultaneity of the rich texture of sensations, the continuity of purpose and meaning in life itself, must arise from statistical processes with certain invariant characteristics, arising in aggregates of millions of neurons. How the occurrence of order in an aggregate of neurons might generate the subjective experience of awareness is a fascinating problem. The physical processes mediating such unexpected properties arising from order in an aggregate, or the organization of energy in a volume of tissue, cannot presently be imagined. That the properties of aggregates cannot always be predicted from study of the individual components is an old truth in science.

Rejection of these speculations on the basis that we know of no mechanisms at present which could accomplish the sensing of its own state by an aggregate would display an immoderate respect for our present level of knowledge. We are ignorant of how the mind arises from the brain. The answer to that riddle is the most challenging unsolved problem for science.

REFERENCES AND AUTHOR INDEX

[Numbers in brackets following each entry indicate the pages on which it is cited.]

ABRAMS, R. (1961). Nucleic acid metabolism and biosynthesis. *Ann. Rev. Biochem.* **30,** 165–188. [126]

ADAM, G., ADEY, W. R., and PORTER, R. W. (1966). Interoceptive conditional response in cortical neurones. *Nature* **209,** 920–921. [257]

ADAMETZ, J. H. (1959). Rate of recovery of functioning in cats with rostral reticular lesions. *J. Neurosurg.* **16,** 85–97. [5]

ADEY, W. R. (1963). Discussion. *In* "Brain Function," (M. A. B. Brazier), Vol. 1, pp. 154–155. Univ. of California Press, Berkeley, California. [237]

ADEY, W. R., DUNLOP, C. W., and HENDRIX, M. S. (1960). Hippocampal slow waves: distribution and phase relationships in the course of approach learning. *Arch. Neurol.* **3,** 74–90. [245]

ADRIAN, E. D., and MATTHEWS, B. H. C. (1934). The interpretation of potential waves in the cortex. *J. Physiol. (London)* **81,** 440. [224]

AGRANOFF, B. W., and KLINGER, P. D. (1964). Puromycin effect on memory fixation in the goldfish. *Science* **146,** 952. [121]

AGRANOFF, B. W., DAVIS, R. E., and BRINK, J. J. (1965). Memory fixation in the goldfish. *Proc. Natl. Acad. Sci. U.S.* **54,** 788–793. [121]

AHMED, Y. Y., and McKENZIE, J. (1963). Changes in the motor neurones after administering muscle relaxant and convulsant drugs. *Nature* **199,** 385–386. [107]

ALBERT, D. J. (1966a). The effect of spreading depression on the consolidation of learning. *Neuropsychologia* **4,** 49–64. [35, 36, 116]

ALBERT, D. J. (1966b). The effects of polarizing currents on the consolidation of learning. *Neuropsychologia* **4,** 65–77. [35, 37, 190]

ALBERT, D. J. (1966c). Memory in mammals: evidence for a system involving nuclear ribonucleic acid. *Neuropsychologia* **4,** 79–92. [35, 116]

ALTMAN, J., and CHOROVER, S. L. (1963). Autoradiographic investigation of the distribution and utilization of intraventricularly injected adenine-^{3}H, uracil-^{3}H and thymidine-^{3}H in the brains of cats. *J. Physiol. (London)* **169,** 770–779. [153]

ALTMAN, J., and DAS, G. D. (1966). Autoradiographic study of the effects of enriched environment on the rate of glial multiplication in the adult rat brain. In press. [43]

AMASSIAN, V. E. (1961). Microelectrode studies of the cerebral cortex. *Intern. Rev. Neurobiol.* **3,** 67–136. [225]

AMOS, H., and MOORE, M. D. (1963). Influence of bacterial ribonucleic acid on animal cells in culture. *Exptl. Cell Res.* **32,** 1–13. [118]

421

References

ANDERSSON, B., and WYRWICKA, W. (1957). The elicitation of a drinking motor conditioned reflex by electrical stimulation of the hypothalamic "drinking area" in the goat. *Acta Psychol. Scand.* **41,** 194–198. [328]

ANOKHIN, P. K. (1960). On the specific action of the reticular formation on the cerebral cortex. *Moscow Colloq. Electroencephalog. Higher Nervous Activity. Electroencephalog. Clin. Neurophysiol. Suppl.* **13,** 257–267. [71]

ANOKHIN, P. K. (1961). Electroencephalographic analysis of cortico-subcortical relations in positive and negative conditioned reactions. *Ann. N.Y. Acad. Sci.* **92,** 899–938. [71]

ARDUINI, A. (1958). Enduring potential changes evoked in the cerebral cortex by stimulation of brain stem reticular formation and thalamus. *In* "Reticular Formation of the Brain," (H. H. Jasper *et al.,* eds.), pp. 333–351. Little, Brown, Boston, Massachusetts. [185]

ARVANITAKI, A. (1942). Effects evoked in an axon by the activity of a contiguous one. *J. Neurophysiol.* **5,** 89–108. [171]

ASHBY, W. R. (1960). "Design for a Brain." Wiley, New York. [17, 88]

ASRATYAN, E. A. (1961). The initiation and localization of cortical inhibition in the conditioned arc. *Ann. N.Y. Acad. Sci.* **92,** 1141–1159. [70]

ASRATYAN, E. A. (1965). Changes in the functional state and pattern of electrical activity in cortical areas involved in the establishment of conditioned connection. *Proc. 23rd Intern. Congr., Intern. Union Phys. Sci., Tokyo, 1965,* Vol. IV, pp. 629–636. [366]

BABICH, F. R., JACOBSON, A. L., BUBASH, S., and JACOBSON, A. (1965a). Transfer of a response to naive rats by injection of ribonucleic acid extracted from trained rats. *Science* **149,** 656–657. [113]

BABICH, F. R., JACOBSON, A. L., and BUBASH, S. (1965b). Cross-species transfer of learning: effect of ribonucleic acid from hamsters on rat behavior. *Proc. Natl. Acad. Sci. U.S.* **54,** 1299–1302. [116]

BAER, A. (1905). Uber Gleichzeitige Electrische Reizung zweier Grosshirnstellen am Ungehemmten Hunde. *Arch. Ges. Physiol. Pflügers* **106,** 523–567. [180, 181]

BALDWIN, B. A., and SOLTYSIK, S. S. (1965). Acquisition of classical conditioned defensive responses in goats subjected to cerebral ischaemia. *Nature* **206,** 1011–1013. [21]

BARLOW, J. S., MORRELL, L., and MORRELL, F. (1965). Some observations on evoked responses in relation to temporal conditioning to paired stimuli in man. *Proc. Intern. Colloq. Mechanisms Orienting Reaction Man, Smolenici and Bratislava, Czechoslovakia.* In press. [354]

BARNES, C. D., and KATZUNG, B. G. (1963). Stimulus polarity and conditioning in planaria. *Science* **141,** 728–730. [100]

BARONDES, S. H., and COHEN, H. D. (1966). Puromycin effect on successive phases of memory storage. *Science* **151,** 594–595. [121, 124]

BARONDES, S. H., and COHEN, M. E. (1967). *Brain Research.* In press. [124]

BARONDES, S. H., and JARVIK, M. E. (1964). The influence of actinomycin-D on brain RNA synthesis and on memory. *J. Neurochem.* **11,** 187–195. [122]

BARTLETT, F., and JOHN, E. R. (1963). Unpublished observations. [84]

BECK, E. C., and DOTY, R. W. (1957). Conditioned flexion reflexes acquired during combined catalepsy and de-efferentation. *J. Comp. Physiol. Psychol.* **50,** 211–216. [194]

BEGLEITER, H., GROSS, M. M., and KISSIN, B. (1965). Evoked cortical responses to affective visual stimuli. *J. Psychophysiol.* In press. [403]

BENJAMIN, F. B., ANASTASI, J. N., and HELVEY, W. M. (1961). The effect of stressor agents on potassium release of rat brain. *Federation Proc.* **20**, 342. [54]

BEURLE, R. L. (1957). Properties of a mass of cells capable of regenerating pulses. *Phil. Trans. Roy. Soc. London* **B240**, 669, 55. [17]

BICKFORD, R. G., JACOBSON, J. L., CADY, D., and THANE, R. (1964). Nature of average evoked potentials to sound and other stimuli in man. *Ann. N.Y. Acad. Sci.* **112**(1), 204–223. [400]

BINDMAN, L. J. (1965). Long lasting changes in firing frequency of neurones in rat cerebral cortex and radial potential gradients. *J. Physiol. (London)* **179**, 14. [229]

BINDMAN, L. J., LIPPOLD, C. J., and REDFEARN, J. W. T. (1962a). The nonselective blocking action of γ-amino-butyric acid on the sensory cerebral cortex of the rat. *J. Physiol. (London)* **162**, 105–120. [185]

BINDMAN, L. J., LIPPOLD, C. J., and REDFEARN, J. W. T. (1962b). Long-lasting changes in the level of the electrical activity of the cerebral cortex produced by polarizing currents. *Nature* **196**, 584. [229]

BINDRA, D. (1959). Stimulus change reactions to novelty and response decrement. *Psychol. Rev.* **66**, 96–103. [68]

BISHOP, G. H., and O'LEARY, J. L. (1950). The effects of polarizing currents on cell potentials and their significance in the interpretation of central nervous system activity. *Electroencephalog. Clin. Neurophysiol.* **2**, 401–416. [48, 184]

BLOCH, S., and SILVA, A. (1959). Factors involved in the acquisition of a maze habit, analysis by means of tranquilizing and sedative drugs. *J. Comp. Physiol. Psychol.* **52**, 550–554. [73]

BLOCK, J. B., and ESSMAN, W. B. (1965). Growth hormone administration during pregnancy: a behavioral difference in offspring rats. *Nature* **205**, 1136–1137. [44]

BONEAU, C. A. (1960). The effects of violations of assumptions underlying the t-test. *Psychol. Bull.* **57**, 49–64. [365]

BORING, E. G. (1933). "The Physical Dimensions of Consciousness." Appleton, New York. [166]

BRATTGÅRD, S. O. (1952). RNA increase in ganglion cells of retina after stimulation by light. *Acta Radiol. Suppl.* **96**, 80. [95]

BRAZIER, M. A. B. (1961). Introductory Comments. *Electroencephalog. Clin. Neurophysiol. Suppl.* **20**, 2–6. [333]

BREEN, R. A., and McGAUGH, J. L. (1961). Facilitation of maze learning with posttrial injections of picrotoxin. *J. Comp. Physiol. Psychol.* **54**, 498–501. [46]

BRIGGS, M. H., and KITTO, G. B. (1962). The molecular basis of memory and learning. *Psychol. Rev.* **69**, 537–541. [126, 151]

BRINK, J. J., and AGRANOFF, B. W. (1966). Effects of puromycin, acetoxycycloheximide and actinomycin-D on protein synthesis in goldfish brain. *Federation Proc.* **25**, 2098. [121]

BRINLEY, F. J., JR., KANDEL, E. R., and MARSHALL, W. H. (1960). Potassium outflow from rabbit cortex during spreading depression. *J. Neurophysiol.* **23**, 246–256. [49]

BROOKHART, J., ARDUINI, A., MANCIA, M., and MORUZZI, G. (1958). Thalamocortical relations as revealed by induced slow potential changes. *J. Neurophysiol.* **21**, 499–525. [185]

BROWN-SEQUARD, C. E. (1884). Existence de l'excitabilité motrice et de l'excitabilité inhibitoire dans les regions occipitales et sphenoidales de l'écorce cérébrale. *Compt. Rend. Mem. Soc. Biol. 8ᵉ Ser., Pt. 1* **36**, 301–303. [180]

BUCHWALD, J. S., HALAS, E. S., and SCHRAMM, S. (1965a). Changes in subcortical

References

and cortical unit activity during conditioning in chronic cats. *Federation Proc.*
24, 522. [257]

BUCHWALD, J. S., HALAS, E. S., and SCHRAMM, S. (1965b). Progressive changes in
efferent unit responses to repeated cutaneous stimulation in spinal cats. *J. Neuro-physiol.* **28**, 200–215. [257]

BUCHWALD, N. A., and HULL, C. D. (1966). Induction of unit inhibition and spind-
ling by stimulation of the lateral geniculate body. *Federation Proc. Abstr.* **25**,
105. [263]

BURCH, N. R. (1959). Automatic analysis of the EEG: a review and classification of
systems. *Electroencephalog. Clin. Neurophysiol.* **11**, 827. [333]

BUREŠ, J. (1959). Reversible decortication and behavior. *In* "The Central Nervous
System and Behavior" (M. A. B. Brazier, ed.), pp. 207–248. Josiah Macy, Jr.,
Found., New York. [25, 26]

BUREŠ, J. (1965). Discussion. *In* "Anatomy of Memory" (D. P. Kimble, ed.), pp. 49–
51. Science and Behavior Books, Inc., Palo Alto, 1965. [257]

BUREŠ, J., and BUREŠOVÁ, O. (1965). Plasticity at the single neuron level. *Proc. 23rd
Intern. Physiol. Congr., Tokyo, 1965* **IV**, 359–364. [25, 257]

BUREŠ, J., BUREŠOVÁ, O., and ZÁHOROVA, A. (1958). Conditioned reflexes and Leão's
spreading depression. *J. Comp. Physiol. Psychol.* **51**, 263–268. [245]

BUREŠ, J., BUREŠOVÁ, O., and WEISS, T. (1960a). Functional consequences of hippocampal spreading depression. *Physiol. Bohemoslov.* **9**, 219–227. [22]

BUREŠ, J., PETRÁŇ, M., and ZACHAR, J., eds. (1960b). "Electrophysiological Methods
in Biological Research." Academic Press, New York. [224]

BUREŠ, J., BUREŠOVÁ, O., WEISS, T., and FIFKOVÁ, E. (1963). Excitability changes in
non-specific thalamic nuclei during cortical spreading depression in the rat.
Electroencephalog. Clin. Neurophysiol. **15**, 73–83. [25]

BUREŠOVÁ, O., BUREŠ, J., and FIFKOVÁ, E. (1962a). Analysis of the effects of cortical
spreading depression on the activity of reticular neurones. *Physiol. Bohemoslov.*
11, 375–382. [25]

BUREŠOVÁ, O., RUDIGER, W., BUREŠ, J., and FIFKOVÁ, E. (1962b). The role of the
hypothalamic drinking centre in unconditioned and conditioned control of water
intake. *Physiol. Bohemoslov.* **11**, 492–496. [25]

BURKHALTER, A. (1963). Effect of puromycin on cholinesterase activity of embryonic
chick intestine in organ culture. *Nature* **199**, 598. [123]

BURNS, B. D. (1954). The production of afterbursts in isolated unanesthetized cerebral
cortex. *J. Physiol. (London)* **125**, 427–446. [28]

BURNS, B. D. (1958). "The Mammalian Cerebral Cortex." Arnold, London. [28]

BURNS, B. D., and MOGENSON, G. (1958). Effects of cortical stimulation on habit
acquisition. *Can. J. Psychol.* **12**, 77–82. [23]

BURNS, B. D., and PRITCHARD, R. (1964). Contrast discrimination by neurones in the
cat's visual cerebral cortex. *J. Physiol. (London)* **175**, 445–463. [13]

BURNS, B. D., and SMITH, G. K. (1962). Transmission of information in the unanesthetized cat's isolated forebrain. *J. Physiol. (London)* **164**, 238–251. [13]

BURNS, B. D., HERON, W., and GRAFSTEIN, B. (1960). Response of cerebral cortex to
diffuse monocular and binocular stimulation. *Am. J. Physiol.* **198**, 200–204. [5, 13]

BUSH, R. R., and MOSTELLER, F. (1955). "Stochastic Models for Learning." Wiley,
New York. [211]

BYRNE, W. L., and SAMUEL, D. (1966). Behavioral modification by injection of brain
extract prepared from a trained donor. *Science* **154**, 418. [114]

BYRNE, W. L., SAMUEL, D., BENNETT, E. L., ROSENZWEIG, M. R., WASSERMAN, E.,

WAGNER, A. R., GARDNER, F., GALAMBOS, R., BERGER, B. D., MARGULES, D. L., FENICHEL, R. L., STEIN, L., CORSON, J. A., ENESCO, H. E., CHOROVER, S. L., HOLT, C. E. III, SCHILLER, P. H., CHIAPPETTA, L., JARVIK, M. E., LEAF, R. C., DUTCHER, J. D., HOROVITZ, Z. P., CARLSON, P. L. (1966). Memory transfer *Science* **153**, 658. [114]

CALLAWAY, E., JONES, R. T., and LAYNE, R. S. (1965). Evoked responses and segmental set of schizophrenia. *Arch. Gen. Psychiat.* **12**, 83–89. [401]

CALVET, J., CALVET, M. C., and SCHERRER, J. (1964). Étude stratigraphique corticale de l'activité EEG spontanée. *Electroencephalog. Clin. Neurophysiol.* **17**, 109–125. [230]

CAMERON, D. E., and SOLYOM, L. (1961). Effects of RNA on memory. *Geriatrics* **16**, 74–81. [108]

CARLINI, G. R. S., and CARLINI, E. A. (1965). Effects of strychnine and cannabis satira (marijuana) on the nucleic acid content in brain of the rat. *Med. Pharmacol. Exptl.* **12**, 21–26. [107]

CARSON, R. C. (1957). The effect of electroconvulsive shock on a learned avoidance response. *J. Comp. Physiol. Psychol.* **50**, 125–129. [70]

CASE, T. J., and FUNDERBUNK, W. H. (1947). An effect of curare on the central nervous system. *Trans. Am. Neurol. Assoc.* **72**, 195–196. [69]

CASPERS, H. (1959). The relations between dendrite potential and direct voltage on the cerebral cortex. *Arch. Ges. Physiol. Pflügers* **269**, 157. [185, 227]

CERF, J., and OTIS, L. S. (1957). Heat narcosis and its effect on retention of a learned behavior in the goldfish. *Federation Proc.* **16**, 20–21. Abstr. [21]

CHAMBERLAIN, T. J., HALICK, P., and GERARD, R. W. (1963). Fixation of experience in the rat spinal cord. *J. Neurophysiol.* **26**, 662–673. [106]

CHANG, H. T. Quoted by Gershuni, G. V. (1959). *Intern. Colloq. Electroencephalog. Higher Nervous Activity Sechenov Physiol. J. USSR (English Transl.)* **45**, 189–199. [208]

CHAPMAN, R. M., and BRAGDON, H. R. (1964). Evoked responses to numerical and non-numerical visual stimuli while problem solving. *Nature* **203**, 1155–1157. [404]

CHEVALIER, J. A. (1965). *J. Comp. Physiol. Psychol.* **59**, 125–127. [20]

CHOROVER, S. L., and SCHILLER, P. H. (1965). Short-term retrograde amnesia in rats. *J. Comp. Physiol. Psychol.* **59**, 73–78. [19]

CHOW, K. L. (1961). Brain functions. *Ann. Rev. Psychol.* **12**, 281–310. [5]

CHOW, K. L. (1964). Bioelectrical activity of isolated cortex. III. Conditioned electrographic responses in chronically isolated cortex. *Neuropsychologia* **2**, 175–187. [188, 246, 302]

CHOW, K. L., and DEWSON, J. (1963). Unpublished observations quoted by Morrell, F. (1963). *In* "Information Storage and Neural Control" (W. S. Fields and W. Abbott, eds.), p. 189. Thomas, Springfield, Illinois. [187, 302]

CHOW, K. L., and DEWSON, J. (1964). Bioelectrical activity of isolated cortex. I. Responses induced by interaction of low and high-frequency electrical stimulation. *Neuropsychologia* **2**, 153–165. [188, 246, 303]

CHOW, K. L., and HUTT, P. J. (1953). The "association cortex" of *Macaca mulatta*: a review of recent contributions to its anatomy and functions. *Brain* **76**, 625–677. [161]

CHOW, K. L., and JOHN, E. R. (1958). Effects of intracerebral injection of anticholinesterase drugs on behavior in rats. *Science* **128**, 781–782. [42, 88]

CHOW, K. L., and JOHN, E. R. (1965). Unpublished observations. [191, 192]

425

References

CHOW, K. L., and RANDALL, W. (1964). Learning and retention in cats with lesions in reticular formation. *Psychonomic Sci.* **1**, 259–260. [5]

CHOW, K. L., and SURVISE, J. (1958). Retention of overlearned visual habit after temporal cortical ablation in monkey. *Arch. Neurol. Psychiat.* **79**, 640–646. [163]

CHOW, K. L., BLUM, J. S., and BLUM, R. A. (1950). Cell ratios in the thalamocortical visual system of macaca mulatta. *J. Comp. Neurol.* **92**, 227–240. [30]

CHOW, K. L., DEMENT, W. C., and JOHN, E. R. (1957). Conditioned electrocortico-graphic potentials and behavioral avoidance response in cat. *J. Neurophysiol.* **20**, 482–493. [309]

CHOW, K. L., GOLLANDER, M., and LINDSLEY, D. F. (1966a). Functional plasticity of lateral geniculate neurons in cats. In preparation. [264]

CHOW, K. L., RANDALL, W., and MORRELL, F. (1966b). Effects of brain lesions on conditioned cortical electropotentials. *Electroencephalog. Clin. Neurophysiol.* **20**, 357–369. [301]

CHRISTENSON, J., FENG, V. S. L., POLLEY, E., and WASE, A. W. (1958). Influence of chlorpromazine on transport of ions into cerebral tissues. *Federation Proc.* **17**, 358. [90]

CICARDO, V. H., and TORINO, A. (1942). Release of potassium by the brain of the dog during electrical stimulation. *Science* **95**, 625. [49]

CLENDINNEN, B. G., and EAYRS, J. T. (1961). The anatomical and physiological effects of prenatally administered somatotrophin on cerebral development in rats. *J. Endocrinol.* **22**, 183–193. [44]

CLYNES, M. (1965). Brain space analysis of evoked potential components applied to chromaticity waves. *Proc. 6th Intern. Conf. Med. Electron. Biol. Eng., Tokyo.* [400, 401]

COHEN, E. P., and PARKS, J. J. (1964). Antibody production by non-immune spleen cells incubated with RNA from immunized mice. *Science* **144**, 1012–1013. [118]

COHEN, H. D., and BARONDES, S. H. (1966). *J. Neurochem.* In press. [122]

COHEN, H. D., ERVIN, F., and BARONDES, S. H. (1966). Puromycin and cyclohex-imide: Different effects on hippocampal electrical activity. *Science* **154**, 1557–1558. [124]

COLFER, H. F., and ESSEX, H. E. (1947). Distribution of total electrolytes, K and Na in the cerebral cortex in relation to experimental convulsions. *Am. J. Physiol.* **150**, 27. [49]

CONWAY, T. W. (1964). On the role of ammonium or potassium ion in amino acid polymerization. *Proc. Natl. Acad. Sci. U.S.* **51**, 1216–1220. [142]

COOK, L., DAVIDSON, A. B., DAVIS, D. J., GREEN, H., and FELLOWS, E. J. (1963). Ribonucleic acid: effect on conditioned behavior in rats. *Science* **141**, 268–269. [109]

COONS, E. E., and MILLER, N. E. (1960). Conflict versus consolidation of memory traces to explain "retrograde amnesia" produced by ECS. *J. Comp. Physiol. Psychol.* **53**, 524–531. [20]

CORDEAU, J. P., and MAHUT, H. (1964). Some long-term effects of temporal lobe resections on auditory and visual discrimination in monkeys. *Brain* **87**, 177–190. [22]

CORLEY, K. (1963). Ph.D. Thesis, Univ. of Rochester, Rochester, New York. [249, 276, 277]

CORNING, W. C. (1966). Retention of a position discrimination after regeneration in planarians. *Psychonomic Sci.* **5**, 17–18. [104]

CORNING, W. C., and FREED, S. (1963). Unpublished observations. [97]

CORNING, W. C., and JOHN, E. R. (1961). Effect of ribonuclease on retention of response in regenerated planarians. *Science* **134**, 1363–1365. [103]

CORSON, J. A. (1966). Personal communication. [8]

CORSON, J. A., and ENESCO, H. E. (1966). Some effects of exogenous RNA on rats. Unpublished ms. [109]

CRAMER, H. (1954). "Mathematical Methods of Statistics." Princeton Univ. Press, Princeton, New Jersey. [337]

CREUTZFELDT, O., and JUNG, R. (1961). Neuronal discharge in the cat's motor cortex during sleep and arousal. *In* "The Nature of Sleep" (G. E. W. Wolstenholme and M. O'Connor, eds.), pp. 131–170. Churchill, London. [234]

CREUTZFELDT, O. D., FROMM, G. H., and KAPP, H. (1962). Influence of transcortical DC currents on cortical neuronal activity. *Exptl. Neurol.* **5**, 436–452. [229]

CREUTZFELDT, O. D., WATANABE, S., and LUX, H. D. (1966a). Relations between EEG phenomena and potentials of single cortical cells. I. Evoked responses after thalamic and epicortical stimulation. *Electroencephalog. Clin. Neurophysiol.* **20**, 1–18. [230]

CREUTZFELDT, O. D., WATANABE, S., and LUX, H. D. (1966b). Relations between EEG phenomena and potentials of single cortical cells. II. Spontaneous and convulsoid activity. *Electroencephalog. Clin. Neurophysiol.* **20**, 19–37. [229, 230]

CUENOD, M., METZGER, H. P., GRYNBAUM, A., and WAELSCH, H. (1966). Effect of conditioning on tritium uptake into brain protein of each hemisphere of the split-brain monkey. *Federation Proc.* **25**, 2964. [120]

CURTIS, D. R. (1963). The pharmacology of central and peripheral inhibition. *Pharmacol. Rev.* **15**, 333–363. [226]

DATTA, R. K., and GHOSH, J. J. (1964). Effect of strychnine sulphate and nialimide on hydrogen-bonded structure of ribonucleic acid on brain cortex ribosomes. *J. Neurochem.* **11**, 357–366. [107]

DAVIS, H. (1964). Enhancement of evoked cortical potentials in humans related to a task requiring a decision. *Science* **145**, 182–183. [401]

DAVIS, R. E., and AGRANOFF, B. W. (1966). Stages for memory formation in goldfish: evidence for an environmental trigger. *Proc. Natl. Acad. Sci. U.S.* **55**, 555–559. [121]

DAWSON, G. D. (1947). Cerebral responses to electrical stimulation of peripheral nerve in man. *J. Neurol. Neurosurg. Psychiat.* **10**, 134–140. [399]

DEUTSCH, J. A., HAMBURG, M. D., and DAHL, H. (1966). Anticholinesterase-induced amnesia and its temporal aspects. *Science* **151**, 221–222. [123]

DEWSON, J. H., III, CHOW, K. L., and ENGEL, J., JR. (1964). Bioelectrical activity of isolated cortex. II. steady potentials and induced surface-negative cortical responses. *Neuropsychologia* **2**, 167–174. [188, 246]

DIAMOND, I. T., and CHOW, K. L. (1962). Biological psychology. *In* "Psychology: A Study of a Science" (S. Koch, ed.), Vol. 4, pp. 158–241. McGraw-Hill, New York. [159]

DI GIORGIO, A. M. (1929). Persistenza nell'animale spinale di assimetrie posturali e motorie di origine cerebellare. Nota I. *Arch. Fisiol.* **27**, 518–542. Quoted in Chamberlain, T. J. (1961). Fixation of experience in the rat spinal cord. M.S. Thesis, Univ. of Michigan, Ann Arbor, Michigan. [106]

DINGMAN, W., and SPORN, M. B. (1961). The incorporation of 8-azaguanine into rat brain RNA and its effect on maze learning by the rat. *J. Psychiat. Res.* **1**, 1–11. [105]

References

Domino, E., Matsuoka, S., Waltz, J., and Cooper, I. (1964). Simultaneous recordings of scalp and epidural somatosensory evoked response in man. *Science* **145**, 1199–1200. [400]

Donchin, E., and Lindsley, D. B. (1965). Visually evoked response correlates of perceptual masking and enhancement. *Electroencephalog. Clin. Neurophysiol.* **19**, 325–335. [400, 402]

Doty, R. W. (1958). Potentials evoked in cat cerebral cortex by diffuse and by punctiform photic stimuli. *J. Neurophysiol.* **21**, 437–464. [5, 262]

Doty, R. W. (1965). Conditioned reflexes elicited by electrical stimulation of the brain in macaques. *J. Neurophysiol.* **28**, 623–640. [347]

Doty, R. W., and Giurgea, C. (1958). Conditioned reflexes established by coupling visual and motor cortex stimulation. *Physiologist* **1**, 17. [193]

Doty, R. W., Rutledge, L., and Larsen, R. M. (1956). Conditioned reflexes established to electrical stimulation of cat cerebral cortex. *J. Neurophysiol.* **19**, 401–415, also personal communications. [193, 194]

Drachman, D. A., and Ommaya, A. K. (1964). Memory and the hippocampal complex. *Arch. Neurol.* **10**, 411–425. [22]

Duncan, C. P. (1949). The retroactive effect of electroshock on learning. *J. Comp. Physiol. Psychol.* **42**, 32–44. [20]

Durup, G., and Fessard, A. (1935). L'électroencéphalogramme de l'homme. *Annee Psychol.* **36**, 1–32. [243, 244, 274]

Eccles, J. C. (1962). Spinal neurones: Synaptic connexions in relation to chemical transmitters and pharmacological responses. *In* "A Symposium on Pharmacological Analysis of Central Nervous System Action" (W. D. M. Paton, ed.), Macmillan (Pergamon), New York. [47]

Eccles, J. C. (1964). "The Physiology of Synapses." Springer, Berlin. [154, 225, 257]

Eccles, J. C. (1965). Possible ways in which synaptic mechanisms participate in learning, remembering, and forgetting. *In* "Anatomy of Memory" (D. P. Kimble, ed.), pp. 12–87. Sci. Behavior Books, Palo Alto, California. [65, 154, 257]

Eiduson, S., Geller, E., and Beckwith, W. (1961). Some biochemical correlates of imprinting. *Federation Proc.* **20**, 345. [97]

Eisenstein, E. M., and Cohen, M. J. (1964). Learning in a single insect ganglion. *Physiologist* **7**, 123. [261]

Elkes, J. (1964). Unpublished lecture at N.Y. Acad. Med. [152]

Elul, R. (1962). Dipoles of spontaneous activity in the cerebral cortex. *Exptl. Neurol.* **6**, 285. [230]

Elul, R. (1966a). Dependence of synaptic transmission on protein metabolism of nerve cells—a possible electrokinetic mechanism of learning. *Nature* **210**, 1127. [150]

Elul, R. (1966b). Brain waves: intracellular recording and statistical analysis help clarifying their physiological significance. Unpublished manuscript. [230]

Epstein, W. (1964). Experimental investigations of the genesis of visual space perception. *Psychol. Bull.* **61**, 115–128. [43]

Erlanger, J. (1939). The initiation of impulses in axons. *J. Neurophysiol.* **2**, 370–379. [171]

Essman, W. B. (1965). Facilitation of memory consolidation by chemically induced acceleration of RNA synthesis. *Abstr. 23rd Intern. Congr. Physiol. Sci., Tokyo* p. 470. [106]

Essman, W. B. (1966). Effect of tricyanoaminopropene on the amnesic effect of electroconvulsive shock *Psychopharmacologia* **9**, 426–433. [106]

ESSMAN, W. B., and JARVIK, M. E. (1961). Impairment of retention for a conditioned response by ether anesthesia in mice. *Psychopharmacologia* **2**, 172. [21]

ESSMAN, W. B., and LEHRER, G. M. (1966). Is there a chemical transfer of training. *Federation Proc.* **25**, 208. [116]

ESTES, W. K. (1955). Statistical theory of distributional phenomena in learning. *Psychol. Rev.* **62**, 369–377. [211]

FARLEY, B. G., and CLARK, W. A. (1954). Simulation of self-organizing systems by digital computer. *IRE, Trans. Inform. Theory* Sept. [16]

FELDMAN, E. J., and CAPRETTA, P. J. (1965). Post conditioning delay and memory transfer through cannibalism. *Worm Runner's Digest* **7**(2), 35–41. [111]

FJERDINGSTAD, E. J., NISSEN, TH., and RØIGAARD-PETERSEN, H. H. (1965). Effect of RNA extracted from the brains of trained animals on learning in rats. *Scand. J. Psychol.* **6**, 1–6. [113]

FLEXNER, L. B., and FLEXNER, J. B. (1966). Effects of acetoxycycloheximide-puromycin mixture on cerebral protein synthesis and memory in mice. *Proc. Natl. Acad. Sci. U.S.* **55**, 369. [124]

FLEXNER, J. B., FLEXNER, L. B., STELLAR, E., DE LA HABA, G., and ROBERTS, R. B. (1962). Inhibition of protein synthesis in brain and learning and memory following puromycin. *J. Neurochem.* **9**, 595–605. [123]

FLEXNER, J. B., FLEXNER, L. B., and STELLAR, E. (1963). Memory in mice as affected by intracerebral puromycin. *Science* **141**, 57–59. [19, 119, 164]

FLEXNER, L. B., FLEXNER, J. B., ROBERTS, R. B., and DE LA HABA, G. (1965a). Loss of recent memory in mice as related to regional inhibition of cerebral protein synthesis. *Proc. Natl. Acad. Sci. U.S.* **52**, 1165–1169. [123]

FLEXNER, L. B., FLEXNER, J. B., DE LA HABA, G., and ROBERTS, R. B. (1965b). Loss of memory as related to inhibition of cerebral protein synthesis. *J. Neurochem.* **12**, 535–541. [123]

FLYNN, J. P., and WASMAN, M. (1960). Learning and cortically evoked movement during propagated hippocampal after discharges. *Science* **131**, 1607. [22]

FOLCH-PI, J. (1952). Discussion. *In* "The Biology of Mental Health and Disease," p. 133. Harper & Row (Hoeber), New York. [55]

FOX, S. S., and O'BRIEN, J. H. (1965). Duplication of evoked potential waveform by curve of probability of firing of a single cell. *Science* **147**, 888–890. [62, 235, 238]

FRIED, C., and HOROWITZ, S. (1964). Contraction: a learnable response. *Worm Runner's Digest* **6**, 3–6. [111]

FROST, J. D., and GOL, A. (1966). Computer determination of relationships between EEG activity and single unit discharges in isolated cerebral cortex. *Exptl. Neurol.* **14**, 506–519. [234]

FUJITA, V., and SATO, T. (1964). Intracellular records from hippocampal pyramidal cells in rabbit during theta rhythm activity. *J. Neurophysiol.* **27**, 1011. [230]

FUSTER, J. M. (1958). Effects of stimulation of brain stem on tachistoscopic perception. *Science* **127**, 150. [57]

FUSTER, J. M., and UYEDA, A. A. (1962). Facilitation of tachistoscopic performance by stimulation of midbrain tegmental points in the monkey. *Exptl. Neurol.* **6**, 384–406. [57]

GAITO, J. (1963). DNA and RNA as memory molecules. *Psychol. Rev.* **70**, 471–480. [127]

GALAMBOS, R. (1961). A glial-neural theory of brain function. *Proc. Natl. Acad. Sci. U.S.* **47**, 129–136. [140]

References

GALAMBOS, R., and SHEATZ, G. C. (1962). An electroencephalograph study of classical conditioning. *Am. J. Physiol.* **203**, 173–184. [331, 332]

GARCIA-AUSTT, E., BOGACZ, J., and VANZULLI, A. (1964). Effects of attention and inattention upon visual evoked response. *Electroencephalog. Clin. Neurophysiol.* **17**, 136–143. [401]

GAVLICHEK, V. (1958). Electroencephalographic characteristics of the conditioned reflex dominant state. *Sechenov Physiol. J. USSR (English Transl.)* **44**, 274–285. [328]

GEIGER, R. S., ADACHI, C., and STEWART, M. (1960). Action of adrenaline and eserine on adult mammalian brain cultures. *Federation Proc.* **19**, 281. [96]

GEISLER, C. D., FRISHKOPF, L. S., and ROSENBLITH, W. A. (1958). Extracranial responses to acoustic clicks in man. *Science* **128**, 1210–1211. [402]

GERARD, R. W. (1955). Biological roots of psychiatry. *Science* **122**, 225–230. [21]

GERSCH, W. (1966). Neural net behavior with antineural elements. Paper presented at Bionics Symposium. [237]

GERSTEIN, G. L. (1961). Neuron firing patterns and the slow potentials. *Electroencephalog. Clin. Neurophysiol. Suppl.* **20**, 68–71 [233]

GILDEN, L., VAUGHAN, H. G., and COSTA, L. D. (1965). Summated human EEG potentials with voluntary movement. Paper presented at *Eastern Psychol. Assoc. Meetings, April.* [400]

GIRDEN, E. (1942a). The dissociation of blood pressure conditioned responses under Erythroidine. *J. Exptl. Psychol.* **31**, 219–231. [69]

GIRDEN, E. (1942b). The dissociation of pupillary conditioned responses under erythroidine. *J. Exptl. Psychol.* **31**, 322–332. [69]

GIRDEN, E. (1942c). Generalized conditioned responses under curare and erythroidine *J. Exptl. Psychol.* **31**, 105–119. [69]

GIRDEN, E. (1947). Conditioned responses in curarized monkeys. *Am. J. Psychol.* **60**, 571–587. [69]

GIRDEN, E., and CULLER, E. (1937). Conditioned responses in curarized striate muscle in dogs. *J. Comp. Psychol.* **23**, 261–274. [11, 69]

GIURGEA, C. (1953). *Studii Cercetari Fiziol. Neurol.* **4**, 41–73. Quoted in R. W. Doty (1959). *Trans. 1st Conf. Central Nervous System Behavior*, p. 250. Josiah Macy, Jr., Found., New York. [193]

GLASKY, A. J., and SIMON, L. N. (1966). Magnesium pemoline: enhancement of brain RNA polymerases. *Science* **151**, 702. [108]

GLASSMAN, E., SCHLESINGER, K., and WILSON, J. (1966). Increased synthesis of RNA in the brains of goldfish during short term learning experiences. *Federation Proc.* **25**, 2962. [97]

GLICKMAN, S. E. (1958). Deficits in avoidance learning produced by stimulation of the ascending reticular formation. *Can. J. Psychol.* **12**, 97–102. [23]

GLICKMAN, S. E. (1961). Perseverative neural processes and consolidation of memory trace. *Psychol. Bull.* **58**, 218–233. [19]

GLIVENKO, E. V., KOROL'KOVA, T. A., and KUZNETSOVA, G. D. (1962). Investigation of the spatial correlation between the cortical potentials of the rabbit during formation of a conditioned defensive reflex. *Fiz. Zh. SSSR Sechenova* **48**(9), 1026. [332]

GOLDBERG, J. M., and NEFF, W. D. (1964). Frequency discrimination after bilateral ablation of cortical auditory areas. *J. Neurophysiol.* **24**, 119–128. [5]

GOLDSTEIN, K. (1940). "Human Nature in Light of Psychopathology." Harvard Univ. Press, Cambridge, Massachusetts. [216]

GOLLUB, L. R., and BRADY, J. V. (1965). Behavioral pharmacology. *Ann. Rev. Pharmacol.* **5**, 235–262. [108]

GOMULICKI, B. R. (1953). The development and present status of the trace theory of memory. *Brit. J. Psychol. Monograph Suppl.* **29**, 1–94. [27]

GOREN, C. (1965). Ribonucleic acid: influence on the maze learning ability of rats. *Worm Runner's Digest* **7**(2), 28–31. [109]

GRAFSTEIN, B. (1963). Potassium release in spreading depression. *In* "Brain Function" (M. A. B. Brazier, ed.), Vol. I, pp. 87–124. Univ. of California Press, Berkeley, California. [49, 139]

GRASTYÁN, E., and KARMOS, G. (1962). The influence of hippocampal lesions on simple and delayed instrumental conditioned reflexes. *Physiol. Hippocampe* Colloq. Intern. No. 107, 1225–1234. C.N.R.S., Paris. [22]

GRASTYÁN, E., LISSÁK, K., and KÉKESI, F. (1956). Facilitation and inhibition of conditioned alimentary and defensive reflexes by stimulation of the hypothalamus and reticular formation. *Acta Physiol. Hung.* **9**, 133–151. [71, 204, 328, 329]

GRASTYÁN, E., LISSÁK, L., MADARASZ, I., and DONHOFFER, H. (1959). Hippocampal electrical activity during the development of conditioned reflexes. *Electroencephalog. Clin. Neurophysiol.* **11**, 409. [245]

GRASTYÁN, E., KARMOS, G., VERECZKEY, L., MARTIN, J., and KELLENYI, L. (1965). Hypothalamic motivational processes as reflected by their hippocampal electrical correlates. *Science* **149**, 91–93. [204, 329]

GREEN, J. D., MAXWELL, D. S., SCHINDLER, W. J., and STUMPF, C. (1960). Rabbit EEG "Theta" rhythm: its anatomical source and relation to activity in single neurons. *J. Neurophysiol.* **23**, 403. [233]

GRIEG, M. E., and HOLLAND, W. C. (1951). Studies on the permeability of erythrocytes. IV. Effect of certain choline and non-choline esters on permeability of dog erythrocytes. *Am. J. Physiol.* **164**, 423–427. [50]

GROSS, C. G., and CAREY, F. M. (1965). Transfer of a learned response by RNA injection: failure of attempts to replicate. *Science* **150**, 1749. [113]

GROSS, C. G., CHOROVER, S. L., and COHEN, S. M. (1965a). Caudate, cortical, hippocampal and dorsal thalamic lesions in rats: alternation and Hebb-Williams maze performance. *Neuropsychologia* **3**, 53–68. [162]

GROSS, M. M., BEGLEITER, H., TOBIN, M., and KISSIN, B. (1965b). Auditory evoked response comparison during counting clicks and reading. *Electroencephalog. Clin. Neurophysiol.* **18**, 451–454. [401]

GROSSMAN, S. P. (1966). Effects of cholinergic stimulation of MRF on conditioned responses. *Federation Proc.* **25**, 108. [57]

GROSSMAN, S. P., and MOUNTFORD, H. (1964). Learning and extinction during chemically induced disturbance of hippocampal functions. *Am. J. Physiol.* **207**, 1387–1393. [22]

GUMNIT, R. J., and GROSSMAN, R. G. (1961). Potentials evoked by sound in the auditory cortex of the cat. *Am. J. Physiol.* **200**, 1219–1225. [190, 227]

GURD, F. R. N., and WILCOX, P. E. (1956). Complex formation between metallic cations and proteins, peptides, and amino acids. *Advan. Protein Chem.* **11**, 312–427. [141]

HAIDER, M., SPONG, P., and LINDSLEY, D. B. (1964). Attention, vigilance, and cortical evoked potentials. *Science* **145**, 180–182. [354, 401]

HANAWALT, N. G. (1937). Memory trace for figures in recall and recognition. *Arch. Psychol.* No. 216, 1–89. [165]

References

HARMON, H. H. (1960). "Modern Factor Analysis." Univ. of Chicago Press, Chicago, Illinois. [337]

HARTRY, A. L., KEITH-LEE, P., and MORTON, W. D. (1964). Planaria: memory transfer through cannibalism reexamined. *Science* 146, 274–275. [111]

HASELKORN, R., and FRIED, V. A. (1964). Cell-free protein synthesis: messenger competition for ribosomes. *Proc. Natl. Acad. Sci. U.S.* 51, 1001–1007. [142]

HEBB, D. O. (1937). The innate organization of visual activity: I. Perception of figures by rats reared in total darkness. *J. Genet. Psychol.* 51, 101–126. [166]

HEBB, D. O. (1949). "The Organization of Behavior." Wiley, New York. [27, 43, 154, 164, 167, 169]

HEBB, D. O., and FOORD, E. N. (1945). Errors of visual recognition and the nature of the trace. *J. Exptl. Psychol.* 35, 335–348. [165]

HECHTER, O., and HALKERSTON, I. D. K. (1964). On the nature of macromolecular coding in neuronal memory. *Perspectives Biol. Med.* 7, 183–198. [152]

HEPPINSTALL, M. E., and GREVILLE, G. D. (1950). In "Electroencephalography" (D. Hill and G. Parr, eds.), pp. 166–202. MacDonald, London. [56]

HERRINGTON, R. N., and SCHNEIDAU, P. (1966). Unpublished observations. [410]

HERTZ, L. (1965). Possible role of neuroglia: a potassium-mediated neuronal-neuroglial-neuronal impulse transmission system. *Nature* 206, 1091–1094. [140]

HESS, W. R. (1954). "The Diencephalon." Grune & Stratton, New York. [204]

HILD, W., and TASAKI, I. (1962). Morphological and physiological properties of neurons and glial cells in tissue culture. *J. Neurophysiol.* 25, 277–304. [225]

HILGARD, E. R., and MARQUIS, D. G. (1940). "Conditioning and Learning." Appleton, New York. [27, 170]

HORI, Y., and YOSHII, N. (1965). Conditioned change in discharge pattern for single neurons of medial thalamic nuclei of cat. *Psychol. Rept.* 16, 241. [257]

HORRIDGE, G. (1962). Learning leg position by the ventral nerve cord in headless insects. *Proc. Roy. Soc. (London)* B157, 33–62. [261]

HORSTEN, G. P. M., and KLOPPER, P. J. (1952). Effects of changes in composition of the CSF on the EEG. *Arch. Intern. Physiol.* 60(4), 491–504. [57]

HOYLE, G. (1965). Neurophysiological studies on "learning" in headless insects. *In* "The Physiology of the Insect Central Nervous System" (J. E. Treherne and J. W. L. Beament, eds.), Academic Press, New York. [261]

HUANG, RU-CHIN, C., and BONNER, J. (1962). Histone, a suppressor of chromosomal RNA synthesis. *Proc. Natl. Acad. Sci. U.S.* 48, 1216–1222. [127]

HUBEL, D. H. (1959). Single unit activity in striate cortex of unrestrained cats. *J. Physiol. (London)* 147, 226–238. [262]

HUBEL, D. H., and WIESEL, T. N. (1962). Receptive fields, binocular interaction and functional architecture in the cat's visual cortex. *J. Physiol. (London)* 160, 106–154. [262]

HUBEL, D. H., and WIESEL, T. N. (1963). Receptive fields of cells in striate cortex of very young, visually inexperienced kittens. *J. Neurophysiol.* 26, 994–1002. [262]

HUGELIN, A., and BONVALLET, M. (1957). Étude éxperimentale des interrelations réticulo-corticales. Proposition d'une théorie de l'asservissement réticulaire a une system diffus cortical. *J. Physiol. (Paris)* 49, 1201–1223. [209]

HUGHES, J. R. (1958). Post-tetanic potentiation. *Physiol. Rev.* 38, 91–113. [49, 184]

HULL, C. L. (1943). "Principles of Behavior: An Introduction to Behavior Theory." Appleton, New York. [166, 211]

HULL, C. L. (1945). The discrimination of stimulus configurations and the hypothesis of afferent neural interaction. *Psychol. Rev.* 52, 133–142. [167]

HUNT, H. F., and BRADY, J. V. (1951). Some effects of electroconvulsive shock on a conditioned emotional response ("anxiety"). *J. Comp. Physiol. Psychol.* **44**, 88–98. [70]

HUNT, H. F., and DIAMOND, I. T. (1957). Some effects of hippocampal lesions on conditioned avoidance behavior in the cat. *Proc. Intern. Congr. Psychol., 15th, Brussels.* [22, 163]

HYDÉN, H. (1960). The neuron. *In* "The Cell" (J. Brachet and A. E. Mirsky, eds.), Vol. IV, Chapt. 5. Academic Press, New York. [149]

HYDÉN, H. (1962). The neuron and its glia—a biochemical and functional unit. *Endeavor* **21**, 144–155. [99, 140]

HYDÉN, H. (1966). *Neurosci. Res. Program, Intensive Study Program.* In press. [100]

HYDÉN, H., and EGYHÁZI, E. (1962). Nuclear RNA changes of nerve cells during a learning experiment in rats. *Proc. Natl. Acad. Sci. U.S.* **48**, 1366–1373. [155]

HYDÉN, H., and EGYHÁZI, E. (1963). Glial RNA changes during a learning experiment with rats. *Proc. Natl. Acad. Sci. U.S.* **49**, 618–624. [98, 99, 140, 155]

HYDÉN, H., and EGYHÁZI, E. (1964). Change in RNA content and base composition in cortical neurons of rats in a learning experiment involving transfer of handedness. *Proc. Natl. Acad. Sci. U.S.* **52**, 1030–1035. [98]

HYDÉN, H., EGYHÁZI, E., JOHN, E. R., and BARTLETT, F. (1966). RNA base ratio changes in planaria during conditioning. *J. Neurochem.* Submitted for publication. [100]

IRWIN, S., and BENAUZIZI, A. (1966). Pentylenetetrazol enhances memory function. *Science* **152**, 100–102. [47]

JACOB, F., and MONOD, J. (1961). Genetic regulatory mechanisms in synthesis of proteins. *J. Mol. Biol.* **3**, 318–356. [127]

JACOB, F., and MONOD, J. (1963). "Cytodifferentiation and Macromolecular Synthesis" (M. Locke, ed.), p. 30. Academic Press, New York. [129]

JACOBSON, A. L., BABICH, R. R., BUBASH, S., and JACOBSON, A. (1965). Differential approach tendencies produced by injection of RNA from trained rats. *Science* **150**, 636–637. [115]

JACOBSON, A. L., FRIED, C., and HOROWITZ, S. D. (1966). Planarians and memory. *Nature* **209**, 599–600. [116]

JARVIK, M. E. (1964). *Ciba Found. Symp. Animal Pharmacol. Drug Action.* (H. Steinberg *et al.*, eds.) [22]

JASPER, H. H. (1954). Functional properties of the thalamic reticular system. *In* "Brain Mechanisms and Consciousness" (J. F. Delafresnaye, ed.). Thomas, Springfield, Illinois. [208]

JASPER, H. H., RICCI, G. F., and DOANE, B. (1958). Patterns of cortical neuronal discharge during conditioned responses in monkeys. *In* "Neurological Bases of Behavior," pp. 277–294. Little, Brown, Boston. [208]

JASPER, H. H., RICCI, G., and DOANE, B. (1960). Microelectrode analysis of cortical cell discharge during avoidance conditioning in the monkey. *Electroencephalog. Clin. Neurophysiol. Suppl.* **13**, 137–155. [245, 256]

JOHN, E. R. (1956). Radioactive tracer exchange in functional brain mapping. *J. Neuropathol. Exptl. Neurol.* **15**, 103–116. [89]

JOHN, E. R. (1961). Higher nervous functions: brain functions and learning. *Ann. Rev. Physiol.* **23**, 451. [72, 220, 243, 295]

JOHN, E. R. (1962). Some speculations on the psychophysiology of mind. *In* "Theories of the Mind" (J. Scher, ed.), pp. 80–121. Free Press, New York. [210]

JOHN, E. R. (1963). Neural mechanisms of decision making. *In* "Information Storage and Neural Control" (W. S. Fields and W. Abbott, eds.). Thomas, Springfield, Illinois. [237, 252, 254]

JOHN, E. R. (1964). Studies on learning and retention in planaria. *In* "Brain Function" (M. A. B. Brazier, ed.), Vol. II. Univ. of California Press, Berkeley, California. [110]

JOHN, E. R., and AHN, H. (1966). Unpublished observations. [254, 366]

JOHN, E. R., and CHESLER, P. (1966). Unpublished observations. [8]

JOHN, E. R., and KILLAM, K. F. (1959). Electrophysiological correlates of avoidance conditioning in the cat. *J. Pharmacol. Exptl. Therap.* **125**, 252. [247, 256, 295, 331]

JOHN, E. R., and KILLAM, K. F. (1960). Electrophysiological correlates of differential approach-avoidance conditioning in the cat. *J. Nervous Mental Disease* **131**, 183. [237, 250, 252, 311, 316, 321]

JOHN, E. R., and LOWY, K. (1962). Unpublished observations. [407]

JOHN, E. R., and SHIMOKOCHI, M. (1966). Unpublished observations. [254, 283, 326, 369, 374]

JOHN, E. R., CHOW, K. L., and DEMENT, W. C. (1957). Unpubl. observations. [299]

JOHN, E. R., WENZEL, B., and TSCHIRGI, R. D. (1958a). Differential effects of reserpine on conditioned responses in cats. *Science* **127**, 25–26. [72]

JOHN, E. R., WENZEL, B., and TSCHIRGI, R. D. (1958b). Differential effects on various conditioned responses in cats caused by intraventricular and intramuscular injections of reserpine and other substances. *J. Pharmacol. Exptl. Therap.* **123**, 193–205. [72, 82, 153]

JOHN, E. R., KILLAM, K. F., WENZEL, B. M., and MASS, M. (1958c). Unpublished observations. [102, 348]

JOHN, E. R., TSCHIRGI, R., and WENZEL, B. M. (1959). Effects of injections of cations into the cerebral ventricles on conditioned responses in the cat. *J. Physiol. (London)* **146**, 550–562. [51, 54, 79]

JOHN, E. R., LEIMAN, A. L., and SACHS, E. (1961). An exploration of the functional relationship between electroencephalographic potentials and differential inhibition. *Ann. N.Y. Acad. Sci.* **92**(3), 1160–1182. [345]

JOHN, E. R., BARTLETT, F., and SACHS, E. (1963a). Unpublished observations. [83]

JOHN, E. R., SACHS, E., and BARTLETT, F. (1963b). Unpublished observations. [90]

JOHN, E. R., RUCHKIN, D. S., and VILLEGAS, J. (1963c). Signal analysis of evoked potentials recorded from cats during conditioning. *Science* **141**, 429–431. [337]

JOHN, E. R., RUCHKIN, D., and VILLEGAS, J. (1964). Signal analysis and behavioral correlates of evoked potential configurations in cats. *Ann. N.Y. Acad. Sci.* **112**, 362–420. [337]

JOHN, E. R., RUCHKIN, D. S., LEIMAN, A., SACHS, E., and AHN, H. (1965). Electrophysiological studies of generalization using both peripheral and central conditioned stimuli. *Proc. 23rd Intern. Congr. Physiol. Sci., Tokyo, 1965* pp. 618–627. [254, 400]

JOHN, E. R., HERRINGTON, R. N., and SUTTON, S. (1967). Effects of visual form on the evoked response. *Science* **155**, 1439–1442. [407, 409]

JUNG, R. (1958). Coordination of specific and non-specific afferent impulses at single neurons of the visual cortex. *In* "Reticular Formation of the Brain" (H. H. Jasper *et al.*, eds.), pp. 423–434. Little, Brown, Boston, Massachusetts. [185, 208]

KAMIKAWA, K., McILWAIN, J. T., and ADEY, W. R. (1964). Response patterns of thalamic neurons during classical conditioning. *Electroencephalog. Clin. Neurophysiol.* **17**, 485–496. [257]

KANDEL, E. R., and SPENCER, W. A. (1961). Electrophysiological properties of an archicortical neuron. *Ann. N.Y. Acad. Sci.* 94(2), 570–603. [230]

KANDEL, E. R., and TAUC, L. (1963). Augmentation prolongée de l'efficacité d'une voie afférente d'un ganglion isolé après l'activation couplée d'une voie plus efficace. *J. Physiol. (Paris)* 55, 271–272. [259]

KANDEL, E. R., and TAUC, L. (1964). Mechanism of prolonged heterosynaptic facilitation in a giant ganglion cell of aplysia depilans. *Nature* 202, 145–147. [259]

KANDEL, E. R., and TAUC, L. (1965a). Heterosynaptic facilitation in neurones of the abdominal ganglion of aplysia depilans. *J. Physiol. (London)* 181, 1–27. [259]

KANDEL, E. R., and TAUC, L. (1965b). Mechanism of heterosynaptic facilitation in the giant cell of the abdominal ganglion of aplysia depilans. *J. Physiol. (London)* 181, 28–47. [259]

KANDEL, E. R., WAZIRI, R., and FRAZIER, W. T. (1965). Conditioning paradigms and cellular neurophysiological analogues of learning in an isolated invertebrate ganglion. *In* "Extensions of Conditioning to Physiological Research," Eastern Psychol. Symp. (D. Shapiro, ed.). [226, 260]

KANDEL, E. R., FRAZIER, W. T., and COGGESHELL, R. (1966). Opposite synaptic actions mediated by different branches of an identifiable interneuron in aplysia. *Federation Proc.* 25, 456. [226]

KAPPERS, C. U. A. (1917). Further contributions on "neurobiotaxis" IX. An attempt to compare the phenomena of "neurobiotaxis" with other phenomena of taxis and trophism. *J. Comp. Neurol.* 27, 261–298. [93]

KATZ, J. J., and HALSTEAD, W. C. (1950). Protein organization and mental functions. *Comp. Psychol. Monograph* 20, No. 103, 1–38. [95]

KATZMAN, R., and LEIDERMAN, P. H. (1953). Brain potassium exchange in normal adult and immature rats. *Am. J. Physiol.* 175, 263–270. [55, 139]

KILLAM, K. F., and HANCE, A. J. (1965). Analysis of electrographic correlates of conditional responses to positive reinforcement: I. Correlates of acquisition and performance. *Abstr. Proc. 23rd Intern. Congr. Physiol. Sci., Tokyo, 1965*, p. 1125. [365]

KLEE, M. R., and OFFENLOCH, K. (1964). Post-synaptic potentials and spike patterns during augmenting responses in cat's motor cortex. *Science* 143, 488–489. [230]

KLEE, M. R., OFFENLOCH, K., and TIGGES, J. (1965). Cross-correlation analysis of electroencephalographic potentials and slow membrane transients. *Science* 147, 519. [229]

KLÜVER, H. (1942). Functional significance of the geniculostriate system. *Biol. Symp.* 7, 263–264. [10]

KOCH, A., RANCK, J. B., and NEWMAN, B. L. (1962). Ionic content of neuroglia. *Exptl. Neurol.* 6, 186–200. [141]

KÖHLER, W. (1929). "Gestalt Psychology." Liveright, New York. [164]

KÖHLER, W. (1940). "Dynamics in Psychology." Liveright, New York. [164, 166]

KOFFKA, K. (1935). "Principles of Gestalt Psychology." Harcourt, Brace, New York. [164, 165]

KONORSKI, J. (1948). "Conditioned Reflexes and Neuron Organization." Cambridge Univ. Press, London and New York. [154]

KONORSKI, J. (1950). Mechanisms of learning. *Symp. Soc. Exptl. Biol.* 4. [212]

KOPP, R. (1966). The temporal gradient of retrograde amnesia to ECS in mice. *Federation Proc.* 25, 416. [21]

References

Kopp, R., Bohdanecky, Z., and Jarvik, M. E. (1966). Long temporal gradient of retrograde amnesia for a well-discriminated stimulus. *Science* **153**, 1547–1549. [21]

Kornberg, A. (1960). Biological synthesis of deoxyribonucleic acids. *Science* **131**, 1503–1508. [126]

Kozhevnikov, V. A. (1958). Some methods of automatic measurement of the electroencephalogram. *Electroencephalog. Clin. Neurophysiol.* **10**, 269–278. [333]

Kraft, M. S., Obrist, W. D., and Pribram, K. H. (1960). The effect of irritative lesions of the striate cortex on learning of visual discriminations in monkeys. *J. Comp. Physiol. Psychol.* **53**, 17–22. [245]

Kral, V. A., and Sved, S. (1963). *Midwest Psychol. Assoc. Meeting, Symp. Nucleic Acids Behavior.* [109]

Krech, D., Rosenzweig, M. R., and Bennett, E. L. (1956). Dimensions of discrimination and level of cholinesterase activity in the cerebral cortex of the rat. *J. Comp. Physiol. Psychol.* **49**, 261. [42]

Krech, D., Rosenzweig, M. R., and Bennett, E. L. (1962a). Relations between brain chemistry and problem solving among cats raised in enriched and impoverished environments. *J. Comp. Physiol. Psychol.* **55**, 801–807. [42]

Krech, D., Rosenzweig, M. R., and Bennett, E. L. (1962b). Effects of environmental complexity and training on brain chemistry. *J. Comp. Physiol. Psychol.* **53**, 509–519. [42]

Krechevsky, I. (1935). Brain mechanisms and "hypotheses." *J. Comp. Psychol.* **19**, 425–448. [42]

Křivánek, J., and Bureš, J. (1960). Ion shifts during Leão's spreading cortical depression. *Physiol. Bohemoslov.* **9**, 494–503. [25, 49]

Krylov, O. A., Danylova, R. A., and Tongur, V. S. (1965). On the participation of RNA in reflectoral activity of white mice. *Life Sci.* **4**, 1313–1317. [103]

Kupferman, I. (1965). Effects of cortical polarization on visual discriminations. *Exptl. Neurol.* **12**, 179–189. [191]

Lajtha, A. (1961). Observations on protein catabolism in brain. In "Regional Neurochemistry" (S. S. Kety and J. Elkes, eds.), pp. 25–36. Macmillan (Pergamon), New York. [94]

Lajtha, A. (1962). The "brain barrier system." In "Neurochemistry" (K. A. C. Elliot, I. H. Page, and J. H. Quastel, eds.), 2nd Ed., pp. 399–430. Thomas, Springfield, Illinois. [117]

Landauer, T. K. (1964). Two hypotheses concerning the biochemical basis of memory. *Psychol. Rev.* **71**, 167–179. [155]

Lansing, R. W. (1965). Electroencephalographic correlates of binocular rivalry in man. Abstr. *Electroencephalog. Clin. Neurophysiol.* **18**, 514. [402]

Lashley, K. S. (1917). The effect of strychnine and caffeine upon rate of learning. *Psychobiology* **1**, 141–170. [45, 69]

Lashley, K. S. (1923). Temporal variation in the function of the gyrus precentralis in primates. *Am. J. Physiol.* **65**, 585–602. [4]

Lashley, K. S. (1924). Studies of cerebral function in learning. VI. The theory that synaptic resistance is reduced by the passage of the nerve impulse. *Psychol. Rev.* **31**, 369–375. [7]

Lashley, K. S. (1929a). Learning. I. Nervous mechanisms in learning. In "The Foundations of Experimental Psychology" (C. Murchison, ed.), pp. 524–563. Clark Univ. Press, Worcester, Massachusetts. [165]

Lashley, K. S. (1929b). Brain Mechanisms and Intelligence: A Quantitative Study of Injuries to the Brain. Univ. of Chicago Press, Chicago, Illinois. [165]

LASHLEY, K. S. (1931). Mass action in cerebral function. *Science* 73, 245–254. [162]

LASHLEY, K. S. (1933). Integrative functions of cerebral cortex. *Physiol. Rev.* 13, 1–42. [162]

LASHLEY, K. S. (1934). Learning. III. Nervous mechanisms in learning. *In* "A Handbook of General Experimental Psychology" (C. Murchison, ed.), pp. 456–496. Clark Univ. Press, Worcester, Massachusetts. [7]

LASHLEY, K. S. (1938). The mechanism of vision: XV. Preliminary studies of the rat's capacity for detail vision. *J. Gen. Psychol.* 18, 123–193. [164, 166]

LASHLEY, K. S. (1942). The problem of cerebral organization in vision. *Biol. Symp.* 7, 301–332. [164, 166, 217]

LASHLEY, K. S. (1950). In search of the engram. *Symp. Soc. Exptl. Biol.* 4, 454–482. [10, 161, 162, 215]

LASHLEY, K. S. (1951). The problem of serial order in behavior. "Cerebral Mechanisms in Behavior" (L. A. Jeffress, ed.), pp. 112–136. Wiley, New York. [204, 218]

LASHLEY, K. S. (1952). Functional interpretation of anatomic patterns. *Res. Publ. Assoc. Res. Nervous Mental Disease* pp. 529–552. [219]

LASHLEY, K. S. (1958). Cerebral organization and behavior. *Proc. Assoc. Res. Nervous Mental Disease* 36, 1–18. [217]

LEIMAN, A. L. (1962). Electrophysiological studies of conditioned responses established to central electrical stimulation. Ph.D. Thesis, Univ. of Rochester, Rochester, New York. [288, 289, 290, 291, 292, 293, 324, 326]

LERNER, R. M. (1959). The representation of signals. *IRE, Trans. Inform. Theory* P 6IT 5, 197. [337]

LIBERSON, W. T., and ELLEN, P. (1960). Conditioning of the driven brain wave rhythm in the cortex and the hippocampus of the rat. *In* "Recent Advances in Biological Psychiatry," Vol. 2, (J. Wortis, ed.). Grune & Stratton, New York. [196, 328]

LIBERSON, W. T., ELLEN, P., and CADELL, T. (1959). EEG studies during avoidance conditioning in rats. *In* "EEG Studies of Conditioning in Animals and Man." Unpublished APA symposium, Chicago. [196, 328]

LINDSLEY, D. F., GOLLANDER, M., and CHOW, K. L. (1966). Dichoptic interactions of lateral geniculate neurons of cats to spot and flash stimulation. In preparation. [264]

LISSÁK, K., and GRASTYÁN, E. (1957). The significance of activating systems and the hippocampus in the conditioned reflex. *Congr. Intern. Sci. Neurol., 1ᵉʳ, Brussels.* [328]

LISSÁK, K., and GRASTYÁN, E. (1960). The changes in hippocampal electrical activity during conditioning. *Moscow Colloq. Encephalog. Higher Nervous Activity* (H. H. Jasper and G. D. Smirnov, eds.). *Electroencephalog. Clin. Neurophysiol. Suppl.* 13, 271–279 [245]

.IVANOV, M. N. (1962). *Proc. 22nd Intern. Congr. Physiol. Leiden, 1962,* p. 899. [338]

LIVANOV, M. N., and KOROLKOVA, T. A. (1951). The influence of inadequate stimulation of the cortex with induction current on the bioelectrical rhythm of the cortex and conditioned reflex activity. *Zh. Vysschei Nervnoi Deyatel'nosti im I.P. Pavlova* 1(3), 332–346. Cited in RUSINOV, V. S., and RABINOVICH, M. Y. (1958). Electroencephalic researches in the laboratories and clinics of the Soviet Union. *Electroencephalog. Clin. Neurophysiol. Suppl.* 8. [195, 308]

References

LIVANOV, M. N., and POLIAKOV, K. L. (1945). The electrical reactions of the cerebral cortex of a rabbit during the formation of a conditioned defense reflex by means of rhythmic stimulation. *Izv. Akad. Nauk. USSR Ser. Biol.* 3, 286. [247, 295]

LLOYD, D. P. C. (1949). Post-tetanic saturation of response in monosynaptic reflex pathways of the spinal cord. *J. Gen. Physiol.* 33, 147–170. [49]

LORENTE DE NÓ, R. (1938). Analysis of the activity of the chains of internuncial neurons. *J. Neurophysiol.* 1, 207–244. [27]

LORENTE DE NÓ, R. (1939). Transmission of impulses through cranial motor nuclei *J. Neurophysiol.* 2, 402–464. [172]

LOUCKS, R. B. (1938). Studies of neural structures essential for learning. The conditioning of salivary and striped muscle responses to faradization of cortical sensory elements, and the action of sleep upon such mechanisms. *J. Comp. Psychol.* 25, 315–332. [193]

LOUCKS, R. B. (1955). The acquisition and retention of responses conditioned to faradic cerebral stimuli administered through electrodes shielded by barriers. *Am. Psychologist* 10, 403. [193, 347]

LOUCKS, R. B. (1961). Methods of isolating stimulation effects with implanted barriers. *In* "Electrical Stimulation of the Brain" (D. E. Sheer, ed.), pp. 145–154. Univ. of Texas Press, Austin, Texas. [193, 347]

LUBIN, M. (1963). A primary reaction in protein synthesis. *Biochim. Biophys. Acta* 72, 345–348. [142]

LUBIN, M. (1964). *In* "The Cellular Function of Membrane Transport" (J. F. Hoffman, ed.), p. 193. Prentice-Hall, Englewood Cliffs, New Jersey. [142]

LUBIN, M., and ENNIS, H. L. (1963). The role of intracellular potassium in protein synthesis. *Federation Proc.* 22, 302. [142]

LUTTGES, M., JOHNSON, T., BUCK, C., HOLLAND, J., and McGAUGH, J. (1966). An examination of "transfer of learning" by nucleic acid. *Science* 151, 834–837. [114]

McADAM, D. W. (1962). Electroencephalographic changes and classical aversive conditioning in the cat. *Exptl. Neurol.* 6, 357. [248]

McCONNELL, J. V. (1962). Memory transfer through cannibalism in planarians. *J. Neuropsychiat.* 3, Suppl. 1, 542–548. [110]

McCONNELL, J. V. (1964). Cannibalism and memory in flatworms. *New Scientist* 21, 465–468. [110]

McCONNELL, J. V., JACOBSON, A. L., and KIMBLE, D. P. (1959). The effects of regeneration upon retention of a conditioned response in the planarian. *J. Comp. Physiol. Psychol.* 52, 1. [103]

McCULLOCH, W. S., and PITTS, W. (1943). A logical calculus of the ideas immanent in nervous activity. *Bull. Math. Biophys.* 5, 115–133. [16]

McGAUGH, J. L. (1961). Facilitative and disruptive effects of strychnine sulphate on maze learning. *Psychol. Rept.* 8, 99–104. [45]

McGAUGH, J. L., and PETRINOVICH, L. (1959). The effect of strychnine sulphate on maze learning. *Am. J. Psychol.* 72, 99–102. [45]

McGAUGH, J. L., and PETRINOVICH, L. (1965). Effects of drugs on learning and memory. *Intern. Rev. Neurobiol.* 8, 139–191. [45]

McGAUGH, J. L., JENNINGS, R. D., and THOMPSON, C. W. (1962). The effect of distribution of practice on the maze-learning of descendants of the Tryon maze bright and maze dull strains. *Psychol. Rept.* 9, 147–150. [47]

MacINTOSH, F. C., and OBORIN, P. E. (1953). Release of acetylcholine from intact cerebral cortex. *Abstr. 19th Intern. Physiol. Congr., Montreal* pp. 580–581. [49]

MAHUT, H. (1962). Effects of subcortical electrical stimulation on learning in the rat.

J. Comp. Physiol. Psychol. **55**, 472–477. [23]

MAHUT, H. (1964). Effects of subcortical electrical stimulation on discrimination learning in cats. *J. Comp. Physiol. Psychol.* **58**, 390–395. [23, 57]

MAJKOWSKI, J. (1958). The electroencephalogram and electromyogram of motor conditioned reflexes after paralysis with curare. *Electroencephalog. Clin. Neurophysiol.* **10**, 503–514. [351]

MAJKOWSKI, J. (1966). Unpublished observations. [298, 351, 353]

MAJKOWSKI, J., and JOHN, E. R. (1966). Unpublished observations. [249, 279]

MARUI, K. (1919). The effect of over-activity on the morphological structure of the synapse. *J. Comp. Neurol.* **30**, 253–282. [140]

MASON, J. W., BRADY, J. V., POLISH, E., BAUER, J. A., ROBINSON, J. A., ROSE, R. M., and TAYLOR, E. D. (1961). Patterns of corticosteroid and pepsinogen change related to emotional stress in the monkey. *Science* **133**, 1596–1598. [55]

MIHAILOVICH, B. D., and JANOVIC, M. (1961). Effects of intraventricularly injected anti-N. caudatus antibody on the electrical activity of the cat brain. *Nature* **192**, 665–666. [117]

MIHAILOVICH, B. D., JANOVIC, M., PETKOVIC, M., and ISAKOVICK, B. (1958). Effect of electroshock upon nucleic acid concentrations in various parts of cat brain. *Experientia* **14**, 144–145. [107]

MILLER, N. E. (1959). Liberalization of basic S-R concepts: extensions to conflict behavior, motivation, and social learning. In "Psychology: A Study of a Science" (S. Koch, ed.), Vol. 2, pp. 196–292. McGraw-Hill, New York. [161]

MILLER, N. E., and COONS, E. E. (1955). Conflict versus consolidation of memory to explain "retrograde amnesia" produced by ECS. *Am. Psychologist* **10**, 394. [20]

MILNER, B., and PENFIELD, W. (1955). The effect of hippocampal lesions on recent memory *Trans. Am. Neurol. Assoc. 80th Ann. Meeting*, pp. 42–48. [22]

MOORE, G. P., PERKEL, D. H., and SEGUNDO, J. P. (1966). Statistical analysis and functional interpretation of neuronal spike data. *Am. Rev. Physiol.* **28**, 493–522. [12]

MORRELL, F. (1957a). Effects of experimental epilepsy on conditioned electrical potentials. *Univ. Minn. Med. Bull.* **29**, 82–102. [245]

MORRELL, F. (1957b). An anatomical and physiological analysis of electrocortical conditioning. *Proc. 1st Intern. Congr. Neurol. Sci., Brussels.* [187]

MORRELL, F. (1958). Some electrical events involved in the formation of temporary connections. In "Reticular Formation of the Brain" (H. H. Jasper et al., eds.), pp. 545–560. Little, Brown, Boston, Massachusetts. [26, 187, 299]

MORRELL, F. (1960). Microelectrode and steady potential studies suggesting a dendritic locus of closure. *Moscow Colloq. Electroencephalog. Higher Nervous Activity* (H. H. Jasper and G. D. Smirnov, eds.). *Electroencephalog. Clin. Neurophysiol. Suppl.* **13**, 65–79. [190, 255, 303]

MORRELL, F. (1961a). Lasting changes in synaptic organization produced by continuous neuronal bombardment. In "Brain Mechanisms and Learning" (J. F. Delafresnaye, ed.). Blackwell, Oxford. [96]

MORRELL, F. (1961b). Effect of anodal polarization on the firing pattern of single cortical cells. *Ann. N.Y. Acad. Sci.* **92**(3), 860–876. [189, 191, 246, 256]

MORRELL, F. (1961c). Electrophysiological contributions to the neural basis of learning. *Physiol. Rev.* **41**, 443. [220, 243]

MORRELL, F. (1961d). Discussion. In "Brain Mechanisms and Learning" (J. F. Delafresnaye, ed.), p. 259. Blackwell, Oxford. [300]

References

MORRELL, F. (1962). Electrochemical mechanisms and information storage in nerve cells. *In* "Macromolecular Specificity and Biological Memory" (F. O. Schmitt, ed.), pp. 73–79. M.I.T. Press, Cambridge, Massachusetts. [145]

MORRELL, F. (1963). Effects of transcortical polarizing currents. *In* "Brain Function" (M. A. B. Brazier, ed.), Vol. I, pp. 125–135. Univ. of California Press, Berkeley, California. [227]

MORRELL, F. (1965). Personal communication. [189]

MORRELL, F., and JASPER, H. (1956). Electrographic studies of the formation of temporary connections in the brain. *Electroencephalog. Clin. Neurophysiol.* **8**, 201–215. [187, 244]

MORRELL, F., and NAITOH, P. (1962). Effect of cortical polarization on a conditioned avoidance response. *Exptl. Neurol.* **6**, 507–523. [190]

MORRELL, F., ROBERTS, L., and JASPER, H. (1956). Effect of focal epileptogenic lesions and their ablation upon conditioned electrical responses of the brain in the monkey. *Electroencephalog. Clin. Neurophysiol.* **8**, 217. [187]

MORRELL, F., NAQUET, R., and GASTAUT, H. (1957). Evolution of some electrical signs of conditioning. Part I. Normal cat and rabbit. *J. Neurophysiol.* **20**, 574. [187]

MORRELL, F., BARLOW, J., and BRAZIER, M. A. B. (1960). Analysis of conditioned repetitive response by means of an average response computer. *In* "Recent Advances in Biological Psychiatry" (J. Wortis, ed.). Grune & Stratton, New York. [188]

MORRELL, F., ENGEL, J., and BOURIS, W. (1966). Unpublished ms. [147, 263, 268, 305, 306, 307]. Presented by Morrell at *Neurosciences Research Program, Boulder, 1966.* (In press).

MÜLLER, G. E., and PILZECKER, A. (1900). Experimentalle Beiträge zur Lehre vom Gedächtnis. *Z. Psychol. Suppl.* **1**, 1–288. [19]

MUSES, C. A., ed. (1962). "Aspects of the Theory of Artificial Intelligence." Plenum Press, New York. [17]

Natl. Physical Lab. Symp. No. 10. (1959). "Mechanization of Thought Processes," Vol. 1 (M. C. Yovits and S. Cameron, eds.). H. M. Stationery Office, London. [17]

NEFF, W. D., NIEDER, P. C., and OSTERREICH, R. E. (1959). Learned responses elicited by electrical stimulation of auditory pathways. *Federation Proc.* **18**, 112. [195]

NIELSON, H. C., DOTY, R. W., and RUTLEDGE, L. T. (1958). Motivational and perceptual aspects of subcortical stimulation in cats. *Am. J. Physiol.* **194**, 427–432. [329]

NIKOLAYEVA, N. (1953). Changes of excitability of nervous structures of the brain during the formation of conditioned reflexes. Ph.D. Thesis, Univ. of Rostov (Russ.). Cited by KOGAN, A. B. (1960). The manifestations of processes of higher nervous activity in the electrical potentials of the cortex during free behavior of animals. *Moscow Colloq. Electroencephalog. Higher Nervous Activity* (H. H. Jasper and G. D. Smirnov, eds.). *Electroencephalog. Clin. Neurophysiol. Suppl.* **13**, 51–61. [193]

NISSEN, TH., RØIGAARD-PETERSEN, H. H., and FJERDINGSTED, E. J. (1965). Effect of ribonucleic acid (RNA) extracted from the brains of trained animals on learning in rats. II. Dependence of RNA effect on training conditions prior to RNA extraction. *Scand. J. Psychol.* **6**, 265–272. [115]

NIU, M. C. (1963). The mode of action of ribonucleic acid. *Develop. Biol.* **7**, 379–393. [118]

NIU, M. C., CORDOVA, C. C., and NIU, L. C. (1961). Ribonucleic acid-induced changes in mammalian cells. *Proc. Natl. Acad. Sci. U.S.* **47,** 1681–1700. [118]

NIU, M. C., CORDOVA, C. C., NIU, L. C., and RADBILL, C. L. (1962). RNA-induced biosynthesis of specific enzymes. *Proc. Natl. Acad. Sci. U.S.* **48,** 1964–1969. [118]

NORTON, T., FROMMER, G., and GALAMBOS, R. (1966). Effects of partial lesions of optic tract on visual discriminations in cats. *Federation Proc.* **25,** 2168. [5, 263]

OCHS, S., HUNT, K., and BOOKER, H. (1960). Spreading depression using chronically implanted electrodes. *Am. J. Physiol.* **200,** 432–444. [25]

OJEMANN, R. G. (1966). Correlations between specific human brain lesions and memory changes. *Neurosci. Res. Program Bull.* **4,** *Suppl.,* 1–70. [11]

OLDS, J. (1956). A preliminary mapping of electrical reinforcing effects in the rat brain. *J. Comp. Physiol. Psychol.* **49,** 281–285. [204]

OLDS, J. (1959). Discussion. In "The Central Nervous System and Behavior," 2nd Conf. (M. A. B. Brazier, ed.), pp. 141–144. Josiah Macy, Jr., Found., New York. [23, 328]

OLDS, J. (1965a). Operant conditioning of single unit responses. *Proc. 23rd Intern. Congr. Physiol. Sci., Tokyo, 1965* **IV,** 372–380. [257]

OLDS, J. (1965b). Operant control of tegmental neuron patterns. *Federation Proc.* **24,** 522. [257]

OLDS, J., and OLDS, M. E. (1961). Interference and learning in paleocortical systems. *In* "CIOMS Symposium on Brain Mechanisms and Learning" (J. F. Delafresnaye, A. Fessard, and J. Konorski, eds.). Blackwell, Oxford. [257]

OTIS, L. S. (1956). Drive conditioning; fear as a response to biogenic drive stimuli previously associated with noxious stimulation. *Am. Psychologist* **11,** 397. [70]

OTIS, L. S. (1957). Drive conditioning: fear as a response to biogenic drive stimuli previously associated with painful stimulation. Ph.D. Thesis, Univ. of Chicago, Chicago, Illinois. [70]

OVERTON, D. A. (1964). State-dependent or "dissociated" learning produced with pentobarbital. *J. Comp. Physiol. Psychol.* **57,** No. 1, 3–12. [68, 73, 75, 77, 78]

OVERTON, D. A. (1966). State-dependent learning produced by depressant and atropine-like drugs. *Psychopharmacologia* **10,** 6–31. [76]

PALLADIN, A. V., ed. (1964). "Problems of the Biochemistry of the Nervous System." Macmillan (Pergamon), New York. [94, 96]

PAVLYGINA, R. A. (1956). The creation of a dominant focus in the hypothalamic region and the examination of its properties. *Trans. Inst. Higher Nervous Activity USSR Acad. Sci. Moscow* **2,** 124. [328]

PEARLMAN, C., and JARVIK, M. E. (1961). Retrograde amnesia produced by spreading cortical depression. *Federation Proc.* **20,** 340. [25]

PEARLMAN, C. A., SHARPLESS, S. K., and JARVIK, M. E. (1961). Retrograde amnesia produced by anesthetic and convulsant agents. *J. Comp. Physiol. Psychol.* **54,** 109. [19, 48, 60]

PETRINOVICH, L. (1963). Facilitation of successive discrimination learning by strychnine sulphate. *Psychopharmacologia* **4,** 103–113. [45, 46]

PETRINOVICH, L., BRADFORD, D., and McGAUGH, J. (1965). *Psychomonic Sci.* **2,** 191. [46]

PICKETT, J. B. E., III, JENNINGS, L. B., and WELLS, P. H. (1965). Influence of RNA and victim training on maze learning by cannibal planaria. *Worm Runner's Digest* **7**(1), 31–38. [111]

PITTS, W., and McCULLOCH, W. S. (1947). How we know universals. *Bull. Math. Biophys.* **9,** 127–147. [209]

References

PLATT, E. E. (1951). The effects of subcutaneous injection of diisopropyl fluorophosphate (DFP) on the rate of learning a discrimination problem by albino rats. Ph.D. Thesis, Ohio State Univ., Columbus, Ohio. [47]

PLOTNIKOFF, N. (1966a). Magnesium pemoline: enhancement of learning and memory of a conditioned avoidance response. Science 151, 703–704. [108]

PLOTNIKOFF, N. (1966b). Magnesium pemoline: antagonism of retrograde amnesia in rats. Federation Proc. 25, 415. [108]

PODSOSSENAIA, L. S. (1958). Cited by RUSINOV, V. S. (1958). Electrophysiological investigation of foci of stationary excitation in the central nervous system. Pavlov J. Higher Nervous Activity (English Transl.) 8, 444–451. [351]

POLLEN, D. H., and SIE, P. G. (1964). Analysis of thalamic induced wave and spike by modifications in cortical excitability. Electroencephalog. Clin. Neurophysiol. 17, 154–163. [230]

PURPURA, D. P. (1958). Organization of excitatory and inhibitory synaptic electrogenesis in the cerebral cortex. In "Reticular Formation of the Brain" (H. H. Jasper et al., eds.), pp. 435–458. Little, Brown, Boston, Massachusetts. [185]

PURPURA, D. P. (1959). Nature of electrocortical potentials and synaptic organizations in cerebral and cerebellar cortex. Intern. Rev. Neurobiol. 1, 47–163. [224, 225]

PURPURA, D. P., and SHOFER, R. J. (1964). Cortical intracellular potentials during augmenting and recruiting responses. I. Effects of injected hyperpolarizing currents on evoked membrane potential changes. J. Neurophysiol. 27, 117–132.

PURF[230, 231], SHOFER, R. J., and MUSGRAVE, F. S. (1964). Cortical intracellular potentials during augmenting and recruiting responses. II. Patterns of synaptic activities in pyramidal and non-pyramidal tract neurones. J. Neurophysiol. 27, 133–151. [230, 231]

QUARTERMAIN, D., PAOLINO, R. M., and MILLER, N. E. (1965). A brief temporal gradient of retrograde amnesia independent of situational change. Science 149, 1116–1118. [20]

RANSMEIER, R. E. (1953). The effects of convulsion, hypoxia, hypothermia, and anesthesia on retention in the hamster. Ph.D. Thesis, Univ. of Chicago. [20]

RANSMEIER, R. E., and GERARD, R. W. (1954). Effects of temperature, convulsion and metabolic factor on rodent memory and EEG. Am. J. Physiol. 179, 663–664. [21]

RAPIN, I. (1964). Evoked responses to clicks in a group of children with communication disorders. Ann. N.Y. Acad. Sci. 112(1), 182–203. [402]

RASCH, E., SWIFT, H., RIESEN, A. H., and CHOW, K. L. (1961). Altered structure and composition of retinal cells in dark reared mammals. Exptl. Cell Res. 25, 348–363. [95]

REINIŠ, S. (1965). Formation of conditioned reflexes in rats after the parenteral administration of brain homogenate. Activitas Nervosa Super. 7, 167. [113]

RÉMOND, H., LESÈVRE, N., and TORRÈS, F. (1965). Average occipital activity in relation to displacement of gaze during visual exploration. Electroencephalog. Clin. Neurophysiol. 20, 208. Abstr. [400]

ROBERTS, E. (1965). Discussion. In "The Anatomy of Memory" (D. P. Kimble, ed.), Sci. Behavior Books, Palo Alto, California. [117]

ROBERTSON, A. D. (1965). Correlation between unit activity and slow potential changes in unanesthetized cerebral cortex of cat. Nature 208, 757–758. [234]

ROBINSON, C. E. (1965). A chemical model of long-term memory and recall. Unpublished ms. [155, 375]

ROSEN, S., and STAMM, J. S. (1966). Intersensory electrocortical conditioning of slow potentials. *Federation Proc.* **25**, 1166. [302]

ROSENBLATT, F. (1958). The perceptron: A probabilistic model for information storage and organization in the brain. *Psychol. Rev.* **65**, 386–408. [17]

ROSENBLATT, F. (1962). "Principles of Neurodynamics." Spartan Books, Washington, D.C. [16]

ROSENBLATT, F., FARROW, J. T., and HERBLIN, W. F. (1966a). Transfer of conditioned responses from trained rats to untrained rats by means of a brain extract. *Nature* **209**, 46–48. [113]

ROSENBLATT, F. R., FARROW, J. T., and RHINE, S. (1966b). The transfer of learned behavior from trained to untrained rats by means of a brain extract. I. *Proc. Natl. Acad. Sci. U.S.* **55**, 548–555. [113]

ROSENBLATT, F. R., FARROW, J. T., and RHINE, S. (1966c). The transfer of learned behavior from trained to untrained rats by means of a brain extract. II. *Proc. Natl. Acad. Sci. U.S.* **55**, 787–792. [113]

ROSNER, B. S. (1962). Psychophysics and neurophysiology. *In* "Psychology: A Study of a science" (S. Koch, ed.), Vol. 4, pp. 280–333. McGraw-Hill, New York. [399]

ROSS, R. B. (1964). Effects of strychnine sulphate on maze learning in rats. *Nature* **201**, 109–110. [48]

ROWLAND, V. (1963). Steady potential shifts in cortex. *In* "Brain Function" (M. A. B. Brazier, ed.), Vol. 1, pp. 136–148. University of Calif. Press, Berkeley, California. [190]

ROYTBAK, A. (1955). Bio-electrical phenomena in the cortex of the cerebral hemispheres. *Acad. Sci. Georgian, SSR, Tiflis.* Transl. by Natl. Med. Lib., Bethesda, Md. [186]

ROYTBAK, A. (1956). Bio-electrical phenomena arising in the cerebral cortex under a combination of stimuli applied to two points of the cortex. *Abstr. 20th Intern. Physiol. Congr., Brussels* pp. 787–788. [186]

RUCHKIN, D., and JOHN, E. R. (1966a). Evoked potential correlates of generalization. *Science* **153**, 209–211. [254, 362, 364, 365]

RUCHKIN, D., and JOHN, E. R. (1966b). Unpublished observations. [389, 397]

RUCHKIN, D. S., VILLEGAS, J., and JOHN, E. R. (1964). An analysis of average evoked potentials making use of least mean square techniques. *Ann. N.Y. Acad. Sci.* **115**(2), 799–826. [337]

RUCHKIN, D. S., TORDA, C., and NEGRIN, J. (1966). Unpublished observations. [410]

RUDENBERG, F. H., and TOBIAS, J. M. (1960). The effect of ribonuclease on the dialysis of calcium from homogenates of lobster nerve and the binding of sodium in the homogenates. *J. Cellular Comp. Physiol.* **55**, 149–157. [141]

RUSINOV, V. S. (1953). An electrophysiological analysis of the connection function in the cerebral cortex in the presence of a dominant focus. *Abstr. Proc. 19th Intern. Congr. Physiol. Sci., 1953 Montreal*, pp. 147–151. [184]

RUSINOV, V. S. (1959). Electroencephalographic studies in conditioned reflex formation in man. *In* "The Central Nervous System and Behavior" (M. A. B. Brazier, ed.), pp. 249–312. Josiah Macy, Jr. Foundation, New York. [354]

RUSSELL, I. S., and OCHS, S. (1963). Localization of memory traces in one cerebral hemisphere and transfer to the other hemisphere. *Brain* **86**, 37–54. [25, 26]

RUSSELL, R. W. (1954). Effects of reduced brain cholinesterase on behavior. *Bull. Brit. Psychol. Soc.* **3**, 6. [47]

RUSSELL, W., and NATHAN, P. (1946). Traumatic amnesia. *Brain* **69**, 280–300. [20]

References

SACHS, E. (1961). The role of brain electrolytes in learning and retention. *Federation Proc.* **20**, 339. [81]

SACHS, E. (1962a). The role of brain electrolytes in learning and retention. Ph.D. Thesis, Univ. of Rochester, Rochester, New York. [51, 52, 56, 68, 81]

SACHS, E. (1962b). Unpublished observations. [55]

SACHS, E. (1965). Personal communication. [53, 85]

SACHS, E., WEINGARTEN, M., and KLEIN, N. W. (1966). Effects of chlordiazepoxide on the acquisition of avoidance learning and its transfer to the normal state and other conditions. *Psychopharmacologia* **9**, 17–30. [78]

SAKHUILINA, G. T. (1955). Certain data concerning the electrophysiology of conditioned reflex switching. *Dokl. Akad. Nauk SSSR* **104**(2), 332–334. [71]

SAKHUILINA, G. T. (1960). Electroencephalograms of dogs in some complex forms of conditioned reflex activity. *Moscow Colloq. Encephalog. Higher Nervous Activity. Electroencephalog. Clin. Neurophysiol. Suppl.* **13**, 211–220. [71]

SAKHUILINA, G. T., and MERZHANOVA, G. K. (1966). Stable changes in the pattern of the recruiting response associated with a well established conditioned reflex. *Electroencephalog. Clin. Neurophysiol.* **20**, 50–58. [366]

SAUNDERS, V. F. (1966). Effect of behavioral and environmental manipulations on central ChE activity in the rat. *Federation Proc.* **25**, 1102. [43]

SCHEIBEL, M. E., and SCHEIBEL, A. B. (1965). The response of reticular units to repetitive stimuli. *Arch. Ital. Biol.* **103**, 279–299. [205, 266]

SCHMITT, F. O., ed. (1962). "Macromolecular Specificity and Biological Memory. pp. 1–6. M.I.T. Press, Cambridge, Massachusetts. [149]

SCHUCKMAN, H., and BATTERSBY, W. S. (1965). Frequency specific mechanisms in learning. I. Occipital activity during sensory preconditioning. *Electroencephalog. Clin. Neurophysiol.* **18**, 44–55. [309]

SCHUCKMAN, H., and BATTERSBY, W. S. (1966). Frequency specific mechanisms in learning. II. Discriminatory conditioning induced by intracranial stimulation. *J. Neurophysiol.* **29**, 31–43. [347]

SEGUNDO, J. P., ROIG, J. A., and SOMMER-SMITH, J. A. (1959). Conditioning of reticular formation stimulation effects. *Electroencephalog. Clin. Neurophysiol.* **11**, 471–484. [328]

"Self-Organizing Systems." (1960). (M. C. Yovits and S. Cameron, eds.). Macmillan (Pergamon), New York. [17]

SELLS, B. H. (1965). Puromycin: effect on messenger RNA synthesis and B-galactosidase formation in *Escherichia coli* LST. *Science* **148**, 371–372. [119]

SHANNON, C. E. (1949). Communications in the presence of noise. *Proc. IRE* **37**, 10–21. [337]

SHANNON, C. E., and WEAVER, W. (1949). "The Mathematical Theory of Communications." Univ. of Illinois Press, Urbana, Illinois. [396]

SHERWIN, A. L., RICHTER, M., COSGROVE, J. B. R., and ROSE, B. (1963). Studies of the blood-cerebrospinal fluid barrier to antibodies and other proteins. *Neurology* **13**, 113–119. [117]

SHIMBEL, A., and RAPOPORT, A. (1948). A statistical approach to the theory of the central nervous system. *Bull. Math. Biophys.* **10**, 41–55. [16]

SHIMOKOCHI, M., and JOHN, E. R. (1965). Unpublished observations. [249]

SHIMOKOCHI, M., and JOHN, E. R. (1966). Unpublished observations. [279]

SHIPLEY, T., JONES, R. W., and FRY, A. (1965). Evoked visual potentials and human color vision. *Science* **150**, 1162–1163. [401]

SHTARK, M. B. (1965). Participation of nucleic metabolism in formation of electrical properties of apical dendrites of cerebral cortex. *Bull. Exptl. Biol. USSR* **59**, 230. [96]

SIEBERT, W. M., and Commun. Biophys. Group (1959). "Processing of Neuroelectric Data," Monograph No. 4. Technol. Press, M.I.T., Cambridge, Massachusetts. [333, 334]

SMIRNOV, A. A. (1955). *Dokl. Akad. Nauk SSSR*, **105**, 185. Cited by Palladin, A. V. (1964). *In* "Problems of the Biochemistry of the Central Nervous System," pp. 311–312. Macmillan (Pergamon), New York. [96]

SMITH, C. E. (1962). Is memory a matter of enzyme induction? *Science* **138**, 889–890. [152]

SMITH, D. R., and DAVIDSON, C. H. (1962). Activity levels and oscillation modes in neural nets. *In* "Biological Prototypes and Synthetic Systems" (E. E. Bernard and M. R. Kare, eds.), Vol. 1, pp. 148–159. Plenum Press, New York. [16]

SNYDER, S., GLOWINSKI, J., and AXELROD, J. (1965). *Life Sciences* **4**, 797. [153]

SOKOLOV, E. M. (1935). Inhibitory conditioned reflex at single unit level. *Proc. 23rd Intern. Physiol. Congr., Tokyo* **IV**, 340–343. [260]

SOKOLOVA, A. (1958). Electrical activity in the visual and motor regions of the cerebral cortex in rabbits during reinforcement of a dominant focus in the motor region by light stimulations. *Zh. Vysshei Nervnoi Deyatel'nosti im I. P. Pavlova* **8**, 593–600. [193]

SOLYOM, L. (1965). *Symp. on Memory, Am. Psychiat. Assoc. Meetings, New York, May.* [110]

SPEHLMAN, R. (1965). The averaged electrical responses to diffuse and to patterned light in the human. *Electroencephalog. Clin. Neurophysiol.* **19**, 560–569. [404, 405]

SPENCER, W. A., THOMPSON, R. F., and NEILSON, D. R. (1964). Analysis of polysynaptic reflex response decrement in the acute spinal cat. *Physiologist* **7**, 262. [260]

SPENCER, W. A., THOMPSON, R. F., and NEILSON, D. R. (1966). Decrement of ventral root electrotonus and intracellularly recorded PSP's produced by iterated cutaneous afferent volleys. *J. Neurophysiol.* **21**, 253–274. [260]

SPEYER, J. F., LENGYAL, P., BASILIO, C., and OCHOA, S. (1962). Synthetic polynucleotides and the amino acid code. *Proc. Natl. Acad. Sci. U.S.* **48**, 63–68. [126]

SPINELLI, D. N., and WEINGARTEN, M. (1966). Afferent and efferent activity in single units of the cat's optic nerve. *Exptl. Neurol.* **15**, 347–362. [264]

SPINELLI, D. N., PRIBRAM, K. H., and WEINGARTEN, M. (1966). Visual receptive field modification induced by non-visual stimuli. *Federation Proc.* **25**, 2173. [264]

SPRAGUE, J. M. (1966). Interaction of cortex and superior colliculus in mediation of visually guided behavior in the cat. *Science* **153**, 1544–1547. [5]

SPYRIDES, G. J. (1964). The effect of univalent cations on the binding of sRNA to the template-ribosome complex. *Proc. Natl. Acad. Sci. U.S.* **51**, 1220–1226. [142]

STAMM, J. S. (1961). Electrical stimulation of frontal cortex in monkeys during learning of an alternation task. *J. Neurophysiol.* **24**, 414–426. [23]

STEFANIS, C. (1963). Relations of the spindle waves and the evoked cortical waves to the intracellular potentials in pyramidal motor neurons. *Electroencephalog. Clin. Neurophysiol.* **15**, 1054. [230]

STENT, G. S. (1964). The operon: on its third anniversary. *Science* **144**, 816–820. [127, 129]

STERN, J. A., ULETT, G. A., and SINES, J. O. (1960). Electrocortical changes during conditioning. *In* "Recent Advances in Biological Psychiatry" (J. Wortis, ed.). Grune & Stratton, New York. [308]

445

References

STILLE, G., and KRÖGER, H. (1957). Behavior of electrolytes in blood, muscle and brain under the influence of analeptics. *Arch. Exptl. Pathol. Pharmakol.* **230,** 14–25. [50]

STRATTON, L. O., and PETRINOVICH, L. (1963). Post-trial injections of an anticholinesterase drug and maze learning in two strains of rats. *Psychopharmacologia* **5,** 47–54. [47]

STRUMWASSER, F., and BAHR, R. (1966). Prolonged in vitro culture and autoradiographic studies of neurons in aplysia. *Federation Proc.* **25,** 1815. [256]

STRUMWASSER, F., and ROSENTHAL, S. (1960). Prolonged and patterned direct extracellular stimulation of single neurons. *Am. J. Physiol.* **198,** 402–413. [256]

SUTTON, S., BRAREN, M., PETERSON, P., ZUBIN, J., and JOHN, E. R. (1965a). Evoked potential correlates of guessing and its consequences. *Eastern Assoc. Encephalographers, EEG Soc.* [405, 407]

SUTTON, S., BRAREN, M., ZUBIN, J., and JOHN, E. R. (1965b). Evoked potential correlates of stimulus uncertainty. *Science* **150,** 1187–1188. [400, 404, 406]

SUTTON, S., TEUTING, P., ZUBIN, J., and JOHN, E. R. (1967). Information delivery and the sensory evoked potential. *Science,* **155,** 1436–1439. [354, 406]

SZILARD, L. (1964). On memory and recall. *Proc. Natl. Acad. Sci. U.S.* **51,** 1092–1099. [152]

TIZZARD, B. (1959). Theories of brain localization from Fluorens to Lashley. *Med. Hist.* **3,** 132–145. [159]

TRYON, R. C. (1940). Genetic differences in maze learning ability in rats. *Yearbook Natl. Soc. Stud. Educ.* **39,** Pt. 1, 111–119. [41]

TSCHIRGI, R. D. (1952). Blood-brain barrier. "Biology of Mental Health and Disease." Harper and Row (Hoeber), New York. [49, 50]

TSCHIRGI, R. D. (1960). Chemical environment of the central nervous system. *In* "Handbook of Physiology: Neurophysiology" (J. Field, ed.), Vol. III, pp. 1865–1890. Am. Physiol. Soc., Washington, D.C. [56, 87, 89]

TUCKER, T., and KLING, A. (1966). Differential effects of early vs. late brain damage on visual duration discrimination in cats. *Federation Proc.* **25,** 106. [5]

UKHTOMSKI, A. A. (1926). Concerning the condition of excitation in dominance. *Novoev Refleksologii i Fiziol. Nervoi Sistemy* **2,** 3–15. Abstr. in *Psychol. Abstr.* 1927 No. 2388. [182]

UNGAR, G. (1966a). Chemical transfer of learning; its stimulus specificity. *Federation Proc. Abstr.* **25,** 109. [114]

UNGAR, G. (1966b). Unpublished observations. Personal communication to J. V. McConnell. [115]

UNGAR, G., and COHEN, M. (1965). Induction of morphine tolerance by material extracted from brain of tolerant animals. *Intern. J. Neuropharmacol.* **5,** 1–10. [114]

UNGAR, G., and OCEGUERA-NAVARRO, C. (1965). Transfer of habituation by material extracted from brain. *Nature* **207,** 301–302. [114]

URBAITIS, J. C., and HINSEY, J. C. (1966). Ablations of cortical and collicular areas in cats: effects on a visual discrimination. *Federation Proc.* **25,** 1167. [5]

UTTAL, W. R. (1965). Do compound evoked potentials reflect psychological codes? *Psychol. Bull.* **64,** 377–392. [399, 401]

VAN HARREVELD, A., and SCHADE, J. P. (1959). Chloride movements in cerebral cortex after circulatory arrest and during spreading depression. *J. Cellular Comp. Physiol.* **54,** 65–84. [25]

Van Harreveld, A., Stamm, J. S., and Christenson, E. (1956). Spreading depression in rabbit, cat, and monkey. *Am. J. Physiol.* **184**, 312–313. [25]

Van Hof, M. W. (1960a). The relation between the cortical responses to flash and to flicker in man. *Acta Physiol. Pharmacol. Neerl.* **9**, 210–224. [400]

Van Hof, M. W. (1960b). Open eye and closed eye occipito-cortical response to photic stimulation of the retina. *Acta Physiol. Pharmacol. Neerl.* **9**, 443–451. [404]

Vasilevs, N. N. (1965). Relationship between background impulse activity of cortical neurons and electrocorticogram phases. *Bull. Exptl. Biol. USSR* **59**, 597. [234]

Vaughan, H. G. (1965). The perceptual and physiologic significance of visual evoked responses recorded from the scalp in man. *Visual Res.* **6**, Suppl. 1, 203–223. [400, 401, 403]

Vertua, R., and Poggi, M. (1960). Serotonina e calcio. Rilievi istoautoradiografici e dosaggi radiochimici sulla distribuzione del Ca45 somministrato da solo o con serotinina. *Ric. Sci.* **30**, 1600–1606. [90]

Verzeano, M. (1963). Las funciones del sistema nervioso; correlaciones entre estructura bioquimica y electrofisiologica. *Acta Neurol. Latinoam.* **9**, 297–307. [233, 234]

Verzeano, M., and Negishi, K. (1960). Neuronal activity in cortical and thalamic networks. *J. Gen. Physiol.* **43** Suppl., 177. [27, 33, 234]

Verzeano, M., Laufer, J., Spear, P., and McDonald, S. (1965). The activity of neuronal networks in the thalamus of the monkey. *Actualités Neurophysiol.* In press. [234, 236]

Vladimirova, Ye. A. (1964). The relationship between different stages of conditioning and the ammonia content of the brain. *In* "Problems of the Biochemistry of the Nervous System" (A. V. Palladin, ed.), pp. 135–146. Macmillan (Pergamon), New York. [142]

Von Foerster, H. (1948). "Das Gedachtnis." Deuticke, Vienna. [95] na. [95]

Vrba, R., Folberger, Ya., Kanturek, V. (1964). Formation of ammonia in brain slices. *In* "Problems of the Biochemistry of the Nervous System" (A. V. Palladin, ed.), pp. 126–134. Macmillan (Pergamon), New York. [142]

Walter, W. G. (1953). "The Living Brain." Norton, New York. [209, 219]

Walter, W. G., Cooper, R., Aldridge, U. J., McCallum, W. C., and Winter, A. L. (1964). Contingent negative variation: an electric sign of sensorimotor association and expectancy in the human brain. *Nature* **203**, 380–384. [246, 403]

Walter, W. G., Aldridge, U. J., Cooper, R., McCallum, C., and Cohen, J. (1965). The interaction of responses to semantic stimuli in the human brain. Abstr. *Electroencephalog. Clin. Neurophysiol.* **18**, 514–515. [404]

Wang, H. H., Tarby, T. J., Kado, R. T., and Adey, W. R. (1966). Periventricular cerebral impedance after intraventricular injection of calcium. *Science* **153**, 1183–1184. [82]

Ward, A. A., Jr., and Malmke, J. H. (1960). Standing potential characteristics of the epileptogenic focus. *Trans. Am. Neurol. Assoc.* **85**, 93–95. [245]

Washizu, Y., Bonewell, G. W., and Terzuolo, C. A. (1961). Effect of strychnine upon the electrical activity of an isolated nerve cell. *Science* **133**, 333–334. [107]

Webster, D. B., and Voneida, T. J. (1964). Learning deficits following hippocampal lesions in split-brain cats. *Exptl. Neurol.* **10**, 170–182. [22]

Wedensky, N. E. (1897). Zeitschrift der rues. Geselhschaft für Volshygiene. Cited in

References

Wedensky, N. E. (1903). Die Erregung, Hemmung, und Narkose. *Arch. Ges. Physiol. Pflügers* **100**, 1–144. [180]

WEINGARTEN, M., and SPINELLI, D. N. (1966). Retinal receptive field changes produced by auditory and somatic stimulation. *Exptl. Neurol.* **15**, 363–376. [264]

WEISS, M. (1962). M.S. Thesis, University of Rochester, Rochester, New York. Cited by John, E. R. (1963). Neural mechanisms of decision making. In "Information Storage and Neural Control." (W. S. Fields and W. Abbott, eds.). Thomas, Springfield, Illinois. [353]

WEISS, P. (1961). The concept of perpetual neuronal growth and proximo-distal substance convection. In "Regional Neurochemistry" (S. Kety and J. Elkes, eds.), pp. 220–242. Macmillan (Pergamon), New York. [96]

WEISS, S. A., and NAKARNOTO, T. (1961). On the participation of DNA in RNA biosynthesis. *Proc. Natl. Acad. Sci. U.S.* **47**, 694–697. [126]

WENZEL, B. M. (1961). Changes in heart rate associated with responses based on positive and negative reinforcement. *J. Comp. Physiol. Psychol.* **54**, 638–644. [72]

WESTBROOK, W. H., and McGAUGH, J. (1964). Drug facilitation of latent learning. *Psychopharmacologia* **5**, 440–446. [46]

WHIPPLE, H. E., ed. (1964). Sensory evoked response in man. *Ann. N.Y. Acad. Sci.* **112**. [399]

WICKE, J. D., DONCHIN, E., and LINDSLEY, D. B. (1964). Visual evoked potentials as a function of flash luminance and duration. *Science* **146**, 83–85. [403]

WIESEL, T. N., and HUBEL, D. H. (1965a). Comparison of the effects of unilateral and bilateral eye closure on cortical unit responses in kittens. *J. Neurophysiol.* **28**, 1029–1040. [263]

WIESEL, T. N., and HUBEL, D. H. (1965b). Binocular interaction in striate cortex of kittens reared with artificial squint. *J. Neurophysiol.* **28**, 1041–1059. [263]

WILSON, J. E., BOGGAN, W. O., ZEMP, J. W., and GLASSMAN, E. (1966). Increased RNA synthesis in mouse brain during learning. *Federation Proc.* **25**, 2963. [98]

WINANS, S. S., and MEIKLE, T. H. (1966). Visual pattern discrimination after removal of the striate visual cortex in cats. *Federation Proc.* **25**, 2167. [5]

WOODBURY, D. M. (1954). Hormones, brain excitability, and electrolytes. *Recent Progr. Hormone Res.* **10**, 65. [50]

WOODBURY, D. M. (1958). Relation between the adrenal cortex and the central nervous system. *Pharmacol. Rev.* **10**, 215–357. [50]

WOODWORTH, R. S. (1918). "Dynamic Psychology." New York. [218]

WURTZ, R. H. (1966). Steady potential correlates of intracranial reinforcement. *Electroencephalog. Clin. Neurophysiol.* **20**, 59–67. [212]

WYRWICKA, W., DOBRZECKA, C., and TARNECKI, R. (1959). On the instrumental conditioned reaction evoked by electrical stimulation of the hypothalamus. *Science* **130**, 336–337. [328]

WYRWICKA, W., DOBRZECKA, C., and TARNECKI, R. (1960). The effect of electrical stimulation of the hypothalamic feeding centre in satiated goats on alimentary conditioned reflexes, Type II. *Acta Biol. Exptl. Polish Acad. Sci.* **20**, 121–136. [328]

YOSHII, N. (1962). Electroencephalographic study on experimental neurosis, a conditioned partly awake state. *Proc. 22nd Intern. Physiol. Congr. Abstr.* **2**, 1088. [308, 353]

Yoshii, N., and Hockaday, W. J. (1958). Conditioning of frequency-characteristic repetitive electroencephalographic response with intermittent photic stimulation. *Electroencephalog. Clin. Neurophysiol.* **10**, 487–502. [187, 188, 299, 301]

Yoshii, N., and Ogura, H. (1960). Studies on the unit discharge of brain stem reticular formation in the cat. I. Changes of reticular unit discharge following conditioning procedure. *Med. J. Osaka Univ.* **11**, 1. [147, 255]

Yoshii, N., Pruvot, P., and Gastaut, H. (1956). A propos d'une activité rhythmique transitoirement enregistrée dans la formation reticulée mesencephalique et susceptible de representer l'expression electroencephalographique de la trace mnemonique. *Compt. Rend.* **242**, 1361. [188]

Yoshii, N., Matsumoto, J., and Hori, Y. (1957a). Electroencephalographic study on conditioned reflex in animals. *1st Intern. Congr. Neurol. Sci., Brussels, 1957.* [328, 353]

Yoshii, N., Pruvot, P., and Gastaut, H. (1957b). Electroencephalographic activity of the mesencephalic reticular formation during conditioning in the cat. *Electroencephalog. Clin. Neurophysiol.* **9**, 595. [187, 247, 301, 332]

Yoshii, N., Shimokochi, M., and Yamaguchi, Y. (1960). Conditioning of frequency characteristic repetitive response with electrical stimulation of some thalamic structures. *Med. J. Osaka Univ.* **10**, 375. [247]

Young, J. Z. (1964). "A Model of the Brain." Oxford Univ. Press (Clarendon), London and New York. [160]

Zal'manson, A. N. (1929). Uslovnyie oboronitel' nyie refleksy pri lokal'nom otravlenii tzentrov kory golovnogo mozga strikhuinom i kokavnom. (Conditioned defensive reflexes after local poisoning of the cortical motor centers with strychnine and cocaine.) *Vysshaya Nervnaya Deyatel'nost, Moscow, Giz* pp. 39–48. [182]

Zamenhof, S., Mosley, J., and Schuller, E. (1966). Stimulation of the proliferation of cortical neurons by prenatal treatment with growth hormone. *Science* **152**, 1396–1397. [43]

Zeigler, H. P. (1957). Electrical stimulation of the brain and the psychophysiology of learning and motivation. *Psychol. Bull.* **54**, 363–382. [23]

Zelman, A., Kabat, L., Jacobson, R., and McConnell, J. V. (1963). Transfer of training through injection of "conditioned" RNA into untrained planarians. *Worm Runner's Digest* **5**, 14–19. [112]

Zinkin, S., and Miller, A. J. (1967). Recovery of memory after amnesia induced by electroconvulsive shock. *Science* **155**, 102–103. [20]

Zubin, J., and Barrera, S. E. (1941). Effect of electric convulsive therapy on memory. *Proc. Soc. Exptl. Biol. Med.* **48**, 596–597. Abstr. [20]

Zuckermann, E. J. (1959). Effect of cortical and reticular stimulation on conditioned reflex activity. *J. Neurophysiol.* **22**, 633–643. [23, 57]

SUBJECT INDEX

A

450

O

S

Subject index